Film N...

BLOOMSBURY FILM GENRES SERIES

Edited by Mark Jancovich and Charles Acland

The *Film Genres* series presents accessible books on popular genres for students, scholars and fans alike. Each volume addresses key films, movements and periods by synthesizing existing literature and proposing new assessments.

Published:
Teen Film: A Critical Introduction
Fantasy Film: A Critical Introduction
Science Fiction Film: A Critical Introduction
Historical Film: A Critical Introduction
Anime: A Critical Introduction

Film Noir

A critical introduction

IAN BROOKES

Bloomsbury Academic
An imprint of Bloomsbury Publishing Inc

B L O O M S B U R Y
NEW YORK • LONDON • OXFORD • NEW DELHI • SYDNEY

Bloomsbury Academic

An imprint of Bloomsbury Publishing Inc

1385 Broadway	50 Bedford Square
New York	London
NY 10018	WC1B 3DP
USA	UK

www.bloomsbury.com

BLOOMSBURY and the Diana logo are trademarks of Bloomsbury Publishing Plc

First published 2017

© Ian Brookes, 2017

Library of Congress Cataloging-in-Publication Data
Names: Brookes, Ian, author.
Title: Film noir: a critical introduction/Ian Brookes.
Description: New York, NY: Bloomsbury Academic, 2017. | Series: Bloomsbury film genres series | Includes bibliographical references and index.
Identifiers: LCCN 2016038797 (print) | LCCN 2016051668 (ebook) | ISBN 9781780933269 (hardback: alk. paper) | ISBN 9781780933139 (pbk.: alk. paper) | ISBN 9781780933245 (ePDF) | ISBN 9781780933177 (ePUB)
Subjects: LCSH: Film noir–History and criticism.
Classification: LCC PN1995.9.F54 B78 2017 (print) | LCC PN1995.9.F54 (ebook) | DDC 791.43/6556–dc23
LC record available at https://lccn.loc.gov/2016038797

ISBN: HB: 978-1-7809-3326-9
PB: 978-1-7809-3313-9
ePDF: 978-1-7809-3324-5
ePub: 978-1-7809-3317-7

Series: Film Genres

Cover design: Burge Agency
Cover image © RKO / REX / Shutterstock, Crossfire 1947, Steve Brodie, Robert Ryan

Typeset by Deanta Global Publishing Services, Chennai, India

Contents

List of illustrations

Fallen Angel (Otto Preminger, 1945).

As it has come down to us through the decades, it is an object of beauty, one of the last remaining to us in this domain, situated as it is between neorealism and the New Wave, after which rounded objects like these will no longer be made. It is an object of beauty because Humphrey Bogart and Lauren Bacall are to be found there, because it is neatly contained in a perfect decade (1945–55), because it is simultaneously defined by its matter (black and white) and by its content (the crime story), because it is strange (see its relation to German expressionism and to psychoanalysis), because one cannot but love it (in contrast to its companion-objects, it is the only one that makes a place for affect and that functions as both a rallying cry and a point of exclusion), because it assures the triumph of European artists even as it presents American actors, because it is a severe critique of faceless capitalism, because it prolongs the reading of detective novels while feeding comparatism, because there is always an unknown film to be added to the list, because the stories it tells are both shocking and sentimental, because it is a great example of cooperation—the Americans made it and then the French invented it—and because a book can be made of all these reasons, in which one would finally have the feeling of having it all. On the whole, film noir is like a Harley-Davidson: you know right away what it is, the object being only the synecdoche of a continent, a history, and a civilization, or more precisely of their representation for nonnatives.

Marc Vernet, "*Film Noir* on the Edge of Doom," trans. J. Swenson, in Joan
    Copjec, ed., *Shades of Noir* (London: Verso, 1993), 1.

Acknowledgments

This book has been many years in the making so my debts go back a long way. Thanks to series editors Charles Acland and Mark Jancovich and, at Bloomsbury, to Mary Al-Sayed, Susan Krogulski, Michelle Chen, Amy Jordan, and the force of nature that is Katie Gallof, our terrific editor. Working with Katie on this book has been a joy. Thanks also to Grishma Fredric and R. Abilash Chandran for their excellent work on the text and production.

Thanks to the staff at the Hallward Library at the University of Nottingham, notably Kenneth Robinson, Anne-Marie Llewellyn, and Alison Stevens, together with a special mention for Philip Bellamy, himself a remarkable noirist, who over several years has tracked down all sorts of out-of-the-way materials that show up in this book. Thanks also to library and archive staff at the British Film Institute, the BFI Reuben Library, the British Library, the American Film Institute, New York Public Library, The Firestone Library at Princeton University, and the Valley Library at Oregon State University at Corvallis.

I am grateful to generous and talented friends who have helped me write this book. In the Department of Culture, Film and Media at the University of Nottingham, thanks especially to Andy Goffey, James Mansell, Tracey Potts, Mark Gallagher, and Alex Simcock. Thanks also to the University's School of American and Canadian Studies, especially to Celeste-Marie Bernier, Jean Darnbrough, Hannah Durkin, Richard King, Pete Messent, Dave Murray, Helen Oakley, Lisa Rull, Graham Taylor, and Douglas Tallack. Special thanks to Nick Heffernan for innumerable discussions about film noir and for his reading of manuscript drafts.

Among other inspirational friends who have lent a helping hand, thanks are due to Jacky Boucherat, Clint Brown, Sandy Bywater, John Stuart Clark, Julia Cooper, Deniz Ertan, Charlotte Fallenius, Geoffrey Fielding, Isabel Jones Fielding, Tim Lathe, Sue and Mark Leitner, Cheryl MacLean, Gill and Dave Murray, Lynne Pettinger, David Purveur, Nick and Janet Sanders, and Sarah Stubbings. I also happily acknowledge a longstanding debt of thanks to Dana Polan. My gratitude to Caroline Robinson goes beyond words. I should also like to thank the students on my film noir courses over many years. Thanks (and apologies) to everyone for enduring the obsessions of a noirophile and, sometimes, for sharing them.

Introduction

This book is designed to provide an introduction to one of the most fascinating, complex, and problematic categories of film. Film noir has generated an enormous amount of academic work over the past few decades, and to the student, it can all look rather daunting: a large and increasingly amorphous field of study.

There are several initial questions we might want to ask about the term. Does "film noir" refer to a specific period of film production? Is its use restricted to films from, say, the 1940s, or can it be used to categorize films made today? Does it apply only to American films? What type of film does it designate? Is it a genre? Why is it a French term rather than an English one (why not just "black film")? Some of these questions may not be that easy to answer. To begin with, there is the problem of how to define the term and there are several impediments to establishing a working definition. "It has always been easier to recognize a film noir than to define the term," says film noir scholar James Naremore, and he has a point.[1] The term was first applied to a group of American films by French critics immediately after the end of the Second World War. One issue arising here is that when these films were originally produced, they weren't known as film noir, a term that was only retrospectively applied.

Another question crops up when we ask what exactly the object of study is supposed to be. The answer may seem obvious. Surely it is the films themselves. But because the term was retroactively projected onto these films, we need to ask another question. Do we study the films called noir *as* noir? That is, do we study them according to the critical apparatus hoisted onto them retrospectively? Or do we study them in terms of their production and consumption at that time, prior to their noir labeling? Even the object of study, then, isn't necessarily clear. I discuss these problems in due course, but for the moment I want to flag up a few of the issues I think would be useful to consider at the outset.

One key issue concerns the parameters of noir. One of my students recounted having a conversation with a housemate about film noir in which they seemed to be talking at crossed purposes. "What do you actually mean by 'film noir,' then?" asked my student. "Well, you know," his housemate replied. "Old films. In black and white." What are we to make of this response? Some might think that the housemate was laboring under a misconception with an answer unlikely to be of much use as a critical definition. But, compared with many definitions of film noir in current circulation, this at least has the merit of indicating a degree of historical specificity ("old"), as well as highlighting a formal feature ("black and white"). For many critics today, "film noir" has come to denote an exceptionally wide category, one that doesn't necessarily specify "old" films at all, nor even ones in black and white (a defining feature for the early French critics). The term has become an increasingly elastic category that now often encompasses a very broad period indeed, from the 1940s, and sometimes earlier, up to the present day. Many studies now routinely incorporate this later period through the concept of "neo-noir," often discussing noir in terms of nostalgia and pastiche. Moreover, noir has also come to be seen in a much wider geographical field as the term has been stretched to incorporate films produced around the world. Film noir, in this sense, has been reproduced as a global phenomenon.

Unlike in other books on film noir, here I make no attempt to extend its geographical boundaries with the addition of more titles, nor do I seek to extend the chronological period in which noir can be said to operate by claiming earlier or later dates, nor do I propose the addition of extra film titles to the ever-expanding noir catalogs and encyclopedias. As I argue below, one of the major problems in film noir studies is the overextended use of the term itself, which now attaches to any and every crime film produced anywhere in the world, rendering it virtually meaningless as a functioning critical tool. It can sometimes seem as if the term has settled over the entire landscape of film studies like a great amorphous black cloud. "Just about everything seems to be labelled film noir these days," says Adam Frost in an entertaining BFI infographic on the subject. "If it's got a detective and a voiceover, it's noir. If we're in a city at night, it's noir, especially if it's raining."[2]

This book is not so much an account of what film noir *is*, but rather what it is said to be. Here, I am using "film noir" with an awareness that it is always an applied term. Like Naremore, I treat the term as a "discursive construct."[3] When I refer to a film noir in this book, I justify my license to use the term on the basis that someone has already applied it previously. In other words, it is a film noir insofar as someone has said it is. My book is about the ways in which the term came to be applied to a particular group of American films of the 1940s and 1950s. In this sense, it treats the term as a historical object of study, as a mode of categorization referring to a specific historical phenomenon, situated in the social, cultural, and political contexts of America in the 1940s and 1950s. It also looks closely at the cultural moment of the inception of the term by the French critics who did much to shape the generic concept. I then go on to consider the factors—industrial, cultural, social, and political—that had a bearing on noir production *avant la lettre*.

We should also bear in mind here one of the fundamental principles of genre criticism. A genre can sometimes seem like the category into which certain films fall and to which they naturally belong. But we should note at the outset that this isn't the case and there is no natural process of categorization. "Genres," as Rick Altman tells us, "are not inert categories shared by all . . . but discursive claims made by real speakers for particular purposes in specific situations."[4] In other words, films don't naturally occupy generic categories, but have been put in them. How, then, did film noir become the generic category into which certain American films from the 1940s and 1950s were put?

Another question concerns the generic status of these films before they became known as noir. The attribution of "film noir" created a new generic grouping of films that were formerly lodged in categories, often as "crime melodrama," but in other categories too. One consequence of this reclassification has frequently involved lifting out the films from their historical contexts to treat them as a thing apart, a category with special status. Throughout the book, I examine noir in relation to other "adjacent" generic categories such as the female gothic, the gaslight film, and, during the war, the home-front melodrama. I also consider other wartime genres such as the conversion narrative and combat film, and take into account the development of the gangster film together with other subcategories of the crime film such as the police procedural, the caper movie, and the "wrong man" film, as well as horror and the social problem film.

Noir scholars are frequently drawn to a small selection of canonical texts in their studies, typically highlighting examples such as *Double Indemnity*, *The Big Sleep* (1946), and *Out of the Past* (1947). I, too, consider these important entries in the noir pantheon, but I also draw on several lesser-known films from the period to look beyond the well-known noir canon in order to problematize the traditional noir constituency. This canon of familiar titles often serves to reaffirm many of the traditional assumptions about film noir, so going beyond it enables us to question some of the habitual generalizations formed from that limited sample.

Film Noir: A Critical Introduction is organized into three parts, each with three chapters. Part One addresses an innocuous enough looking question, "What is film noir?" only to find in answer something of a complicated critical morass. Chapter 1 charts the critical evolution of the category and, where much noir criticism pays scant attention to the historical conditions of its invention, I undertake a more thoroughgoing excavation of the term to raise questions about the predisposing factors in French culture and society which gave rise to the term, and to the anomalous question of why a group of American films should come to be known by a French name. Another issue I examine is how noir criticism has worked to impose an order of classification on what were often quite disparate films.

The stylistic look and narrative themes of film noir have often been seen as its defining and unifying characteristics. Many critics have placed particular emphasis on visual style. Recognizable by its low-key lighting with chiaroscuro effects and unusual shadow patterns with distorted camera angles, noir's visual style is linked to an iconography featuring dark cityscapes and rain-soaked streets at night, characteristics suggesting the stylistic influence of German expressionism. Noir has also been associated with such narrative themes as a haunted past, malign fate, the dark city, and the "absent family." It is this confluence of visual style, iconography, and narrative themes that is often seen as the defining characteristic of noir, and Chapter 2 examines these claims. The chapter also assesses the widely held view that film noir uniquely provides narrative expressions of a "postwar malaise" in American society. This chapter provides detailed analysis of noir style, although it's worth bearing in mind that this isn't a component that can be seen in isolation, and I return often to the subject of visual style throughout the book.

For many, the appeal of noir derives from its treatment of gender. Two of its paradigmatic characterizations, the femme fatale and the private eye, are often seen as emblematic of noir. Feminist criticism has highlighted the significance of the femme fatale as a transgressive figure, challenging patriarchal structures of power and authority, while noir's representations of masculinity have often been linked to uncertainties about the socioeconomic conditions of life in postwar America. Chapter 3 examines the cultural background of these figures, taking into account some of the "hard-boiled" pulp fiction that provided the source for many films noir, raising questions about why gender is seen as such a key element in film noir.

Noir studies often fail to make much of a distinction between the historical periods in which it was produced, often lumping the films together as part of a general, generically determined category. Part Two provides a historical framework for noir comprising three periods: wartime (1939–45), postwar (1945–50), and a late period (1950–58). The chapters in Part Two examine these historical phases by drawing on a range of film-related sources including studio publicity materials and reviews in addition to the film texts themselves. This enables us to identify some illuminating disparities between the retroactive noir modes of categorization of the films and the ways in which they were seen on original release.

Chapter 4 charts the "prehistory" of film noir and examines the emergence and early development of film noir during the war years in the context of the "genre work" of Hollywood's wartime production cycles such as the combat film and the home-front melodrama. Although the postwar years are usually credited as the definitive period of noir filmmaking, it was wartime itself that gave rise to a group of films working as narrative refractions of wartime concerns mapped onto criminal narratives. This chapter considers noir's place in the generic landscape of wartime America to ask how its "dark" narratives may have been at odds with the ideological imperatives evident in Hollywood's other genres. I also examine wartime factors affecting Hollywood film production such as the effects of government restrictions on studio expenditure and wartime censorship regulations, both of which had an impact on the development of noir stylistics.

In Chapter 5, I cover the postwar years, the period most strongly associated with the production of "classic" noir such as *The Big Sleep* and *Out of the Past*. In contrast to a self-consciously affirmative narrative like *The Best Years of Our Lives* (1946), films noir were seen to reflect a dark and disillusioned vision of postwar America. This chapter examines critical claims for the generic distinctiveness and coherence of postwar noir. I also discuss existentialism, one of the key philosophical ideas associated with film noir. In this connection, I also examine low-budget filmmaking practices, predominantly with reference to Edgar G. Ulmer's *Detour* (1945), widely seen as the ne plus ultra of low-budget noir. I also consider here the place of adjacent genres such as the manifestation of the "corporation" gangster in such films as *I Walk Alone* (1948) and *Force of Evil* (1948), and also the modern gothic in *Sorry, Wrong Number* (1948) together with two Max Ophuls films, *Caught* (1949) and *The Reckless Moment* (1949).

The noir titles in the late period became increasingly diverse in terms of both visual style and narrative themes. Films such as *Outrage* (1950), *Kiss Me Deadly* (1955), and *Touch of Evil* (1958) were markedly different from each other. What united them, however, was that they were all productions of the Cold War, and Chapter 6 accounts for the ways in which late noir in its various subcategories can be seen in relation to fears and anxieties generated by the Cold War. The chapter examines how noir criticism worked to ensure the persistent application of a term that was struggling to categorize an increasingly fragmentary body of films, often separated widely in terms of style, theme, and—in the context of the Cold War—political stance as well. In this chapter I consider the relation between film noir in the 1950s and other generic categories such as the social problem film and the caper film. For many critics, the "classic" period of film noir draws to a close with *Touch of Evil*, and sometimes a little later with titles such as *The Crimson Kimono* (1959), *Odds Against Tomorrow* (1959), and *Cape Fear* (1962) (a film that I discuss in Chapter 8). Although this book is principally concerned with the specified historical period, I also discuss some of the ramifications of "post-noir" or the "post-classical" development of "neo-noir."

I have mentioned earlier how film noir is often seen to speak on behalf of a dark mood or "postwar malaise" in American society (I discuss "Zeitgeist noir" in Chapter 2). This view reflects one of the tendencies in noir criticism to make vague presumptions about what it takes to be the social conditions instrumental in shaping the production of film noir. Many accounts of noir remain disconnected from their historical moment and lack historical grounding. Part 3 presents a historical case study of what was then known as "the veteran problem," and it is my contention that social concerns with the figure of the returning veteran permeated postwar noir. After the end of the war, the veteran became the focus of intense scrutiny and speculation. His "readjustment" became the subject of overarching social concern, and he was invariably seen as a social problem. A vast quantity of sociological and popular literature on "the veteran problem" began to appear before the end of the war, and this case study demonstrates how these concerns were refracted through noir narratives.

Chapter 7 examines the discourse of veteran "readjustment" by drawing together a wide range of contemporaneous writings on the veteran problem: from advice to wives on how to assist with their husband's emotional readjustment to accounts by psychiatrists and criminologists warning of veteran violence, criminality, and the dangers of his "stranger" status. Concerns with the veteran problem repeatedly surfaced in the postwar narratives of film noir. These concerns often appeared in what we might call the "readjustment narrative," often identifiable as a subset of postwar noir. In contrast to the kind of affirmative narrative of veteran homecoming in *The Best Years of Our Lives*, noir films such as *Cornered* (1945), *The Blue Dahlia* (1946), *Dead Reckoning* (1947), and *Ride the Pink Horse* (1947) would suggest a dismal future and, sometimes, no future at all. Largely passed over in most noir scholarship, the discourse of the returning veteran figures significantly in film noir, and this discourse constitutes the focus of Chapter 8. The chapter also includes an analysis of the star persona of Humphrey Bogart, a figure readily identifiable with films noir.

Finally, in Chapter 9, I address one of the main concerns in the discourse of readjustment: the perception that the experience of military service would have engendered a conformist disposition in the veteran. This notion of military conformity was linked to wider concerns with a condition of conformity inherent in American society. For many social commentators, large-scale forms of corporate organization were becoming a defining feature of postwar American life, and it seemed to them as if the veteran had left one type of "total institution" only to arrive at another, becoming, in William H. Whyte's telling phrase, an "organization man." At the same time there were concerns that America had become a failing democracy. As postwar narratives would often show, it was precisely here in the ordinary small-town community that democracy was seen as especially vulnerable to incursive totalitarian influence. In my discussion of *The Stranger* (1946), I highlight the political implications of a narrative in which active citizenship is set up as a bulwark against the resurgence of postwar fascism as an internal threat to postwar America.

Notes

1 James Naremore, *More than Night: Film Noir in its Contexts* (Berkeley: University of California Press, 1998), 9.

2 Adam Frost, "Infographic: What makes a Film Noir?" (BFI, July 22, 2015). http://www.bfi.org.uk/news-opinion/news-bfi/features/infographic-what-makes-film-noir (Accessed June 27, 2016).

3 Naremore, *More than Night*, 6.

4 Rick Altman, *Film/Genre* (London: BFI, 1999), 101.

PART ONE

What is film noir?

1

Genre and the problem of film noir

"When *I* use a word," Humpty Dumpty said, in rather a scornful tone, "it means just what I choose it to mean—neither more nor less."

"The question is," said Alice, "whether you *can* make words mean so many different things."

"The question is," said Humpty Dumpty, "which is to be master— that's all."

LEWIS CARROLL, *Through the Looking-Glass and What Alice Found There* (1879)[1]

Film noir! . . . I never heard that expression in those days.

BILLY WILDER[2]

What does it mean to speak of film noir as a "problem" when it hardly looks very problematic? After all, doesn't film noir appear as one of the most obviously recognizable categories of film? Anyone with a basic knowledge of cinema would surely be capable of giving at least a rudimentary account of it. When teaching my own courses on film noir, I often ask students at the outset to jot down their preliminary ideas about what it is. Almost everyone can provide at least some kind of response. They typically talk about crime films from the 1940s, black and white cinematography, urban settings, and characterizations such as the femme fatale and the private eye. When asked for representative titles, they usually come up with a handful from the period, such as *Double Indemnity* (1944) or *The Big Sleep* (1946). Sometimes, they mention more contemporary titles as well, such as *Fight Club* (1999), *Brick* (2006) or Christopher Nolan's

Batman trilogy.[3] There is also a tendency for particular directors to feature prominently in their examples: David Lynch, for instance, with *Blue Velvet* (1986), *Lost Highway* (1997) and *Mulholland Drive* (2001); Quentin Tarantino, for *Reservoir Dogs* (1992), *Pulp Fiction* (1994), and *Jackie Brown* (1997); and Joel and Ethan Coen, for *Fargo* (1996), *The Big Lebowski* (1998) and *The Man Who Wasn't There* (2001).

What invariably emerges from these sessions is widespread disagreement. On the question of periodization, for example, some see noir in terms of a distinct historical period with a beginning and an end. This period is usually seen to run from the early 1940s (sometimes earlier) to the late 1950s (sometimes later). For others, the term describes an ongoing category of film running more or less continuously from the early 1940s to the present. Here, "film noir" operates in contemporary critical discourse to provide terms of reference drawn from the earlier decades to denote a category of films produced afterward, usually designated as "neo-noir." One of the first problems we have to contend with, then, is whether film noir is what James Naremore calls "an extinct genre," one that constitutes a discrete historical object of study, or whether it is a more contemporary form of classification with an ongoing existence.[4]

My students' responses demonstrate something of the contentious nature of noir criticism and, indeed, they often find it gratifying to discover that their own struggles to account for the term are reflected more widely in academic debates. The term denotes one of the most complicated categories of film as well as the most intellectually challenging and exciting. Even the term itself has a complex history and one of the most useful questions we can ask is why a group of American films should be known by a French name. I'll return to this question later when I discuss how the term came into being and why it achieved such widespread currency.

Another problem arises from the fact that when these films were originally produced they weren't known as film noir, a term that was only retrospectively applied by critics. Neither the film industry nor its audiences were aware of the term at the time. It may seem odd for us today to discover that when Billy Wilder was making *Double Indemnity* (1944)—often seen as *the* quintessential noir—he didn't know he was making a film noir and nor did audiences realize they were watching one. Film noir, as a generic category, is unique in the sense of being constituted as a post hoc critical invention. But what kind of category?

Given that this book appears in a series on film genres, we should at least be able to presume that film noir is a genre, but it isn't that simple. Although some critics have seen film noir as a genre, it has also been described as a cycle, a series, a movement, a visual style, a lighting technique, and a mood or tone. Michael Walker has provided a useful summary of the disparate ways in which critics have defined noir:

> The cycle of 'forties and 'fifties Hollywood films that retrospectively became known as films noirs seems at first sight to be rather too diverse a group to be constituted with any precision as a generic category. Nevertheless, various critics have sought different unifying features: motif and tone (Durgnat, 1970), social background and artistic/cultural influences (Schrader, 1971), iconography, mood and characterisation (McArthur, 1972), visual style (Place & Peterson, 1974), the "hard-boiled" tradition (Gregory, 1976), narrative and iconography (Dyer, 1977), representation and ideology (Kaplan, 1978), a master plot paradigm (Damico, 1978), conditions of production (Kerr, 1979), paranoia (Buchsbaum, 1986 . . .) and patterns of narration (Telotte, 1989).[5]

To complicate the situation still further, Jon Tuska sees noir as "both a screen style . . . and a perspective on human existence and society."[6] How can we make sense of all these competing claims? Whatever noir is, it isn't a genre in the generally accepted sense of the term as, say, the western or the musical are.

As Walker's summary suggests, viewpoints about what constitutes the "unifying features" of noir are so widely disputed that the functioning capability of the term itself can be called into question. Walker also identifies another major problem when he says that the group of films held by critics to constitute film noir seems "too diverse" to be categorized together under the rubric of noir. Most of the surveys on noir literature show an extraordinarily heterogeneous grouping of films. If, for example, we look at some of the entries in one of the standard encyclopedic reference books on film noir, the generic range and diversity appear striking, often including titles that might be thought to require the very widest latitude of definition for inclusion.[7] For example, if film noir of the 1940s is assumed to have contemporary urban settings, a Hollywood cycle of period melodramas from the middle of the decade— including *Gaslight* (1944), *Hangover Square* (1945), and *The Spiral Staircase* (1945)—has Victorian or Edwardian settings and is more usually categorized in the female gothic or gaslight genres. At the other generic extreme, and also well represented in the *Encyclopedia*, is science fiction. Titles such as *The Day the Earth Stood Still* (1951), *Invaders from Mars* (1953), *Invasion of the Body Snatchers* (1956), and *Them!* (1954) are usually categorized in the cycle of science fiction/horror films of the 1950s. In addition to science fiction, there are several entries for the western in the *Encyclopedia*, including *Duel in the Sun* (1946), *I Shot Jesse James* (1949), *Johnny Guitar* (1954), *The Naked Spur* (1953), and *Rancho Notorious* (1952). There is even an entry for *The Black Book* (1949), also known as *Reign of Terror*, a narrative treatment of Maximilien Robespierre's Paris after the French Revolution.[8] How, then, can we account for a category that seems to incorporate all these other genres?

This leads to another complicating factor in the various noir subcategories. There is, for example, the noir western, including *Pursued* (1947), *Ramrod* (1947), *Blood on the Moon* (1948), *Yellow Sky* (1948), and *Devil's Doorway* (1950); and the noir musical, including *The Band Wagon* (1953) and *Carmen Jones* (1954). According to one critic, there is a category of "noir musical films," which includes *The Red Shoes* (1948), a British film with a ballet subject by Michael Powell and Emeric Pressburger; *Young at Heart* (1954), the Doris Day and Frank Sinatra musical; and Leonard Bernstein's *West Side Story* (1961), an updated version of Shakespeare's *Romeo and Juliet* with its rival families transposed as warring teenage gangs in New York City.[9] There is also the category of comedy noir, including *Lady on a Train* (1945) and *My Favorite Brunette* (1947), together with several comedies by Preston Sturges such as *The Miracle of Morgan's Creek* (1944), *Hail the Conquering Hero* (1944), and *Unfaithfully Yours* (1948). The British Ealing comedy *Kind Hearts and Coronets* (1949) used to be called a black comedy but is now often called *comédie noire*.

Another of the noir fusion-phrases is "tech-noir." Tech-noir, a hybrid of noir and dystopian science fiction, is named after the nightclub in *The Terminator* (1984), "TechNoir," where Sarah Connor (Linda Hamilton) attempts to evade the cyborg assassin programmed to kill her. Tech-noir includes such films as *Alien* (1979) and its sequels, and *Blade Runner* (1982), itself the subject of a study under the rubric of "Future Noir."[10] Emily E. Auger sees tech-noir as characterized by a futuristic technology that "has become an aggressively destructive force that threatens to transform the environment into a wasteland and forever alter the forms of human individuality, relationships, and ways of living."[11] Auger's book provides another extensive catalog of film titles including *A Clockwork Orange* (1971), *Westworld* (1973), *Videodrome* (1983), *Brazil* (1985), *RoboCop* (1987), *Total Recall* (1990), and *The Truman Show* (1998). Even this brief list of titles indicates the sheer range and disparate nature of films being categorized under subcategories of noir.

These encyclopedic entries are indicative of a tendency in noir criticism to attract "inventory" approaches, and since the 1970s there has been a plethora of encyclopedias, catalogs, dictionaries, guidebooks, and filmographies of the kind exemplified by Silver and Ward's pioneering *Film Noir*, first published in 1979. It was subsequently published in a third edition as *Film Noir: An Encyclopedic Reference to the American Style* (1992) and is, at the time of writing, in its fourth, with additional editors James Ursini and Robert Porfirio, as *Film Noir: The Encyclopedia* (2010). Each successive edition represents a significant expansion of its predecessor in the number of film titles it contains. There are many examples of such encyclopedic approaches.[12] There is also a plethora of websites similarly preoccupied with inventories.[13]

FIGURE 1.1 Two contenders for the "first" film noir: left, *The Maltese Falcon* (John Huston, 1941), showing the interior of Sam Spade's apartment; and right, the nightmare sequence in *Stranger on the Third Floor* (Boris Ingster, 1940).

So voluminous is the quantity of work on film noir that it constitutes by far the largest body of work on any film category. Much of this work is based on a critical proclivity for cataloging and, indeed, list-making can be seen to constitute something of a methodology in noir studies. The ever-lengthening list of film titles constitutes what Shannon Clute and Richard Edwards have called the "seductive amplitude" of noir, an exercise incapable of ever being completed.[14] Certainly, the profusion of inventory studies illustrates the kinds of problems inherent in critical attempts to produce a coherent taxonomy for film noir. By probing those attempts to impose an order of categorization on these films, we can start to question the functioning nature of the term. One interesting place to begin would be to ask of the two films often held to bookend the classical noir period, *The Maltese Falcon* (1941) and *Touch of Evil* (1958): What is it they have in common? We could ask the same question of *The Maltese Falcon* and *Stranger on the Third Floor* (1940), the latter being a film that many critics now cite as having replaced *The Maltese Falcon* as the "first" film noir (see Figures 1.1 and 1.2). How have these films, each markedly different from the other, been linked under the rubric of noir?

FIGURE 1.2 The "last" film noir: Orson Welles as Captain Quinlan in *Touch of Evil* (Orson Welles, 1958).

The encyclopedias and catalogs that form such a characteristic feature of noir criticism have a great deal in common with the fictional encyclopedia of animals, "The Celestial Emporium of Benevolent Knowledge," which appears in an essay by Jorge Luis Borges. Fascinated by the "wonderment of this taxonomy," Michel Foucault draws our attention to Borges's passage at the outset of his book, *The Order of Things*:

> This passage quotes a "certain Chinese encyclopaedia" in which it is written that "animals are divided into: (a) belonging to the Emperor, (b) embalmed, (c) tame, (d) sucking pigs, (e) sirens, (f) fabulous, (g) stray dogs, (h) included in the present classification, (i) frenzied, (j) innumerable, (k) drawn with a very fine camelhair brush, (l) *et cetera*, (m) having just broken the water pitcher, (n) that from a long way off look like flies."[15]

Foucault recalls how the passage kept him laughing and it's easy to see why. The bizarre entries and surreal juxtapositions of Borges's fantastical taxonomy read like a ready-made satire on some of the encyclopedic studies of film noir. It also serves to highlight the dubious authority of the encyclopedia as a scholarly text with its ludicrous and unsubstantiated claims.

And yet however fantastical Borges's passage appears, it may not seem quite as far fetched in comparison with some of the entries classified as noir. In Patrick Brion's *Le Film Noir*, for example, we find situated between the entries for Hitchcock's *Shadow of a Doubt* (1943) and Siodmak's *Phantom Lady* (1944) the title *Who Killed Who?* (1943), a Tex Avery animated short. Its inclusion in Brion's catalog raises questions about what constitutes a representative example of film noir from "*the Golden Age of American Crime Films*," the subtitle of his book. The film itself has no discernible traces of film noir at all but rather plays with the tropes of a traditional ghost story linked to an old-fashioned whodunit.[16] Its inclusion in a book about film noir is a mystery.

Andrew Spicer is surely right to describe the sheer volume of work on film noir as "evidence of a thriving minor industry that shows no signs of abating."[17] His own work has made a significant contribution to that industry through several books seeking to extend the parameters of film noir. His *European Film Noir*, for example, features accounts of French, British, German, Spanish, and Italian film noir and neo-noir, while his *Historical Dictionary of Film Noir* attempts to extend the geographical boundaries of film noir yet further, incorporating entries from countries such as Argentina, New Zealand, and South Korea, to name but a few. The global reach of film noir, according to this view, seems practically inexhaustible, although the *Dictionary* is by no means comprehensive.[18] There are several instances of this globalizing tendency.[19]

This globalizing "extension" in noir criticism has created other problems. Spicer is one of many critics who see film noir as "exploring the dark underside of the American dream," but this becomes a more difficult concept to deal with in a transnational context. "Because that dream forms the core mythology of global capitalism," he says, "film noir, handled intelligently, is not merely a commodified style, but an important and continuously evolving cultural phenomenon that, even if it cannot be defined precisely, remains a crucial vehicle through which that mythology can be critiqued and challenged."[20] For "globalists" like Spicer, a great deal of critical ingenuity is deployed in attempts to transform noir into a global configuration, especially here, as an ideological critique. But the problem with this kind of statement is that it is impossible to pin down. It's unclear, for example, how the American Dream is supposed to export to global capitalism. What does it mean to say "film noir, handled intelligently"? Can the lack of a precise definition be brushed aside so lightly? Spicer's "revisionist impulse" that works to extend the geographical constituency of noir beyond its original American one looks difficult to sustain.

This notion of widening the parameters of film noir as an object of study can seem like an attractive one, especially when compared with what Spicer sees as the limited focus on the "national exclusivity" of American cinema which, he claims, is "a serious distortion of noir."[21] However, it is here, in these ever-widening geographical boundaries that the student is likely to encounter one of the major problems of definition. For example, Spicer criticizes Raymond Borde and Étienne Chaumeton for their pioneering 1955 text, *Panorama du film noir américain 1941-1953*, on the grounds that its object of study is American when it would be difficult to see how it could be otherwise given the historical circumstances in which they were writing and when the object of their study was intentionally that of American film. I discuss these circumstances in more detail below, but for the moment let me say that this book takes what might be called a post-revisionist view, and certainly a more skeptical attitude toward what I will argue is the overextended use of the term itself. Part of that overextended use has seen the term become almost synonymous with the crime film. In fact, the term is in such wide circulation and so casually used by critics, fans, and scholars that it gets attached to virtually any crime film produced anywhere, often rendering the term effectively meaningless. This ever-expanding body of film noir together with the lack of any agreed definition has enabled critics to draw selectively from the catalog of titles in order to demonstrate the particular critical viewpoint they wish to argue. Film noir, in this broad sense, can mean anything a critic wishes it to mean when evidence for that view is provided by the selective use of a film text that "fits" the argument. This is one of the reasons why noir has proved such a critically attractive field of study.

Another problematic assumption in noir criticism is the notion held by Spicer and others of a "distortion" of noir. Critics often lay claim to what might be described as the *degree* of "noirness" to be found in a given film text, and this is evident in much of their work, especially in the kind of encyclopedic studies I have mentioned earlier. Here, we will often find commentaries that criticize a film noir for a perceived deficiency or shortfall of some kind, preventing it from being a "true" noir and therefore ineligible for the attribution of full noir status. But this, of course, is to presuppose that there exists in the first place a pure undistorted noir text, although it is by no means clear what that text is supposed to be.[22]

Cultural noir

Let Revlon take you back to the days of Film Noir with our Ultra HD Lipstick

Revlon advertisement (2015).[23]

"Noir" is complicated further by its wider cultural appeal. Beyond a mere film category, the term has acquired a pervasive cultural spread, traversing perfume, makeup, tailoring, lingerie, chocolates, tobacco, hairdressing salons, bars, clubs, and video games (giving rise to another noir subcategory, "game noir").[24] Noir, as Naremore suggests, "has become one of the dominant intellectual categories of the late twentieth century, operating across the entire cultural arena of art, popular memory, and criticism."[25] Why should the term have this kind of cultural resonance beyond that of a film category? Certainly, it's suggestive of some kind of intrinsic cultural value deriving, perhaps, from the films it describes and the period in which they were made. As Ian Cameron puts it, "even at the most rudimentary level of recognition, *noir* almost invariably has positive connotations: as a descriptive (or evocative) term, *film noir* carries an undertone of almost automatic approbation that, say, [the] western or musical do not."[26]

Examples of "cultural noir" abound, and I have chosen as an illustrative example of noir's evocative cultural reach a work by a musician. In 1997 singer-songwriter Carly Simon released an album called *Film Noir*. Accompanied by a promotional film, *Songs in Shadow: The Making of Carly Simon's Film Noir*, the album tells us a great deal about the cultural legacy of film noir at the end of the twentieth century.[27] The album comprises a collection of standards rendered in Hollywood's characteristic orchestral idiom of the 1940s with a few drawn explicitly from film noir soundtracks, such as Johnny Mercer's "Laura" from Otto Preminger's *Laura* (1944) and Frank Loesser's "Spring Will Be A Little Late This Year" from Robert Siodmak's *Christmas Holiday* (1944), all with accompanying vocals by Simon and an orchestral ambience self-consciously designed to evoke classical Hollywood noir. *Songs in Shadow* works to recreate a period sense of recording a film soundtrack as we see Simon, producer Jimmy Webb, and the session musicians in rehearsal intercut with scenes of nightclubs, dark corridors, and foggy streets at night, all replicating the familiar iconography of film noir. The opening credits are seen against a black background with backlit cigarette smoke, two of the more obvious signifiers of 1940s' noir, with Simon wearing dark glasses and a black dress. The CD liner notes are written by Martin Scorsese, himself an authority on film noir and director of several "neo-noir" films, thereby helping to authenticate the noir credentials of the album's concept.

What does all this have to tell us about film noir? In one sense, noir provides a certain type of packaging for the collection of songs and the singer. There is little in the songs and their arrangements to justify the title of the collection per se, and musically several of them sound like reworked treatments reminiscent of Brill Building pop from the 1960s or power ballads from the 1970s. We see Simon looking chic and elegant, evoking 1940s' style and fashion, and smiling widely in all the photographs in the liner notes. There is nothing in the pictures to suggest the dark themes and somber look of 1940s' film noir, nor the enigmatic glamor of the femme fatale she seems to be emulating. Rather, the noir packaging works as pastiche, where "film noir" provides a kind of ready-made package designed to replicate an age more stylish and romantic than our own. It appeals to us in part because it was an age in which it wasn't just permissible to smoke cigarettes but almost compulsory to do so, the stylish accoutrements to illicit sex and looking cool, especially in contrast to our own age of prohibitive health warnings.

Some of these issues are taken up in Marc Vernet's account of the appeal of film noir in the passage that appears as the epigraph at the beginning of this book. Vernet, a noir skeptic, nicely enumerates the various ways in which noir exercises its allure as "an object of beauty." But he then goes on to dispel the illusory nature of noir's attraction: it can be an object of beauty only insofar as it remains critically uninspected and this, he argues, is what has happened. To speak about film noir, he says, means "being installed in repetition, in taking up the unanalysed discourse of [one's] predecessors, with pre-established definitions . . . that are impossible to criticize." One reason he gives for this—"who has seen and studied all the films listed by Silver and Ward?"—reminds us of the sheer weight of catalog studies of noir. Vernet also suggests that the successors to Borde and Chaumeton's "founding" *Panorama* book "have only lengthened the list of films to be included, adding photographs and more extensive technical documentation: a look at these works' general presentations shows that the argumentation has remained fundamentally the same, without innovation."[28] Ultimately, we find ourselves in the curious position of studying a subject whose very existence is in doubt. As Steve Neale puts it: "As a single phenomenon, *noir*, in my view, never existed. That is why no one has been able to define it, and why the contours of the larger *noir* canon in particular are so imprecise."[29]

"The Americans made it and then the French invented it"

What we can determine, however, are the historical circumstances in which the term emerged and developed. How, then, did a group of American films become known by a French name? Noir critics generally agree that the first occurrence of the term being applied to American films can be found in an article by Nino Frank in the French film journal *L'Écran Français* in 1946, and in a second, by Jean-Pierre Chartier, appearing three months later in *La Revue du Cinéma*.[30] Critics often mention these early noir proponents in passing before going on to discuss the American films they highlight. However, these articles are foundational texts in the critical invention of film noir, and we should therefore pay close attention not only to what they say but also to the cultural moment in postwar France that gave rise to them.

In 1946, following the years of German Occupation—what the French call *les années noires*—France received a sudden influx of American films previously prohibited by the Nazi administration. For cineaste critics like Frank and his contemporaries, these films had been eagerly awaited after a hiatus of five years, and when they eventually arrived in the summer of 1946 they were exhibited en bloc, notably at the Cinémathèque Française in Paris, a central venue for what was then a thriving French cineaste culture. It was in these circumstances, then, that Frank and Chartier first saw this backlog of American films. These back-to-back screenings enabled the French critics more readily to pick up on what they saw as the similarities between these films and to take note of how different they were from prewar Hollywood productions. As R. Barton Palmer puts it:

> Enthusiastic admirers of a cinema they thought more vital and lively than their own, many French critics were struck by what they perceived as a radical change in American crime films, a loose category encompassing several established genres, including gangster, detective, and police procedural films as well as crime melodrama.[31]

It's noteworthy to see how this early stage in the critical construction of film noir involves a drawing together of different genres.

Frank lists seven films he found "particularly masterful:" *Citizen Kane* (1941), *The Little Foxes* (1941), and *How Green Was My Valley* (1941) together with *Double Indemnity*, *Laura*, *The Maltese Falcon*, and *Murder, My Sweet* (1944). He singled out the last four as belonging to a class that used to be called the crime film but would be best described as "criminal psychology." For Frank, the old-fashioned crime film was like the traditional detective story which, in the works of Edgar Allen Poe, Émile Gaboriau, and Arthur Conan Doyle, had become predictable and formulaic. The detective-hero in such stories was merely "a thinking machine" in narratives encumbered with lengthy explications at the end. Only *Laura* belongs to this "outdated genre," but the other three are different in that they are seen as "true to life." The detective here, says Frank, "is not a mechanism but a protagonist." This represents a shift away from the puzzle-solving formula of the traditional whodunit to an altogether different kind of narrative. For Frank, this new kind of *policier* is a significant development in terms of genre, particularly because he sees it as having "superseded" the traditional western. Now, "chases on horseback and idylls in coaches" have been displaced by "the dynamism of violent death and dark mysteries," and with the notion of a "fantastic social order."

Another characteristic of the detective figure identified by Frank and evident in both *The Maltese Falcon* and *Murder, My Sweet* is that he is now a private eye, situated "on the fringe of the law."[32] These "noir" films are linked to what Frank describes as a "third dimension," a call for "true-to-life" verisimilitude: "There is nothing remarkable in the fact that today's viewers are more responsive to this stamp of verisimilitude, of 'true to life' ['*vécu*'], and, why not, to the kind of gross cruelties which actually exist." Then, in a scarcely concealed acknowledgment of the *années noires*, he notes that "the struggle to survive is not a new invention."[33]

Frank also identified another development in formal narrative technique that, he found, served his "true-to-life" criterion, "the intervention of a narrator or commentator" enabling a "fragmentation of the narrative." The use of flashback and voice-over narration in films such as *Double Indemnity*, as Frank points out, was not in itself new but had a French antecedent. Sacha Guitry had used both techniques in *Le Roman d'un Tricheur* [*Confessions of a Cheat*] (1936). For Frank, the advent of these American "noir" films raised a question of national rivalry, leading him to ask: "Has Hollywood definitively outclassed Paris?" Certainly, he detected a schism between an old guard of "museum objects" represented by John Ford and William Wyler against a new "class of authors" like Billy Wilder, Otto Preminger, and John Huston. Although Ford's *How Green Was My Valley* and Wyler's *The Letter* (1940) may have been "admirable," they were also "profoundly boring," with production values "written in capital letters" or as "filmed theatre in all its splendor. . . . Both are devoid of life, of truth, of depth, of charm, of vitality, of real energy— of that 'third dimension' that I prefer," he says.[34]

Like Frank, Jean-Pierre Chartier also detected a new tendency in the recent American films. He similarly focuses on *Double Indemnity* and *Murder, My Sweet* together with *The Postman Always Rings Twice* (1946) and Wilder's *The Lost Weekend* (1945). He begins by drawing attention to the inscription on posters for *Double Indemnity*, "She kisses him so that he'll kill for her," emblazoned over a blood stain. The same line, Chartier says, would work as well for both *Murder, My Sweet* and *The Postman Always Rings Twice* in which "all the characters are more or less corrupt." Whereas Frank had championed the new "noir" films, Chartier was repelled by their antihumanism. "It is hard to imagine sinking deeper into pessimism and disgust with humanity," he says.[35] Nevertheless, he was impressed with some of the formal features of *Murder, My Sweet*, particularly when the detective is repeatedly rendered unconscious, "and each time the screen tries to render the experience of someone being knocked out: a play of twisted shapes, which makes us think of the experiments of 'pure cinema', of the presentation of a nightmare and disturbed vision in the manner of the old school of avant-garde filmmakers."[36] Chartier is resistant to claims for a French prewar school of film noir in films such as Marcel Carné's *Le Quai des brumes* [*Port of Shadows*] (1938) and *Hôtel du Nord* (1938), films that would be subsequently categorized as "*réalisme poétique*" ("poetic realism"). These, he argues, "contain some glimmer of resistance to the dark side, where love provides at least the mirage of a better world, where some re-vindication of society opens the door for hope, and even though the characters may despair they retain our pity and our sympathy." But there is none of that in the American noir films, Chartier says. "These are monsters, criminals and psychopaths without redemptive qualities who behave according to the preordained disposition towards evil within themselves."[37]

These two articles highlight several factors in the French critical reception of these American films. To begin with, it is significant that Frank should include Raymond Chandler in his list of admired "authors," and make repeated reference to Dashiell Hammet. These so-called "hard-boiled" writers found a receptive readership in France in the 1930s. Hammett's *Red Harvest* (1929) and *The Glass Key* (1931) were both published there in translation in 1932, soon after their American publication. These writers, many of whose novels would become known as films noir, can be seen as a precursor to the French import of the film adaptations themselves. At the same time, the 1930s saw the emergence of a new generation of French crime writers. The most important of these was Georges Simenon, whose popular Maigret novels were frequently adapted for film. Jean Renoir's *La Nuit du Carrefour* [*Night at the Crossroads*] (1932), Jean Tarride's *Le Chien jaune* [*The Yellow Dog*] (1932), and Julien Duvivier's *La Tête d'un homme* [*A Man's Head*] (1933) were the first of a series of Maigret adaptations that, as Ginette Vincendeau has argued, "constitute the beginning proper of French film noir."[38] We can see here in the emergence and confluence of crime fiction and film in 1930s' France a sense in which French critics observing the new American "noir" films could identify affinities with their own literary and cinematic traditions.[39]

As M. E. Holmes has pointed out, in the week of July 3–9, 1946, the week before the American films arrived in France, Parisian cinemas were showing several of the *réalisme poétique* films banned during the Occupation, including *Pépé le Moko* (1937), *La Bête Humaine* [*The Human Beast*] (1938), *Le Jour se lève* [*Daybreak*] (1939), and *La Règle du jeu* [*The Rules of the Game*] (1939). Cinemagoers were consequently able to see these prewar French films side-by-side with the new American ones.[40] If "film noir" emerged as a postwar term, it also had a significant application in prewar France when, as Charles O'Brien has pointed out, it was in common critical parlance as a negative or pejorative term with connotations of "immorality and scandal."[41] Moreover, with the imminent prospect of war, France's *avant guerre* culture was hardly conducive to film narratives characterized by desolate, demoralizing themes and stylistics. By 1939 it seemed that "the vogue for *film noir* had ended, the genre's melodramatic despair and expressionistic visual style made obsolete by new ideological conditions linked to the impending war."[42]

There is a significant issue here, usually overlooked by noir critics: the effect on French critical thinking of the *années noires* themselves. Naremore suggests that the end of the war in Paris "gave rise to what might be called a noir sensibility," and he examines the cultural and intellectual currents that he sees as instrumental in the production of that sensibility.[43] It's important to note that this "noir sensibility" would surely have been affected by the Occupation. Certainly, as Jean-Paul Sartre saw it shortly after the liberation of Paris in 1944, the experience of life under German Occupation was all-pervasive and practically incommunicable to anyone who wasn't there. The "most painful feature," says Sartre, was "the abstract, ambient horror, inspired by an invisible enemy" which "formed the fabric of our consciousness and influenced the whole meaning of the world."[44] Sartre also recalls the defining ambivalence of everyday life: "Everything we did was equivocal," he says, "we never quite knew whether we were doing right or doing wrong; a subtle poison corrupted even our best actions."[45] French critical receptivity to the new American "noir" films tends to highlight the kind of aesthetic values that resonate with the experience of the *années noires*. Frank's preoccupation with criminal psychology, violence, and "*vécu*" realism together with the formal techniques that worked to fragment the narratives can all be seen as bearing the traces of life under the Occupation.[46]

Articles on American noir occasionally appeared after those by Frank and Chartier. For example, two years later, Henri-François Rey discussed two additional films, both by Fritz Lang, *The Woman in the Window* (1945) and *Scarlet Street* (1945), noting that by then "noir" had become "the fashionable expression."[47] The first major French study of noir was Raymond Borde and Étienne Chaumeton's *Panorama of American Film Noir, 1941-1953*.[48] Borde and Chaumeton identified a "series" of American noirs which included, in addition to the initial wave of titles identified by Frank, *This Gun for Hire* (1942), *The Killers* (1946), *The Lady in the Lake* (1947), *Gilda* (1946), and *The Big*

Sleep (1946). Borde and Chaumeton defined "series" as "a group of nationally identifiable films sharing certain common features (style, atmosphere, subject)."[49] Although they defined it as a series, they are actually describing a generic cycle with a given life span, and they describe with some precision that series in terms of a rise-and-fall pattern in the chapters "the war years and the formation of a style (1941–1945)," "the glory days (1946–1948)," "decadence and transformation (1949–1950)," and finally, "the demise of a series (1951–1953)." The *Panorama* represents an important stage in the development of film noir as a critical construct, coming nearly a decade after the first use of the term by Frank and Chartier and drawing on a decade of French critical commentary in the interim. Here, they attempt to define, codify, and assess their selected group of films, adopting a method that involves "studying the most typical characteristics of films the critics have generally deemed to be noir."[50] What does their critical enterprise contribute to the development of French criticism of film noir?

They identified five key adjectives in the description of noir: "oneiric, strange, erotic, ambivalent, and cruel."[51] Recalling Frank's phrase about "the dynamism of violent death," they note how in just a few years the series has "accumulated so many hideous acts of brutality and murder." Sordid or strange, death always emerges at the end of a tortuous journey. "Film noir," they say, "is a film of death."[52] One of their main concerns is how "film noir has given a new lease of life to the theme of violence," and central to noir's violence is what they call "the ceremony of killing."[53] Here, the conventions of the adventure film, notably "combat with equal weapons," are abandoned along with any notion of a "fair fight." Noir is replete with instances of elaborately staged ritualized killings, and they cite several examples such as those in *The High Wall* (1947), *The Enforcer* (1951), *Red Light* (1949), *Kiss of Death* (1947), *Brute Force* (1947), and *Border Incident* (1949) (see Figure 1.3).[54]

Borde and Chaumeton describe an additional series in the noir field, the "*documentaire policier*"—what we would call today the police procedural—which includes *The House on 92nd Street* (1945), *Boomerang!* (1947), *Call Northside 777* (1948), *The Naked City* (1948), *Port of New York* (1949), and *Panic in the Streets* (1950). The main difference between these two series, they say, is that the procedural "considers a murder 'from an official police viewpoint,' and film noir from the criminal's, 'as a psychology of crime.'" In procedurals, the criminals "traverse the screen solely in order to be tailed, spied on, interrogated, hunted down, or killed." They are disparaging of this kind of "edifying" procedural, which is actually "a documentary to the glory of the police."[55] It's clear which of the two series they value, championing Joseph H Lewis's "incontestably noir opus" *Gun Crazy* (1950) over his film *The Undercover Man* (1949) from the previous year in which Lewis, they dismissively observe, "described the work of some tax officials."[56]

FIGURE 1.3 The "ceremony of killing": prison informant Wilson (James O'Rear), driven to his death in the workshop's pressing plant in *Brute Force* (Jules Dassin, 1947).

Borde and Chaumeton also saw the popularization of psychoanalysis as an influential factor in the development of film noir, with the "wide therapeutic diffusion" of psychiatry dating from 1935 and continuing through the 1940s. They noted, accurately, how wartime testing on army recruits "detected a significant percentage of neuropaths and psychopaths," and that after the end of the war, "the increase in admissions to psychiatric hospitals and clinics focused general attention on the social problem of psychological maladjustment."[57] The first "explicitly psychoanalytic" film, *Blind Alley* (1939), involving "the description and final explication of a case history," was followed by other "case" noirs such as *The Snake Pit* (1948), *Home of the Brave* (1949), and *Spellbound* (1945). Borde and Chaumeton also identified a group of films characterized by an "implicit psychoanalysis" which "restitute a psychological atmosphere" in which characters have "complexes" that remain deliberately unresolved, as in *Gilda* (1946), *Leave Her to Heaven* (1946), and *White Heat* (1949). "In any event," they say, "psychoanalysis has furnished the detective film with many features of a noir psychology." The psychoanalytic noir "has underlined the irrational character of criminal motivation" in which the love of money is often "a cover for libidinal fixation or infantile conflict" and psychiatry "knows that criminal behavior patterns often hide self-destructive reactions or guilt complexes." The "ambience of this 'depth psychology' . . . with its ambiguous or secret meanings . . . is transposed in the enigmatic situations of film noir, in imbroglios of intentions and of traps whose ultimate meaning remains remote and appears to recede indefinitely."[58]

Another factor identified by Borde and Chaumeton in the development of noir was the increasing importance of the wartime documentary ("propaganda or newsreels") in cinema programs with a corresponding emphasis on cinematic realism. This, they suggest, engendered three new genres: "the war film, the police documentary, and . . . film noir." But there was also a sense in which wartime events themselves "habituated people to violence and prepared the way for a crueler kind of cinema," intensified by public awareness of German and Japanese atrocities after the end of the war. Such atrocities, being distanced from American soil, "retained an exotic, unreal aspect" and in America film noir was able "to create a synthesis between realism and cruelty."[59] This is a sharp observation from a critical vantage point less than a decade after the end of the war.

One of the key issues arising from the critical invention of noir by French critics like Borde and Chaumeton concerns the question of whether prewar French cinema had "anticipated" American film noir, a question previously raised by Nino Frank. Borde and Chaumeton saw only limited French influence and although the "three greats" of French cinema—Julien Duvivier, Jean Renoir, and Marcel Carné—"had created a certain noir realism," this was somewhat limited. "Did *Pépé le Moko*, *Quai des brumes*, and *La Bête Humaine* announce American film noir? We think not."[60] Remakes were another matter, however, and Borde and Chaumeton go on to highlight how Hollywood had remade several "of the best French noir works." *Pépé le Moko* was remade twice, first as *Algiers* (1938) and second as *Casbah* (1948); Renoir's *La Chienne* [*The Bitch*] (1931) was remade by Fritz Lang as *Scarlet Street* (1945); Carné's *Le Jour se lève* was remade by Anatol Litvak as *The Long Night* (1947); and Henri-Georges Clouzot's *Le Corbeau* [*The Raven*] (1943) was remade by Otto Preminger as *The 13th Letter* (1951). It seems odd to attempt to minimize the influence of French cinema on American noir after compiling such a list of remakes. Rather, as Naremore has suggested, "the French were . . . predisposed to invent American noir because it evoked a golden age of their own cinema."[61]

For Borde and Chaumeton the war years were crucial in the formation of American noir style, but there was an anomaly in the period. Although, like Frank, they identified *The Maltese Falcon* as the earliest instance of a "typical work," they noted that there were few other examples: von Sternberg's *The Shanghai Gesture* (1942), Frank Tuttle's *This Gun for Hire* (1942), Stuart Heisler's *The Glass Key* (1942) and, "maybe," Norman Foster's *Journey into Fear* (1943). They argue that the "real advent of the series" didn't occur until 1946 with *The Lady in the Lake*, *Gilda*, *The Big Sleep*, and *The Dark Corner* (1946). "Why this false start," they ask, when *The Maltese Falcon* was followed by a "long silence" with only a few intermittent examples of "the new style." They attribute this lacuna to the intrinsically "anti-social" nature of film noir in its depictions of a characteristically "ambivalent" hero together with "a venal, debased milieu," the kind of depictions that were "out of place" in wartime when American soldiers were fighting on behalf of national values. There was in film noir, then, "an obvious discrepancy with official ideology."[62]

If there was a cultural predisposition for French critics to create noir, one of the predominant currents in French culture to influence their thinking was surrealism. It's significant, then, that Borde and Chaumeton's *Panorama* should bear the imprimatur of Marcel Duhamel who wrote its preface, and apposite that his preface should be so eccentric. Duhamel was an important figure in the French cultural context that engendered noir. One of the proponents of surrealism in the 1920s, he founded Gallimard's *Série noire* in 1945, an imprint specializing in French translations of American "hard-boiled" crime fiction by authors including Dashiell Hammett, Raymond Chandler, James M Cain, and Horace McCoy. Duhamel's preface serves to underscore the relation between surrealism and noir. His sentiments are revealing in that they highlight both the importance of film and filmgoing to the surrealists.

Here, Duhamel reminisces fondly about his own filmgoing experiences in Paris in the 1920s in the company of fellow surrealists Jacques Prévert, Yves Tanguy, André Breton, and Raymond Queneau: "Solely the noir kind," he improbably suggests, throwing the term around with some abandon.[63] He recalls William Wellman's *Chinatown Nights* (1929) as "the masterpiece of silent noir gangster film" together with some George O'Brien features, "that were curious, nonconformist, and as noir as you could wish."[64] Recalling the silent period, Duhamel claims that the origins of film noir can be traced back to early cinema such as in *L'Assassinat du Duc de Guise* (1908) and Louis Feuillade's *Les Vampires* (1915–16), a silent crime-film serial in ten episodes.[65] Here, too, early American film style (what the French called "American montage") was making an impact, especially at Gaumont where Feuillade's *Les Vampires* was itself influenced by the American melodrama serial *The Perils of Pauline* (1914).

Feuillade was greatly admired by the Parisian avant-garde, notably for his serial adaptations of the popular *Fantômas* novels by Marcel Allain and Pierre Souvestre (1913–14).[66] It's easy to see why these early films chimed with a nascent surrealist imagination and to constitute what Robin Walz sees as one of "the mass-culture 'stimulators' of surrealism." Walz identifies four motifs in the *Fantômas* serial, all of which can be seen as precursors of noir: "displaced identities, endless detours, uncanny objects, and sublime horror."[67] With their bizarre juxtapositions of ordinary city locations and fantastic incidents, the spectral figure of Fantômas himself seems to represent a weird anarchic terrorist, sinister and cruel, a shadowy, shape-shifting phantom. The serial also represented a cultural phenomenon that had huge popular appeal with the figure of its masked antihero bestriding the city becoming part of the cultural fabric of Paris, as John Ashbery has pointed out. "Plastered on billboards, on kiosks and *colonnes Morris*, on walls of corridors in the Métro, his image multiplied throughout the city."[68] In this metropolitan milieux, where the familiar and everyday is transmogrified into the fantastic and uncanny, narratives are fractured by detours, improbabilities, and far-fetched coincidences. The affinities between American noir and the surrealist imagination can be readily identified.[69]

For Duhamel and his fellow surrealists, cinemagoing became a compulsive experience: they were dedicated fans, in thrall to cinema. However, it was an experience removed from any conventional sense of coherent narrative viewing. The early surrealists

> would randomly pop in and out of fleapit theatres for brief periods of time, sampling the imagery. . . . Wilfully disrupting narrative continuities, they savored the cinematic mise-en-scène. . . . At certain moments, even in ordinary genre films or grade-B productions, it could involuntarily throw off bizarre images, strange juxtapositions, and erotic plays of light and shadow on human bodies, thus providing an opportunity for the audience to break free of repressive plot conventions.[70]

As the surrealists favored disrupted narratives—physically achieving such an effect by their comings and goings during film screenings—the disrupted narrative structures that often characterized film noir through the use of flashback and plots of labyrinthine complexity proved particularly attractive.

Certain kinds of film were particularly well suited to the surrealists' agenda for what Naremore calls "the destruction of bourgeois art and the desublimation of everyday life." That agenda, as he observes, was played out in films with "improbable, confusing, or incoherent narratives: the bad film, the crazy comedies, the horror film, and—especially in the post-World War II era—the Chandleresque detective film, which often lost control of its plot and became a series of hallucinatory adventures in the criminal underworld."[71] Surrealist writings on cinema often shared, and sometimes anticipated, noir characteristics.[72] For example, an article by Louis Aragon, "On Décor," which appeared in 1918 in *Le Film*, draws attention to the capability of film to render everyday objects strange,

> those dear old American adventure films that speak of daily life and manage to raise to a dramatic level a banknote on which our attention is riveted, a table with a revolver on it, a bottle that on occasion becomes a weapon, a handkerchief that reveals a crime, a typewriter that's the horizon of a desk, the terrible unreeling ticker tape with its magic ciphers that enrich or ruin bankers.[73]

Aragon's article highlights the attraction of American film which locates within the very ordinariness of everyday life a way of seeing the dramatic potential of ordinary objects. Moreover, all these objects "speak to daily life" as criminal per se, where even the ticker tape machine, as the technology of capitalism,

FIGURE 1.4 The dramatic potential of ordinary objects: the incriminating lighter in *Strangers on a Train* (Alfred Hitchcock, 1951).

bespeaks criminal enterprise. As we shall see, American films noir were filled with precisely such strangely rendered objects. Think, for instance, of the opening shot of the revolver on the desk in *The Big Heat* (1953) or the abnormal coffee cup in the diner in *Detour* (1945) (see Figure 1.4).

This, then, is the first "wave" of French criticism that saw the invention of film noir as a critical term. At this stage, the extent of noir criticism has been conducted on a modest scale in terms of the number of films under discussion. Frank, Chartier, and Rey nominated a total of seven films noir between them, while Borde and Chaumeton listed a total of twenty-one in their appendix of "Film Noirs."[74] As Steve Neale points out, seen in proportion to Hollywood's total output for the period, these numbers are miniscule.[75] How, then, did "film noir" come to be such a pervasive term? Indeed, "film noir" is one of several French terms that feature in film studies which suggestively provide a certain cultural status or cachet to the object of study. To put it another way, the term sounds "classier" than in its English translation. This is hardly surprising. As film noir gained critical currency in France in the 1950s, it formed part of a more general development in film theory and criticism whereby French critics sought to validate the importance of Hollywood hitherto seen as a commercialized, mass-produced cinema, unworthy of serious study.

Notes

1 Lewis Carroll, *Through the Looking-Glass and What Alice Found There* (1879) in Martin Gardner, ed., *The Annotated Alice* (London: Penguin, 2001), 224.

2 Quoted in Martin Scorsese and Michael Henry Wilson, *A Personal Journey with Martin Scorsese Through American Movies* (London: Faber and Faber, 1997), 110.

3 *Batman Begins* (2005), *The Dark Knight* (2008), and *The Dark Knight Rises* (2012).

4 James Naremore, *More than Night: Film Noir in its Contexts* (Berkeley: University of California Press, 1998), 2–3.

5 Michael Walker, "Film Noir: Introduction," in Ian Cameron, ed., *The Movie Book of Film Noir* (London: Studio Vista, 1992), 8.

6 Jon Tuska, *Dark Cinema: American Film Noir in Cultural Perspective* (Westport CT: Greenwood Press, 1984), xv–xvi.

7 Alain Silver, Elizabeth Ward, James Ursini, and Robert Porfirio, eds., *Film Noir: The Encyclopedia* (New York: Overlook Duckworth, 2010).

8 Inclusion of *The Black Book* is attributable to the fact that it was directed by Anthony Mann with John Alton as director of photography, two of the most widely acknowledged visual stylists in 1940s' noir.

9 Sheri Chinen Biesen, *Music in the Shadows: Noir Musical Films* (Baltimore: Johns Hopkins University Press, 2014).

10 Paul M. Sammon, *Future Noir: The Making of Blade Runner* (New York: Harper, 1996).

11 Emily E. Auger, *Tech-Noir Film: A Theory of the Development of Popular Genres* (Bristol: Intellect, 2011), 11.

12 Robert Ottoson's *A Reference Guide to the American Film Noir, 1940-1958* (Metuchen, NJ: Scarecrow Press, 1981); Lee Server, Ed Gorman, and Martin H. Greenberg, *The Big Book of Noir* (New York: Carroll & Graff, 1998); Geoff Mayer and Brian McDonnell, *Encyclopedia of Film Noir* (Westport, CT: Greenwood Press, 2000); Michael L. Stephens, *Film Noir: A Comprehensive, Illustrated Reference to Movies, Terms and Persons* (Jefferson, NC: McFarland, 2006); Alexander Ballinger and Danny Graydon, *The Rough Guide to Film Noir* (London: Rough Guides, 2007); Jim Hillier and Alastair Phillips, *100 Film Noirs* (London: BFI, 2009); Andrew Spicer, *Historical Dictionary of Film Noir* (Lanham, MD: Scarecrow Press, 2010); John Grant, *A Comprehensive Encyclopedia of Film Noir: The Essential Reference Guide* (Milwaukee: Limelight, 2013); Andrew Spicer and Helen Hanson, eds., *A Companion to Film Noir* (Oxford: Wiley Blackwell, 2013); Paul Duncan and Jürgen Müller, eds., *Film Noir: 100 All-Time Favorites* (Köln: Taschen, 2014). In addition, Silver and Ursini have edited no fewer than four Film Noir *Readers*.

13 See, for example, "250 Quintessential Noir Films (1940-1964)" at "They Shoot Pictures, Don't They?" http://www.theyshootpictures.com/noir250noirs1.htm. (Accessed January 15, 2016). The site also includes an additional 500 "American noir or noir-related films" from the same period. This list is divided into three subcategories of titles which are cited as film noir: (a) "often," (b), "quite often," and (c) "not often." See: http://www.theyshootpictures.com/noirmoreamerican.htm (Accessed January 15, 2016).

14 Shannon Clute and Richard L. Edwards, *The Maltese Touch of Evil: Film Noir and Potential Criticism* (Dartmouth: Dartmouth College Press, 2011), 13.

15 Michel Foucault, *The Order of Things: An Archeology of the Human Sciences* (New York: Vintage, 1994), xv.

16 Patrick Brion, *Le Film noir: L'âge d'or du film criminel américain d'Alfred Hitchcock à Nicholas Ray* (Paris: Éditions Nathan, 1991), 62–65.

17 Spicer and Hanson, eds., *Companion to Film Noir*, 12.

18 Andrew Spicer, ed., *European Film Noir* (Manchester: Manchester University Press, 2007); Spicer, *Historical Dictionary of Film Noir* (Lanham, MD: Scarecrow Press, 2010).

19 See for example, Dennis Broe, *Class, Crime and International Film Noir: Globalizing America's Dark Art* (New York: Palgrave Macmillan, 2014); Gyan Prakash, ed., *Noir Urbanisms: Dystopic Images of the Global Modern City* (Princeton, NJ: Princeton University Press, 2010); Jennifer Fay and Justus Nieland, *Film Noir: Hard-Boiled Modernity and the Cultures of Globalization* (Abingdon: Routledge, 2010).

20 Ibid., xlix.

21 Spicer, "Introduction: The Problem of Film Noir," in Spicer and Hanson, eds., *Companion*, 3.

22 Perhaps that text is *Double Indemnity* (1944). It was surely inevitable that criticism would eventually render "noir" as a superlative. "So which is the noirest film ever?" asks Adam Frost in the BFI "Infographic" we have looked at in the Introduction. Frost amusingly nominates a set of criteria by which film noir can be identified, only to discover that there is only one film, *Double Indemnity*, that meets all the criteria and that consequently there exists only one film noir. See Adam Frost, "Infographic: What makes a Film Noir?" (BFI, July 22, 2015). http://www.bfi.org.uk/news-opinion/news-bfi/features/infographic-what-makes-film-noir (Accessed June 27, 2016).

23 Advertising copy for a lipstick commercial by Revlon called "Film Noir" (2015). See: https://www.youtube.com/watch?v=HLrVYUTqEug (Accessed June 27, 2016).

24 See, for example, *L.A. Noire* (Rockstar Games, 2011).

25 Naremore, *More than Night*, 2.

26 Cameron, ed., *Movie Book of Film Noir*, 6.

27 Carly Simon, *Film Noir* (Arista, 1997); *Songs in Shadow: The Making of Carly Simon's Film Noir* (Surreal Life Productions, AMC, 1997).

28 Marc Vernet, "*Film Noir* on the Edge of Doom," in J. Swenson, trans., Joan Copjec, ed., *Shades of Noir: A Reader* (London: Verso, 1993), 1, 2.

29 Steve Neale, *Genre and Hollywood* (London: Routledge, 2000), 173–74.

30 Nino Frank, "Un nouveau genre 'policier': L'aventure criminelle" ("A New Kind of Police Drama: The Criminal Adventure," trans. Alain Silver), *L'Écran Français* (August 1946), repr. in Alain Silver and James Ursini, eds., *Film Noir Reader 2* (New York: Limelight, 1999), 15–19; Jean-Pierre Chartier, "Les Américaines aussi font des films 'noirs'" ("Americans Also Make *Noir* Films," trans. Alain Silver) in *La Revue du Cinéma* (November 1946), repr. in Silver and Ursini, eds., *Film Noir Reader 2*, 21–23.

31 R. Barton Palmer, *Hollywood's Dark Cinema: The American Film Noir* (New York: Twayne, 1994), 7. We take for granted today the ready availability of films on DVD and online but for these critics, writing before the age of the internet, they were often difficult or impossible to access. In postwar Paris, it must have been tantamount to an American "season" of screenings.

32 Frank, "New Kind of Police Drama," 15–16.

33 Ibid., 18.

34 Ibid., 18–19. See also Frank, "Et la troisième dimension?" *L'Écran Français* (July 24, 1946), 5.

35 Chartier, "Americans Also Make *Noir* Films," 21.

36 Ibid., 23.

37 Ibid.

38 Ginette Vincendeau, "French Film Noir," in Spicer, ed., *European Film Noir*, 25. See also Vincendeau, "Noir Is Also a French Word: The French Antecedents of Film Noir," in Cameron, ed., *Movie Book of Film Noir*, 57–58.

39 See Robin Buss, *French Film Noir* (London: Marion Boyars, 1994).

40 M. E. Holmes, *Nino Frank: From Dada to Film Noir*, Chapter 4, "Nino Frank and the Fascination of Noir," http://rememberninofrank.org/chapters/nino-frank-and-the-fascination-of-noir.html (Accessed January 5, 2016).

41 Charles O'Brien, "Film Noir in France: Before the Liberation," *Iris* 21 (Spring 1996), 8, 10.

42 Ibid., 8.

43 Naremore, *More than Night*, 11. See also 11–27.

44 Jean-Paul Sartre, "Paris Under the Occupation," *La France libre* (November 15, 1944), in J. G. Weightman, ed., *French Writing On English Soil: A Choice of French Writing Published in London Between November 1940 and June 1944* (London: Sylvan Press, 1945), 125–26.

45 Ibid., 131.

46 On the Occupation years, see Ian Ousby, *Occupation: The Ordeal of France, 1940-1944* (London: John Murray, 1977); Julian Jackson, *France: The Dark Years, 1940-1944* (New York: Oxford University Press, 2001); Richard Vinen, *The Unfree French: Life under the Occupation* (London: Allen Lane, 2006).

47 Henri-François Rey, "Hollywood Makes Myths Like Ford Makes Cars (Last Installment): Demonstration by the Absurd: Films Noirs," *L'Écran Français* (June 1948), in R. Barton Palmer, ed., *Perspectives on Film Noir* (New York: G.K. Hall, 1996), 29.

48 Raymond Borde and Étienne Chaumeton, *A Panorama of American Film Noir, 1941-1953,* trans. Paul Hammond (San Francisco: City Lights, 2002). First published as *Panorama du film noir américain, 1941-1953* (Paris: Éditions de Minuit, 1955).

49 Ibid., 1.

50 Ibid., 5.

51 Ibid., 2. As translator Paul Hammond points out, the French word *insolite*, given here as "strange," is difficult to translate: its connotations can encompass unusual, peculiar, unaccustomed, odd, and uncanny. See translator's note, 4.

52 Ibid., 5.

53 Ibid., 9, 10.

54 Ibid.

55 Ibid., 6, 7.

56 Ibid., 6.

57 Ibid., 18.

58 Ibid., 19–20. For a study of film noir and psychiatry, see Marlisa Santos, *The Dark Mirror: Psychiatry and Film Noir* (Lanham, MD: Lexington, 2011).

59 Borde and Chaumeton, *Panorama*, 21–22.

60 Ibid., 23.

61 Naremore, *More than Night*, 15.

62 Borde and Chaumeton, *Panorama*, 29.

63 Marcel Duhamel, "Preface," xxiii.

64 Ibid., xxiv.

65 Ibid.

66 *Fantômas* (1913), *Juve contra Fantômas* (1913), *Le Mort qui tue* (1913), *Fantômas contra Fantômas* (1914) and *Le Faux Magistrat* (1914).

67 Robin Walz, "Serial Killings: *Fantômas*, Feuillade, and the Mass-Culture Genealogy of Surrealism," *Velvet Light Trap* 37 (Spring 1996), 51.

68 John Ashbery, "Introduction to *Fantômas*," in Marcel Allain and Pierre Souvestre, eds., *Fantômas* (1911; London: Picador, 1986), 2.

69 For a thoroughgoing account of *Fantômas* in French cinema history, see Richard Abel, *The Ciné Goes to Town: French Cinema 1896-1914* (Berkeley: University of California Press, 1998), 370–80.

70 James Naremore, "A Season in Hell or the Snows of Yesteryear?" in Borde and Chaumeton, eds., *Panorama*, xi.

71 Naremore, *More Than Night*, 18.

72 On surrealist film writing, see Paul Hammond, "Available Light," in Paul Hammond, ed., *The Shadow and Its Shadow: Surrealist Writings on the Cinema* (3rd edn, San Francisco: City Lights, 2000), 1–48.

73 Louis Aragon, "On Décor," *Le Film* (September 1918), repr. in Hammond, ed., *Shadow and Its Shadow*, 57.

74 Borde and Chaumeton, *Panorama*, 161.

75 Neale, *Hollywood and Genre*, 155–56.

2

Visual style and narrative themes

For spectators who grew up during the postwar period and its aftermath, there existed an internalized movie whose characters circled warily around each other in a world of nightclubs and truck stops, a backlit theater of memory where women's faces disappeared in cigarette smoke and the world was erased by the blare of rumba bands. All men were named Steve and hadn't shaved in three days, had been wounded in battle or betrayed in the bedroom, stopped off for coffee but couldn't get that tune out of their heads, had been out of work since they got back from the war, took no satisfaction in anything but a grim, worn-out lucidity of purpose. The women were isolated, cynical, haunting, ruthless, frightened, doomed. Their intentions were crucial but definitively illegible. The rest of the world—cops, soda jerks, small-time hoods and con artists, rubes on the town flashing their wads, hatcheck girls dreaming of movie careers, cunning drunkards, eccentric night clerks—didn't care anyway. The el rumbled by, indifferent to the lovers dying in the shadow.

GEOFFREY O'BRIEN[1]

Visual style

Years ago, when in pictures we showed Jimmy Valentine cracking a safe, he usually carried the typical flashlight in one hand, while with the other he worked on the safe combination. In some scenes the flashlight was placed beside him on the floor. In either case the light source was established as a low one. To create an authentic effect, the cameraman lit the character from a low light which illuminated the face from an unusual angle. It distorted the countenance, threw shadows seldom seen in everyday life across the face. This light, which exaggerates features, became so popular that even in our films of today, when we want to call the attention of the audience to a criminal character, we use this type of illumination.

JOHN ALTON, "Criminal Lighting," in *Painting With Light* (1949).[2]

The visual style and narrative themes of film noir have often been seen as its defining and unifying characteristics. Many critics have placed particular emphasis on a visual style (although, oddly, none of the original French critics discussed it at all). This style is characterized by low-key lighting, chiaroscuro effects of light and shade and unusual shadow patterns. Noir cinematography often works to produce distorted effects through devices such as canted camera angles (Dutch angles) or unconventional camera positions. Critics have also charted an iconography for film noir, characterized by the figures of the femme fatale and the private eye, and featuring cityscapes of rain-soaked streets at night, flashing neon lights, and locales such as seedy bars, cheap hotels, roadside diners, and ritzy nightclubs. The narrative themes usually attributed to noir include a protagonist with a haunted past, malign fate, and criminal corruption. Narrative structures are often complex with the use of subjective narration told in voice-over and flashback in a disordered narrative chronology. It is this confluence of visual style, iconography, and narrative themes that is often held to define noir.

Following the first phase of noir criticism in France, American and British critics began to develop film noir studies, which consolidated and extended the earlier French ones. Much of this work, published predominantly in the 1970s, focused on visual style and narrative themes, often in relation to what critics took to be a connection between the films and the historical period that gave rise to them. The earliest explication of the term in English can be found in Charles Higham and Joel Greenberg's study of *Hollywood in the Forties*, in a chapter titled "Black Cinema."

A dark street in the early morning hours, splashed with a sudden downpour. Lamps form haloes in the murk. In a walk-up room, filled with the intermittent flashing of a neon sign from across the street, a man is waiting to murder or be murdered . . . the specific ambience of *film noir*, a world of darkness and violence, with a central figure whose motives are usually greed, lust and ambition, whose world is filled with fear. . . . A *genre* deeply rooted in the nineteenth century's vein of grim romanticism, developed through U.F.A. and the murky, fog-filled atmosphere of pre-war French movies. . . . Standard lamps fallen on pile carpets, spilling a fan of light about the face of a corpse; interrogation rooms filled with nervous police, the witness framed at their centre under a spotlight, heels clicking along subway or elevated platforms at night; cars spanking along canyon roads, with anguished faces beyond the rain-splashed windscreen . . . here is a world where it is always night, always foggy or wet, filled with gunshots and sobs, where men wear turned-down brims on their hats and women loom in fur coats, guns thrust deep in their pockets. . . . And above all, shadow upon shadow upon shadow . . . every shot in glistening low-key, so that rain always glittered across windows or windscreens . . . faces were barred deeply with those shadows that usually symbolised some imprisonment of body or soul.[3]

This account is interesting for several reasons, not least because it creates something of a template for much of the noir criticism to follow. Specifically, it provides a mixture of the different components seen to make up noir, drawing together both its stylistic and thematic concerns. With an emphasis on the visual style and "ambience" of the films, the account lists several instances of noir lighting together with some of the characteristic sets and locations. These elements combine to constitute an aesthetic linked to trapped conditions. The account also represents an early attempt to situate 1940s' noir in the context of its sources and influences, such as in the wider cultural sweep of nineteenth-century Romanticism and its twentieth-century manifestations through German expressionism of the 1920s and the French *réalisme poétique*' of the 1930s, all the while inflected with a sense of darkness which physically and metaphorically pervades the narratives.

For Janey Place and Lowell Peterson, in their influential article "Some Visual Motifs of *Film Noir*," visual style is *the* defining aspect of noir and "the consistent thread that united the very diverse films that together comprise this phenomenon."[4] For them, the "photographic style" of noir was contrary to standard studio practice. "*Noir* lighting," they say,

is "low-key." The ratio of key to fill light is great, creating areas of high contrast and rich, black shadows. Unlike the even illumination of high-key lighting which seeks to display attractively all areas of the frame, the low-key *noir* style opposes light and dark, hiding faces, rooms, urban landscapes—and, by extension, motivations and true character—in shadow and darkness which carry connotations of the mysterious and the unknown.[5]

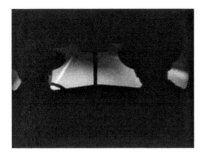

FIGURE 2.1 Noir lighting: "Small areas of light seem on the verge of being completely overwhelmed by the darkness that now threatens them from all sides." *The Killers* (Robert Siodmak, 1946).

Place and Peterson provide some detailed frame analysis in support of their claims for the primacy of visual style in noir. "Above all," they say, "it is the constant opposition of areas of light and dark that characterizes *film noir* cinematography. Small areas of light seem on the verge of being completely overwhelmed by the darkness that now threatens them from all sides"[6] (see Figure 2.1). Another key area highlighted by Place and Peterson is the departure from the standard industry practice of shooting night scenes "day-for-night" whereby night scenes were shot in daylight with lens filters that produced a night effect. The advent of noir saw a shift to shooting night scenes "night-for-night" where they were actually shot at night with artificial light sources to provide the required illumination. This had the effect of yielding the highest levels of contrast and producing the richest, darkest blacks, in contrast to the gray tones typically produced by day-for-night techniques.

Place and Peterson also highlight the importance of camerawork, notably the expressive effects of increased depth of field and wide-angle lenses in creating, respectively, a "closed universe" or of drawing the viewer into the picture.[7] Another key area is that of a mise-en-scène "designed to unsettle, jar, and disorient the viewer in correlation with the disorientation felt by the *noir* heroes" where "compositional balance within the frame is often disruptive and unnerving." In marked contrast to the conventional industry practice of "harmonious triangular three-shots and balanced two-shots" are "bizarre, off-angle compositions of figures placed irregularly in the frame, which create a world that is never stable or safe, that is always threatening to change drastically and unexpectedly."[8] Subsequent criticism has similarly emphasized a visual style characterized by compositional disunity and disequilibrium, often with such disruptive effects as the well-known trope of the splintered shadows of venetian blinds.

One of the problems with this analysis is that many of these formal features could be claimed for other genres too. Indeed, it would be possible to substitute "horror" or "gothic thriller" for "noir" and make the same case. Another problem is that many of the films noir deemed as "classic" have few or none of these features. Take, for instance, Howard Hawks's *The Big Sleep* (1946), shot throughout with the director's characteristic eye-level shooting style and devoid of most of the stylistic characteristics itemized by Place and Peterson.[9] Similarly, another problem arises in the prominence they attribute to certain kinds of camerawork. "The archetypal *noir* shot," they say, "is probably the extreme high-angle long shot, an oppressive and fatalistic angle that looks down on its helpless victim to make it look like a rat in a maze."[10] In fact, this shot is seldom in evidence and is far from being "archetypal." This kind of generalized claim can reveal the limitations of a study based on a small sample of films.

The most influential article from this 1970s' period is Paul Schrader's "Notes on *Film Noir*." Schrader's "Notes" stress the importance of visual style in the definition of film noir and, after Borde and Chaumeton, the most significant attempt to codify the term. Like Place and Peterson, Schrader sees lighting as one of noir's important "recurring techniques," and he is one of the first critics to argue for the influence of German expressionism in noir's visual style. Schrader also draws attention to an expressionist visual style where "oblique and vertical lines are preferred to horizontal. Obliquity adheres to the choreography of the city, and is in direct opposition to the horizontal American tradition of [D.W.] Griffith and [John] Ford. Oblique lines tend to splinter a screen," Schrader says, "making it restless and unstable."[11]

Film noir and German expressionism

Cameron Crowe: "Were you influenced [on *Double Indemnity*] by the
    German expressionist films?"
Billy Wilder: "No. There was *some* dramatic lighting, yes, but it was
    newsreel lighting. That was the ideal."[12]

German expressionism in cinema was a cultural phenomenon of the 1920s and formed part of a broader cultural movement which began roughly around the turn of the century. It was characterized by a highly stylized and artificial mise-en-scène that deployed unreal sets of distorted appearance. Buildings, staircases, and trees are slanted and twisted out of shape. Expressionism features false perspectives with fractured spaces, oblique angles, and zigzagged lines, together with chiaroscuro lighting and its extreme contrast between light and dark. The crazy world depicted works as an expression of a disordered mind, especially an insane one. Robert Wiene's *Das Kabinet des Dr. Caligari* [*The Cabinet of Dr. Caligari*] (1920) is widely acknowledged as the locus classicus of German expressionism.[13]

Following Schrader, the influence of German expressionism on film noir became widely accepted by critics and most descriptions of noir include an account of it as one of its key sources, especially in those studies that posit a "genealogy" approach.[14] Raymond Durgnat, for instance (writing shortly before Schrader), says it "heavily influences American *films noirs*, in which German directors . . . loom conspicuously."[15] There is a tendency in many such accounts to assume that German expressionism was imported into Hollywood where it displaced the studios' standard shooting and lighting techniques, providing a radical alternative to its conventional procedures. The influence of German expressionism, according to this view, was facilitated by the large numbers of German and East European émigrés who fled to America from Nazi Germany in the 1930s. In some ways this appears convincing. Schrader's "Notes" include a substantial list of émigrés working as directors, cinematographers, screenwriters, and composers, and this would make for a strong colony of influence in Hollywood.[16]

This view, however, has not gone unchallenged. Billy Wilder wasn't the only émigré associated with noir to repudiate the influence of expressionism. Otto Preminger, credited as the director of several noir titles, rejected the term too. "What you call Expressionism," he told Robert Porfirio in a 1975 interview, "are lousy sets."[17] Marc Vernet has also raised objections to the presumed influence of expressionism. He argues that "expressionist" lighting techniques weren't new to Hollywood in the 1940s but were already in evidence much earlier, "from at least 1915." He cites several film examples, one of the most revealing being *The Big Gamble* (1931) which, as he rightly points out, contains a number of interior and exterior scenes with light sources producing "noir" effects, and this in a film coming nearly a decade before what critics take to be the beginning of film noir. Vernet also draws attention to the use of "noir" lighting in gothic films well before such exemplary 1940s' titles as Jacques Tourneur's *Cat People* (1942). It was already evident in Todd Browning's collaborations with Lon Chaney in the 1920s, in the work of cinematographer Lee Garmes in Rouben Mamoulian's *City Streets* (1931), and in Josef von Sternberg's *Shanghai Express* (1932). The cinematographers responsible for films noir weren't "callow youths seeking to impose a new style," says Vernet, but usually Hollywood "veterans" who had been working there since the 1910s and 1920s.[18] For Vernet, "American cinema had, ever since the 1910s, a long and important tradition of '*noir*' lighting, whether in gothic or detective films, or simply in order to give greater pathos to scenes set at night."[19] In other words, Hollywood's use of "expressionist" lighting actually predated the advent of German expressionism itself.

It's also worth noting that German expressionism is a term that, like film noir itself, cannot be seen as a monolithic entity. Robert Porfirio has argued that German expressionism has two different phases and that it was in its second or "compromised" phase that the "forerunner" of film noir can be identified. This is in contrast to the preceding "classic" phase which, with its "extreme visuals," was more readily identified with the horror film, exemplified by Universal's *Son of Frankenstein* (1939). This second phase, according to Porfirio, saw the "fluid visual style" of cinematographers Fritz Wagner and Karl Freund displace "the static, fixed camera of pure expressionism" together with the development of expressive editing techniques by directors such as G. W. Pabst and F. W. Murnau as well as "more subtle shades of lighting" affecting the mood and atmosphere (*stimmung*) of the *Kammerspielfilm* (chamber-drama film) and the shift from the artificiality of studio sets toward the "sociological interest" of the *Strassenfilm* (street film). These factors, Porfirio argues, serviced the "psychological realism" of the *Kammerspielfilm* which "had its analogue in the noir cycle where virtually every entry has a psychological dimension and where a variety of devices (visual and aural) were put to use to portray 'inner states.'"[20] The *Kammerspielfilm* was based on the chamber dramas staged by Max Reinhardt at his Berlin theater, the *Kammerspiele*. These were small-scale, "slow-burn" productions staged for small audiences with a focus on character psychology. Settings were typically downbeat and endings unhappy. In a related development, the *Strassenfilm* cycle in Weimar Germany in the 1920s covered a wide range of urban-set narratives, often with a focus on the social problems of an urban milieu such as poverty, crime, and violence. The *Strassenfilm* is linked to the *Neue Sachlichkeit* (New Objectivity) and it is concerned with social realism. *Strassenfilm* melodramas often depicted the social decline of a bourgeois protagonist, seduced by the excitement of the city, such as in Karl Grune's *Die Strasse* (1923).[21]

Beyond their emphasis on expressionism, Schrader's "Notes" are important for their attempt to synthesize the different conditions or "catalytic elements" affecting Hollywood in the 1940s, elements he sees as instrumental in engendering film noir. Like Borde and Chaumeton, he sees film noir in historical terms, as "a specific period of film history," and his article is the first attempt, after theirs, to historicize the period in distinct phases.[22] But he also draws on the same kind of transhistorical motifs and archetypes as Durgnat had done in his "genealogy" study. Durgnat's cultural sweep is broad indeed, encompassing "Greek tragedy, Jacobean drama and the Romantic Agony" as "earlier responses to epochs of disillusionment and alienation." "The first detective thriller," he says, "is *Oedipus Rex*" and identifies the "Clytemnestra plot" in innumerable films noirs such as *The Postman Always Rings Twice* (1946).[23]

Schrader also offers an explanation for the longstanding critical neglect of film noir in America. "For a long time, *film noir*, with its emphasis on corruption and despair, was considered an aberration of the American character. The western, with its moral primitivism, and the gangster film, with its Horatio Alger values, were considered more American than the *film noir*."[24] Schrader's "Notes" would become one of the key critical texts in the 1970s to address that neglect and would form part of a growing body of work on film noir that formed part of the emergence and development of film studies as an academic discipline. Schrader's "Notes" would acquire further resonance a few years later when he acquired critical recognition as the screenwriter of Martin Scorsese's *Taxi Driver* (1976). This film, as Naremore has suggested, "did as much as any critical essay to make noir seem relevant to the period."[25]

Schrader's essay had also drawn attention to the low-budget, "B" film status of film noir as a possible explanation for its neglect, a notion developed in another important 1970s' essay by Paul Kerr. Kerr notes the failed attempts by critics to provide film noir with a "respectable pedigree" through recourse to the various perceived influences—"sociological, psychological, philosophical, political, technological and aesthetic"—claimed as the "progenitors" of noir. In an entertaining catalog of such "ancestors" of noir—reminiscent of that Borgesian "Emporium" we saw in the previous chapter—Kerr lists the following:

> the influx of German emigrés and the influence of expressionism; the influx of French emigrés and the influence of existentialism; Ernest Hemingway and the "hard-boiled" school of writing; Edward Hopper and the "ash can" school of painting; pre-war photo-journalism, wartime newsreels and post-war neorealism; the creators of [*Citizen*] *Kane*—Citizens [Herman] Mankiewicz, [Gregg] Toland and [Orson] Welles; the Wall Street crash and the rise of populism; the Second World War and the rise of fascism; the Cold War and the rise of McCarthyism.[26]

Also included in Kerr's list are some other vague "sources" such as "general American fears about bureaucracy, the bomb . . . the big city . . . the industrialisation of the female work-force during the war and the escalating corporatism of American capital throughout the 1940s."[27] Kerr highlights several of the assumptions that, by the late-1970s, were beginning to accrete around film noir, especially those loose kinds of "family-tree" studies such as Durgnat's. Kerr's study is particularly useful insofar as it represents one of the earliest attempts to provide a thoroughgoing analysis of a historically specific conjunction of industrial and economic factors affecting the modes of film production, distribution, and exhibition of the B-film noir.

"Docu-Noir"

There is another complicating factor in determining noir's visual style because this was subject to change during the period, embracing several different stylistic modes. The expressionistic visual style often seen by critics as a distinguishing feature of film noir was more evident in the earlier period. The postwar period saw an increase in a semidocumentary style, a style that Alain Silver has called "docu-noir."[28] Several factors were instrumental in this development. Wartime conditions had imposed restrictions on studio set-building, which led to an increase in location shooting which was facilitated by technological developments such as lighter cameras, portable lighting equipment, and faster film stock. The stylistics of the semidocumentary were influenced by the "realism" of newsreel journalism and the wartime documentary together with the impact of Italian neorealism and, more specifically, by a group of films by the producer Louis de Rochement who had previously made *The March of Time* newsreels that regularly featured in movie theaters throughout the 1940s.

The first of the semidocumentaries to establish the form was *House on 92nd Street* (1945), a narrative reconstruction of a real-life espionage case directed by Henry Hathaway and produced by de Rochement. The film utilized a number of devices to create verisimilitude, beginning with the opening title cards that stated that scenes were photographed "in the localities of the incidents depicted." Another de Rochement/Hathaway collaboration was *13 Rue Madeleine* (1947), based on case files from the Office of Strategic Studies (OSS). Other examples of the semidocumentary include Rochemont's *Boomerang!* (1947), *The Naked City* (1948), shot almost entirely on location in New York, and *Panic in the Streets* (1950), which was shot in New Orleans (see Figure 2.2). The subcategory also includes *The Street with No Name* (1948), *The Undercover Man* (1949), *Armored Car Robbery* (1950), *Mystery Street* (1950), *Union Station* (1950), and *The Racket* (1951). *The House on 92nd Street*, which began the cycle, works virtually as a public relations exercise on behalf of the FBI and the ensuing films follow suit in narratives that are paeans to the work of the police and agencies. The cycle also demonstrates a conservative if not downright right-wing narrative agenda where the voice-over, formerly the means of a subjective mode of narration, is deployed as an authoritarian mouthpiece, speaking on behalf of the agency. Borde and Chaumeton had already deprecated the "perfect" government agents in *The Undercover Man* (1949) and *Port of New York* (1949) as "puerile, cartoon-style police officers."[29] It would be interesting, then, to know what they would have made of *The F.B.I. Story* (1959), a film that surely represents the apotheosis of government agency promotional advertizing that is tantamount to an official history of the Bureau. Made with the full cooperation of the Agency, it even

FIGURE 2.2 "Docu-Noir": location shooting in New Orleans in *Panic in the Streets* (Elia Kazan, 1950).

featured J. Edgar Hoover himself in an uncredited role, extolling the efficiency of the organization of which he was director. The notion of yoking together under the same rubric of film noir both expressionist and semidocumentary stylistics is certainly to stretch the term.

Nevertheless, there was another aspect of location shooting which was linked to wider debates about realism and a more "serious" dimension to postwar American film. As Brian Neve has pointed out, "the physical detachment from studio sound stages not only added an element of documentary to films, but away from line and executive producers, directors could in some circumstances exercise greater autonomy." Mark Hellinger, producer of *The Naked City* (1948) and several other such documentary-style films noir, "still regarded a proposal to shoot *The Naked City* on the streets of New York as risky and 'experimental' in early 1947."[30] It is for similar reasons that some commentators have admired the low-budget "B" noir as being relatively free of studio control, thereby enabling a greater degree of artistic independence not only of style but also of sociopolitical critique. (I discuss low-budget noir in Chapter 5)

This "naked-city" realism also provided another source for the visual style of postwar noir. "*Naked City*" first appeared as the title of a book by New York photographer Weegee (Arthur Fellig) in 1945, with Hellinger having acquired the rights to the title for his film from Weegee.[31] Weegee was a tabloid photographer specializing in flash-lighted black-and-white pictures of urban night scenes, often depicting in stark and morbid detail the aftermath of violent crime, including the corpses of murdered criminals. Equipped with a shortwave police radio, he was able to gain immediate access to a crime scene, often arriving there before the police, and processed his pictures in a makeshift darkroom out of the trunk of his car. His photographs featured regularly in newspapers such as the *New York Post* and *Daily News*, bringing a style of tabloid realism to low-life subjects who looked as if they had been caught in the moment. A "docu-noir" like *The Naked City* with its location shooting had affinities not only with Italian neorealism and newsreel journalism but also with the visual style of Weegee's photojournalism.[32]

Another problem with accounting for visual style is that film noir, as Robert Sklar has suggested, "describes the psychology and the look not simply of a genre, but of a surprisingly pervasive tone in Hollywood films of the 1940s." This is apparent in films "quite distinct" from film noir but which nevertheless "share its feelings of claustrophobia and entrapment" such as the Preston Sturges wartime comedies *The Miracle of Morgan's Creek* (1944) and *Hail the Conquering Hero* (1944).[33] Paul Schrader concurs that "[al]most every dramatic Hollywood film from 1941 to 1953 contains some *noir* elements."[34] Sklar and Schrader are right to highlight this "pervasive" trend, which is indeed prevalent in a wide range of films across Hollywood's entire generic range. Let us take two examples, almost at random. The first example, Max Ophuls's *Letter From an Unknown Woman* (1948), usually categorized as melodrama or "fallen-woman" film, might seem like a far cry from film noir with its *fin-de-siècle* Vienna setting. However, its narrative structure, told in flashback with voice-over narration, is characteristics of noir narrative, as is its dark, low-key lighting for both street scenes and interiors. The letter of the title is written by Lisa (Joan Fontaine) to her former lover Stefan (Louis Jordan) as she is dying, though in the narrative present she is already dead. Stefan too is introduced under the shadow of his own impending death in a sequence that shows him arriving home late at night in a horse-drawn carriage on a deserted street in heavy rain. With its narrative themes of doomed love, preordained death and, in the forthcoming duel, a ritual of killing, the film can be stylistically and thematically linked to film noir. Note particularly the scene in which Lisa leaves Stefan's apartment for the last time and is shown on an artificial street set from a high-angled shot, a diminutive figure reduced to pure diagonal shadow, walking away under the street lamps.[35]

The second example is Frank Capra's *It's a Wonderful Life* (1946), a film that has inexplicably acquired a reputation as an optimistic affirmation of the values of family and community life. A suicidal George Bailey (James Stewart), wishing that he'd never been born, is shown the consequences of his wish in the "unborn sequence" where Bedford Falls is rendered as its dark other, Pottersville. This is a night world of urban decadence, a chaotic, crowded, electrified metropolis, its flashing neon signs signaling a world of vice and corruption. For the anguished "non-existant" George, the city is the ultimate nightmare in which he goes unrecognized, looking very like a noir protagonist in extremis. In both films there are strong elements of noir visual style and narrative themes, each providing instances of the "pervasive" noir tone across Hollywood's generic landscape.

Iconography

For many, the iconography of film noir is one of its most obvious and recognizable features. Anyone reading Geoffrey O'Brien's descriptive "montage" at the top of this chapter or the account by Higham and Greenberg would have little difficulty in recognizing that these are descriptions of film noir. But how would they know? Iconography is a central concept in genre recognition. The western, for example, is unmistakably recognizable through a system of recurrent visual motifs. "Almost every frame of a western movie identifies it as such by the objects within it," says Richard Maltby, "whether these generic signifiers be setting, characters, costumes, or accoutrements."[36] This sense of iconographic identity is similarly true of the gangster film. These "objects" are the generic hallmarks that help to constitute their respective genres: in each case, they provide a precise and comprehensive set of visual "data" which designates the genre. But despite appearances to the contrary, there is a problem with the iconography of film noir in that it lacks a generic set of objects to compare with those evident in the western and the gangster film. This isn't to suggest that there isn't a discernible iconography for film noir, but rather that it isn't as distinctive or consistent as its generic counterparts.

One of the most iconic images associated with film noir is that of the city, especially at night. Several noir critics have seen the city as a defining focus.[37] Many films noir actually have "city" in their titles.[38] It's significant too that the cover of the first edition of Borde and Chaumeton's *Panorama* should feature as a representative image of film noir an image from *Night and the City* (1948), featuring a tightly cropped image of a haunted-looking Richard Widmark as Harry Fabian.[39] Certainly, film noir is characterized by various urban settings. Take for example one of Nino Frank's original titles, *Murder, My Sweet* (1944). The opening shot depicts a tightly framed group of detectives interrogating a man with heavily bandaged eyes, a lamp illuminating the tabletop with the rest of the frame in darkness. The injured man, Philip Marlowe (Dick Powell), begins to recount the story that has brought him there, signaling a flashback as the camera moves from the interrogation room to a city street at night with its flashing neon signs as we hear Marlowe's voice-over narration. The camera moves up from the street to the window of Marlowe's office, its sign telling us that he is a private investigator. Illuminated intermittently by the flashing sign, we see from the inside of the office Marlowe's reflection in the window and then, suddenly, that of another figure looming large above him (see Figure 2.3). The first few minutes of the film provide a series of images often associated with the iconography of noir: the precinct interrogation, the city streets at night, the neon lights, the private eye's office, the arrival of a client with an enigmatic brief.

FIGURE 2.3 The opening sequence of *Murder, My Sweet* (Edward Dmytryk, 1944) with Dick Powell as private eye Philip Marlowe.

Another common trope in noir iconography is a macro perspective of the city at large, an establishing shot of the city at night such as the multiple shots of New York at the beginning of *Kiss of Death* (1947) or the silhouetted New York skyline in the credit sequence of *Cry of the City* (1948). *The Naked City* opens with a montage sequence of New York City locations at night. *Double Indemnity* (1944) begins with a car frenetically careering through the dark streets of Los Angeles. Most noirs are set in cities, particularly New York, Chicago, San Francisco, or Los Angeles, but many are set in small towns. *Boomerang!* (1947), for example, opens with a depiction of the streets of an ordinary Connecticut town during the day before cutting to a night scene of a murder on one of the same streets. Other films will give a micro perspective of the city through interiors, often deploying a kind of banal realism or quotidian ordinariness around what will become the site of a crime. For example, the opening scene in *Deadline at Dawn* (1946) shows the interior of a nondescript boarding house—before abruptly cutting to a close-up of a woman's face with a fly moving across it. She is asleep but looks dead, an image that presages her subsequent murder.

FIGURE 2.4 The Naked City: left, *Kiss of Death* (Henry Hathaway, 1947) and right, *The Naked City* (Jules Dassin, 1948).

The iconography of film noir includes a number of city locations such as police precincts, nightclubs, bars, railway stations and bus terminals, apartment buildings, rooming houses, hotel lobbies, newspaper offices, gyms, poolrooms, hospitals, prisons, and junkyards, although noir doesn't have a monopoly on these locations of course. Another part of this iconography can be seen in the spaces occupied by the cast of characters inhabiting the noir world: private eyes, detectives, and police officers, district attorneys, FBI agents, and officials from other government agencies, flatfoot cops, ex-convicts, strong-arm men, button men, and small-time hoods; there are also nightclub singers, showgirls, waitresses, hatcheck girls, or taxi dancers such as June Goffe (Susan Haywood) in *Deadline at Dawn* and Ginny Tremaine (Gloria Grahame) in *Crossfire* (1947).[40]

We should also note a narrative function of noir's iconography, often realized through the transitory spaces of its locations. As Vivian Sobchack has persuasively suggested, "the cocktail lounges, hotel bars, diners, roadhouses, and motels that spacialize film noir . . . are made for transients and transience." These are "quasi places that substitute perversely for the hospitable and felicitous places and 'domesticity' of a proper home."[41] During the postwar 1940s, the notion of "home" would take on particular significance, especially for a population that was perpetually in transit, having endured the disruptions and dislocations of the war years. Here, then, noir iconography is interesting for what it shows us and what it doesn't. As Sobchack says, "in noir, homes are given to us only in glimpses—as something lost or something fragile and threatened."[42] In a wartime culture of temporary accommodation and its filmic representations in noir, "the rooms of hotels and motels and boardinghouses figure as spaces of social dislocation, isolation, and existential alienation."[43] Illustrations of such "quasi places" are also evident in the kinds of interior spaces depicted in the paintings of Edward Hopper, whose work has been seen as a correlative to film noir, most famously in *Nighthawks* (1942).[44]

Narrative themes

Film academics have employed the term *film noir* as a blanket definition for any movie without a happy ending, from *King Kong* to *Citizen Kane*.

CARLOS CLARENS[45]

According to Paul Schrader, "Hollywood lighting grew darker, characters more corrupt, themes more fatalistic and the tone more hopeless."[46] One of the ways in which film noir appears to achieve coherence across its disparate narratives is often implied through its film titles. These are often stripped down to a single, stark adjective that encapsulates a sense of isolation and entrapment: *Abandoned* (1949), *Bewitched* (1945), *Caged* (1950), *Caught* (1949), *Convicted* (1950), *Cornered* (1945), *Desperate* (1947), *Framed* (1947), *Possessed* (1947), *Railroaded* (1947), *Spellbound* (1945), and *Trapped* (1949). Other titles speak of obstacles, restrictions, traps, diversions, impediments, illusions, and thwarted progress: *Backfire* (1950), *Criss Cross* (1949), *The Crooked Way* (1949), *The Crooked Web* (1955), *Deception* (1946), *Decoy* (1946), *Detour* (1945), *Drive a Crooked Road* (1954), *The High Wall* (1947), *Lured* (1947), *The Narrow Margin* (1952), *No Escape* (1953), *No Way Out* (1950), *One Way Street* (1950), *Phantom Lady* (1944), *Pitfall* (1948), *Quicksand* (1950), *Roadblock* (1951), *Sorry, Wrong Number* (1948), *Strange Illusion* (1945), *Strange Impersonation* (1946), *The Steel Trap* (1952), *The Street with No Name* (1948), *Tight Spot* (1955), *Undercurrent* (1946), *The Web* (1947), *Where the Sidewalk Ends* (1950), and *The Wrong Man* (1956). Many noir titles explicitly evoke darkness and night: *Appointment with a Shadow* (1958), *The Big Night* (1951), *Between Midnight and Dawn* (1950), *Clash by Night* (1952), *Dark City* (1950), *The Dark Corner* (1946), *The Dark Mirror* (1946), *Dark Passage* (1947), *The Dark Past* (1948), *Dark Waters* (1944), *Fear in the Night* (1947), *He Walked by Night* (1948), *The Long Night* (1947), *Man in the Dark* (1953), *Night Has a Thousand Eyes* (1948), *The Night Holds Terror* (1955), *The Night of the Hunter* (1955), *The Night Runner* (1957), *Night Without Sleep* (1952), *Nightfall* (1957), *Nightmare* (1956), *Nightmare Alley* (1947), *Shadow of a Doubt* (1943), *Shadow of a Woman* (1946), *Shadow on the Wall* (1950), *So Dark the Night* (1946), *Somewhere in the Night* (1946), *Strangers in the Night* (1944), *They Drive by Night* (1940), and *They Live by Night* (1948). These titles often work as a kind of shorthand for noir's narrative themes.

In these and other titles, one of the principal themes is violence or the threat of violence. As we have seen in Chapter 1, French critics had highlighted the theme of violence inherent in the films noir they saw. "An unprecedented panoply of cruelties and sufferings unfolds in film noir," say Borde and Chaumeton.[47] Violence might erupt inexplicably, particularly in everyday locations and often in unexplained circumstances that seem at odds with the ordinariness of the surroundings. In the opening scene of *The Killers* (1946), for instance, two heavies arrive at a nondescript small-town diner where they start humiliating and menacing the proprietor although without any specific threats until they announce they are there to kill "the Swede," one of the regular diners there. There is no apparent reason for this, and it is the lack of any explanation that accentuates the threat of incipient violence. Similarly, in *The Big Night* (1951), a man accompanied by his henchmen, enters a bar where, in a ritual of humiliation and self-debasement, he instructs the proprietor to take off his shirt ("I want to see some skin") and kneel on the floor where he is brutally beaten with a walking stick in front of his son and the customers who watch passively. We don't know what this punishment is for, nor why it should take the form of a public ritual, nor why the victim so passively accepts it.

Film noir abounds with examples of set-piece domestic violence, often murder. See, for instance, the frenzied ice-pick stabbing of Kitty March (Joan Bennett) by Chris Cross (Edward G. Robinson) in *Scarlet Street* (1945), a *crime passionnele*; or the almost identical murders of the husbands in *Double Indemnity* and *The Postman Always Rings Twice*, clubbed to death by an assailant hidden in the back of the family car, each the lover of the husband's wife who is driving. These are calculated, premeditated, and, for the period, extremely brutal, especially in their domestic settings. Violent crime is no longer committed by an external perpetrator, but by a spouse or her lover.

There were also innumerable acts of casual violence, often unexpected and disquieting. In *Kiss of Death* (1947), for instance, a giggling psychopath, Tommy Udo (Richard Widmark), sadistically pushes a wheelchair-bound old woman down a flight of stairs, killing her. Other examples will see a jarringly casual treatment of the human body. In *Inner Sanctum* (1948), for example, following the accidental killing of a woman, Harold Dunlap (Charles Russell) takes advantage of a train slowly pulling out of the station to dump her body on the observation deck of a railway car. In *The Naked City*, we follow the camera peering through the venetian blinds of a window to reveal two men in hats and suits strangling an unknown woman and manhandling her lifeless, floppy body. Although obviously dead, we see gloved hands turning on the bath taps: "Gotta be sure," says one of the men unceremoniously.

"Wrong man" noir

Eleanor Johnson (Ann Sheridan): "But Frank's done nothing wrong."
Cop: "Oh yes he has. He was in the wrong place at the wrong time."

Woman on the Run (1950)

Frank Bigelow (Edmond O'Brien): "I want to report a murder."
Detective: "Sit down. Where was this murder committed?"
Bigelow: "San Francisco, last night."
Detective: "Who was murdered?"
Bigelow: "I was."

D.O.A. (1950)

Another noir theme, which constitutes something of a noir subcategory, is the "wrong man" narrative, named after Hitchcock's *The Wrong Man* (1957) in which an innocent man is falsely accused of a crime. In Hitchcock's film, the weight of circumstantial evidence that accumulates against the innocent Manny Balestrero (Henry Fonda) seems less like a spate of unfortunate coincidences and more like an incontrovertible force emanating from the city, working to frame him. The "wrong man" trope also appears in *Black Angel* (1946), *Boomerang!* (1947), *They Won't Believe Me* (1947), *Call Northside 777* (1948), *Impact* (1949), *Convicted* (1950), *Mystery Street* (1950), *Where the Sidewalk Ends* (1950), *The Unknown Man* (1951), and *Murder Is My Beat* (1955). Some of these films, including Hitchcock's, were based on true stories previously published and much is made of their verisimilitude. *Call Northside 777*, directed by Henry Hathaway, is a documentary-style treatment of an investigation by *Chicago Times* journalist James P. McGuire into the wrongful conviction of Joe Majczek for the murder of a Chicago police officer. With McGuire acting as technical adviser, the film was based on a *Reader's Digest* article about the case. Much of the film was shot on location in Chicago and opens with the statement: "This is a true story."[48]

Similarly, *The Wrong Man* opens with Hitchcock directly addressing the audience to announce that "this is a true story, every word of it," while appearing in long-shadowed silhouette. Hitchcock's film, about "an average sort of fellow," was based on a *Life* magazine account of the case of a New York musician accused of a string of robberies, who is ultimately found to be innocent.[49] While in other genres this might yield a "happy ending," here it is cold comfort as the trauma endured by Manny's wife Rose (Vera Miles) has driven her to a nervous breakdown for which she is treated in a sanatorium. An epilogue states that two years after the incident, Rose "walked out of the sanatorium completely cured," but the text is at odds with a narrative closure that cannot adequately compensate for the ordeal she has suffered. "An innocent man has nothing to fear," says Lieutenant Bowers (Harold J. Stone) to Balestrero, a reassurance wholly contradicted by narrative events. The theme of unjust accusation would become a significant theme in film noir, often with an emphasis on the susceptibility of ordinary people to random chance.

The "wrong man" narrative fits into the wider noir theme of existential happenstance in which ordinary people going about their everyday lives get caught up in random incidents (I discuss this aspect of existential noir in Chapter 5). For example, in *Woman on the Run*, Frank Johnson (Ross Elliott) is out walking his dog one night when he sees a man being shot dead, a murder in which he himself becomes implicated; or Frank Bigelow in *D.O.A.* (1950), fatally poisoned by accident, who, in the last few hours of life remaining to him, investigates the circumstances of his own murder.

"Postwar malaise" and Zeitgeist noir

It's hardly surprising that the noir critics who had identified all those familiar noir themes—disillusionment, fear, anxiety, alienation, fatalism, angst, paranoia—would seek to explain what caused them. There are a number of problems in their attempts to do so. To begin with, in what can be termed a Zeitgeist theory of noir, critics have often identified, or taken for granted, a correlation between film noir and the "dark mood" of postwar America. Critics have often speculated that it is these films that uniquely reflect a "postwar malaise" in American society. One of the earliest attempts to link film noir with the socioeconomic or sociopolitical conditions of the period is Colin McArthur's 1972 study of the crime film, *Underworld U.S.A.* Like many subsequent critics, McArthur sees the 1940s as characterized by "a general mood of fear and insecurity" with a future of "uncertainty" "paralleled in the general mood of malaise, the loneliness and *angst* and the lack of clarity about the characters' motives in the [noir] thriller." McArthur also talks about how the "obvious cruelty" in these films was related to a society newly familiar with "the horrors of Auschwitz and Hiroshima and other atrocities" of the war. For McArthur, *The Dark Corner* (1946) "is a cry of loneliness and despair in a sick world."[50] Also, bearing in mind that McArthur was writing at a time when auteur theory was prevalent, he highlights those émigré directors associated with the "black thriller" of the 1940s—Fritz Lang, Robert Siodmak, Billy Wilder—who had fled prewar Europe, "their sensibilities, forged in the uncertainty of Weimar Germany and decaying Austria-Hungary, were much more sour and pessimistic than the more buoyant vision of native American directors such as Ford and Capra."[51] As a catchall generalization, "postwar malaise" would become the standard epithet used to pathologize the period and one of the most overworked phrases in noir criticism.

Another problem arises in the assumptions about what is taken to be that noir mood. There is substantial critical consensus about what this broadly encompasses, and, indeed, critics often provide virtually interchangeable lists. Place and Peterson, for example, see "characteristic . . . moods of claustrophobia, paranoia, despair, and nihilism."[52] Ottoson sees "despair, alienation, disillusionment, moral ambiguity, pessimism, corruption, and psychoses."[53] Noir criticism often identifies a dark underworld in which criminality stands metaphorically for a destabilized American society. Telotte, for example, identifies a focus "on urban crime and corruption, and on sudden upswellings of violence in a culture whose fabric seems to be unraveling." Consequently, he says, "noir seems fundamentally about violations: vice, corruption, unrestrained desire."[54] Framed within the spaces of this stylistically and thematically dark world are noir's archetypal characterizations: figures trapped in inhospitable or hostile environments, marginalized, estranged, and alienated from society at large. They are often seen to articulate a pessimistic commentary on the uncertainties of contemporary American society as figures who personify, as it were, pictures of a darkened psyche. Silver and Ward claim that these narratives "consistently evoke the dark side of the American persona" and that their "central figures . . . caught in their double binds, filled with existential bitterness, drowning outside the social mainstream, are America's stylized vision of itself, a mirror of the mental dysfunction of a nation in uncertain transition."[55] Telotte sees in noir what he describes as an "abrogation of the American dream's most basic promises— of hope, prosperity, and safety from persecution."[56] As Foster Hirsch sees it:

> Beneath its repeated stories of double and triple crosses, its private passions erupting into heinous crimes, the sleazy, compromised morality of many of its characters, can be glimpsed the political paranoia and brutality of the period. In its pervasive aura of defeat and despair, its images of entrapment, the escalating derangement of its leading characters, *noir* registers, in a general way, the country's sour postwar mood. This darkest, most downbeat of American film genres traces a series of metaphors for a decade of anxiety, a contemporary apocalypse bounded on the one hand by Nazi brutality and on the other by the awful knowledge of nuclear power.[57]

Hirsch's account is in some ways representative of the kind of quasi-historical criticism that can seem quite persuasive at face value. It seeks to correlate a set of narrative tropes with what is taken to be a certain postwar mood. Nevertheless, we should be wary that this is painted in very broad brushstrokes indeed.

As Richard Maltby argues in a key essay to take issue with this Zeitgeist tendency, critics "have identified a *noir* sensibility, traced it across a body of films, and then sought to attach it to a general American cultural condition of 'postwar malaise.'"[58] The problem identified by Maltby is caused by the lack of any clear attempt to locate these films within the historical context of their production and consumption, depending instead on generalizations and their presumed causal link to the films.

There is another related problem arising from this critical tendency. Film noir is often assumed to have a uniquely privileged position relative to any other generic category in being able to articulate a picture of a postwar American Zeitgeist. But as we've already seen, even with the widest latitude of definition, the number of films that can be classified as film noir during the period is relatively small. Why should film noir lay claim to speak on behalf of a national mood? Here, as Fredric Jameson suggests:

> It has often been said that every age is dominated by a privileged form, or genre, which seems by its structure the fittest to express its secret truths; or perhaps, if you prefer a more contemporary way of thinking about it, which seems to offer the richest symptom of what Sartre would have called the "objective neurosis" of that particular time and place.[59]

Certainly, if we look at Hollywood's general output during the immediate postwar period, we can identify several different genres, including comedies, such as *The Egg and I* (1947) and *The Bachelor and the Bobby-Soxer* (1947), and musical comedies such as *Road to Utopia* (1946), *Mother Wore Tights* (1947), and *Easter Parade* (1948). As Maltby suggests, no one seems to have made any claims that films such as *Magic Town* (1947) or *The Bishop's Wife* (1947) should be seen in relation to the Zeitgeist, or why a film noir like *Out of the Past* should be seen as any more "*zeitgeistig*" than the others.[60] And yet that is precisely what much noir criticism has assumed.

Notes

1 Geoffrey O'Brien, "The Return of Film Noir!" *New York Review of Books* (August 15, 1991), 43.

2 John Alton, *Painting With Light* (1949; Berkeley: University of California Press, 1995), 54–55. Alton is referring to *Affairs of Jimmy Valentine* (1942) on which he was cinematographer. Alton was associated with several key noir productions to which he brought a distinctive visual style, particularly the series he made with Anthony Mann—*T-Men* (1947), *Raw Deal* (1948), *Border Incident* (1949)—and also in other notable examples such as *Hollow Triumph* (1948), *He Walked by Night* (1948), *The Crooked Way* (1949), *Mystery Street* (1950), *Talk About a Stranger* (1952), *Witness to Murder* (1954), and Joseph H. Lewis's *The Big Combo* (1955). The minimal lighting techniques described by Alton were well suited to low-budget noir filmmaking, avoiding the need for costlier standard setups.

3 Charles Higham and Joel Greenberg, *Hollywood in the Forties* (New York: A.S. Barnes, 1968), 19–21.

4 Janey Place and Lowell Peterson, "Some Visual Motifs of *Film Noir*," in *Film Comment* (January/February 1974) in Silver and Ursini, *Film Noir Reader*, 65.

5   Ibid., 66.

6   Ibid., 67.

7   Ibid.

8   Ibid., 68.

9   See for instance Ian Brookes, "Who the Hell Is Howard Hawks?" in Brookes, ed., *Howard Hawks: New Perspectives* (London: Palgrave/BFI, 2016), 4–5.

10   Place and Peterson, "Some Visual Motifs," 68.

11   Paul Schrader, "Notes on *Film Noir*," *Film Comment* (Spring 1972) in Silver and Ursini, *Film Noir Reader*, 57.

12   Cameron Crowe, *Conversations with Wilder* (New York: Alfred A. Knopf, 1999), 53.

13   On German expressionism, see for instance Kristin Thompson and David Bordwell, *Film History: An Introduction* (New York: McGraw-Hill, 1994), 108–15. See also Lotte H. Eisner's classic study, *The Haunted Screen: Expressionism in the German Cinema and the Influence of Max Reinhardt*, trans. Roger Greaves (London: Thames & Hudson, 1969).

14   See, for example, Foster Hirsch, *Film Noir: The Dark Side of the Screen* (1981; New York: Da Capo, 1983), 53–58.

15   Raymond Durgnat, "Paint It Black: The Family Tree of the *Film Noir*," *Cinema* (1970), repr. in Silver and Ursini, eds., *Film Noir Reader*, 39.

16   Schrader's list includes: "Fritz Lang, Robert Siodmak, Billy Wilder, Franz Waxman, Otto Preminger, John Brahm, Anatole Litvak, Karl Freund, Max Ophuls, John Alton, Douglas Sirk, Fred Zinneman, William Dieterle, Max Steiner, Edgar G. Ulmer, Curtis Bernhardt, [and] Rudolph Maté," all names strongly associated with film noir productions. Schrader, "Notes," 55.

17   Quoted in Robert Porfirio, "Interview with Otto Preminger," in Robert Porfirio, Alain Silver and James Ursini, eds., *Film Noir Reader 3: Interviews with Filmmakers of the Classic Noir Period* (New York: Limelight, 2002), 96. See also Preminger's remarks about Max Reinhardt and expressionism in German theater, 93–95.

18   Vernet, "*Film Noir*," 9–10. Vernet doesn't mention any specific Browning titles, but see for example, *The Unknown* (1927), a gothic horror using expressionist lighting techniques.

19   Ibid., 12.

20   Robert Porfirio, "The Strange Case of Film Noir," in Spicer and Hanson, eds., *Companion to Film Noir*, 23.

21   See Thompson and Bordwell, *Film History*, 115–16; 122–24; Eisner, *Haunted Screen*, 177–221; 251–68.

22   Schrader, "Notes," 53; 58–61.

23   Durgnat, "Paint It Black," 37.

24   Schrader, "Notes," 62.

25   Naremore, *More Than Night*, 34. Naremore sees in Schrader's "Notes" a "structuring absence" of the Vietnam War. The visual style and narrative themes in *Taxi Driver*, with its Vietnam veteran Travis Bickle (Robert De Niro), are "analogous to all those returning World War II soldiers in Hollywood thrillers of the 1940s." Ibid., 33, 34.

26 Paul Kerr, "Out of What Past? Notes on the B *Film Noir*," *Screen Education* (Autumn/Winter 1979/1980), repr. in Silver and Ursini, eds., *Film Noir Reader*, 107.

27 Ibid.

28 See Alain Silver and James Ursini, "Docu-Noir," in Paul Duncan, ed., *Film Noir* (Köln: Taschen, 2004), 80–95.

29 Borde and Chaumeton, *Panorama*, 88.

30 Brian Neve, *Film and Politics in America: A Social Tradition* (London: Routledge, 1992), 149–50.

31 Weegee, *Naked City* (New York: Essential Books, 1945).

32 On Weegee and film noir, see Alain Bergala, "Weegee and Film Noir," in *Weegee's World* (Boston: Bullfinch, 2000), 69–117.

33 Robert Sklar, *Movie-Made America: A Cultural History of American Movies* (1975 rev. edn, New York: Vintage, 1994), 253.

34 Schrader, "Notes," 54.

35 Ophuls went on to make two films noir, both released in the following year: *Caught* (1949) and *The Reckless Moment* (1949).

36 Richard Maltby, *Hollywood Cinema* (Oxford: Wiley Blackwell, 1995), 117.

37 See for example, Spencer Selby, *Dark City: The Film Noir* (Jefferson, NC: McFarland, 1884); Nicholas Christopher, *Somewhere In the Night: Film Noir and the American City* (New York: Owl, 1997); Eddie Muller, *Dark City: The Lost World of Film Noir* (London: Titan, 1998).

38 See for instance, *City For Conquest* (1940), *Cry of the City* (1948), *The Naked City* (1948), *Dark City* (1950), *Night and the City* (1950), *The Sleeping City* (1950), *The Captive City* (1952), *City That Never Sleeps* (1953), *While the City Sleeps* (1956), and *City of Fear* (1959).

39 Borde and Chaumeton, *Panorama du film noir américain, 1941-1953* (Paris: Éditions de Minuit, 1955), 1.

40 The taxi dancer or "dime-a-dance" girl appears in several films noir as one of the denizens of its downbeat urban milieu, sometimes as a euphemism for casual prostitution. See also *Tomorrow Is Another Day* (1951), *Killer's Kiss* (1955), and *I Died a Thousand Times* (1955).

41 Vivian Sobchack, 'Lounge Time: Postwar Crises and the Chronotype of Film Noir' in Nick Browne, ed., *Refiguring Film Genres: Theory and History* (Berkeley: University of California Press, 1998), 138.

42 Ibid., 139.

43 Ibid., 155.

44 Other examples of Hopper's affinities with noir iconography include *Automat* (1927), *Office at Night* (1927), *Night Windows* (1928), *Hotel Lobby* (1943), and *Hotel Window* (1955). For these and other examples, see Sheena Wagstaff, ed., *Edward Hopper* (London: Tate Publishing, 2004).

45 Carlos Clarens, *Crime Movies: An Illustrated History of the Gangster Genre From D.W. Griffith to Pulp Fiction* (1980 rev. edn, New York: Da Capo, 1997), 194.

46 Schrader, "Notes," 53.

47 Borde and Chaumeton, *Panorama*, 10.

48 "Tillie Scrubbed On," *Reader's Digest* (December 1, 1946), 81–84.

49 See Herbert Brean, "A Case of Identity," *Life* (June 29, 1953), 97–107.

50 Colin McArthur, *Underworld U.S.A.* (London: Secker & Warburg, 1972), 67.

51 Ibid., 68.

52 Place and Peterson, "Some Visual Motifs," 65.

53 Robert Ottoson, *A Reference Guide to the American Film Noir, 1940-1958* (Metuchen, NJ: Scarecrow Press, 1981), 1.

54 Telotte, *Voices in the Dark: The Narrative Patterns of Film Noir* (Urbana: University of Illinois Press, 1989), 2.

55 Alain Silver, Elizabeth Ward, James Ursini, and Robert Porfirio, eds., *Film Noir: The Encyclopedia* (New York: Overlook Duckworth, 2010), 22.

56 Telotte, *Voices in the Dark*, 2.

57 Hirsch, *Film Noir*, 21.

58 Richard Maltby, "The Politics of the Maladjusted Text," in Cameron, ed., *Movie Book of Film Noir*, 41.

59 Fredric Jameson, *Postmodernism, Or, the Cultural Logic of Late Capitalism* (New York: Verso, 1991), 67.

60 Maltby, "Politics of the Maladjusted Text," 41.

3

Genre and gender

"Baby, I don't care"

There's a scene from the movie *Out of the Past* . . . where Robert Mitchum has been sent down to Mexico to pick up Bad Girl Jane Greer, who shot Kirk Douglas and stole 40 grand from him. Mitchum has seen her in a bar, and you take one look at him as he sees this woman, and you know he's going to flush his fucking life down the toilet for this woman. In the chaste manner of '40s melodramas, they meet a couple of times for a drink, speak elliptically, and they end up on the beach one night and the waves are breaking, and they're holding each other and she says to him, You don't want me. You don't need me. I'm no good, I shot Kirk Douglas, I stole 40 grand from him, I'm bad, I'm evil, you don't want me, you don't need me; and Mitchum draws the woman to him and says, Baby, I don't care. And that's it, essentially, for me. I'm too ambitious and circumspect to flush my life down the toilet for a woman, and I'm happily married to a woman who's eminently good and strong and sane; but I love the romantic notion of it.

JAMES ELLROY[1]

Gender and sexuality are often seen as *the* defining elements in film noir, underpinning its narrative concerns and characterizations. "For many commentators," Steve Neale has suggested, "the principal hallmarks of *noir* include a distinctive treatment of sexual desire and sexual relationships, a distinctive array of male and female character types, and a distinctive repertoire of masculine and feminine traits, ideals, characteristics and forms of behaviour."[2] Many critics have seen these concerns with gender and sexuality as expressions of contemporaneous social factors that "help not only to define *film noir*, but also to account for its existence."[3]

Moreover, because noir is often seen as a "masculine" film category—or at least one that deals primarily with a masculine narrative viewpoint—critics have often pointed to the predicaments of men in noir films as markers of a "crisis" in masculinity. Richard Dyer, for example, sees film noir as "characterised by a certain anxiety over the existence and definition of masculinity and normality."[4] For Frank Krutnik, film noir reveals "an obsession with male figures who are both internally divided and alienated from the culturally permissible (or ideal) parameters of masculine identity, desire and achievement."[5] Krutnik sees in the sheer numbers of the noir "tough thriller" of the late 1940s "evidence of some kind of crisis of confidence within the contemporary regimentation of male-dominated culture."[6] Deborah Thomas sees a tendency in film noir "to dramatise a particular crisis in male identity," while Florence Jacobowitz sees noir "as the genre wherein compulsory masculinity is presented as a nightmare."[7]

Why is gender seen as such as such an integral element in film noir? What kind of role does gender play in the discourses of noir? A useful starting point for discussion of these issues is *Out of the Past* (1947), described by Robert Ottoson as "quite simply the *ne plus ultra* of forties *film noir*."[8] Here, we can find two of the most iconic and emblematic characterizations of film noir, crystallized in the figures of the private eye and the femme fatale. Jeff Bailey (Robert Mitchum) runs a garage in a small town. When a former associate, Joe Stefanos (Paul Valentine), tracks him down there, he tells his girlfriend Ann (Virginia Huston) about his past. A former private detective now living under an assumed name, he describes to her the circumstances in which he was hired by Whit Sterling (Kirk Douglas) to locate Kathie Moffat (Jane Greer) who, after shooting Sterling, fled to Mexico with $40,000 of his money. From the instant he first sees her, stepping out of the sunlight in her white dress and into the darkened cantina toward him, he becomes irrevocably trapped in a series of events emanating from that narrative moment.

Many of the key thematic, stylistic, and narrational aspects of film noir can be seen to coalesce in *Out of the Past*. Jeff narrates his story in voice-over and in flashback, describing the events from his past from which he cannot now escape. Here, we see Mitchum's private eye in trademark trench coat and fedora, permanently smoking a cigarette. It's an image that will come to stand as a virtual synecdoche for film noir (see Figure 3.1). In that moment, he falls hopelessly for Greer's femme fatale in an *amour fou* that will ultimately destroy them both as well as any prospect of a future life he might have had with Ann. We see him laconic and feckless, in a kind of existential paralysis, unable or unwilling to act. In Mitchum's somnambulant look, we see him drained of self-will, drifting toward his own demise and, literally, not caring. This is the iconic moment of irresistible infatuation described by James Ellroy at the top of the chapter.

Hard-boiled fiction and the private eye

Taggart Wilde: "What are you getting for it all?"
Philip Marlowe: "Twenty-five dollars a day and expenses."

RAYMOND CHANDLER, *The Big Sleep* (1939)[9]

Anne Riordan to Philip Marlowe: "Oh – a hard-boiled gentleman."

RAYMOND CHANDLER, *Farewell, My Lovely* (1940)[10]

Out of the Past is an adaptation of a novel by Geoffrey Homes (Daniel Mainwaring), *Build My Gallows High* (1946). The novel belongs to a category of "hard-boiled" crime fiction, one that provided several source novels for films noir in the 1940s and 1950s. We've already seen in Chapter 1 how French critics like Nino Frank admired the new American films because they were so different from prewar Hollywood. Part of what made them different was their breakaway from the old-fashioned detective-story format of the so-called "golden age" of detective fiction that flourished between the wars. The new American film noir derived from an alternative literary source and from a different generation of writers such as Dashiell Hammett, Raymond Chandler, and James M. Cain. In fact, the three films singled out by Frank for special mention are all adaptations of these authors' work: *The Maltese Falcon* (Hammett), *Murder, My Sweet* (Chandler), and *Double Indemnity* (Cain)

Borde and Chaumeton similarly emphasized the importance of these writers in the development of film noir, specifically the "hard-boiled" characteristics of their fiction. "The immediate source of film noir," they say, "is obviously the hard-boiled detective novel of American or English origin," and they credit

FIGURE 3.1 Robert Mitchum as private eye Jeff Bailey in *Out of the Past* (Jacques Tourneur, 1947): a virtual synecdoche for film noir.

Hammett as "the creator of this new American literary current" with Chandler as "the group's most important author."[11] This hard-boiled literary provenance of American films noir was a significant one in shaping their critical reception in France. Critics like Frank were already familiar with the hard-boiled crime fiction of these American authors, available in translation through Gallimard's *Série noire* imprint, and consequently "primed" for the arrival of their film adaptations in postwar Paris. When Frank reviewed *The Maltese Falcon* in *L'Écran Français*, he discussed the film almost exclusively in terms of Hammett's hard-boiled novel.[12]

There is a world of difference between these hard-boiled writers and "golden-age" crime fiction. First, the fictional world of writers like Agatha Christie and Dorothy L. Sayers is a "closed" world in the sense that its characteristic location, typically a country house, is enclosed and set apart from the modern urban world. Second, as these country mansion locations suggest, the settings are British, or more specifically English, and tied to an upper-middle-class social milieu. Third, its narrative structure is shaped by a treatment of the crime, invariably a murder, as a clue-puzzle or whodunit plot mechanism. This crime is usually committed before or soon after the beginning of the novel. The role of the detective is one that works backward, gathering and assessing the evidence to determine the circumstances of the crime and the identity of the murderer, eventually to be revealed at the denouement in an instance of what Stephen Knight has neatly called "the death-detection-explanation model."[13]

In his apologia for hard-boiled fiction, "The Simple Art of Murder" (1944), Raymond Chandler famously lambasts this form of detective fiction. He is even more scornful than Frank about the traditional detective story with its quaint conventions and artificial settings. Chandler satirizes what he saw as the ludicrous characteristics of this fiction, "of how somebody stabbed Mrs. Pottington Postlethwaite III with the solid platinum poniard just as she flatted on the top note of the 'Bell Song' from *Lakmé* in the presence of fifteen ill-assorted guests."[14]

Chandler championed Hammett as the master of a hard-boiled realism that was the antithesis of the golden age. "Hammett took murder out of the Venetian vase and dropped it into the alley, says Chandler." He "gave murder back to the kind of people that commit it for reasons, not just to provide a corpse." For Chandler, Hammett's writing "had a basis in fact; it was made up of real things."[15] And so it was: Hammett had experience of what he was writing about, having worked as a private detective for the Pinkerton National Detective Agency before becoming a writer. His short stories were published in the 1920s in *Black Mask* magazine, the most important of a proliferating number of popular titles under the rubric of pulp fiction ("the pulps"), named after the cheap paper on which they were printed. His first novel, *Red Harvest*, was serialized in *Black Mask* and later published, more prestigiously, by Alfred A. Knopf in 1929 when it was widely reviewed and critically acclaimed. Herbert Asbury, for example, writing in *The Bookman*, was one of several reviewers who recognized in Hammet's first novel an altogether new departure in crime fiction:

> It is doubtful if even Ernest Hemingway has ever written more effective dialogue than may be found within the pages of this extraordinary tale of gunmen, gin and gangsters. [Hammett] displays a style of amazing clarity and compactness, devoid of literary frills and furbelows, and his characters, who race through the story with the rapidity and destructiveness of machine guns, speak the crisp hard-boiled language of the underworld. Moreover, they speak it truly, without a single false or jarring note.[16]

Asbury makes some astute observations about Hammett's writing and his review highlights a number of its hard-boiled characteristics. The comparison with Hemingway, for example, is one that many commentators would subsequently stress, largely because Hemingway also made use of a pared-down, quick-paced prose style with an emphasis on dialog to drive the action forward.[17]

Red Harvest also inaugurated a different kind of characterization in the figure of the private eye, a figure that would later become one of the most recognizable archetypes in film noir. Known in this incarnation only as the "Continental Op," he made his first appearance in several earlier short stories in *Black Mask* and later, more famously, as Sam Spade in *The Maltese Falcon* (1930). At the beginning of *Red Harvest*, the Op arrives at Personville (also known as "Poisonville") and describes what he sees there.

> The city wasn't pretty. . . . The smelters whose brick stacks stuck up tall against a gloomy mountain to the south had yellow-smoked everything into uniform dinginess. The result was an ugly city of forty thousand people, set in an ugly notch between two ugly mountains that had been all dirtied up by mining. Spread over this was a grimy sky that looked as if it had come out of the smelters' stacks.
>
> The first policeman I saw needed a shave. The second had a couple of buttons off his shabby uniform. The third stood in the center of the city's main intersection . . . directing traffic, with a cigar in one corner of his mouth.[18]

This is a far cry from the world of Agatha Christie. Much of what can be considered "hard-boiled" can be seen at work in this passage and central to this world is the figure of the private eye. Here, he is an anonymous figure (we never get to know his name), his identity defined solely by his job description and his role as a private investigator. The depiction of the cityscape itself is grim, stained by industrial pollution. Its disheveled police officers look unequal to their task and there is from the outset a sense of inadequacy about the forces of law and order in a city that we soon see to be a morass of corruption and criminality. There is also a sense in which "hard-boiled" describes a prose style with a tough, terse, vernacular speech derived from a tough urban milieu. It is written in the first-person by a narrator who is "there" in Personville, describing what he sees and what he knows, a protagonist tough enough to be able to take care of himself as he navigates his way through a deceptive, corrupt, and violent environment. Also here, as well as in other hard-boiled detective fiction, the narrative sees the protagonist dealing with and responding to a series of ongoing events. This is all at considerable remove from the settings, characters, prose style, and "death-detection-explanation model" of classical detective fiction.

The amateur detectives of the golden age—Miss Marple, Hercule Poirot, Lord Peter Wimsey—were being challenged by the professional private eye. For him—and it was a him—crime isn't some exotic aberration from the norm but part of the everyday fabric of modern urban life. He found himself operating in a dangerous and threatening environment where even his own clients might be as duplicitous and untrustworthy as the criminals he comes up against. For Chandler, this environment necessitated a new kind of "hero."

> But down these mean streets a man must go who is not himself mean, who is neither tarnished or afraid. . . . He must be a complete man and a common man and yet an unusual man. He must be, to use a rather weathered phrase, a man of honor—by instinct, by inevitability, without thought of it, and certainly without saying it. He must be the best man in his world and a good enough man for any world. I do not care much about his private life. . . . He is a relatively poor man, or he would not be a detective at all. He is a common man or he could not go among common people. He has a sense of character, or he would not know his job. He will take no man's money dishonestly and no man's insolence without a due and dispassionate revenge. He is a lonely man and his pride is that you will treat him as a proud man or be very sorry you ever saw him. He talks as the man of his age talks—that is, with rude wit, a lively sense of the grotesque, a disgust for sham, and a contempt for pettiness. . . . The story is this man's adventure in search of a hidden truth, and it would be no adventure if it did not happen to a man fit for adventure. He has a range of awareness that startles you, but it belongs to him by right, because it belongs to the world he lives in.[19]

It's clear from all this that Chandler is talking about a masculine world and a masculine hero. He is setting out a kind of code of practice for the private eye, and it's interesting to see the values it contains, especially as this figure would feature in film noir as one of its most iconic figures. In some ways it's a code of professional practice, but it's also suggestively romantic with an implicit chivalric code. Moreover, in contrast to the middle-class or aristocratic sleuths of the golden age, Chandler's private eye is a blue-collar worker, even one with a proletarian slant, and grounded in a wage-labor economy. (There may be few things we know for certain about him, but we know exactly what his daily rate of pay is because he always tells us.) If we think of Hammett's Sam Spade as a representative example, even his name sounds like the antithesis of a Lord Peter Wimsey. It's a pair of monosyllabic, alliterative names: American, demotic, with a surname suggestively evoking the stock-in-trade spade work of the private eye, digging in the dirt. In both speech and action, he is drawn from a tough urban milieu. This is a masculine register, in contrast to what we might see as the more feminized social milieu of classical detective fiction.[20]

The archetypal hard-boiled private eye fashioned by Hammett and Chandler became a key figure within the investigative structure of film noir. Characterized by a cynical, wisecracking wit, he was beholden to nobody. Chandler might have added to his "code" that his detective isn't to be bought by anybody, even if it occasionally appears as if he might be. He isn't a company man but works for himself, although he is for hire even to the most disreputable and dishonest client. A detective like Sam Spade may be a "man of honor," although not so much that he is above having an affair with his partner's wife and with the client who murdered his partner. He is not so much a hero as an antihero, necessarily "tarnished" by his environment but also *of* it in such a way as to make him uniquely qualified to undertake the job in hand. As Richard Maltby suggests:

> Uncertainly adrift in a world of treachery and shifting loyalties, the investigator of the *noir* movie was himself less than perfect, frequently neurotic, sometimes paranoid, and often managed to re-establish a stable world in the film only by imposing an arbitrary resolution on the other characters.[21]

Most commentators on film noir have routinely accepted the premise suggested by Borde and Chaumeton that the hard-boiled detective novel is "obviously" a source for film noir.[22] We should be mindful, however, that the influence of hard-boiled detective fiction on film noir is not so obviously the case as it might appear. Dashiell Hammett's first success in Hollywood was with an MGM adaptation of his last novel, *The Thin Man* (1934), followed by five sequels, all of which were a far cry from the hard-boiled world of Sam

Spade.[23] These films were part romantic comedy and part amateur detective story, based on the relationship between Nick Charles (William Powell), a retired private eye, and his wife Nora (Myrna Loy), a wealthy socialite, who together lead a stylish lifestyle. The dialog is witty rather than hard-boiled and the elegant sets more closely resemble those in, say, RKO's series of Fred Astaire and Ginger Rogers musicals of the same decade.

Marc Vernet has argued that there are several factors that complicate assumptions about the influence of hard-boiled fiction on film noir. First, there is the seemingly unexplained chronological gap between initial publication of source novels and their film adaptations. In the case of *The Maltese Falcon*, for example, there is a gap of over ten years between the novel's publication and John Huston's film. Another factor is that there were adaptations of this and other hard-boiled novels during the 1930s, that is, well before the period when film noir is presumed to begin. With *The Maltese Falcon*, Warner Brothers had already acquired the rights to the book before the end of its serial publication in *Black Mask* magazine. In fact, *The Maltese Falcon* had already been the subject of two previous film adaptations, *The Maltese Falcon* (1931) and *Satan Met a Lady* (1936), neither of which are considered as films noir. Another example given by Vernet is Frank Tuttle's *The Glass Key* (1935), an adaptation of Hammett's novel serialized in *Black Mask* in 1930. Vernet justifiably asks why Tuttle's version of the Hammett novel, which meets "all" the criteria of film noir, isn't seen as such. The same applies to the first adaptation of Chandler's 1942 novel *The High Window* (a Philip Marlowe story), made by Herbert Leeds as *Time To Kill* (1942). As Vernet suggests, "adaptations of hard-boiled novels made during the 1930s have been occulted," and "numerous films are swept under the rug in order to attempt to maintain an artificial purity and isolation of *film noir*."[24]

There are yet further problems with the figure of the hard-boiled detective itself, especially as it has become such an emblematic figure of film noir. Contrary to appearances, this figure, at least in its Hammett/Chandler incarnations, appears in only a handful of films. After Sam Spade in *The Maltese Falcon*, the first film to feature Chandler's Philip Marlowe was Edward Dmytryk's *Murder, My Sweet* (1944), an adaptation of his 1940 novel *Farewell, My Lovely*, with Dick Powell as Marlowe. The Marlowe role was reprised by Humphrey Bogart in Howard Hawks's *The Big Sleep* (1946), by Robert Montgomery in *The Lady in the Lake* (1947), and then by George Montgomery in John Brahm's *The Brasher Doubloon* (1947), an adaptation of Chandler's *The High Window*. This makes a total of only five films.[25] The anomaly here is that one of the most emblematic figures of film noir is actually drawn from a fraction of its films. There is also a sense that much of the iconic power of that representation derives from Bogart's performances, playing both Spade and Marlowe (see Figure 3.2). (I discuss Bogart's "noir persona" in Chapter 8.)

FIGURE 3.2 Humphrey Bogart as private eye Philip Marlowe in *The Big Sleep* (Howard Hawks, 1946).

Nevertheless, given the inaugural status of *The Maltese Falcon* as the "first" film noir and its importance to French critics, it's worth examining the interplay of masculinities in the narrative, especially vis-à-vis Bogart's Spade. As Richard Dyer has suggested, "film noir abounds in colourful representations of decadence, perversion, aberration etc. Such characters and milieux vividly evoke that which is not normal, through connotations (including of femininity, homosexuality, and art) of that which is not masculine. By inference," says Dyer, "the hero, questing his way through these characters and milieux, is normal and masculine."[26] How, then, can *The Maltese Falcon*, be seen in terms of Dyer's polarized masculinities? Certainly, there is a marked contrast throughout the narrative between the "normal" masculinity of Bogart's Spade and the other male characters he encounters.

Despite the fabulous monetary value of the falcon, it's the pursuit of the "rara avis" in itself which provides the *raison d'être* for all the narrative's criminal acts. It is valued as the desired object of unique rarity rather than for its financial worth. Although the criminal objective is to steal the falcon, the purpose of the quest more closely resembles a desire to acquire the article for a private collection. Gutman (Sydney Greenstreet) is a collector of exquisite taste and refinement for whom ownership of the falcon is really a matter of connoisseurship, as indeed is the quest itself as a kind of extended carnivalesque artwork. Even when thwarted in his attempt to acquire the falcon, he almost gleefully determines to renew his attempt to locate it. Gutman himself is a dedicated aesthete, a figure in noir often coded as a "foreigner." Although German by name (a self-reflexive joke), the fastidious tailoring of his morning suit together with his bowler hat and rolled umbrella all signify an anachronistic form of Englishness, while his clipped diction and penchant for archaic phrasing ("By Gad, sir!") imply a quasi-aristocratic

FIGURE 3.3 Left, Kasper Gutman (Sydney Greenstreet) and right, Joel Cairo (Peter Lorre) in *The Maltese Falcon* (John Huston, 1941).

decadence. With his vast girth and in his silk dressing gown, he lords it over his "queer" entourage at the Belvedere hotel. When Spade arrives at his hotel suite, Gutman links arms with him, holding his hand, in a gesture that is all exaggerated courtesy and high camp. Even Gutman's suite is luxuriant and feminized in contrast to the masculinized space of Spade's apartment which is spare and functional (see Figure 3.3).

Gutman's gang, a camp vaudevillian troupe of grotesques, includes Joel Cairo (Peter Lorre), an effeminate homosexual (in the novel, unequivocally "queer") (see Figure 3.3). His arrival at Spade's office is announced by Spade's secretary, Effie Perrine (Lee Patrick), who presents his Gardenia-scented card to Spade's evident amusement. Throughout his ensuing conversation with Spade, he toys with a silver-tipped cane which he suggestively presses to his lips. Cairo is by turns an effete dandy, a hysterical crybaby, and a would-be tough guy. His indeterminate accent, affected vocal mannerisms, and punctilious syntax suggest another kind of foreigner, here of Eastern European extraction. His multiple passports further obscure any clear sense of his national identity.

The third member of the gang is Wilmer Cook (Elisha Cook, Jr), the "boy" or "gunsel." Wilmer isn't so much a heavy as one who acts out the role to the point of self-parody (as when we see him tailing Spade, he walks down the street shouldering his way into passersby). In his unsmiling demeanor, hood's dress and gangster patois—"The cheaper the crook, the gaudier the patter," says Spade—he is a caricature of a gangster. There is also the implication that within Gutman's retinue he serves in a sexual role ("gunsel" denotes not only a gun-toting criminal but also a catamite), and he even has a girl's name. With scarcely a single male character who could be said to represent any kind of social normality, Bogart's Spade represents a certain kind of tough American masculinity pitted against these foreign others with their aberrant sexuality and feminized aestheticism.

We can note parallels in other films noir such as *Gilda* (1946), in which the "normal" working-class masculinity of Johnny Farrell (Glenn Ford) is contrasted with the homosexual aesthete foreigner Ballin Mundson (George Macready) who, like Joel Cairo, carries a phallic cane (here, more insidiously, a swordstick). Another example can be seen in Detective Mark McPherson (Dana Andrews) against Waldo Lydecker (Clifton Webb) in *Laura* (1944).[27]

The femme fatale

Don Blake (Don DeFore): "Looking for something?"
Jane Palmer (Lizabeth Scott): "My lipstick."
Don Blake: "Colt or a Smith and Wesson?"

Too Late for Tears (1949)

"That's a honey of an anklet you're wearing, Mrs Dietrichson."

WALTER NEFF (Fred MacMurray) to Phyllis Dietrichson
(Barbara Stanwyck) in *Double Indemnity* (1944).

Many of the commonly held generalizations about noir focus on representations of women and, according to most critics, one of the paradigmatic characterizations in film noir is that of the femme fatale—literally, "deadly woman"—the predatory, treacherous, and duplicitous figure of the sexual temptress. We saw an example of what is often held to be the progenitor of this figure in Brigid O'Shaughnessy (Mary Astor) in *The Maltese Falcon*, a sociopath who adopts a series of guises to get what she wants: the upper-class sophisticate, the anxiously protective "sister," the naïve and vulnerable

FIGURE 3.4 Brigid O'Shaughnessy, aka Miss Wonderly (Mary Astor), in *The Maltese Falcon* (John Huston, 1941).

innocent, and the calculating murderess who comes close to ensnaring Sam Spade (see Figure 3.4). What makes her so dangerously alluring is her inscrutability and unpredictability. "The femme fatale is the figure of a certain discursive unease," says Mary Ann Doane, "a potential epistemological trauma. For her most striking characteristic, perhaps, is the fact that she never really is what she seems to be. She harbors a threat which is not entirely legible, predictable, manageable."[28]

Feminist criticism in the 1970s highlighted the significance of the femme fatale as a transgressive figure, economically and sexually independent, challenging patriarchal structures of power and authority. For many critics, the figure of the femme fatale is seen as an expression of anxieties about the change in women's roles during wartime. Feminists gravitated to film noir because its representations of women differed notably from those traditionally associated with Hollywood productions. For E. Ann Kaplan, writing in the introduction to her seminal collection *Women in Film Noir*, a genre such as the western—she cites John Ford's *My Darling Clementine* (1946) and *The Searchers* (1956)—typically saw women "in their fixed roles as wives, mothers, daughters, lovers, mistresses, whores, simply [to] provide the background for the ideological work of the film which is carried out through men." In contrast, women in film noir became "central to the intrigue of the films" and not "safely" positioned in such familiar roles as those in the western.

> Defined by their sexuality, which is presented as desirable but dangerous to men, the women function as the obstacle to the male quest. The hero's success or not depends on the degree to which he can extricate himself from the woman's manipulations. Although the man is sometimes simply destroyed because he cannot resist the woman's lures . . . often the work of the film is the attempted restoration of order through the exposure and then destruction of the sexual, manipulating woman.[29]

Such sexually defined women may be punished at the end of the narrative, as Brigid O'Shaughnessy is at the end of *The Maltese Falcon*, seen through the "prison bars" of the descending elevator, but the transgressor's comeuppance doesn't necessarily see the impact of her power curtailed. As Sylvia Harvey has suggested: "Despite the ritual punishment of acts of transgression, the vitality with which these acts are endowed produces an excess of meaning which cannot finally be contained. Narrative resolutions cannot recuperate their subversive significance."[30]

The notion of a dangerously seductive and destructive femininity isn't new, of course, as Janey Place suggests. "The dark lady, the spider woman, the evil seductress who tempts man and brings about his destruction is among the oldest themes of art, literature, mythology and religion in western culture."[31] Its antecedents can be seen in the Sirens in the *Odyssey*, luring seamen to their deaths through the enchanting power of their song as well as in biblical figures like Salome and Delilah. A Hollywood precursor of the femme fatale can be seen in the "vamp" of silent cinema. This was a vampiric figure with an exotic sexuality and foreign background, exemplified by stars such as Theda Bara and Pola Negri who appeared in contrast to the more innocent and wholesome "American" stars like Mary Pickford and Lillian Gish. There is a dichotomy here that is often played out in terms of what feminist noir critics have seen as opposing female types. As Christine Gledhill sees it, the investigative structure of film noir presupposes a male hero in a male world. "Women in this world," she says,

> tend to split into two categories: there are those who work on the fringes of the underworld and are defined by the male criminal ambience of the thriller—bar-flies, night-club singers, expensive mistresses, *femmes fatales*, and ruthless gold-diggers who marry and murder rich old men for their money; and then there are on the outer margins of this world, wives, long-suffering girlfriends, would-be fiancees who are victims of male crime, sometimes the object of the hero's protection, and often points of vulnerability in his masculine armour.[32]

Like Gledhill, Janey Place also sees a dichotomy between two kinds of women in noir: the "spider woman" or femme fatale, and the "nurturing woman" or redeemer.[33] This dichotomy can be seen in *Out of the Past* and the two women with whom Jeff has relationships. Ann is the small-town girl, dependable and dull, while Kathie is dangerous, destructive, and exciting.[34]

Part of the attraction of film noir to these feminist critics was their perception that it represented a critique of marriage and family life. Sylvia Harvey emphasizes the absence of family, while Gledhill notes how in the world of the noir thriller "the norm of the bourgeois family becomes markedly absent and unattainable" through films that "challenge the ideological hegemony of the family."[35] In contrast to the conventional "happy ending" and the presumed notion of "living happily ever after," film noir presents family relations as "broken, perverted, peripheral or impossible."[36] For Place, consignment to domestic normality and the nice girl option isn't much of an option at all.

> On the rare occasions that the normal world of families, children, homes and domesticity appears in film noir, it is either so fragile and ideal that we anticipate its destruction . . . or, like the "good" but boring women who contrast with the exciting, sexy *femmes fatales*, it is so dull and

constricting that it offers no compelling alternative to the dangerous but exciting life on the fringe.[37]

Indeed, Deborah Thomas sees "the so-called redemptive woman" constituting as much of a threat to the noir male as the femme fatale who, with a conservative agenda, "is intent on the hero's domestication and the restoration of the status quo."[38]

An alternative to the "absent family" view has been suggested by Nina C. Leibman, who argues that "the family is very much present" in film noir which comes with an "ideological agenda . . . heavily embedded in the traditional hegemony of the nuclear family unit."[39] As Leibman points out, a film like *The Big Heat* (1953) shows family life in a "positive" way and the relationship between Dave Bannion (Glenn Ford) and his wife Katie (Jocelyn Brando)—is shown as almost idyllic: "we have the perfect marriage," he tells her. Leibman describes their "softly lit" home—the antithesis of noir's low-key lighting—in a *mise-en-scène* displaying "open doorways, neatly stacked dishes in glass cabinets. . . . The dishwashing scene between Katie and Dave is affectionate— there are no oblique room dividers separating the couple."[40] Certainly, we see Dave Bannion at home with Katie, deeply rooted in a domestic environment as a loving husband and father. But of course, as both Place and Harvey have suggested, it's *too* "ideal" and cannot survive, and Katie is killed just outside the family home by a car bomb intended for her husband.

The figure of the femme fatale frequently appears as emblematic of noir at large, often through her image on film posters. Take, for example, the famously iconic image of Rita Hayworth in the title role of *Gilda*. Hayworth is wearing the well-known Jean Louis black satin strapless dress and smoking a cigarette, an image that stands as a virtual synecdoche for film noir (see Figure 3.5). We can recall from Chapter 1 how Jean-Pierre Chartier began his discussion of *Double Indemnity* with reference to the inscription on the film poster: "She kisses him so that he'll kill for her." That quotation makes for as good a definition of "femme fatale" as any other, describing a woman who uses sex for her own murderous ends. Phyllis Dietrichson (Barbara Stanwyck) in *Double Indemnity* is often seen as the personification of this figure, enlisting her lover Walter Neff (Fred MacMurray) to kill her husband. Another example, also based on a Cain novel, is Cora Smith (Lana Turner) in *The Postman Always Rings Twice*, who similarly manipulates her lover to kill her husband. Contemporaneous advertising for film noir often exploited this idea of a murderous female. Many noir posters drew on the graphic style of pulp fiction book covers, often featuring a seductive woman in a state of *déshabillé*, sometimes armed, as in such films noir as *Blonde Alibi* (1946), *Blonde Ice* (1948), *The Lady From Shanghai* (1948), *Gun Crazy* (1950), *A Blueprint For Murder* (1953), *The Glass Web* (1953), *Naked Alibi* (1954), *Accused of Murder*

(1956), and *Cop Hater* (1958). Sometimes, as in the *Double Indemnity* poster, a relationship between sex and death was suggestively implied. In *A Kiss Before Dying* (1956), for example, there is some ambivalence about whether the poster image depicts a sex act or a murder. This ambivalence can be seen in the poster for Hitchcock's *Dial M For Murder* (1954) depicting a female figure in what may be either the throes of death or orgasm. By the 1950s, the femme fatale had become a central figure on the covers of pulp fiction, echoing the iconography and plots of mid-1940s' film noir. As Lee Horsley has suggested in his study of the noir thriller, "the femme fatale often holds a gun on the cover and has by the end of the narrative pulled the trigger."[41]

The initial appearance of a femme fatale in a noir narrative is invariably beguiling, as we've seen with the entrance of Kathie Moffat in *Out of the Past*. We can see two other such moments in parallel scenes in *Double Indemnity* and *The Postman Always Rings Twice* (1946), each involving a married woman. In the former, the insurance salesman Walter Neff (Fred MacMurray) arrives at the Dietrichsons' house in order to renew their automobile insurance. He first glimpses Phyllis Dietrichson wrapped in a towel at the top of the stairs (see Figure 3.5). A few moments later, as she walks down the stairs buttoning up her dress, his eyes follow her with a tracking shot tightly framed on her legs. She goes to the mirror and applies lipstick. Later, he becomes transfixed by the anklet she's wearing, repeatedly mentioning it in the few minutes' conversation he has with her. "I kept thinking of Phyllis Dietrichson," he later recalls in voice-over, "and the way that anklet of hers cut into her leg." His eroticized recollection of her has become one of a sadistic, fetishized image.

In *The Postman Always Rings Twice*, Frank Chambers (John Garfield) arrives at a roadside diner where he sees Cora Smith (Lana Turner) for the first time. Her appearance is presaged by the sound of her dropped lipstick rolling across the floor toward him and it is this which first catches his attention. The camera follows his gaze across the floor, resting on her bare legs and white peep-toe shoes, then to a full-figure shot showing her dressed in pristine white, and then to a close-up of her face framed with a white turbaned headdress (see Figure 3.5). She is looking at herself in a compact mirror, applying the lipstick that he has returned to her. She closes the door on him, shutting him out. In both cases, we witness the moment in which each protagonist is caught up in the machinations of the femme fatale. It's as if the highly fetishized shots of these female accoutrements (anklet, lipstick) work as erotic traps. In each case, from this moment, each man will become the woman's lover and each will bludgeon her husband to death at her behest.

The figure of the femme fatale looms large in critical discourse where it is often assumed to be an intrinsic characterization in noir films.[42] However, this is by no means true. When Nino Frank first applied the term noir to his

FIGURE 3.5 Femmes Fatales: left, Gilda Mundson (Rita Hayworth) in *Gilda* (Charles Vidor, 1946); right, Phyllis Dietrichson (Barbara Stanwyck) in *Double Indemnity* (Billy Wilder, 1944); and bottom, Cora Smith (Lana Turner) in *The Postman Always Rings Twice* (Tay Garnett, 1946).

set of American films in 1946, his "sample" included *Laura* (1944), a film that has no such characterization at all. In fact, it would be possible to make a very long list of all those films noir that lacked any femme fatale, including many of the best-known examples from *Shadow of a Doubt* (1943) to *A Touch of Evil* (1958). The assumption here is that if it is a film noir, therefore it must have a femme fatale. This in turn has led to the attribution of "femme fatale" to any vaguely seductive female character and ultimately to any "bad" female character. However, a femme fatale type has been deployed in various different forms in ways that demonstrate that the term wasn't restricted to noir. Steve Neale has noted how one study from 1950 identified a character type known as "the bitch." If "the bitch" is exemplified by Kitty (Joan Bennett) in an "archetypal" noir like *Scarlet Street* (1945), says Neale, "she is also exemplified by Mrs. Macomber (Joan Bennett again) in *The Macomber Affair* (1947)," a melodrama that no one has ever described as a film noir.[43] Another study, Michael Renov's *Hollywood's Wartime Women* (1988), discusses such female types of the period as the "Inscrutable Female" and the "Evil Woman."

While films noir like *Laura* and *Gilda* are examples of the former category, "so too are comedies and westerns like *Ball of Fire* (1941) and *The Ox-Bow Incident* (1943)." And while a film like *The Dark Mirror* (1946) features an "Evil Woman" type, so too do melodramas like *Manpower* (1941) and *The Razor's Edge* (1946), as well as a film like *Orchestra Wives* (1942), a musical featuring Glenn Miller and his Orchestra.[44] We can see, then, how an awareness of this historical context can complicate the blanket attribution of "femme fatale."

Film noir and gaslight melodrama

Mrs Mannigham: "I begin to doubt, don't you see? I begin to believe I imagine everything. Perhaps I do. Are you here? Is this a dream, too? Who are you? I am afraid they are going to lock me up."

PATRICK HAMILTON, *Gas Light* (1939)[45]

"Now we can make it look like suicide."

MRS HUGHES (Dame May Whitty) to her son Ralph (George Macready), overheard by Julia Ross (Nina Foch) in *My Name Is Julia Ross* (1945).

We have already seen in Chapter 1 some of the difficulties involved in establishing a definition of film noir and its complicated situation among different genres. The relation between film noir and "adjacent" genres such as the female gothic or "woman's film" is a case in point. It's clear that for several critics film noir is strongly identified as a masculine-oriented form. On original release, however, many of the films we know today as films noir were categorized as melodrama. As Steve Neale has pointed out, films such as *Cornered* (1945), *The Locket* (1947), and *Shockproof* (1949)—together with *Murder, My Sweet*—were all typically described in both studio publicity and press reviews as melodrama (or in *Variety*'s abbreviated form, "meller"). These, says Neale, "were by far the commonest terms used to describe what are often now called *noirs*, whether they were hard-boiled detective films, gangster films, gothic thrillers, and woman's films, paranoid thrillers, psychological thrillers, police films or semi-documentaries."[46] Examples abound, but take for instance a "quintessential" film noir like *Double Indemnity* described in the *New York Times* on release as a "tough melodrama."[47] This use of "melodrama" is at odds with the ways in which it functions as a category in film studies where, as Ben Singer has suggested, it is "all but synonymous with a set of subgenres that remain close to the hearth and emphasize a register of heightened emotionalism and sentimentality: the family melodrama, the woman's film, the weepie, the soap opera, etc."[48] Melodrama, in this historical sense, refers to much more than just the narrowly defined genre it would become in academic discourse. What, then, are we to make of the attribution of "crime melodrama" to what would subsequently become film noir, and what of the implicit gender divide between film noir (male) and melodrama (female)?

As Elizabeth Cowie has argued, there is a sense in which the noir narrative itself functions as melodrama. "In *film noir*," she says, "a narrative of an external enigma, a murder or a theft, replaces the melodrama's plot of an external event of war, poverty or social circumstance." But also, "the element of fate, of chance and coincidence, which produces the characteristic under-motivation of events in melodrama, is also central to the *film noir* as characters 'feel compelled by forces and passions beyond their reason to act as they do—in a form of *amour fou*.'" Consequently, film noir can be seen as a "development of melodrama so that whereas earlier the obstacles to the heterosexual couple had been external forces of family and circumstance, wars or illness, in the *film noir* the obstacles derive from the characters' psychology or even pathology as they encounter external events."[49] In this sense, then, the notion that melodrama and film noir exist in contradistinction to each other across some kind of gendered divide is called into question as "crime melodrama" can be seen as a telling description encompassing several different narrative types.

Another problem arises in the relation between film noir and the "female-gothic" cycle of the 1940s in films such as *Rebecca* (1940), *Suspicion* (1941), *Dark Waters* (1944), *Gaslight* (1944), *Jane Eyre* (1944), *Experiment Perilous* (1944), *My Name Is Julia Ross* (1945), *Shock* (1946), *The Spiral Staircase* (1946), *Undercurrent* (1946), *Dragonwyck* (1946), *Bury Me Dead* (1947), *Sleep, My Love* (1948), *Sorry, Wrong Number* (1948), *Caught* (1949), and *Whirlpool* (1950), some of which are included in lists of film noir. Take *Ivy* (1947) for example, an Edwardian melodrama that centers on a woman, Ivy Lexton (Joan Fontaine), who murders her husband by poisoning him. This film has generally been seen as female gothic rather than film noir, at least until recently. It didn't appear in any of the previous editions of the Silver and Ward *Encyclopedia*, although it does have an entry in the current edition where it's described in terms of "gaslight melodrama" with Fontaine's Ivy described as the "first femme fatale in a gaslight noir."[50] This seems odd. It suggests a contradiction in terms and serves to illustrate the extent to which generic definitions can be stretched to accommodate almost anything.

Gaslight melodrama, which draws on a gothic revival following the success of Daphne Du Maurier's novel *Rebecca* (1938), is named after Patrick Hamilton's stage play *Gas Light* (1938) and its ensuing film adaptations, the British *Gaslight* (1940) and its MGM remake (1944) by George Cukor. Its narrative sees a husband contrive to have his wife believe that she is going mad. As

Tania Modleski has argued, the gothic revival that gave rise to the "gaslight" subgenre or cycle coincided with the adaptations of hard-boiled fiction into film noir, and while films noir received considerable critical attention, their gaslight counterparts were largely ignored. Noir is seen to have greater sociological interest than the gaslight cycle, Modleski says, "because it reveals male paranoid fears, developed during the war years, about the independence of women on the home front. Hence the necessity . . . of destroying or taming the aggressive, mercenary, sexually dynamic 'femme fatale' whose presence is indispensable to the genre." The gaslight films, though, "reflect *women's* fears about losing their unprecedented freedoms and being forced back into the homes after the men returned from fighting to take over the jobs and assume control of their families."[51] Hence the narrative concerns of gaslight films with female characters in extremis, trapped in domestic spaces that are themselves inscribed with menace, suspicion, paranoia, fear, and anxiety. Certainly, as Neale suggests, the female gothic (and its gaslight variant) can be seen to have much in common with film noir, not least through what Andrea Walsh has called the "culture of distrust" generated by wartime and postwar conditions.[52] There is no reason to suppose, as many noir critics do, that these conditions uniquely informed film noir. Where there has been a tendency for critical interest to focus on the predicament of the male protagonist in film noir rather than on his female counterpart in the gothic, it is because, as Neale suggests, much of the critical interest in noir has stressed its affiliation with the hard-boiled novel rather than the stage thriller and gothic romance.[53] This tells us something not only about the relation between generic categories but also shows up a critical hierarchy of genres in which the masculine (noir) has traditionally taken precedence over the feminine (gothic/gaslight).

Notes

1 Quoted in Todd Erickson, "James Ellroy: Crime Fiction Beyond Noir," *L.A. Weekly* (July 21, 1989), 19–20.

2 Neale, *Genre and Hollywood*, 160.

3 Ibid.

4 Richard Dyer, "Resistance Through Charisma: Rita Hayworth and *Gilda*," in E. Ann Kaplan, ed., *Women in Film Noir* (London: BFI, 1978), 91.

5 Frank Krutnik, *In a Lonely Street: Film Noir, Genre, Masculinity* (London: Routledge, 1991), xiii.

6 Ibid., 91.

7 Deborah Thomas, "How Hollywood Deals With the Deviant Male," in Cameron, ed., *Movie Book of Film Noir*, 60; Florence Jacobowitz, "The Man's Melodrama: *The Woman in the Window* and *Scarlet Street*," in Cameron, ed., *Movie Book of Film Noir*, 153.

8 Robert Ottoson, *A Reference Guide to the American Film Noir, 1940-1958* (Metuchen, NJ: Scarecrow, 1981), 132.

9 Raymond Chandler, *The Big Sleep* (1939; Harmondsworth: Penguin, 1976), 111.

10 Raymond Chandler, *Farewell, My Lovely* (1940; Harmondsworth: Penguin, 1976), 62.

11 Raymond Borde and Étienne Chaumeton, *A Panorama of American Film Noir, 1941-1953*, trans. Paul Hammond (San Francisco: City Lights, 2002), 15.

12 Nino Frank, "An Exciting . . . Put-You-To-Sleep Story," *L'Écran Français* (August 7, 1946) in William Luhr, ed., *The Maltese Falcon: John Huston, Director*, trans. Connor Hartnett (New Brunswick, NJ: Rutgers University Press, 1995), 130–31.

13 Stephen Knight, *Crime Fiction, 1800-2000: Death, Detection, Diversity* (Basingstoke: Palgrave Macmillan, 2004), 136.

14 Raymond Chandler, "The Simple Art of Murder: An Essay" in *The Simple Art of Murder* (New York: Vintage, 1988), 10. What Chandler is satirizing here resembles *Cluedo*, a board game devised in the 1940s. Players determine who committed a murder, where, and with what implement (it might be Colonel Mustard in the conservatory with a candlestick). *Cluedo* is a whimsical and nostalgic treatment of the classic English whodunit reduced to an absolute formula.

15 Chandler, "Simple Art of Murder," 14.

16 Herbert Asbury, "Fiction," *The Bookman* (March 1929), 92.

17 For a useful example of Hemingway's "hard-boiled" style, see his short story "The Killers" (1927), later adapted as Robert Siodmak's film noir *The Killers* (1946).

18 Dashiell Hammett, *Red Harvest* (1929; New York: Vintage/Black Lizard, 1992), 3–4.

19 Chandler, "Simple Art of Murder," 18.

20 This is not to suggest that the "new" detective was necessarily a male figure. For a useful corrective to that view, see Philippa Gates, "Independence Unpunished: The Female Detective in Classic Film Noir," in Robert Miklitsch, ed., *Kiss the Blood Off My Hands: On Classic Film Noir* (Urbana: University of Illinois Press, 2014), 17–36.

21 Richard Maltby, "The Politics of the Maladjusted Text," in Cameron, ed., *Movie Book of Film Noir*, 39.

22 See for example Crowther, *Film Noir*, 13–37; Hirsch, *Dark Side of the Screen*, 22–51, Walker, "Film Noir," 9–16.

23 *The Thin Man* (1934), *After the Thin Man* (1936), *Another Thin Man* (1939), *Shadow of the Thin Man* (1941), *The Thin Man Goes Home* (1945), and *Song of the Thin Man* (1947).

24 Marc Vernet, "*Film Noir* on the Edge of Doom," in Joan Copjec, ed., *Shades of Noir: A Reader* (London: Verso, 1993), 14.

25 Marlowe would have a significant "afterlife" with later adaptations including *Marlowe* (1969), an adaptation of Chandler's *The Little Sister* (1949) with James Garner in the title role; Robert Altman's *The Long Goodbye* (1973) with Elliott Gould; and remakes of *Farewell, My Lovely* (1975) and *The Big Sleep* (1978), both with Robert Mitchum as Marlowe.

26 Dyer, "Resistance Through Charisma," 92.

27 On hard-boiled fiction and film noir, see Geoffrey O'Brien, *Hardboiled America: Lurid Paperbacks and the Masters of Noir* (1981; New York: Da Capo, 1997); William Hare, *Pulp Fiction to Film Noir: The Great Depression and the Development of a Genre* (Jefferson, NC: McFarland, 2012); Lee Horsley, *The Noir Thriller* (London: Palgrave Macmillan, 2009); Bran Nicol, *The Private Eye: Detectives in the Movies* (London: Reaktion, 2013).

28 Mary Ann Doane, *Femme Fatales: Feminism, Film Theory, Psychoanalysis* (New York: Routledge, 1991), 1.

29 E. Ann Kaplan, "Introduction." in Kaplan, ed., *Women in Film Noir* (London: BFI, 1978), 2–3.

30 Sylvia Harvey, "Woman's Place: The Absent Family of Film Noir," in Kaplan, ed., *Women in Film Noir*, 33.

31 Janey Place, "Women in Film Noir," in Kaplan, ed., *Women in Film Noir*, 35.

32 Christine Gledhill, "*Klute* 1: A Contemporary Film Noir and Feminist Criticism," in Kaplan, ed., *Women in Film Noir*, 14. Kaplan's collection contains two essays by Gledhill on *Klute* (1971) and it's worth noting the prominence of this later film in discussions of "classic" noir.

33 Place, "Women in Film Noir," 42–50; 50–54.

34 Ibid., 50.

35 Harvey, "Woman's Place;" Gledhill, "*Klute* 1," 15, 19.

36 Harvey, "Woman's Place," 25.

37 Place, "Women in Film Noir," 50.

38 Thomas, "How Hollywood Deals With the Deviant Male," 59.

39 Nina C. Leibman, "The Family Spree of Film Noir," *Journal of Popular Film and Television* 16, no. 4 (Winter 1989), 169.

40 Ibid., 172–73.

41 Horsley, *Noir Thriller*, 130. See also, 125–52. Horsley's book is one of many to reproduce the famous image of Rita Hayworth as Gilda on its cover.

42 See for example Kaplan, ed., *Women in Film Noir*; Crowther, *Film Noir*, 115–38; Hirsch, *Dark Side of the Screen*, 152–57. See also Karen Burroughs Hannsberry, *Femme Noir: Bad Girls of Film* (Jefferson, NC: McFarland, 1998); Dominique Mainon and James Ursini, *Femme Fatale: Cinema's Most Unforgettable Lethal Ladies* (Milwaukee: Limelight, 2009).

43 Neale, *Genre and Hollywood*, 163.

44 Ibid.

45 Patrick Hamilton, *Gas Light* (London: Constable, 1939), 34.

46 Neale, *Genre and Hollywood*, 179–80.

47 Bosley Crowther, "The Screen: 'Double Indemnity,' a Tough Melodrama, With Stanwyck and MacMurray as Killers, Opens at the Paramount," *New York Times* (September 7, 1944), 21.

48 Quoted in Neale, *Genre and Hollywood*, 181.

49 Cowie, "*Film Noir* and Women," in Copjec, ed., *Shades of Noir*, 130.

50 Silver and Ward et al., eds., *Film Noir: The Encyclopedia*, 153.

51 Tania Modleski, *Loving With a Vengeance: Mass Produced Fantasies For Women* (Hamdon, CO: Archon, 1982), 21.

52 Quoted in Neale, *Genre and Hollywood*, 163.

53 Ibid., 163–64.

PART TWO

The history of film noir

4

Prehistory and the wartime period, 1939–45

Critics often talk about film noir as if it were a discrete entity, separate from other generic categories, and viewed in critical isolation. It is important to remember, though, that noir first existed among other film genres and indeed, it *is* other genres. All the films that critics today categorize as noir had a "pre-noir" life with a different categorization. We have seen in previous chapters something of the composite relations of film noir with other genres. We have also noted how noir is said to speak to a dark national mood. But how does film noir fit into the generic landscape of wartime America? If noir is supposed to articulate a pessimistic view of American society, what other views were being articulated during the war years? To draw on Thomas Doherty's phrase, what kind of "genre work" was undertaken by Hollywood in its wartime role and how did film noir relate to that role?[1]

Film noir and the "genre work" of wartime

> If it is an "escape" picture, will it harm the war effort by creating a false picture of America, her Allies, or the world we live in?
>
> Question addressed to Hollywood filmmakers in *Government Information Manual for the Motion Picture Industry*, 1942.[2]

The war period saw the emergence of two predominant production cycles: the combat film and the home-front melodrama. But as Thomas Schatz has pointed out, "virtually all of Hollywood's major genres were affected by the war and might in some way be included under the general rubric of 'war film'."[3] All wartime productions, then, were *of* the war and, to a lesser or greater extent, about it.

The combat film is routinely seen as a flag-waver, providing uncomplicated national propaganda that looks like the antithesis of noir's downbeat narratives. The combat film represents wartime Americanism through what Jeanine Basinger has called "the concept of the unified group," mobilized by wartime necessity "to work together as a group, to set aside individual needs, and to bring our melting pot tradition together to function as a true democracy since, after all, that is what we are fighting for: the Democratic way of life."[4] The locus of this democratic Americanism was to be found in the democratically constituted platoon that, as a microcosm of American society, became a staple element in the combat film. As the core unit of military organization, the platoon was constructed out of unified diversity and harmonized by common purpose. Its strength and integrity are derived from its multiethnic, multiracial, multidenominational composition, a combination that emphasized America's geographical diversity, drawing on characters who variously signified the local value of their home through the personification of town, city, or state.[5] These films work to enact the core values of American democracy in action.

The second wartime production cycle was the home-front melodrama. Films such as *Mrs Miniver* (1942) and *Since You Went Away* (1944) dealt explicitly with wartime hardship and loss in narratives that centered on the figure of a stoical matriarch. Some home-front melodramas dealt with specific wartime issues such as women working in the war industries.[6] Others proved adaptable in incorporating wartime themes without actually mentioning the war. The woman's film, for example, a staple genre in the 1930s, could take its female protagonist and place her in situations she might typically face in a wartime context. Even a romantic melodrama like *Now, Voyager* (1942) could use a "woman's picture" narrative to speak to women in wartime. The story of Charlotte Vane (Bette Davis) tells of her transformation from "ugly duckling" spinster to beautiful romantic lover, but it also demonstrates how a woman can successfully change the course of her life, acquire independence, take on new responsibilities, and stand up for herself at a time when millions of American women were themselves having to face new challenges in their lives.

Similarly, *Mildred Pierce* (1945), a generic hybrid combining film noir and maternal melodrama, contains scarcely any traces of the war. The only specific reference to wartime is when Monte Beragon (Zachary Scott) mentions that "nylons are out for the duration" and Ida (Eve Arden) vaguely alludes to a "manpower shortage." As with James M. Cain's source novel (1941), there is an ambient sense of the Depression era. Desperately trying to find work as a waitress following her husband's departure, Mildred Pierce (Joan Crawford) has to provide for her children alone. Mildred's story, then, about a working mother, can be seen as a variation of the home-front melodrama with an unspecified homefront (see Figure 4.1). Even in a period musical like *Meet Me in St Louis* (1944), the focus on its female household and imminent family

FIGURE 4.1 Home-front melodrama and film noir: Mildred Pierce (Joan Crawford) in *Mildred Pierce* (Michael Curtiz, 1945).

relocation to New York all chime with the upheavals of a wartime nation. We can also see in Tootie's (Margaret O'Brien) burial of her "dead" dolls a morbid hint of the casualties of the unmentioned war. What these wartime genres had in common was a narrative capability to lend themselves to the expression of a purposeful and affirmative sense of endeavor about the war, in contrast to the darker and more pessimistic themes of film noir.

As the combat film stressed the collective enterprise of the group and the homefront melodrama that of female solidarity, many "coded" narratives focus on an individual who has failed to commit to the war effort. Here, in what Dana Polan has called the "conversion narrative," a character is seen to be disengaged from any purposeful role. The conversion narrative witnesses that character undergo a transformation in attitude, leading him, and sometimes her, to acknowledge the indispensable contribution that each must make in accordance with national war aims.[7] Film noir represents a counterpoint to the "genre work" of the conversion narrative: it would be difficult to imagine any noir character making common cause with national wartime interests.

The conversion narrative made for a significant wartime cycle and there are many instances mapped onto most existing genres. Perhaps the best-known example is Rick Blaine (Humphrey Bogart) in *Casablanca* (1942). Two years later, Bogart effectively reprised the role, as Harry Morgan, in *To Have and Have Not* (1944). Other examples were displaced onto the First World War settings: the arrogant Private Plunkett (James Cagney) in *The Fighting 69th* (1940); the conscientious objector Alvin York in *Sergeant York* (1941); and the careerist stage performer Harry Palmer (Gene Kelly) who deliberately injures himself to evade the draft in *For Me and My Gal* (1942). Other examples use foreign settings such as the embittered deserter Clive Briggs (Tyrone Power) in *This Above All* (1942); the self-serving profiteer Joe Adams (Cary Grant) in *Mr Lucky* (1943); and the cowardly French schoolmaster Arthur Lory (Charles Laughton) in *This Land Is Mine* (1943).

Women were also subject to "conversion" and brought into line with the national ideology of wartime. Women were seen as potentially disruptive to national wartime interests because of their pursuit of independence and social equality. As Lary May has pointed out, "empowered women" had featured in many 1930s' films, personified by stars such as Bette Davis, Joan Crawford, and Myrna Loy, often in working roles. But wartime necessitated a more complex ideological role for women, occasioning a "split" in female identity.[8] "She saw her work as a means to support her man fighting abroad, yet she focused her identity on providing in the home the freedom and personal fulfillment that were being lost in the larger public realm."[9] This notion of an identity "split" is a useful way of conceptualizing the kind of patriotic role women were being asked to play for the duration. We can see this role played out in *Since You Went Away* (1944) where the wife of a serviceman serving overseas, Anne Hilton (Claudette Colbert), undertakes work in a munitions factory while her daughters work as nurses. With their men away, their "dangerous desires" for independence, freedom, and sexual expression are channeled into the home. But although her war work "symbolizes women's participation in the war effort," it can only be as "an extension of her new identity as mother and wife." The message, May says, "is not only that ideal women will make the guns to win the war, but also that their true identity is found in creating a vision of love and beauty that men can expect to find when they return from the front."[10] There are some important implications for film noir here. If the "empowered woman" had assumed a role of "patriotic domesticity" in the national wartime interest, by the end of the war her work was done, and it was assumed that she would resume her role as homemaker for her returning husband. This would not necessarily turn out to be the case.

The crime film and film noir

An obvious starting point to explore the prehistory of noir is the crime film. We have already considered some of the thematic and stylistic characteristics of noir in Chapter 2, but how do these compare with those of American crime films prior to *Stranger on the Third Floor* (1940) and *The Maltese Falcon* (1941), the films usually taken to herald the arrival of film noir? What were the features of the other Hollywood genres that would have a bearing on the development of film noir? We considered German expressionism as one of the attributed influences on noir, but what other influences were there? Which filmmakers had an impact on the development of noir at this time?

Crime has featured in film narratives from the earliest days of American cinema. Some historical accounts of film noir make brief reference to the 1930s, but usually to only three gangster films made during the period in what has come to be known as the classic gangster cycle: *Little Caesar* (1931), *The Public Enemy* (1931), and *Scarface* (1932). These were indeed important and influential films, but they were instances of only one of several production cycles featuring gangster stories in the 1920s and 1930s, and it is useful to see the period in terms of such production cycles. For example, another important gangster film, *The Doorway to Hell* (1930), is seldom mentioned today, and yet this was the first of an early 1930s' cycle to draw on the life of Al Capone and proved highly influential in its depiction of an "attractive" gangster figure, here in Louie Ricarno (Lew Ayres).[11]

Josef von Sternberg's Paramount silent, *Underworld* (1927), was a major influence in triggering the vogue for gangster films of the early sound era, and von Sternberg was himself a major figure in the development of both thematic and stylistic characteristics which preempted noir. Von Sternberg's reputation today is largely based on three characteristics of his work, all of which can be seen as influential in the development of film noir. First, there is the series of films he made with Marlene Dietrich, the first of which was the *The Blue Angel* (1930), an early incarnation of the figure of a seductive female that pointed toward noir's femme fatale.[12] Second, *Underworld*'s Bull Weed (George Bancroft) marked a significant shift in criminal characterizations which had been represented hitherto as unequivocal villains. Bull Weed is a far more ambivalent figure, characterized with chutzpah and panache. He would serve as a model for several of the gangster characterizations of the early 1930s such as Tom Powers (James Cagney) in *Public Enemy*, Rico Bandello (Edward G Robinson) in *Little Caesar*, and Tony Camonte (Paul Muni) in *Scarface*.

Third, von Sternberg's *Underworld* and *The Docks of New York* (1928) utilized a low-key lighting style, later to become a primary element in noir's visual style. It's as a visual stylist that von Sternberg is most influential, and many of his scenes in *Underworld* exploit stylistic effects foreshadowing those of film noir. Note, for example, the heightened artificiality of the film's

FIGURE 4.2 Josef von Sternberg, visual stylist: left, *Underworld* (Josef von Sternberg, 1927) and right, *Docks of New York* (Josef von Sternberg, 1928).

exteriors, often with an expressionistic appearance. Scenes are usually designed with low-key lighting to provide striking contrasts between light and dark, where blocks of shadow create diagonal shapes often with large areas in darkness and objects like ladders casting strong shadow patterns (see Figure 4.2). Figures are often picked out purely in silhouette form. Von Sternberg's visual style also incorporates small domestic details and quirky surrealistic touches. Note, for example, the peculiar moment when Feathers (Evelyn Brent) arrives at the café. After she has adjusted her dress, we witness a solitary strand from her feather boa floating downward, the camera following its progress until it is caught by the cleaner Rolls Royce (Clive Brook), just above the floor. Note also the kitten on window ledge, seen in curious juxtaposition with the bullet hole in the window behind the lace curtains.

There is an even stronger evocation of a Sternbergian visual style in *Docks of New York*, especially in its fogbound dockside. Here, we witness the suicidal leap of Sadie (Betty Compson), rendered as a blurred silhouetted shape reflected in the rippling water (see Figure 4.2). Sadie is rescued by Bill Roberts (George Bancroft), a stoker on shore leave. Later that night, improbably, they get married. Sadie is attempting to escape her hopeless life as a prostitute, working the dockside dancehall. Situated in this port location, typical of the kind of liminal spaces occupied by the denizens of film noir, these characters live quite literally at the margins of society. In this sense, they share some affinities with the French poetic-realist films of the ensuing decade such as Jean Vigo's *L'Atalante* (1934), Marcel Carné's *Hotel du Nord* (1938), and *Le Quai des brumes* [*Port of Shadows*] (1938). Like *Docks of New York*, these films draw on a visual style that exploits the contrived ambience of studio-bound sets, the artificial habitat of its disillusioned figures. Although von Sternberg is less well known today, for French critics like Borde and Chaumeton he was a major figure in the development of film noir and they discuss him at length, not only for his introduction of the new gangster figure in *Underworld* but also for *The Shanghai Gesture* (1940) which they saw as a key work in the formation of noir style, not least for its "oneirism and eroticism."[13]

This is not to suggest that von Sternberg inaugurated the gangster film with *Underworld*. One of the problems in histories of the crime film, notably the gangster film, is that they are often partial in their accounts and selective in their choice of films. As Steve Neale has suggested of such histories, "so many films, and so many cycles of films, are ignored," and "routine productions" are bypassed.[14] Conversely, certain films are singled out and lauded, but often divorced from their industry contexts in which they often formed part of a generic pattern or production cycle. Commentators now tend to mention D. W. Griffith's short *The Musketeers of Pig Alley* (1912) as the earliest instance of the gangster film, although this too was only one of several crime films produced during that period.[15]

The (Other) *Maltese Falcon*

The version of *The Maltese Falcon* that impressed French critics was the third Warner Brothers' adaptation of Hammett's novel, and it's instructive to consider why the first version, directed by Roy Del Ruth (1931), fails to appear on anyone's list of films noir. Although it remained quite faithful to the novel and retained a substantial amount of its original dialogue, the film is markedly different in almost every other way. The Del Ruth version, in generic terms, seems like a kind of anachronistic parody of its more familiar successor, and it's striking to see scenes in which the familiar dialogue of the later version is rendered in such a different register. One of the main differences between these two versions is that the first was made before censorship regulations became more strictly enforced under the Production Code Administration (PCA). Del Ruth's film showed the kind of risqué material typical of pre-Code productions. At the beginning of the film we see a silhouette of Sam Spade (Ricardo Cortez) kissing a woman behind his office door followed by a close-up of her legs as she makes what is clearly a postcoital adjustment of her stockings. As he takes down the "Busy Don't Disturb" sign hanging suggestively on his door, we see that the office couch has evidently been the site of a sexual encounter between Spade and the woman. We later learn that he is sleeping with his client, Ruth Wonderly (Bebe Daniels) whom we see in his bed and in his bath. When his partner's widow Iva Archer (Thelma Todd) arrives unexpectedly, we learn that he has been having an affair with her too. "Who's that dame wearing *my* kimonah?" she demands on finding Wonderly installed in his apartment. Clad in silk dressing gown and polka-dot pajamas and seen filing his fingernails, Cortez's Spade is a leering ladies' man. His foppish appearance is in marked contrast to Bogart's, and indeed, it is a characterization that wouldn't be out of place in Gutman's entourage in Huston's film. This is an altogether racier version, played more as a sex comedy, and has none of the dark-toned sexuality of its successor.

German Hollywood

There are several significant international developments in the prewar years which had a bearing on film noir, not least of which were factors affecting the film industry in Germany. Critics often discuss the influence of German expressionism on film noir in terms of visual style (see Chapter 2), but there are several other important factors in the relation between German cinema and "pre-noir" Hollywood. Although there is a tendency in film studies to link generic categories to national cinemas (Soviet montage, Italian neorealism,

German expressionism), this can be misleading in its implication of nationally discrete categories when transnational crosscurrents were common.

We can see a case in point if we return to von Sternberg's early sound film *The Blue Angel*. The film was made at the German studio Universumfilm Aktiengesellschaft (UFA) in two different language versions, English and German (as *Der Blaue Engel*). Von Sternberg had previously been working in Hollywood, as had the film's co-star Emil Jannings, and he returned there to make his other films with Dietrich. Another German filmmaker associated with UFA was F. W. Murnau who worked there before coming to Hollywood to make the silent melodrama *Sunrise: A Song of Two Humans* (1927) for the Fox Film Corporation, a film often seen as an example of "proto-noir." Fritz Lang made several films in Germany during the Weimar period and established a formidable reputation as one of Germany's leading filmmakers.[16] He fled the country soon after Hitler came to power, continuing his career in Hollywood where he established himself as a director strongly associated with film noir throughout the 1940s and 1950s.

The transatlantic cultural crossings of Murnau and Lang were not isolated cases. It is also worth noting how commercial arrangements between German and American studios created a more highly developed sense of transnational cross-fertilization than is usually acknowledged. As Sheri Chinen Biesen has pointed out, in 1926–27 the American studios Paramount and MGM invested substantial capital in UFA under an international distribution agreement called "ParUfaMet," an arrangement that helped to bolster UFA's film production during the economically unstable Weimar era.[17] In other words, there were formal arrangements in place which facilitated the exchange of filmmakers between Germany and America well before the migration of filmmakers and other creative personnel during the 1930s following the rise of Nazism across Europe. The ParUfaMet alliance, says Biesen, "enabled Hollywood to tap into Germany's vulnerable film industry and raid UFA's creative talent."[18] With the rise of the Third Reich in the 1930s and the Nazi appropriation of UFA, the dark expressionist aesthetic of films like *M* were discountenanced as "degenerate", the favored Nazi term ("Entartete Kunst") to deride modernist art, especially art associated with the Weimar period, including German expressionism.

There is a tendency to see the migratory movement of European filmmakers as one-way traffic to America, but, in fact, it went both ways. Note, for example, the case of Alfred Hitchcock's early career. Hitchcock, like Lang, would later play a significant role in the development of American noir, gaining formative experience at UFA on a visit there in 1924 at the behest of the British studio Gainsborough, for which he was then working. Already steeped in the early work of Lang, Murnau, and Pabst, Hitchcock was a beneficiary of the studio partnership agreement between Gainsborough and Ufa (Ufa-Gainsborough). Hitchcock's experience at UFA's Neubabelsberg studio in

Berlin enabled him to study German filmmaking practices at first hand, establish working collaborations with UFA personnel such as cinematographer Theodore Sparkhul, and observe major directors like Murnau working on the set.[19] Another example of this two-way flow can be seen in the career of Louise Brooks who achieved international fame as the femme fatale Lulu in Pabst's *Die Büchse der Pandora* [*Pandora's Box*] (1929) after the director had seen her in Howard Hawks's Fox production, *A Girl In Every Port* (1928).[20]

Many of the German émigrés fleeing the Third Reich, including Lang, arrived first in Paris before departing to the United States.[21] For Lang and his compatriots, Paris in the 1930s was the site of a large émigré community, many of whom—Robert Siodmak, Max Ophüls, and Billy Wilder—had worked in the French film industry during a period that, as Biesen reminds us, coincided with the "*réalisme poétique*" film cycle of France's own national cinema.[22] As we saw in Chapter 1, Jean-Pierre Chartier had already drawn attention to these French films in his account of American noir. These French poetic-realist films are often seen by critics as a significant influence on American noir. This influence can be seen in various ways, notably in the number of them that would later appear as American remakes.[23] These French films had a significant influence on American cinema in terms of both stylistic and thematic concerns through these and other seminal examples of poetic realism, including Carné's *Hotel du Nord* (1938) and *Quai des brumes* [*Port of Shadows*] (1938). By the late 1930s and the imminent Occupation of France, most of the émigrés who had sought refuge in Paris left for America and many ended up in Hollywood where they made extensive contributions to the development of film noir. This didn't mean, as some accounts suggest, that Hollywood effectively imported German expressionism into film noir via the filmmakers who arrived there en masse fleeing Nazi Europe. Their contributions were more complex than that. Indeed, those émigré filmmakers who found work in Hollywood studios were active across different genres, as we shall see.

The émigré filmmakers who arrived in Hollywood were leaving their homeland as well as their homes and their work, often in the most difficult circumstances and in the knowledge of what was happening across Europe under the encroaching shadow of the Third Reich. Although noir critics generally emphasize the cultural background of these filmmakers, many of whom had worked in expressionist cinema and theater in the Weimar period, we should also remember the conditions that forced them to leave Europe. The "sensibility" of film noir, as historian Gerd Gemünden has pointed out,

> certainly entertains close affinities to the sense of loss and cultural despair which many German language exile filmmakers experienced in 1930s and 40s America. These films frequently revolve around questions of (war) trauma, psychosis, memory, and amnesia, split or doubled identity,

featuring men driven from their home, outsiders who cannot comprehend the political and social forces that determine their existence.[24]

The genre with which many of these émigrés were associated was horror—a genre often seen to have affinities with film noir. Many of the émigré directors and other filmmaking personnel associated with film noir in the 1940s also worked in American horror in the 1930s. It is also the case that films seen as classics of German expressionism like Wiene's *Das Kabinet des Dr. Caligari* [*The Cabinet of Dr. Caligari*] (1920) and Murnau's *Nosferatu: eine Symphonie des Grauens* [*Nosferatu: A Symphony of Horrors*] (1922) have also been categorized as psychological horror. Many of the émigrés worked on Hollywood's horror cycles of the 1930s, notably at Universal. Their careers can sometimes demonstrate a trajectory from German expressionism via horror to film noir. For example, Todd Browning's *Dracula* (1931), which inaugurated the studio's horror cycle, and Robert Flory's *Murders in the Rue Morgue* (1932) both had Karl Freund as cinematographer and Freund himself later directed *The Mummy* (1932). Freund had previously worked at UFA on a number of expressionist films such as Paul Wegener's *Der Golem: wie er in die Welt kam* [*The Golem: How He Came into the World*] (1920) and later photographed such films noir as *Undercurrent* (1946), *Two Smart People* (1946), and *Key Largo* (1948). The assumption that German filmmakers came to Hollywood and made film noir there is something of a simplification, and it's important to be aware of the "traffic" of émigré personnel between horror and noir in the 1940s.[25]

The émigrés in Hollywood often made films at odds with an affirmative wartime agenda and they often seemed more difficult to categorize than their noir labels might suggest. An interesting example of wartime noir which draws together several generic elements is Siodmak's *Christmas Holiday* (1944) at Universal. Set for the most part in New Orleans, the narrative is a curious combination of female gothic, southern gothic, and psychological melodrama, all mapped onto a contemporary wartime setting (see Figure 4.3). On Christmas Eve, Lieutenant Charles Mason (Dean Harens) learns from a "Dear John" telegram that his fiancée has just married someone else. While flying home to San Francisco, bad weather forces his aircraft to hold over at New Orleans. There, he is introduced to Jackie Lamont (Deanna Durbin), a name she has assumed after her husband Robert Manette (Gene Kelly) was convicted of murder and imprisoned. Jackie is working as a singer or "hostess" in what is identifiably a brothel. A flashback depicts the early months of her married life, living at the sinister gothic mansion which is the family home together with Robert's forbidding mother (Gale Sondergaard). It becomes clear to Abby, as Jackie was then known, that her husband is not what he seems as he introduces her to his low-life gambling haunts (the naïve Abby doesn't even know what a bookmaker is). At home, she finds both her husband and his

FIGURE 4.3 Female gothic, wartime melodrama, and film noir: Deanna Durbin and Gene Kelly in *Christmas Holiday* (Robert Siodmak, 1944).

mother repeatedly lying to her and their behavior increasingly inexplicable. After Robert's trial, Abby's voice-over tells how "a psychoanalyst said that Robert's relations with his mother were pathological. . . . He wasn't just her son, he was . . . her everything."

Universal exploited Durbin's wholesome star image as the vulnerable young wife of a murderous psychopath. *Christmas Holiday* is one of several wartime films noir that work as a negation of the kind of affirmative narrative endorsement of home and family life typically found in home-front melodrama. In fact, *Christmas Holiday* is a wholly ironic title, seemingly calculated to mislead audiences who would have been unprepared to see Durbin and Kelly in such roles. Indeed, an affronted Bosley Crowther in the *New York Times* found it "really grotesque and outlandish what they have done to Miss Durbin in this film."[26] Casting a star like Durbin in such a noir role, like Fred MacMurray's in *Double Indemnity*, became a feature of wartime noir, with the effect of demonstrating how the noir landscape wasn't the exclusive preserve of a criminal class, but rather one in which ordinary, innocent people could get caught up in a chain of events not of their making. *Christmas Holiday* also shows marriage as a hopelessly failed institution.

Another of the émigrés to play an important role in the development of wartime noir was Alfred Hitchcock. The director of a series of British crime thrillers, Hitchcock began his American career with *Rebecca* (1940), the first of the 1940s' cycle of female gothic thrillers, followed by *Suspicion* (1941) and *Shadow of a Doubt* (1943), both in similar vein, featuring an imperiled female whose life is threatened by her husband and uncle, respectively. These were followed by *Spellbound* (1945), and *Notorious* (1946), all of which are usually categorized as film noir. One of the most significant characteristics of Hitchcock's visual style, as Patrick McGilligan points out, can be traced to his UFA experience of a German cinema that placed particular emphasis on set design and atmosphere, with a style characterized by "shadows and glare, bizarre angles, extreme close-ups, and mobile camera work" together with what would become Hitchcock's trademark "floating camera" after its use by Murnau.[27] Oddly enough, Hitchcock's position as a noir director has often been overlooked, and commentators have tended to place him at some distance from directors more closely identified with noir, especially the German émigrés like Siodmak and Lang. One of the few noir critics who does recognize Hitchcockian noir is Foster Hirsch for whom Hitchcock "is pre-eminently a noir stylist."[28] Although Hitchcock specialized in thrillers, his oeuvre is more generically complex and wide-ranging, encompassing the female gothic to "wrong man" narratives. There are several reasons why Hitchcock has been marginalized in writings on film noir. As James Naremore has suggested, Hitchcock was "a kind of genre unto himself" and he provides some speculative explanations for Hitchcock's marginalised noir status, not least his "wrong" sense of Britishness.[29] One of the main points arising from Naremore's study reveals the limitations of noir criticism when faced with a subject that doesn't "fit" its critical agenda.

The "suggestive background" of wartime noir

For many critics, film noir is predominantly, if not exclusively, a postwar phenomenon. Its films are often seen as narrative refractions of the aftermath of the war and the social problems besetting postwar America. This might seem odd, given that the French critics who first gave rise to the term were talking exclusively about films produced during the war years. Wartime films noir, as Sheri Chinen Biesen has suggested, "reflect a different set of anxieties from those we see in the films noir of the postwar era and result from a different set of circumstances in the Hollywood production system."[30] What, then, were these circumstances affecting Hollywood production and what were the anxieties they reflected? What were the characteristics of wartime noir and how did these differ from the postwar period? I will deal with postwar noir in the following chapter but for the moment I want to consider some other historical contexts in which wartime noir was produced. For Biesen, films noir such as *Phantom Lady* (1944), *Murder, My Sweet* (1944), and *Double Indemnity* "represent the most expressionist, stylistically black phase of film noir." Wilder's *Double Indemnity*, she rightly says, "is darker in visual style than his 1950 film *Sunset Boulevard*," while "Lang's *Ministry of Fear* [1944] and *Scarlet Street* [1945] are darker than his 1950s films noir, such as *The Big Heat* (1953)."[31]

We should note that wartime saw an unprecedented increase in moviegoing. The upheaval of war precipitated massive demographic change and an unprecedented scale of relocation to meet the needs of wartime production. As millions moved to new jobs in the war industries and millions of servicemen shipped abroad, few remained unaffected by the effects of dislocation and separation. Wartime moviegoing assumed a new kind of social and cultural significance when, as Thomas Schatz suggests, "the moviegoing experience remained the central, unifying wartime ritual for millions of Americans, from the war-plant worker in Pittsburgh to the foot soldier in the Pacific."[32] Its significance was recognized by government agencies as the means by which the tenets of wartime Americanism could be most effectively disseminated. For civilians at home, the movie theater acquired new meaning as the locus of wartime community. As Thomas Doherty says, "theaters were natural places to disseminate information, sell war bonds, hold rallies, solicit money for charities, and collect goods for the war effort."[33] Theaters also doubled as emergency shelters for servicemen in transit and as unofficial churches for community singing.[34] In wartime Hollywood, distribution and exhibition became as important as production in signifying the war effort. For servicemen abroad, "the movies" signified home and numerous articles reported on G.I. moviegoing, often in improbably makeshift circumstances, "in muddy jungle clearings, ice-covered Quonset huts, battered barns, open-air amphitheaters, on hillsides, beaches, on ship decks in the moonlight and jammed into reeking heat below decks while in enemy waters."[35] Hollywood provided the cultural texts and social practices that symbolized wartime America and, in conjunction with the government and the military, defined for popular consumption the cultural meaning of America at war. This wartime context, often neglected in noir studies, is important when the culture of America's everyday life was suffused with the presence of the war.

With the attack on Pearl Harbor on December 7, 1941, Hollywood was itself suddenly transformed into a war industry. Its wartime role was linked to a wider picture in which the nation at large geared up for conversion to a wartime economy. Several government agencies were involved in the regulation of Hollywood's output, notably the War Production Board (WPB), the agency responsible for the allocation and rationing of materials in short supply such as gasoline, rubber, and metal. The WPB imposed restrictions on the industry, including a reduction in the amount of available raw film stock. Limits were imposed on studio spending and it was from such constraints on the use of scarce resources that film noir would derive some of its characteristic stylistic features. With national shortages of lumber and steel, the WPB imposed a budgetary limit of $5,000 on set construction. This was a severe restriction when, according to one newspaper report, set expenditure of $50,000 was "frequent" and $100,000, for a production such as How Green Was My Valley (1941), was "not unusual."[36] Studios were consequently required to make more economical use of their allocated resources and to increase the practice of recycling materials.[37]

These restrictions were widely reported in the trade press and elsewhere, usually as an inevitable wartime necessity to economize, but occasionally as a measure that might bring aesthetic benefits as well. Bosley Crowther, for example, writing in the *New York Times*, saw potential advantages in these limitations. Such restrictions, for example, would necessitate a reduction in the spaces routinely allocated for the camera—"space to dolly or make full-figure shots"—previously built in excessive proportions. But the major consequence of set-rationing for film noir was that it might encourage "more fanciful invention in the use of suggestive background."[38] A "suggestive background" could serve as a description of film noir production, where sets might need to be only partially built and, where low-key lighting was deployed, could dispense with the need for costly paraphernalia. If much of a set was in darkness, it wasn't necessary to show what could be concealed. Moreover, filmmakers could use the budgetary restrictions to advantage through "fanciful invention," making more creative use of what was available and exploiting the expressive potential of a tighter budgetary aesthetic.

Another solution was to dispense with studio sets altogether and make use of location shooting. Several Hollywood directors had enlisted in the services where they made military documentaries.[39] I have already mentioned in Chapter 2 how the documentary realism of newsreel journalism and the wartime documentary would play into the development of postwar noir, but the immediate impact of documentary realism occurred during the war years, influenced by location shooting. Bosley Crowther was one of several commentators to applaud the "promising" opportunities afforded by location shooting and he singles out Hitchcock's *Shadow of a Doubt* (1943) at Universal as a case in point. Universal was able to avoid the construction costs of building sections of "a small American city" at the studio as it "dispatched the whole company to a California town [Santa Rosa], where virtually all of the picture was made."[40] It's an odd paradox, though, that a wartime noir like *Shadow of a Doubt* should be stylistically shaped by the exigencies of a patriotic wartime measure to show a dark obverse of Hollywood's more affirmative wartime family melodramas.

Audiences seeing wartime films noir like *Shadow of a Doubt* and *Double Indemnity* on first release did so as part of the staple program typically provided in movie theaters, comprising commercial newsreels, official combat reports, nonfiction shorts, screen magazines, and independent documentaries. All this, we should remember, was happening in a pretelevision age when newsreels provided the main source of news. While the radio provided more immediate and up-to-date coverage of breaking news, the newsreel provided what Doherty describes as "verification and coherence" to the complex narrative of the war. "The newsreels," says Doherty, "made sense of the thing."[41] To those audiences, the films noir they intermittently saw as part of the staple program were embedded in the context of that wartime narrative.

"She kisses him so that he'll kill for her": *Double Indemnity*

> Yes, I killed him. I killed him for money, for a woman. And I didn't get the money, and I didn't get the woman. Pretty, isn't it?
>
> WALTER NEFF (Fred MacMurray), *Double Indemnity* (1944).

Double Indemnity, like *The Maltese Falcon* and *Out of the Past*, is often cited by critics as a paradigmatic example of film noir. This reputation has tended to obscure the fact that the film was exceptionally innovative in several respects. It was widely recognized by American critics on release as an altogether new kind of film.[42] An adaptation of the novella by James M. Cain, the story was inspired by the notorious Snyder-Gray murder case of 1927. Ruth Snyder, together with her lover Henry Judd Gray, plotted the murder of her husband having first taken out a "double indemnity" insurance policy on his life. Both were found guilty and executed the following year. The Snyder-Gray case also provided the basis for Cain's novel *The Postman Always Rings Twice* (1934).[43] The story received widespread and lurid coverage in the press. Snyder's execution was caught by a photographer with a concealed camera and appeared on the front page of the *New York Daily News*, becoming one of the iconic crime pictures of the decade.[44] Perhaps Billy Wilder had the Snyder-Gray executions in mind when he devised and shot the original ending for *Double Indemnity* which shows Neff's execution in a gas chamber, an ending he abandoned.[45]

FIGURE 4.4 Confessional flashback: Fred MacMurray as Walter Neff in *Double Indemnity* (Billy Wilder, 1944).

Another "new" feature of *Double Indemnity* was its depiction of domestic crime. Although violent domestic crime is commonplace in films today, *Double Indemnity*'s story, in which the two leads conspire to carry out a brutal murder, dispose of the body, and demonstrate the detailed planning and execution of the murder, was then quite exceptional and represented a significant shift in what could be shown under PCA regulations. With its focus on crime, sex, and violence, film noir continuously tested the Code's strictures on what was permissible on screen. Cain was a notorious figure in PCA casework whose stories were repeatedly discountenanced by the PCA as unacceptable for film production. Cain's *Double Indemnity* was a case in point after Paramount's attempt to film the story in 1935 was blocked by the PCA's Joseph Breen who objected to its "low tone and sordid flavor."[46] Cain's 1934 novel *The Postman Always Rings Twice* caused even more problems for MGM and the PCA. Tay Garnett's film noir adaptation wouldn't appear until over a decade later (1946), following shifts in both public attitudes and a relaxation in censorship restrictions.[47]

For Cain, the popularity of the "so-called hard-boiled crime pictures" like *Double Indemnity* "is simply that the producers are now belatedly realizing that these stories make good movies" for a public "fed up with the old-fashioned melodramatic type of hokum."[48] At the same time, though, it was actually the liberalization in censorship that facilitated public interest in these new crime films. Raymond Chandler (who cowrote the *Double Indemnity* screenplay with Wilder) suggested that "the studios have gone in for these pictures because the Hays office [PCA] is becoming more liberal. . . . I think they're okaying treatments now which they would have turned down ten years ago, probably because they feel people can take the hard-boiled stuff nowadays."[49]

We should also note that *Double Indemnity* was released in a wartime context, when a substantial amount of Hollywood's output was tailored to what could often seem like a "promotional" ideological agenda on behalf of wartime Americanism. David O. Selznick's home-front melodrama *Since You Went Away* (1944), for example, released in the same year as *Double Indemnity* concerns a family facing the hardships of wartime in a purposeful and optimistic narrative built around "the Unconquerable Fortress: the American Home." This is a long way from the "American home" occupied by the Dietrichsons in *Double Indemnity*. Selznick's prestigious film—the most expensive Hollywood production since *Gone with the Wind* (1939)—was sentimental and patriotic in its affirmation of family values. The narrative deals with the privations and sacrifices of wartime family life through the experience of Anne Hilton (Claudette Colbert), wife, mother, and stalwart custodian of the American home, who ultimately sees the safe return of her husband after serving overseas. Against this, *Double Indemnity* shows the disintegration of home and family, going against the grain of the more official kind of wartime ideology embedded in home-front melodramas.

Another new feature about *Double Indemnity* was the casting of Fred MacMurray as the insurance salesman Walter Neff (see Figure 4.4). This was casting against type as MacMurray's career to date at Paramount had seen him in lightweight roles, often as a romantic-comic lead, playing decent, affable characters. Wilder wanted a "sympathetic" character for the role of Neff, "someone with a decent, average-Joe image."[50] This, of course, has the effect of rendering the murder of Mr. Dietrichson (Tom Powers) not as the act of a criminal type, of a killer, but as the act of an ordinary, everyday kind of man, previously a law-abiding salesman.

Another unusual feature of the narrative is its treatment of both the crime and the criminal. Screen versions of the classic detective story popular in the 1930s were based on a formula that, as we saw in Chapter 3, found the detective solving the crime as a conundrum. But another important aspect of this form, as R. Barton Palmer has pointed out, is how the spectator identifies with the detective. "Classic detective fiction," says Palmer, "not only distances the spectator emotionally from the crime (which exists, as it were, only to be solved) but makes him or her hope for the eventual identification of the criminal, the social or psychological meaning of whose motives is ultimately irrelevant."[51]

The identification of the spectator with the point of view of the detective also sees an alignment with the perspective of the law. In *Double Indemnity*, this point of identification is radically reversed as the spectator is drawn into the criminal's viewpoint. Neff's perspective is conveyed in a narrative structure designed to make the spectator privy to his subjective point of view. This is achieved through his own subjective voice-over narration, given largely in the form of a recorded confession, and through the narrative's flashback structure through which *his* version of the story unfolds. Also, the narrative present

FIGURE 4.5 Phyllis Dietrichson (Barbara Stanwyck) in the driving seat during her husband's murder in *Double Indemnity* (Billy Wilder, 1944).

reveals from the outset that Neff is already fatally wounded and unlikely to survive. So when he admits to Dietrichson's murder, telling us that he did it for money and a woman, we are immediately caught up in his account of the *amour fou* and the murder he plans and executes, just as he is caught up in it. His fears and anxieties in the aftermath of the murder become ours too. Think of the scene after Neff and Phyllis Dietrichson (Barbara Stanwyck) have disposed of her husband's body on the railway track and are about to make good their escape in her car. She turns over the engine several times, but it won't start. Ask yourself how you feel when watching the scene (Remember that we have just witnessed them commit a brutal, premeditated murder as Neff strangles Dietrichson, the camera remaining fixedly on her chilling, sexually charged expression.) (see Figure 4.5). This kind of suspense-inducing device is a familiar trope today, but at the time it was new and worked to create not only a moment of narrative tension but also a sense of complicity in the spectator.[52] We, like them, want the car to start. Our feeling about the crime is further complicated by the fact that Dietrichson himself is presented as an unsympathetic character, boorish and domineering, and although his murder is depicted as vicious and cold-blooded, we are unlikely to care much about him.

Although there is a "detective" working to solve the crime, he is not with the police department but with the insurance company, appearing in the form of claims manager Barton Keyes (Edward G. Robinson), and it is Keyes who fulfills the traditional function of official investigator. If the spectator has been led to empathize with Neff rather than with the detective figure, Keyes is in many ways an admirable character, especially through Robinson's bravura performance. He makes a number of smart, rapid-fire speeches that demonstrate tremendous acumen and expertise: his rendition of the actuarial tables on suicide, for example, is a tour de force. Nevertheless, Keyes remains the ultimate company man, driven by actuarial data and thoroughly inculcated with the investigatory ethos of his job.

Having rejected Keyes's offer of a "desk job" as claims investigator, Neff determines to take on the corporation, using his knowledge of the company's procedures in a calculated gesture of defiance in the knowledge that he will be subject to the full force of its investigation. Although he says he has killed Dietrichson for money and a woman, it is this transgressive act against his corporate employers as much as money or sexual desire that is the *raison d'être* for his crime. The roots of that transgressive impulse can be traced to an old story told by the newspaperman Arthur Krock about an incident that occurred at the *Louisville Times*, an incident that Krock recounted to the young writer, Cain.

> There was an ad in the paper for women's underwear . . . and it was
> supposed to say, "If these sizes are too big, take a tuck in them." But as

Krock was reading through that night's first edition, he saw that somebody had changed the first letter in the word "tuck." Krock ordered the ad changed for the next edition, then summoned the printer and demanded an explanation. The printer couldn't provide one. He couldn't understand how such an embarrassing accident could have happened. Krock remained suspicious. Two days later, he went and interrogated the printer again. . . . The printer confessed. "Mr. Krock," he said, trying finally to explain, "you do nothing your whole life but watch for something like that happening, so as to head it off, *and then*, Mr. Krock, you catch yourself watching for chances to do it."[53]

Cain, who had worked as an insurance salesman himself, drew on the idea of a corporate employee who could exploit the specialized knowledge he had acquired at work to commit "the perfect crime" as Walter Neff would try to do. He recounts his rationale to Keyes:

It was all tied up with something I'd been thinking about for years, since long before I ran into Phyllis Dietrichson. Because, you know how it is, Keyes, in this business you can't sleep for trying to figure out all the tricks they could pull on you. You're like the guy behind the roulette wheel watching the customers to make sure they don't crook the house. And then, one night, you get to thinking how you could crook the house yourself, and do it smart, because you've got the wheel under your hands, you know every notch of it by heart.

In both the stories there is an implication that the transgressive impulse is a reaction against the routines of longstanding corporate employment. It is surely significant that Neff's impulse had been latent "long before" he met Phyllis Dietrichson. Here, then, we can see a wartime instance of film noir as a critique of the corporation which, as we shall see in the next chapter, will gather momentum in the postwar period.[54]

Notes

1 Thomas Doherty, *Projections of War: Hollywood, American Culture, and World War II* (New York: Columbia University Press, 1993), 85–121.

2 *Government Information Manual for the Motion Picture Industry* (Office of War Information, Bureau of Motion Pictures, 1942), quoted in Clayton R. Koppes and Gregory D. Black, *Hollywood Goes to War: How Politics, Profits, and Propaganda Shaped World War II Movies* (New York: Free Press, 1987), 66.

3 Thomas Schatz, *Boom and Bust: American Cinema in the 1940s* (Berkeley: University of California Press, 1999), 222.

4   Jeanine Basinger, *The World War II Combat Film: Anatomy of a Genre* (New York: Columbia University Press, 1986), 36–37.

5   Key examples include *Bataan* (1943), *Air Force* (1943), *Sahara* (1943), *Destination Tokyo* (1944), *Back to Bataan* (1945), and *The Story of G.I. Joe* (1945).

6   See for instance *Swing Shift Maisie* (1943), *Rosie the Riveter* (1944), and *Tender Comrade* (1944).

7   Dana Polan, *Power and Paranoia: History, Narrative, and the American Cinema. 1940-1950* (New York: Columbia University Press, 1986), 75–76.

8   Lary May, "Making the American Consensus: The Narrative of Conversion and Subversion in World War II Films," in Lewis A. Erenberg and Susan E. Hirsch, eds., *The War in American Culture: Society and Consciousness During World War II* (Chicago: University of Chicago Press, 1996), 87, 89.

9   Ibid., 89.

10 Ibid., 90.

11 See Richard Maltby, "The Spectacle of Criminality," in J. David Slocum, ed., *Violence and the American Cinema* (New York: Routledge, 2001), 117–52.

12 See also *Morocco* (1930), *Dishonored* (1931), *Shanghai Express* (1932), *Blonde Venus* (1932), *The Scarlet Empress* (1934), and *The Devil Is a Woman* (1935). *The Blue Angel* (1930) narrates the ruin of Professor Rath (Emil Jannings) who falls for Lola Lola (Dietrich), cabaret singer at the Blue Angel nightclub.

13 Borde and Chaumeton, *Panorama*, 38. See also 33–37.

14 Neale, *Genre and Hollywood*, 77.

15 Ibid., 78.

16 Lang's German films include *Der müde Tod* [*Destiny*] (1921), *Dr. Mabuse, der Spieler* [*Dr. Mabuse, The Gambler*] (1922), *Metropolis* (1926), *Spione* [*Spies*] (1928), *Frau im Mond* [*Woman in the Moon*] (1929), and *M: Eine Stadt sucht einen Mörder* [*M: A City Searches for a Murderer*] (1931).

17 Sheri Chinen Biesen, *Blackout: World War II and the Origins of Film Noir* (Baltimore: Johns Hopkins University Press, 2005), 16.

18 Ibid.

19 Patrick McGilligan, *Alfred Hitchcock: A Life in Darkness and Light* (Chichester: Wiley, 2003), 62–63.

20 See for instance Ian Brookes, "Who the Hell Is Howard Hawks?" in Brookes, ed., *Howard Hawks: New Perspectives* (London: Palgrave/BFI, 2016), 13.

21 Lang often recounted a story, possibly apocryphal, about a meeting he had with the Nazi Propaganda Minister Josef Goebbels who offered him the post of overseeing the development of Nazi cinema, a story that reads like a scene from one of his own films noir. See Tom Gunning, *The Films of Fritz Lang: Allegories of Vision and Modernity* (London: BFI, 2000), 8–10.

22 Biesen, *Blackout*, 16–17.

23 Jean Renoir's *La Chienne* [*The Bitch*] (1931) was remade by Lang as *Scarlet Street* (1945) and *La Bête Humaine* (1938) as *Human Desire* (1954); Julien Duvivier's *Pépé le Moko* was remade twice, first as *Algiers* (1938)

and second as a musical, *Casbah* (1948); Marcel Carné's *Le Jour se lève* [*Daybreak*] (1939) was remade as *The Long Night* (1947) by Anatole Litvak.

24 Gerd Gemünden, *A Foreign Affair: Billy Wilder's American Films* (New York: Berghahn, 2008), 33.

25 See, for example, Peter Hutchings, "Film Noir and Horror," in Spicer and Hanson, eds., *Companion to Film Noir*, 111–24.

26 Bosley Crowther, "The Screen: 'Christmas Holiday,' Presenting Deanna Durbin in Serious and Emotional Role, Supported by Gene Kelly, Opens at Criterion," *New York Times* (June 29, 1944), 16.

27 McGilligan, *Alfred Hitchcock*, 63. For instances of Hitchcock's "floating camera," see, for example, the opening scenes of *Rope* (1948), *Rear Window* (1954), and *Psycho* (1960).

28 Foster Hirsch, *The Dark Side of the Screen: Film Noir* (New York: Da Capo, 1981), 139.

29 James Naremore, "Hitchcock at the Margins of Noir," in *An Invention Without a Future: Essays on Cinema* (Berkeley: University of California Press, 2014), 139–55.

30 Biesen, *Blackout*, 3.

31 Ibid.

32 Schatz, *Boom and Bust*, 132.

33 Doherty, *Projections of War*, 82.

34 Ibid., 82, 84.

35 Editors of *Look*, "Beachhead Bijou," in *Movie Lot to Beachhead: The Motion Picture Goes to War and Prepares for the Future* (New York: Doubleday, Doran, 1945), 104.

36 Walter Wanger, "Upheaval in Hollywood," *Los Angeles Times* (November 15, 1942), H4.

37 Schatz, *Boom and Bust*, 132, 143–44.

38 Bosley Crowther, "It's an Ill Wind—But the Recent War Restrictions on Film Production Bode Some Good," *New York Times* (September 27, 1942), X3.

39 John Ford made *Battle of Midway* (1942); John Huston, *Report From the Aleutians* (1943) and *The Battle of San Pietro* (1945); William Wyler, *The Memphis Belle: A Story of a Flying Fortress* (1945) and Frank Capra, the *Why We Fight* series (1942–45).

40 Crowther, "It's an Ill Wind."

41 Doherty, *Projections of War*, 231.

42 See, for example, Philip K. Scheuer, "Film History Made by 'Double Indemnity,'" *Los Angeles Times* (August 6, 1944), C1, 3.

43 On Cain's treatments of the case, see William Marling, *The American Roman Noir: Hammett, Cain, and Chandler* (Athens: University of Georgia Press, 1995), 148–161.

44 "DEAD!" *New York Daily News* (January 13, 1928), 1.

45 These scenes are presumed lost. On the original ending, see Naremore, *More Than Night*, 90–95.

46 Quoted in Leonard J. Leff and Jerold L. Simmons, *The Dame in the Kimono: Hollywood, Censorship, and the Production Code from the 1920s to the 1960s* (London: Weidenfeld and Nicolson, 1990), 127.

47 On the censorship history of *The Postman Always Rings Twice*, see ibid., 128–36; see also the AFI entry on the film. The American adaptation was preceded by a French version, Pierre Chenal's *Le dernier tournant* [*The Last Turn*] (1939), and an Italian one, Luchino Visconti's *Ossessione* [*Obsession*] (1943), both countries with fewer censorship restrictions.

48 Quoted in Lloyd Shearer, "Crime Certainly Pays on the Screen: The Growing Crop of Homicidal Films Poses Questions for Psychologists and Producers," *New York Times* (August 5, 1945), 37.

49 Quoted in Shearer, "Crime Certainly Pays," 37.

50 Kevin Lally, *Wilder Times: The Life of Billy Wilder* (New York: Henry Holt, 1996), 134.

51 R. Barton Palmer, *Hollywood's Dark Cinema: The American Film Noir* (New York: Twayne, 1994), 46–47.

52 See Lally, *Wilder Times*, 138.

53 Otto Friedrich, *City of Nets: A Portrait of Hollywood in the 1940s* (London: Headline, 1987), 160.

54 Wilder's own critique of the corporation continued in his later films, notably *The Apartment* (1960), a romantic comedy with noir elements which also features Fred MacMurray. See Ian Brookes, "The Eye of Power: Postwar Fordism and the Panoptic Corporation in *The Apartment*," *Journal of Popular Film & Television* 37, no. 4 (Winter 2009): 150–60.

5

The postwar period, 1945–50

For many critics, the postwar period represents the major era of film noir production. Borde and Chaumeton saw the years 1946–48 mark both "the ascension and the apogee of film noir"[1] and other critics have followed suit, often identifying within this period many of the films seen as quintessential examples of the category such as *The Big Sleep* (1946), *The Postman Always Rings Twice* (1946), *The Killers* (1946), and *Out of the Past* (1947). The patriotic impulse driving wartime genres like the combat film and home-front melodrama disappeared at the end of the war, and critics identified a more pessimistic vein in postwar film noir. Paul Schrader detected a widespread sense of disillusionment across virtually all sections of society from small businessmen, housewives, and factory workers that was "mirrored in the sordidness of the urban crime film."[2] This chapter examines films noir of the period in a wider generic context than is usual in noir studies in order to test habitual critical claims for the generic distinctiveness of postwar noir. Specifically, I locate noir in relation to the gangster film, modern gothic, and domestic melodrama while also considering the generic impact of existentialism, performance, and low-budget filmmaking practices on the development of postwar film noir.

"Haphazard": Film noir and existentialism

June Mills (Alice Faye): "Tired?"
Eric Stanton (Dana Andrews): "Maybe I am, waiting for something to happen."
June Mills: "Nothing's going to happen."

Fallen Angel (1945)

Fay (Coleen Gray): "Johnny, you've got to run!"
Johnny Clay (Sterling Hayden): "Ah, what's the difference?"

The Killing (1956)

One of the major themes to become associated with postwar noir was existentialism. French critical interest in American film noir originally came out of a Left Bank intellectual culture then under the sway of existential ideas in philosophy and literature. Although the surrealist tradition in French culture played an influential role in predisposing critics toward American noir, existentialism would provide them with a different kind of emphasis in their readings of the films. James Naremore provides a useful comparison between the two strains of thought. "Existentialism was despairingly humanist rather than perversely anarchic," he says, so "if the surrealists saw the postwar American thriller as a theater of cruelty, the existentialists saw it as a protoabsurdist novel. For critics who were influenced by existentialism, film noir was attractive because it depicted a world of obsessive return, dark corners, or *huis-clos* [no exit]."[3] But what is existentialism and why is it significant to film noir?

One of the seminal essays on existentialism is Robert Porfirio's "No Way Out: Existential Motifs in the *Film Noir*," first published in *Sight and Sound* in 1976, and the first sustained analysis to argue for the "black vision" of existentialism as the main unifying factor of film noir.[4] Porfirio suggests that existentialism was unknown in America until after the Second World War when it was popularized through the writings of its principal exponents, Jean-Paul Sartre and Albert Camus. Existentialism had previously failed to make inroads in the United States because, Porfiro argues, it went against the American grain of an instinctual optimism. This sense of optimism had been "successively challenged" by such factors as the Depression, totalitarianism, fear of communism, the loss of insular security, and a sense of individual initiative compromised by the growth of the technocratic state.[5] For Porfirio, existentialism emanated from the margins of the same Romantic tradition "which led to surrealism, expressionism and literary naturalism," that is, to the other main cultural movements that would become associated with film noir. Porfirio characterizes existentialism in terms of "a disoriented individual facing a confused world that he cannot accept." It emphasizes "man's contingency in a world where there are no transcendental values or moral absolutes, a world devoid of any meaning but the one man himself creates."[6] The existential world Porfirio describes is one in which there is no place for any conventional hero but only one of a "non-heroic" kind.[7] He highlights the trope of the Hemingway hero as one "to whom something has been done" as well as one who bears a sense of loss—and an awareness of that loss—of the ties that bind him to a community.[8] Existentialism, then, encompasses conditions of alienation, the futility of action, the arbitrariness of events, and the meaninglessness and absurdity of existence.

Porfirio astutely links the casting and performance of Hollywood's stars to the realization of the existential noir "non-hero" and recognizes the significance of certain kinds of noir star personae and existential performance.

> Vulnerability and a sense of loss were suggested in Humphrey Bogart's lined face and slightly bent posture; in Alan Ladd's short stature and a certain feminine quality about his face; in the passivity and heavy-lidded eyes of Robert Mitchum; in the thinly veiled hysteria that lay behind many of Richard Widmark's performances; in Robert Ryan's nervous manner.[9]

For Porfirio, this vulnerability is embodied in the figure of the Swede (Burt Lancaster) in Siodmak's version of Hemingway's story, "The Killers." Lancaster, "whose powerful physique ironically dominated the cinematic frame . . . passively awaits death at the hands of the hired assassins."[10] Such noir "non-heroes" were also positioned within the stylistic apparatus of film noir, obscured in shadows, dissected by lines, and confined in small spaces in mise-en-scènes which emphasized his entrapment, isolation, and loneliness.[11]

This aspect of existential performance is worth further exploration, especially as the study of noir performance is an underdeveloped one. One of the noir critics who has addressed this issue is Foster Hirsch who has described the noir actor as being "part of the decor" in a performance which is linked to the noir "mood and ambience."[12] Obviously, there is a very wide range of stars and performance styles to be included in an account of noir performance, but let us take just two of Hirsch's examples, Alan Ladd and Veronica Lake, both stars strongly associated with film noir in the 1940s, appearing together in three notable noirs at Paramount: *This Gun for Hire* (1942), *The Glass Key* (1942), and *The Blue Dahlia* (1946). "Their faces barely move," says Hirsch. "Their unblemished beauty has a manufactured quality" and they appear "mannikin-like." Together, "they make convincing victims, suggesting, beneath their masks, a weakness and vulnerability."[13] Their vocal delivery is flat, monotonous, and as oddly artificial as the way they look.

Ladd's persona as the killer Raven in *This Gun for Hire* is the first incarnation of such a character. The scene in which he comes across a little girl wearing leg braces sitting on the stairs provides an instance of his inscrutable mask (see Figure 5.1). Having carried out his contract killings in an upstairs apartment, he encounters her again on the way down, still sitting in the same place. We see him momentarily consider killing her too, as a witness placing him at the scene, before wordlessly returning her ball to her and leaving. But in Ladd's performance, there is a silent intimation that he *could* kill the child. We should remember that *This Gun for Hire* was singled out by Borde and Chaumeton as a seminal film noir, and one of the main points of attraction for them was Ladd's "most disturbing" role as this killer. Their comments are revealing:

> His slight frame and his overly docile baby face, with its limpid eyes, its gentle, unobtrusive features, appear to have come from some other planet, after all the huge and brutal killers who peopled prewar gangster films. Only his expressionless features in situations of great tension reveal a fearsome, inhuman frigidity in this fallen angel.[14]

In *The Glass Key*, an adaptation of Hammett's novel of the same name, Ladd's Ed Beaumont sees him with a different but comparable persona, the unresisting victim of sadomasochistic torture in which his passivity seems almost to embrace the brutal punishment meted out to him, his diminutive frame and feminized features make him appear especially vulnerable. "You're a strange man," Ellen Graham (Lake) says to him later. "Tell me, why did you take such a beating?"

French critics were predisposed toward noir partly because they identified in its narratives a kinship with the existential currents in French intellectual life. We should also remember that French intellectuals had long admired American writers like Hammett, Chandler, and Cain, identifying in their hard-boiled fiction instances of their own existential interests. Existentialism is known as a French philosophical phenomenon, but as Stephen Faison suggests, America had developed its own version of existentialism "at least several years before Sartre and Camus published their first existential works."[15] Faison argues that American existentialism can be seen both in film noir and the hard-boiled fiction that provided much of its source material. According to this argument, then, French critics were responding to American film and fiction in which they saw reflections of their own philosophical concerns, as well they might. It's worth bearing in mind that French existentialism itself owed some kind of debt to hard-boiled American fiction. Cain's 1934 novel *The Postman*

FIGURE 5.1 "This fallen angel": Alan Ladd as Philip Raven in *This Gun for Hire* (Frank Tuttle, 1942).

Always Rings Twice—a novel which had been available in French translation since 1937 and was "extremely popular" in Paris in the late 1930s—was an acknowledged influence on Camus in his own "existential" novel, *L'Étranger* (*The Stranger*), published in France in 1942 (and in America in 1946). Camus may also have seen the French film version of *The Postman Always Rings Twice*, *Le Dernier Tournant* [*The Last Turn*] (1939).[16]

For a "homegrown" instance of American existentialism, we can return to Hammett's *The Maltese Falcon* and an episode in the novel which, oddly, doesn't appear in any of the film versions. Sam Spade tells Brigid O'Shaughnessy a story about a man named Flitcraft who left his office to go to lunch one day and never returned: his family never saw him again. He had seemed moderately and unremarkably successful. "He owned his house in a Tacoma suburb, a new Packard, and the rest of the appurtenances of successful American living."[17] Spade recounted how five years later he was working with a detective agency in Seattle when Mrs. Flitcraft came in and reported that a man resembling her husband had been seen in Spokane. Spade located him. Flitcraft told him that he was now living there under an assumed name with a new wife and child in a suburban home and with a successful business, in circumstances which virtually replicated those he had abandoned in Tacoma five years earlier. Spade recounted Flitcraft's story:

> Here's what had happened to him. Going to lunch he passed an office-building that was being put up—just the skeleton. A beam or something fell eight or ten stories down and smacked the sidewalk alongside him. It brushed pretty close to him, but didn't touch him, though a piece of the sidewalk was chipped off and flew up and hit his cheek. It only took a piece of skin off, but he still had the scar when I saw him. He rubbed it with his finger—well, affectionately—when he told me about it. He was scared stiff of course, he said, but he was more shocked than really frightened. He felt like somebody had taken the lid off life and let him look at the works.[18]

Until that moment, Flitcraft had lived his life as "a clean orderly sane responsible affair" but "a falling beam had shown him that life was fundamentally none of these things." It was an epiphanic moment for him. "He, the good citizen-husband-father, could be wiped out between office and restaurant by the accident of a falling beam. He knew then that men died at haphazard like that, and lived only while blind chance spared them."[19] The story works as a kind of existential viewpoint *avant la lettre*. The incident resonates in an existential context because Spade understands what Flitcraft is saying ("I got it all right"), and we can readily imagine the inclusion of this scene being played by Bogart's Spade. Existential elements would feature in many postwar films noir, especially in low-budget productions.

Low-budget noir: Edgar G. Ulmer's *Detour*

Eddie Dmytryk always said, "What is this film noir? . . . We gotta make a picture in four weeks? We've only got so much money to make it? We've got to condense the sets and photograph it really good because we can't afford the proper sets?" And "we didn't know we were making film noir. We were making a picture for a price!"

RICHARD WIDMARK (2002)[20]

Well before the financial restrictions imposed by wartime regulations, Hollywood had an established tradition of low-budget filmmaking. In the 1930s the major studios began to feature the "B" movie or "programmer" as a supplement to the "A" picture on the program, providing Depression-era audiences with two films for the price of one.[21] Later in the decade, there was a proliferation of so-called Poverty Row studios such as Republic and Monogram which specialized in low-budget productions. They were joined in the following decade by the Producers Releasing Corporation (PRC).[22] The "B film" designation implies an inferior product, literally something second rate. "When one mentions the term *B movie*," says Arthur Lyons in his study of the subject, "most people think 'B' stands for 'bad'."[23] Bad they may have been, but they also provided what can be seen as creative workshops for filmmakers who learned to make do with minimal sets and truncated shooting schedules.

It was in these circumstances that Edgar G. Ulmer's *Detour* (1945) was made at PRC (see Figure 5.2). Ulmer's film has acquired an almost mythical reputation among fans and scholars as a definitive film noir that seems to have all the requisite noir credentials, not only in its narrative themes and visual stylistics but also in the way it was fashioned from such meager resources. Ulmer, who was born in the Czech Republic, was one of the European émigrés

FIGURE 5.2 Al Roberts (Tom Neal) in *Detour* (Edgar G. Ulmer, 1945).

to come to Hollywood early, accompanying Murnau there to work with him on *Sunrise* (1927). He had previously worked in Germany as an assistant to Max Reinhardt, Murnau, Lang, and Ernst Lubitsch, and as codirector with Siodmak on *Menschen am Sonntag* [*People on Sunday*] (1930). Following these illustrious associations, Ulmer's own directorial career in Hollywood began with *Damaged Lives* (1933), an exploitation film about a man who contracts syphilis after a casual sexual encounter ("His Life of Debauchery Brought Disease To His Wife!"). Myron Meisel has described how "Ulmer worked on the lowest depths of Poverty Row, far beyond the pale of the B film into the seventh circle of the Z picture, shooting his films in dingy studios on makeshift sets, on lightning swift schedules."[24] The working conditions at PRC were certainly restrictive. "Most of my PRC pictures were made in six days," Ulmer told Peter Bogdanovich. "Just try to visualize it—eighty setups a day."[25]

The world of *Detour* is so unremittingly harsh and unsympathetic that it conveys an almost farcical sense of hopelessness, a world in which any future possibilities are already foreclosed, where there is only the prospect of a kind of unfuture for its protagonist Al Roberts (Tom Neal). The narrative shows his "road-world" perspective as he undertakes a westward journey from New York to join his fiancée Sue (Claudia Drake) in Los Angeles. Al is seen for the first time trudging along a dark roadside, dirty, disheveled, and broke. If he once had a promising future as a concert pianist ("which couldn't have been brighter if I'd embroidered it with neon lights"), his artistic ambitions are failed from the outset. Despite Sue's encouragement that he will "make Carnegie Hall yet," he can only envisage a role for himself there as a janitor ("I'll make my debut in the basement"). Unable or unwilling to do anything purposeful to realize his ambition, the focus of his attention suddenly shifts to Sue and to an insistent preoccupation with their marriage. They are seen together in an early flashback performing in a New York nightclub where he is a pianist and she a singer. Their relationship at first seems to suggest a promising future together, at least according to Al, and his voice-over narration describes an auspicious romance:

> There was Sue, who made working there a little like working in heaven. But how we felt about each other, well, there's nothing very unusual in that. I was an ordinary healthy guy and she was an ordinary healthy girl and when you add those two together you get an ordinary healthy romance, which is the old story, sure, but somehow the most wonderful thing in the world. All in all I was a pretty lucky guy.

Al's narration struggles awkwardly to present a conventional kind of romance, but his account is contradicted by the actual depiction of their relationship. Al is an unreliable narrator, as Andrew Britton has pointed out, and his commentary, through which we are led to understand the story, is "profoundly self-deceived and systematically unreliable."[26] After Sue's departure, for example, when Al resolves to go and see her, it's clear from their telephone conversation that some time has elapsed since they last spoke. The sequence suggests that the call is of considerable moment, rendered ironically as kind of absurd visual hyperbole as it shows a series of switchboard operators and telegraph lines (clearly stock footage) functioning to provide their connection, a transnational link between east and west and, seemingly, the reconnection of their romance. But the conversation is largely one-sided: Sue is seen listening but it is Al who does all the talking, reiterating his desire to get married "right away."

When Sue is seen on the phone, it is only for the briefest moment, sitting still and impassively. The scene is one of several in the film that demonstrates how "B" picture productions would typically dispense with time-consuming entrances and exits. We see Al making the call, but she doesn't come to the phone: she is already there with the receiver in her hand. As Flynn and McCarthy suggest, the elimination of such "stage business" can give "B" films "a strange, almost cryptic air of flatness and unreality." Directors like Ulmer, they say, "developed a kind of visual shorthand to turn these minimal resources into expressive devices."[27] Certainly, the brief scene showing Sue conveys a "flat" effect in her response to Al.

Al hitchhikes west and gets a ride from Charles Haskell (Edmund MacDonald). Later, he takes over the wheel and is seen driving at night. Looking into the rearview mirror, the mundane view of the receding road behind is transmogrified with a dissolve into a sequence in which Sue is singing "I Can't Believe That You're In Love With Me" in a performance which is, for him, not only redolent of their former romance but also his fantasy projection of her success as a star vocalist. In a minimalist representation, the sequence conveys an opulent and stylish setting with Sue fronting a "big" band with the bandsmen and their instruments silhouetted behind her. Like the mirror from which Roberts conjures the sequence, the frame is tilted. The stylistic effect is akin to the iconography associated with the dance bands of the swing era, although here it simultaneously implies a sense of dislocation. As an expression of his yearning, for romance and success, it too is rendered out of kilter.

Haskell's accidental death sets in motion a sequence of events that see an inversion of the ordinary world around Roberts. Having acquired Haskell's clothes and car, he also assumes his identity before picking up a hitchhiker, Vera (Ann Savage). If Roberts's marriage to Sue can only be an elusive fantasy, his "marriage" to Vera becomes a grotesque parody of married life. For Vera too, the road signifies little more than hopelessness. Staring at the road ahead, she appears to be in a catatonic trance, her posture resembling that of Haskell's before his death. She too is dying, of tuberculosis. Like Haskell, she dies an accidental death, leaving Roberts the victim of bizarre circumstances as he is implicated in two murders. The roadhouse outside Reno from which Al narrates his story is a kind of limbo between east and west, rendered as a kind of stasis. It is as if the entire country has been rendered as a vast borderland through which his journey pointlessly continues, where he is consigned to oblivion and exile until the moment, sooner or later, of his inevitable arrest for the murders he hasn't committed ("Some day a car will stop to pick me up that I never thumbed").

Al's westward journey takes him through a series of inhospitable landscapes in which America is seen as a continuing wasteland, a succession of nondescript roadside locations like the diner, motel, and gas station. New York City had been represented through a minimal stage set of a fogbound street, while Los Angeles is reducible to a used-car lot. But in Ulmer's mise-en-scène, this is ordinariness in extremis. Ordinary objects and everyday occurrences become in themselves unstable and unpredictable. A coffee cup looms larger than life in an almost hallucinatory distortion. A car door and a telephone inadvertently become instruments of death. Al's journey also resonates with a sense of the west embedded in American mythology, although by now, with his five o' clock shadow and disheveled appearance, he is a grim parody of the promise of professional success and romantic love. The same is true of Hollywood where Sue has become not the movie star of his fantasy but a "hash-slinger."

Inconceivable coincidences ending in death occur not just once but twice and in circumstances so absurd as to defy any ordinary sense of narrative logic. A travel montage sequence begins with a purposeful sense of Al's westward progression toward his destination. But as John Belton has pointed out, *Detour* presents such a sequence only to subvert it. "After the map montage," says Belton, "the journey continues with shots of Roberts hitchhiking from the wrong side of the highway and with cars driving on the wrong side of the road. Though the direction of Roberts' movements remains consistent, the logic of his actions and that of the traffic around him do not." The montage ends just before Haskell picks him up and his subsequent detour takes him into "uncharted territory."[28]

The extraordinary amount of critical interest in *Detour* can be at least partly explained by the "fit" between the film's budgetary aesthetic and its narrative concerns. The film's unique critical status as *the* definitive low-budget noir owes something to its uncompromising critique of the American Dream. But perhaps its main appeal is through the way in which the fatalistic despair and hopelessness of the narrative is actually conveyed through the very limitations imposed on Ulmer's filmmaking. The almost ridiculously cheap sets of his shoestring budget seem appropriate to a critique of Hollywood and seem to offer proof of a more authentic mode of filmmaking, its trashy production values are at a considerable distance from the big budgets and happy endings of Hollywood's. To some, *Detour* confers on Ulmer an almost heroic stature as a guerrilla filmmaker. Moreover, Ulmer made these films not as a director unable to obtain work in the major studios. Rather, as Meisel points out, "Ulmer *chose* to make these films."[29]

In some ways, Poverty Row filmmaking could produce films that were more difficult to categorize, often with a more complex generic make up. Take for example, Jack Bernhard's little-known Monogram film *Decoy* (1946). Usually categorized as a film noir, it has much in common with horror. The film opens enigmatically with a close-up of a filthy washroom sink in which someone is washing his hands. We then see his reflection in a broken mirror. Leaving the washroom, his movements are inexplicably strange with his fixed expressionless stare and zombie-like walk. Later, in flashback, we learn that he is Dr. Lloyd Craig (Herbert Rudley), now fatally wounded. With its wooden box, buried treasure, and maps torn in half, the film is like a cross between *Treasure Island* adventure and *Frankenstein* horror, while anticipating some of the tropes of the "mad science" films of the following decade. Margot Shelby (Jean Gillie) wants to obtain the stolen $400,000 her boyfriend Frank Olins (Robert Armstrong) has hidden. In prison, Olins is due to face execution in a gas chamber; but Shelby has devised an intricate scheme to reclaim Olins's body and administer an antidote to the cyanide gas, having enlisted the help of Dr. Craig for this purpose. Having removed Olins's "corpse" from the prison, Craig brings his body back to life in a sequence reminiscent of innumerable horror films when we see a series of close-ups of medical equipment used to resuscitate him. "I'm alive!" he exclaims, echoing one of the characteristic tropes of countless horror films. Such Poverty Row filmmaking could complicate conceptions of more conventional studio genres.

Film noir and the gangster film

"I'm going to build an organization along scientific lines," says the gangster Alec Stiles (Richard Widmark) in *The Street with No Name* (1948). Other gangsters would follow suit. Concerns with new forms of criminal organization underwrite several of the period's films noir, often with an emphasis on an intrinsic gangsterism in corporate organizations. As we saw in Chapter 4, the crime film would provide a template for a critique of postwar corporatism.

A scene in *I Walk Alone* (1948) shows the gangster Frankie Madison (Burt Lancaster) recently released from prison. Having served out his sentence, he returns to see his former partner from the old bootlegging days, Noll "Dink" Turner (Kirk Douglas), to claim his share of the proceeds from their nightclub. Frankie's brother Dave (Wendell Corey), now the accountant for

Dink's new business, enters the room carrying a set of account books. Dink sardonically refuses Frankie's demand. The scene self-consciously highlights a transition in the narrative representation of the gangster of the early 1930s to a new criminal type of the 1940s. The traditional figure of the gangster was receding from view and so too was his traditional setting. The meeting between Frankie and Dink takes place in a room that bears no resemblance to the archetypal gangster venues of the preceding decade. One of Frankie's henchmen exclaims on entering the businesslike boardroom—"What a layout!"—a reaction that inadvertently describes a comprehensively different business setup with a new kind of organization. We know these are gangsters but they no longer look like gangsters. The conventional iconography of earlier Prohibition-era narratives has become obsolete and the old-time gangster an anachronism. Postwar criminal enterprise is seen to have acquired a corporate organization in which the criminal now looked more like a businessman than a gangster.[30]

Frankie angrily demands redress in the only way he knows how, through tough-guy bravado ("There's only one way to handle you . . ."), the kind of threat now reminiscent of a bygone era. Dink derisively replies, "Kill me?" Frankie perseveres with his confrontational stance: "If I have to, yeah! A guy's got to fight for what's his." Dink, in turn, taunts Frankie with his obsolescence in the new corporate order, scornfully evoking the old Prohibition days. "You and your boys," he says, with a wry glance at Frankie's gang.

> This isn't the Four Kings, no hiding out behind a steel door and a peephole. This is big business. We deal with banks, lawyers, and a Dun and Bradstreet rating. The world's spun right past you, Frankie. In the twenties, you were great. In the thirties, you might've made the switch. But today, you're finished. As dead as the headlines the day you went to prison.

Frankie desperately attempts to make sense of this "big business" talk and demands a straightforward explanation, only to be told that there are no "simple answers." He questions his brother about the new organizational structure, beginning with what he takes to be an obvious assumption. "Dink's got the full say around here, right?" "Yes," replies Dave, who has been reciting a list of their corporate interests, "except that it's revocable by a vote of the board of directors of Reed and Associates." An exasperated Frankie demands to know, "Just what does Dink own?" Dave replies, "in which corporation?" Bewildered and uncomprehending, Frankie can't understand this new business organization that has rendered him redundant, nor can he speak its language, derived from the *Wall Street Journal*.

Similar concerns can be seen in Abraham Polonsky's *Force of Evil* (1948), a narrative that draws on several noir conventions in its depiction of a criminal organization. An establishing shot shows the familiar noir trope of city buildings, here the office buildings of New York's financial district, while an accompanying voice-over announces: "This is Wall Street." (see Figure 5.3) Image and narration work together to establish through a documentary style an authentic sense of time and place. The scene is viewed from an elevated perspective from which the camera pans down slowly to the street far below where diminished sidewalk figures look incidental in comparison with the towering buildings that dominate both street and skyline. "Wall Street" here is both the city location and, symbolically, the focal expression of American capitalism. The opening narration is spoken by Joe Morse (John Garfield), a "corporation lawyer" who works for Ben Tucker (Roy Roberts) at Tucker Enterprises. Joe is first seen arriving at his Wall Street office, conservatively dressed in a dark suit. Like the accountant Dave in *I Walk Alone*, Joe looks like a conventional businessman. His role at Tucker Enterprises, however, is to supervise the transition of the corporation's illegal gambling operation to a legitimate business footing, "to make it legal, respectable, and very profitable." Banking on the prediction that the next day's lottery on the fourth of July will entail heavy betting on the number 776 ("the old Liberty number"), Tucker and Joe plan to fix that result so that all the small-time numbers operators will be hit so hard by the ensuing payout that they will be forced out of business, enabling Tucker to move in and take over.

Joe's description of the scheme, for all its ruthlessness, remains within the limits of normal corporate enterprise as an ordinary instance of corporate takeover in a free market economy: "Tomorrow night," says Joe, "every bank in the city is broken. And we step in and lend money to who we want while we let the rest go to the wall. We're normal financiers." Joe's older brother Leo (Thomas Gomez) is one of those small operators, and Joe attempts to persuade him that he can only survive from a position within the corporation. Leo, as a small-time businessman, sees himself as different from Joe and

FIGURE 5.3 "This is Wall Street": *Force of Evil* (Abraham Polonsky, 1948).

Tucker ("I do my business honest and respectable!"), but he is also tied into the same corporatist system. Leo can only delude himself that he is "an honest man" by clinging desperately to the fantasy of a small-time business ethic, even when confronted with irrefutable evidence to the contrary. All business is tainted with criminality, the narrative is saying, and everyone is implicated in the same corrupt system.

Although the narrative deals mainly with Joe and Leo, it is also concerned with the effects of this corporatist system on the "little people" too. Wall Street might provide a legitimate and prestigious front for the numbers organization, but it also operates through a covert network of insalubrious cells located, as Joe describes them, "behind pool rooms, in lofts and cellars, or hidden in slum apartments like Leo's." Leo's "bank" is dingy and shabby with the blinds furtively drawn and the door permanently chained. It is small and overcrowded, like a sweatshop, with an odd assortment of employees, all involved in its nickel-and-dime operations. But there is nothing about them to suggest that they are criminals and they are characterized in both appearance and demeanor by their ordinariness. These miscellaneous characters include the old, the sick, and the phobic together with the young Doris Lowry (Beatrice Pearson), all characterized as innocents, although they are all active participants in the illegal operation of Leo's business.

The premises appear particularly narrow and confined, especially when raided by the police, like a claustrophobic trap in which everyone is caught. This is most evident in the bookkeeper Freddy Bauer (Howland Chamberlain). Freddy is clerical-looking: slight, bespectacled, balding, and dressed in a rumpled suit. With his hunched posture and haunted look, nervously clutching his hat, Freddy is a figure of acute anxiety. During the raid he is like a cornered animal, frantic with fear, desperately trying to escape. As the corporatist world begins to close in on him, he will do anything to quit. For Freddy, escape has become impossible and his desperate desire to "quit" becomes an incantatory refrain of unremitting hopelessness as he begs Leo to be released ("Please, Mr Morse, all I want is to quit, that's all, nothing else. They won't let me quit and I want to quit. I'll die if I don't quit"). This is prophetic both for Freddy and Leo. Fear, sickness, and anxiety are seen throughout the narrative as symptomatic of the intrinsic corruption of the corporate world. When Freddy says, "I'm sick of this place," it is literally true. Leo too is sick and dying ("I'm a man with heart trouble. I die almost every day myself. That's the way I live"). Even Joe, for all the vigor of his self-conviction, experiences fear as an absolute and permanent condition. For Freddy, Leo, and Joe, locked into the corporatist structure, there can be no escape. As Tucker says: "Nobody quits, understand, not even the janitor."

This structure is represented through the narrative's recurrent images of ascent and descent. *Force of Evil* begins with a high perspective of the corporation building in which the trajectory of Joe's success could be measured visually by his office "up in the clouds." Following his rise, the film ends with his fall, represented visually through a sequence of descent. Leaving his office for the last time, Joe is seen from a similarly high perspective as a diminutive and solitary figure, walking along the deserted streets in the gray light of dawn. Later, beneath the George Washington Bridge, he descends yet further to find Leo's body, his voice-over narration one of unremitting hopelessness, expressed in an unusually heightened poetic form:

> I was feeling very bad there when I went down there. It was all going down, and I went down. I was by myself and I went down. I just kept going down and down there, down to the bottom of the world.

We can see in this emphasis on diminution and descent a repudiation of the classic gangster trajectory where even violent death is at least a spectacular finale to what has been an ascendant life. For Leo, in contrast, there is only the degradation and anonymity of an unseen death "down there" in the river.

This power of the organization to diminish and overwhelm is a recurrent trope in postwar noir, and this is especially evident in the crime-investigation film, a significant subset of postwar noir. In what can be seen as a postwar mutation of the classic gangster, Cody Jarrett (James Cagney) in *White Heat* (1949) represents the old gangster, now unable to survive against the modernized technological and bureaucratized forces of law and order which have themselves been transformed into new forms of organizational power against the criminal ones. But Jarrett isn't just an anachronistic reprise of Cagney's 1930s' gangster roles: now, as the postwar gangster, he can become the nonconformist outsider only through a kind of nihilistic madness, through his spectacular self-immolation on top of the exploding gas tanks.[31]

The law, and Jarrett's nemesis, is personified by FBI agent Hank Fallon (Edmond O'Brien), a bland and impersonal character, the kind of interchangeable "stock" figure to be found in many postwar "agency" crime-investigation noirs. These agents were actually named after their agencies, and so "G-Man" is "Government-Man" and stands for any special agent of the government, usually an FBI agent, and "T-Man" for "Treasury-Man." These agents were often characterized as components in the techno-bureaucratic apparatus of their agencies in narratives that emphasized procedural rather than human agency. Such crime-investigation noirs as *T-Men* (1948) and *Trapped* (1949), with their pointed acknowledgments to the Treasury Department, adopt narrative perspectives of the government agencies and often seem like public information films produced on behalf of the agencies themselves. By the late 1940s, the faceless agency man was taking over from the more idiosyncratic private eye, a figure used to operating *outside* official law enforcement agencies.[32]

The forces of law and order close in on Jarrett and ultimately destroy him, but his fall is an ambivalent one. The narrative, as Jonathan Munby has pointed out, is capable of two contradictory readings. On the one hand, it could suggest "a valorization of institutional power and its 'organization man'," while on the other, "the appeal of Cagney's performance rests in part on his rejection of the sinister aspects of a conforming culture embodied in Edmond O'Brien's faceless . . . undercover FBI agent."[33] If we side with Munby's second reading, Jarrett's defiance can be seen as a kind of heroically crazy gesture in the face of an all-encompassing organizational force, which Dana Polan has described as "a cold, calculating, encircling rationalism."[34] Moreover, Jarrett's insane proclamation—"Made it, Ma! Top of the world!"—is strangely reminiscent of the neon sign message in *Scarface*—"THE WORLD IS YOURS"—and hence, the old gangster trajectory remains implicit, in mutated form, through the markedly older Cagney and his new incarnation.[35] In contrast to the organization that has brought Joe and Leo "down to the bottom of the world," Jarrett's psychopathic self-destruction is at least a momentary assertion of ascendancy over the "encircling rationalism" of the organizational power of the law enforcement agencies.

The world of the gangster is predominantly a masculine world with a public setting, but there is another strand of postwar noir located in the domestic world and with feminine concerns. Although the femme fatale is often assumed to be the dominant version of noir femininity, this is far from being the case. One of the most prevalent forms of female representation is that of a wife and mother caught up in a home and family life that goes badly wrong. Many postwar films see a conflation of different genres such as the woman's film and the female gothic drawing on noir tropes such as a condition of being trapped, often where it is home and marriage that are the traps. "Marriage hovers over the woman's film like a black cloud," says Jeanine Basinger, and the notion of home is frequently presented as a space of danger, threat, and alienation.[36]

Film noir and the modern gothic

Cab Driver: "Whose funeral is it, lady?"
Barbara Carlin (June Lockhart): "Mine."

Bury Me Dead (1947)

We saw in Chapter 3 how film noir was conjoined with the female gothic through gaslight melodrama, but the gothic could also lend itself to contemporary adaptations. *My Name Is Julia Ross* (1945) is one of several postwar films noir with a modern gothic setting, directed by Joseph H. Lewis.[37] Julia Ross (Nina

Foch) begins a new job as private secretary to Mrs. Hughes (Dame May Whitty) and wakes up to find herself in a strange house with a new identity as Marion Hughes, her nightgown bearing the monogram of her new name, "M.H." She is horrified to discover a wedding ring on her finger and that she is, apparently, married to Ralph Hughes (George Macready), the psychopathic son of Mrs. Hughes. Although the narrative uses several traditional gothic tropes (old cliff-top house, secret passage, black cat), it is rooted in contemporary life. We first see Julia in London, scanning the classified ads in desperate need of a job and owing back rent on the shabby rooming house where she lives. Securing a job through a bogus agency, she becomes the victim of an elaborate conspiracy in which her "husband" and his mother as well as everyone else she encounters are all playing roles to convince her that she is mentally ill. This is because they plan to fake her suicide in order to cover up Ralph's earlier murder of the real Marion Hughes.

As Dana Polan has suggested of gothic films of the 1940s, these are not so much drawn from the literary gothic domain of such fiction as *The Castle of Otranto* (1764) or *The Monk* (1796), in which evil emanating from the devil emerges in "devilish places," but rather in the familiar spaces of everyday life. And so, says Polan, "the menace of the modern gothic is the menace of an all-too-natural world."[38] Julia wakes up to find herself locked in a gothic oak-paneled chamber, but we later see its windows equipped with modern steel bars, making her room resemble a prison cell in a house resembling a high-security mental hospital. To the extent that the film works as a kind of gothic nightmare, it is marriage that represents the threat to who she is. All traces of her previous identity are destroyed by her sinister "mother-in-law" in preparation for her sacrificial marriage to the sinister Ralph.

The tropes of a modern gothic and its concerns with marriage can be found in several films noir of the period. Even a period gothic like Siodmak's *The Spiral Staircase* (1946), set in 1906, has a modern touch, beginning with a murder committed in a room above the screening of a moving picture show. The film retains many of the traditional features of the earlier female gothic narratives like *Rebecca* (1940) and *Gaslight* (1944) with its "haunted" house, thunderstorms, shadowy visual style, and imperiled female protagonist. Helen McCord (Dorothy McGuire) is a mute maidservant who, because of her disability, is vulnerable to a murderer whose victims all have physical afflictions of one kind or another (see Figure 5.4). (This is an early example of the subcategory of the serial killer crime film with links to both noir and the gothic.) Helen is seen in a fantasy sequence where she bears witness to a grim parody of a wedding ceremony, her own. The wedding takes place at the house that is spectacularly decked out with flowers but darkly lit in somber tones, making it look more like a funeral than a wedding. When called upon to say, "I do," she cannot speak, thereby suffering an expressionist nightmare in

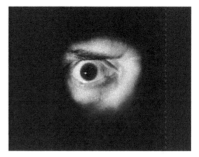

FIGURE 5.4 Period gothic and film noir: maidservant Helen McCord (Dorothy McGuire) under the watchful eye of Professor Warren (George Brent) in *The Spiral Staircase* (Robert Siodmak, 1946).

which she becomes the subject of silent judgment by the congregation, before whom she shows herself incapable of fulfilling her obligation to get married.

The serial killer is revealed to be Professor Warren (George Brent), and there is a sense in which he is the kind of "dastardly" villain characteristic of traditional gothic tales (see Figure 5.4). But there is another kind of narrative inflection here that goes beyond the old-fashioned, diabolical, gothic evildoer or the noir trope of the murderous psychopath. "What a pity my father didn't live to see me become strong," Warren tells Helen, "to see me dispose of the weak and imperfects of the world whom he detested." The utterance seems less typical of the wicked villain of the old gothic world or the abnormal psychology of the serial killer and more resonant with Nazi ideology and the Final Solution, increasing evidence of which was screened on newsreel reports at this time.[39]

There are similar gothic elements in Max Ophuls's *Caught* (1949), where the fantasy of marriage to a wealthy husband comes horrifically true for Leonora Eames (Barbara Bel Geddes). Her husband, Smith Ohlrig (Robert Ryan), sees her literally "caught" in a gothic castle and repeatedly shown in a mise-en-scène which emphasizes spatial entrapment. Ohlrig is an autocratic industrialist who lords it over his minions and terrorizes his wife in a vast gloomy castle, its spaces reminiscent of the great hall in Charles Foster Kane's Xanadu. Ohlrig, like Kane, is a tyrant who personifies absolute power, summoning her at will at any time of night, even during her pregnancy, and threatening her with taking custody of the child solely as a way of asserting his power over her. "When you have money," he tells her, "you can always get enough people to swear to anything you want." From the outset, Leonora has aspired to a lifestyle fantasized from the pages of upmarket fashion magazines. Once achieved, however, marriage, home, and family turn into a nightmare for her. Extricating herself from Ohlrig's tyrannical regime comes at the price of a miscarriage before she can abandon him and begin a new life with more modest aspirations with Doctor Larry Quinada (James Mason), a pediatrician working with poor patients in an East Side medical practice.

By the late 1940s, the gothic cycle was almost over, although the "modern gothic" home continued to feature in a number of noir narratives. Take, for example, Ophuls's last American film, *The Reckless Moment* (1949). Here we see Lucia Harper (Joan Bennett) continuously trying to negotiate with the incursion of a criminal into her home, while simultaneously managing the domestic routines of family life and, most importantly, keeping up appearances. In some ways the narrative is reminiscent of the warfront melodrama with Lucia's permanently absent husband Tom away in Europe, existing only as the recipient of Lucia's letters or a disembodied voice on the telephone. (Like Lucia, we never see him.)

Lucia intercedes in the relationship her daughter Bea (Geraldine Brooks) is having with reprobate Ted Darby (Shepperd Strudwick), warning him off seeing Bea again. Bea and Darby meet secretly at the boathouse at the family home when Darby is accidentally killed. Finding his body the next morning and fearing that her daughter will be implicated in a scandal, Lucia disposes of it in the bay. Afterwards, a man called Donnelly (James Mason) calls at the house, intending to blackmail Lucia with incriminating letters from Bea to Darby in his possession. A relationship between Lucia and her blackmailer begins to develop, a curious kind of counter-marriage. We see him helping with her grocery order, making small decisions about what he imagines the household needs, worrying about her smoking too much, and slipping a gift for her into the bag of groceries. When she asks him for change for the phone and he gives it to her, they have the look of a couple quite familiar with each other and, by this stage, they are working together almost as partners. Although at first sight Donnelly is a menacing figure and a threatening intrusion into the family home, he later becomes an intensely sympathetic character. Lucia finds that she and Donnelly have come to share an empathy and intimacy of a kind that she does not have with her husband and she grieves terribly at his death (see Figure 5.5). Donnelly's Irish characterization here is reminiscent of Mason's role as another romantic criminal, the IRA man Johnny McQueen in Carol Reed's British film *Odd Man Out* (1947) two years previously, a film often seen to have thematic and stylistic affinities with noir.[40]

The depiction of Lucia's home and married life is interesting in several ways. The family home is pleasant and spacious, a well-appointed oceanfront house situated in what a voice-over describes as the "charming community" of Balboa in California. But as we saw in Ophuls's representation of the Ohlrig house in *Caught*, the mise-en-scènes in the Harper home depict Lucia in spaces designed to convey a sense of claustrophobic entrapment. She seems restrained and repressed within the family home. In her appearance she always looks smartly dressed and repeatedly admonishes her son for his

FIGURE 5.5 Modern gothic: Lucia Harper (Joan Bennett) mourns the death of Martin Donnelly (James Mason) in *The Reckless Moment* (Max Ophuls, 1949).

casual appearance. With an exaggerated sense of propriety and a compulsion to maintain a domestic façade, there is an altogether incongruous aspect to her buttoned-up look, especially in the scenes on the beach and in the boat, lugging a heavy corpse. In the concluding scene, we see her called to the phone to speak to her husband immediately after we have seen her lying on her bed, distraught after Donnelly's death. But then, having composed herself and come downstairs, we hear her reassuring Christmas platitudes to her husband while we see her positioned behind the banister, its vertical columns having the appearance of prison bars. Well might she lament the death of Donnelly because the prospect of her future married life in this depiction of the postwar American home is made to appear virtually like a cage. In some ways she is as trapped and terrorized as Helen in the more traditional female gothic of *The Spiral Staircase*.

If Lucia's home seems comfortable and secure, it is actually anything but that—the intrusion of blackmailers into the family home is not the only cause of the domestic disruption. It's clear that the Harper family are living beyond their means. Even worse, though, is when Lucia tries to raise the money herself to pay off Donnelly, only to discover that, as a wife, she isn't allowed to borrow on her own account. As the bank won't lend her the money and she can do nothing without her husband's signature, she is obliged to deal with insalubrious moneylenders and pawnbrokers. So unaccustomed is she to dealing with financial matters that she stumbles over the wording of her request when dealing with a loan shark, unsure whether to "make" or "get" a loan. She does all this in order to protect her family, but Donnelly recognizes that she is as trapped in her world as he is in his, a dead-end world of petty crime. He is the only one who understands her. He asks her, "Do you never get away from your family?" "No," she answers. "You don't know how a family can surround you at times," she tells him. We can be sure that she has never

FIGURE 5.6 Barbara Stanwyck as bedridden invalid Leona Stevenson in *Sorry, Wrong Number* (Anatole Litvak, 1948).

said that to anyone else before. The only other figure with whom Lucia shares a real affinity is the black housekeeper Sybil (Frances Williams), and there is an implication that Sybil, like Donnelly, understands her predicament when others, including her family, do not.

Another kind of updated gothic treatment of domestic space can be seen in Anatole Litvak's *Sorry, Wrong Number* (1948). Leona Stevenson (Barbara Stanwyck), invalid daughter of pharmaceutical magnate James Cotterell (Ed Begley), overhears on a crossed telephone line two men planning to murder a woman that night (see Figure 5.6). Unknown to her then, she is the intended victim of the murder that has been planned by her husband Henry (Burt Lancaster). The film's flashback structure provides an account of the events leading inexorably to the murder that she is powerless to prevent. Like Ophuls, Litvak uses a highly mobile camera, with traveling shots around Leonora's bedroom. The traveling camera has a mobility that the bedridden Leonora does not and serves to emphasize her stricken condition which sees her literally embedded in the domestic space of her bedroom. She might live in a luxurious apartment, but this does not make it any less of a prison for her. Indeed, as the wealthy heiress to her father's business empire, the narrative shows her as spoiled and neurotic, but with nothing physically wrong with her. As in Ohlrig's house in *Caught*, there is a kind of pathology inherent in the homes of the rich.

There is another traveling shot deployed as the prelude to Leonora's murder with the camera moving around the bedroom and out of the window to the street below, glimpsing the shadow of the man who will kill her. Where a husband like, say, Johnny Aysgarth (Cary Grant) in *Suspicion* is an ambivalent figure throughout the narrative but ultimately "proved" to be innocent, there is no such ambivalence in *Sorry, Wrong Number*. Leonora's husband has arranged her murder, admitting as much to her in the last call she receives before her death.[41]

Film noir and domestic melodrama

Now, Sam. Do it now. Set me free, set both of us free. He fell down the stairs and fractured his skull, that's how he died. Everybody knows what a heavy drinker he was. Oh, Sam, it can be so easy.

MARTHA IVERS (Barbara Stanwyck)
to Sam Masterson (Van Heflin) In *The Strange Love of Martha Ivers* (1946)

A couple of hours ago down at the Sunset Beach Hotel a room registered to a Mr Sam Grover caught on fire and a body went hurtling all in flames out the window. After that all they could've possibly found was a body so badly burned and smashed that they'd never be able to tell who it was, except that it had on Sam's watch and ring.

EDNA GROVER (June Vincent) in *Shed No Tears* (1948)

When Martha Ivers (Barbara Stanwyck) urges Sam Masterson (Van Heflin) to kill her alcoholic husband Walter O'Neil (Kirk Douglas) in *The Strange Love of Martha Ivers* (1946), it is difficult not to recall Stanwyck's previous incarnation as the murderous wife, Phyllis Dietrichson, in *Double Indemnity* two years previously. We saw in Chapter 3 how Stanwyck's Dietrichson came to be seen as the quintessential femme fatale together with other examples such as Cora Smith in *The Postman Always Rings Twice* and Kathie Moffatt (Jane Greer) in *Out of the Past*. As I have suggested, one of the problems with the general attribution of "femme fatale" has been to create an assumption that the characterization is an intrinsic element in film noir. *Double Indemnity* is widely seen to have created the template for the characterization, but there are actually very few films in which this "paradigmatic" figure occurs. This has resulted in a disproportionate emphasis on a figure presumed to predominate in postwar noir, but which in fact does not. This is not to suggest that there are no narrative representations of women who commit domestic murders, but rather that there is a wide range of domestic crime committed by female characters who do not belong in noir's preordained category of the femme fatale.

Take for example Irene Williams (Helen Walker) in *Impact* (1947). Already married, Irene plots with her lover Jim Torrence (Tony Barrett) to murder her husband Walt Williams (Brian Donleavy), a wealthy industrialist. Unlike the Dietrichsons in *Double Indemnity* or the Smiths in *The Postman Always Rings Twice*, Walt is happily married, or so he believes. He is a loving husband, devoted to his wife, showering her with flowers, gifts, and endearments. She is devoted to a high-living lifestyle and seen predominantly in a luxurious apartment with a servant waiting on her. She is called a femme fatale, but it's not clear why.[42] Her circumstances are completely different from those of Phyllis Dietrichson and Cora Smith.

If the femme fatale is a relatively rare figure in postwar noir, at least as the figure identified by noir critics, she does occasionally occur, more usually in some of the Poverty Row noirs. In *Blonde Ice* (1948), for example, Claire Cummings (Leslie Brooks) uses "serial" marriage and murder purely as the most expedient way of obtaining the wealth, status, and power she wants, almost securing the ultimate prize of a congressman and a fine address in Washington. "You're not a normal woman," Les Burns (Robert Paige) tells her. "You're cold, like ice. Yeah, like ice. Blonde ice." Another low-budget example can be found in *Shed No Tears* (1948) which, like *Double Indemnity*, involves a life insurance scam. Edna Grover (June Vincent) and her husband Sam (Wallace Ford) fake his death in a hotel fire to claim his life insurance. But Edna plans to double-cross Sam and take off with the money and her lover Ray Belden (Robert Scott). Edna's low-life world is macabre and grotesque, matched by the low-budget production values. "Whose body was it?" asks Belden. "Just a corpse Sam got from an undertaker in some sort of deal," she nonchalantly replies.

There is a comparable characterization in Jenny Hager (Hedy Lamarr) in Edgar Ulmer's period melodrama *The Strange Woman* (1946).[43] Like Claire Cummings, Hager is a "wanton" who exploits her sexual allure to get what she wants and to climb the social ladder. "This isn't the life I was born for," she tells her impecunious alcoholic father. "Men like me, and it's the men who have the money in this world." Here, though, there is also an implication of childhood abuse and a sadomasochistic dimension to her behavior. After a whipping from her father, she flees to the house of Ephraim Poster (Louis Hayward). Realizing that he is watching her as the housekeeper dresses her wounds, she turns coquettishly toward him, exposing her bare shoulder, aware of the sexual attraction she has for him. Nevertheless, the hardship and abuse of Jenny's early life link the melodramatic aspects of her story to the social problem film in ways that complicate its classification as film noir.

Another curious entry in the noir catalog is *Guest in the House* (1946), especially in the attribution of "femme fatale" to Evelyn Heath (Anne Baxter).[44] The film makes for an unusual film noir in that there is no crime as such (confounding even the most basic assumption about film noir, that it necessarily involves crime). Evelyn arrives at the family home of her fiancé to convalesce after a mental illness. She is welcomed into the house—an unusual depiction of a communal and rather bohemian household—although she is a manipulative and disruptive presence, obsessively determined to destroy its domestic harmony. But there is little in her appearance or behavior to suggest a femme fatale. One of the main problems arising from all these films is that they demonstrate such a wide range of thematic, stylistic, and generic concerns that make it difficult for them to coexist meaningfully under the rubric of film noir.

One of the odder entries in noir catalogs is John Stahl's *Leave Her to Heaven* (1946) which, in a category generally defined by its black-and-white cinematography, is in color and Technicolor at that. A Technicolor noir seems like a contradiction in terms: it's a process that makes for a saturated color effect, producing a heightened sense of artificiality. This quality, as Borde and Chaumeton acknowledge in their account of the film, saw its use hitherto as the preserve of adventure films and musicals.[45] This is, then, a very different kind of film "noir." A melodrama about Ellen Berent (Gene Tierney) and her marriage to Richard Harland (Cornel Wilde), the pair meet on a train where we see the first of a series of scenes that exploit Tierney's appearance to convey a sense of madness (see Figure 5.7). In the first, we see her glacial beauty, her flawless facial features an inscrutable mask (recalling those of Alan Ladd and Veronica Lake). Harland is immediately smitten with her although discomfited by her extraordinary stare, held by her intense gaze in a remarkable shot held for almost a minute. In the second, we see her early the next morning on horseback, rapt, scattering the ashes of her father. The third provides, paradoxically, one of the most iconic images of 1940s' noir. Ellen is sitting in a boat on a lake where Richard's paraplegic younger brother Danny (Darryl Hickman) is swimming. Danny gets into difficulties in the water and drowns while Ellen, seen in close-up in white robe and dark glasses, looks on with calculating appraisal. Fearful that she would have to look after Danny, she lets him die.[46] In the fourth scene, the pregnant Ellen throws herself down stairs to induce a miscarriage. Finally, she plans her own death, having arranged for several pieces of incriminating evidence to implicate Richard and her hated sister Ruth (Jeanne Crain) in her murder as a weapon to destroy them.

FIGURE 5.7 Technicolor Noir: Gene Tierney in *Leave Her to Heaven* (John Stahl, 1946).

A different kind of psychotic figure to those usually depicted in 1940s' noir, Ellen's murderous nature is driven by an obsessive love transferred from her father to her husband. "There's nothing wrong with Ellen," says her mother Margaret (Mary Philips). "It's just that she loves too much." Borde and Chaumeton admired the "audacious" film, even as its Technicolor palette and country locations might seem to take it outside their own definition of noir. But with scenes in "the color of dried blood," and where the landscape is "a state of soul," Ellen's madness is inscribed in the wilderness itself.[47] Even by the "anti-domestic" standards of postwar noir, there is no character who so thoroughly repudiates the notion of a nurturing female, nor who visits such destructive force on home and married life as Ellen does.

Notes

1 Raymond Borde and Étienne Chaumeton, *A Panorama of American Film Noir, 1941-1953*, trans. Paul Hammond (San Francisco: City Lights, 2002), 53.

2 Paul Schrader, "Notes on *Film Noir*," *Film Comment* (Spring 1972) in Silver and Ursini, *Film Noir Reader*, 55.

3 James Naremore, *More than Night: Film Noir in its Contexts* (Berkeley: University of California Press, 1998), 22.

4 Robert Porfirio, "No Way Out: Existential Motifs in the *Film Noir*," *Sight and Sound* (Autumn 1976), repr. in Silver and Ursini, eds., *Film Noir Reader* (New York: Limelight, 1996), 77–93.

5 Ibid., 80.

6 Ibid., 81.

7 Ibid., 83–85.

8 Ibid., 84.

9 Ibid.

10 Ibid., 85.

11 Ibid.

12 Foster Hirsch, *Film Noir: The Dark Side of the Screen* (New York: Da Capo, 1981), 146.

13 Ibid., 147.

14 Borde and Chaumeton, *Panorama of American Film Noir*, 37.

15 Stephen Faison, *Existentialism, Film Noir, and Hard-Boiled Fiction* (Amherst, NY: Cambria Press, 2008), 2.

16 See David Madden, *Cain's Craft* (Metuchen, NJ: Scarecrow, 1985), 79.

17 Dashiell Hammet, *The Maltese Falcon* (1930; New York: Vintage Crime/Black Lizard, 1992), 62.

18 Ibid., 63.

19 Ibid., 64.

20 Quoted in an interview with Adrian Wootton at the National Film Theater, London (July, 2002). DVD Extra on *Kiss of Death* (BFI, 2007).

21 Schatz, *Boom and Bust*, 41, 43.

22 Todd McCarthy and Charles Flynn, "The Economic Imperative: Why Was the B Movie Necessary?" in Todd McCarthy and Charles Flynn, eds., *Kings of the Bs: Working Within the Hollywood System: An Anthology of Film History and Criticism* (New York: Dutton, 1975), 18–19.

23 Arthur Lyons, *Death on the Cheap: The Lost B Movies of Film Noir!* (New York: Da Capo, 2000), 29.

24 Myron Meisel, "Edgar G. Ulmer: The Primacy of the Visual," in McCarthy and Flynn, eds., *Kings of the Bs*, 148.

25 Peter Bogdanovich, "Edgar G. Ulmer," in McCarthy and Flynn, eds., *Kings of the Bs*, 387.

26 Andrew Britton, "Detour," in Cameron, ed., *Movie Book of Film Noir*, 174.

27 McCarthy and Flynn, "Economic Imperative," 22–23.

28 John Belton, "Film Noir's Knights of the Road," *Bright Lights Film Journal* 12 (Spring 1994): 5–15.

29 Meisel, "Edgar G. Ulmer," 149.

30 The classic gangster was showcased through flamboyant dress. In *Public Enemy* (1931), for example, the heist scene cuts immediately to the tailor's shop ("and remember, *six* buttons") as Tom Powers (James Cagney) aspires to the status of Nails Nathan (Leslie Fenton), appearing in a succession of fastidious "costumes." Similarly, in *Little Caesar* (1931), Joe Massara (Douglas Fairbanks, Jr.) anticipates the sartorial potential of city life ("Gee, the clothes I could wear!"); and when Rico (Edward G. Robinson) sees Diamond Pete Montana (Ralph Ince), he cannot help but glance at his ostentatiously jeweled tie-pin and ring, pointedly shown in close-up. In *Scarface* (1932), Tony Camonte (Paul Muni) attempts to impress Poppy (Karen Morley) with an exhibition of his shirts. Conversely, the postwar gangster wore inconspicuous business suits so as *not* to draw to attention to himself, although flashes of the old bravado could still occasionally be seen. "Buy yourself a closet full of clothes," says Alec Stiles (Richard Widmark) to Eugene Cordell (Mark Stevens) in *The Street with No Name* (1948), proffering a wad of cash. "I like my boys to look sharp."

31 Jarrett's characterization retains the old Cagney gangster persona, drawn cumulatively from the succession of his 1930s' roles. His last major gangster role had been a decade earlier, as Eddie Bartlett in *The Roaring Twenties* (1939), a film that can be seen as the last in a cycle of sympathetic portrayals of gangster figures. Dying in the arms of Panama Smith (Gladys George) on the steps of a church—"He used to be a big-shot," she tells a police officer at the scene—the film seems like a requiem for the old gangster and its final image resembles nothing less than a *pietà*.

32 It would be impossible to imagine Sam Spade or Philip Marlowe as agency men, especially as played by Humphrey Bogart. Although previously a detective himself, the private eye was too much of an outsider, often operating at the margins of the law. He was usually contemptuous of its "flatfoot" procedures and "by-the-book" bureaucracy.

33 Jonathan Munby, *Public Enemies, Public Heroes: Screening the Gangster from Little Caesar to Touch of Evil* (Chicago: Chicago University Press, 1999), 118–19.

34 Dana Polan, *Power and Paranoia: History, Narrative, and the American Cinema, 1940-1950* (New York: Columbia University Press, 1986), 165.

35 Another small instance of Von Sternberg's influence on the gangster film can be seen in *Underworld*'s neon sign "THE CITY IS YOURS" five years before *Scarface*.

36 Jeanine Basinger *A Woman's View: How Hollywood Spoke To Women, 1930-1960* (London: Chatto & Windus, 1994), 319.

37 This is the first of a series of key films noir by Lewis who went on to make *So Dark the Night* (1946), *The Undercover Man* (1949), *Gun Crazy* (1949), and *The Big Combo* (1955).

38 Polan, *Power and Paranoia*, 281.

39 Other 1940s' gothics deal with female trauma explicitly in wartime settings. See for instance *Dark Waters* (1944) and *Shock* (1946).

40 The film makes for an interesting combination of expressionistic noir stylistics and prefigures Reed's *The Third Man* (1949) two years later. Virtually the entire narrative is built on McQueen's protracted death and his doomed, tragic antihero owes a great deal to the French poetic realism of the 1930s.

41 Hitchcock uses a similar idea of a murder being heard on the telephone in *Dial M For Murder* (1954).

42 See for example the entry on the film in Alain Silver, Elizabeth Ward, James Ursini, and Robert Porfirio, eds., *Film Noir: The Encyclopedia* (New York: Overlook Duckworth, 2010), 149.

43 Critics often focus on Ulmer's *Detour* at the expense of his other noir films such as *Strange Illusion* (1945), a fascinating treatment of "gothic-psychiatric" noir.

44 See for example the account of the film in Silver and Ward, *Film Noir: The Encyclopedia*, 120–21.

45 Borde and Chaumeton, *Panorama of American Film Noir*, 47.

46 Ellen resembles Cora in *The Postman Always Rings Twice*, whose husband planned to take her to Canada to care for his paralyzed sister. She describes her fear of being trapped in "some miserable little dump of a town where I'll rot the rest of my life away waiting on him and his half-dead sister!"

47 Borde and Chaumeton, *Panorama of American Film Noir*, 47–48. *Leave Her to Heaven* can be seen as a precursor of Douglas Sirk's melodramas of the ensuing decade, characterized by the saturated color schemes of their "Sirkian" *mise-en-scènes*. The iconic image of Ellen on the lake is also an instance of the kind of surreal incongruity used by Hitchcock, as in the scene of an elegantly fur-coated Melanie Daniels (Tippi Hedren) in a rowing boat on Bodega Bay in *The Birds* (1963).

6

The late period, 1950–58

Hollywood Fails to Clean Out Reds, Probers Charge: Communist Infiltration in Filmland Unabated, Says House Committee

HEADLINE IN LOS ANGELES TIMES (FEBRUARY 17, 1952)[1]

We have seen in preceding accounts of the earlier historical periods how film noir has been stretched in various ways by critics to accommodate a diverse range of titles. If we take more or less at random a handful of the canonical noir titles of this late period across the 1950s, it reveals an even more disparate group, reminding us again of that fantastical animal taxonomy by Borges that we have discussed in Chapter 1. The titles included under the rubric of film noir during this period became increasingly diverse in terms of both visual style and narrative themes. Films such as *Outrage* (1950), *The Big Heat* (1953), *The Big Combo* (1955), *Kiss Me Deadly* (1955), and *Touch of Evil* (1958) were as much different as they were alike. In this chapter, I consider the relation between film noir in the 1950s and other generic categories such as the social problem film and the caper film. The chapter considers the context of the Cold War and its bearing on the different kinds of political stance adopted in Cold War noir. Also, along with the end of the classical period at the end of the decade, I discuss the "post-classical" development of what critics would call "neo-noir."

In their *Panorama*, Borde and Chaumeton described the period, 1951–53 as "the demise of a series," characterized by different production trends that they saw as unconducive to noir filmmaking. "Hollywood," they say, "is on the lookout for new formulas in which 'escapism' is the order of the day."[2] Although they don't say so, it was during this period of demise that some of the directors most strongly identified with noir production in its earlier and more critically validated period abandoned it for other kinds of filmmaking. Some abandoned Hollywood altogether for the "exoticism" of location shooting in European cities, often renting studios there as well. John Huston made *Moulin Rouge* (1953) and *Beat the Devil* (1954), and William Wyler *Roman Holiday* (1953) in Europe. Technological developments in Technicolor encouraged a turn toward spectaculars such as Robert Siodmak's *The Crimson Pirate* (1952) and Edward Dmytryk's *Mutiny* (1952).[3] Elsewhere, Borde and Chaumeton saw a conservative shift away from noir toward "more conformist channels" such as the "patriotic productions" of Sam Fuller's *The Steel Helmet* (1951) and Mark Robson's *I Want You* (1951). They also noted how the spy thriller had been reconfigured. "All that was needed in order to do this," they say, "was replace the word 'Nazi' with the word 'Russian'."[4] With few exceptions they remained unimpressed with "the bland heritage of the noir series," although did note its positive influence on "the social film."[5]

Film noir and the "social film"

One "social film" not mentioned by Borde and Chaumeton is Ida Lupino's *Outrage*, although it is an example of the kind of social problem film, shot with noir stylistics, that would fit their bill. Made by her own production company, The Filmakers [*sic*], *Outrage* is one of the earliest narrative treatments of rape— hitherto a taboo subject for the Production Code Administration—to appear in a mainstream film.[6] The film shows Ann Walton (Mala Power) leaving her office after working late, aware that she is being followed by a man. Frightened and desperate, she flees into a trucking depot, the shadowed figure of the man trailing her. The scene is stark and spare, with low-key lighting, shot with a combination of tilted camera angles and high-angled crane shots looking down on her, rendering her exposed in the open spaces of the parking lot. One high shot of Ann shows her under a street lamp throwing long shadows, highlighting her vulnerability and uncertainty about which way to run. Tracking shots move along with her as she tries to evade the man among the trucks, the face of her attacker blurring in oblivion as she loses consciousness. In some ways, the scene is reminiscent of some of the tropes of the female gothic that we have considered in Chapter 3, its imperiled female menaced by a male assailant. After the rape, the narrative shifts to concerns with how Ann deals with the trauma of violent sexual assault while living in a conspicuously masculine world. The narrative dramatizes the aftermath of her trauma in a way that encourages the audience to empathize with her ordeal. This is one of several films in which Lupino can be seen to combine a "social problem" film subject with noir stylistics.

Lupino is an important if marginalized figure in film noir.[7] She appeared in *They Drive by Night* (1940) and *High Sierra* (1941) with Humphrey Bogart at Warner Brothers and subsequently in a string of other noir titles: *Road House*

(1948), *Woman in Hiding* (1949), *On Dangerous Ground* (1952), *Beware, My Lovely* (1952), *Private Hell 36* (1954), *The Big Knife* (1955), *Strange Intruder* (1956), and Fritz Lang's *While the City Sleeps* (1956). Lupino is also important because of her independent role as both director and producer. In an industry dominated by men, the degree of control she had over her own filmmaking was unprecedented, especially through her own production companies between 1949 and 1953. The films she made there had unconventional and controversial "social" subjects, such as teenage pregnancy in *Not Wanted* (1949)[8] and bigamy in *The Bigamist* (1953). *Not Wanted* is a particularly interesting example of Lupino's social problem noir melodrama with an empathetic narrative treatment of its protagonist: a low-budget film with a flashback structure, semidocumentary style, location shooting, and expressionistic scenes. The requisite noir crime here is the "kidnapping" of a baby by a woman suffering from postnatal depression, whom we see as the victim of a harsh and unsympathetic social system. Lupino also made *The Hitch-Hiker* (1953), a film that deals with the noir subject of random fate intervening into ordinary life when two men on a fishing trip pick up a hitchhiker who turns out to be a psychotic killer.[9]

Mystery Street (1950) provides another example of female empathy, albeit an unusual one. The film is a late contribution from MGM to the semidocumentary noir style with much of the film shot on location in Boston, at Harvard University, and Cape Cod. Through John Alton's cinematography, there is a split between the typical flat gray lighting of the documentary style and the rich low-key lighting of noir (see Figure 6.1). The film is significant in several ways to the development of late noir, not least for breaking new ground in its treatment of forensic pathology. Although the film draws on the familiar tropes of what we might call "boarding-house gothic"—note the shabby cluttered room of the landlady Mrs. Smerrling (Elsa Lanchester)—it also anticipates the later narrative treatment of forensic investigation and analysis in, say, a television series such as *CSI: Crime Scene Investigation* (CBS, 2000–15).

Sometime after "B-girl" Vivian Heldon (Jan Sterling) has gone missing, skeletal remains are discovered on the beach at Cape Cod. An investigation ensues, headed by Lieutenant Peter Moralas (Ricardo Montalban) who enlists the help of Dr. McAdoo (Bruce Bennett) at Harvard's Department of Legal Medicine, and there is considerable narrative emphasis on forensic pathology. This emphasis differs from more typical "agency" procedurals where forensics are used for the identification and apprehension of the criminal. Here, they are used to identify the remains of an unknown person with little to go on but some bone fragments and hair follicles. There is also an element of gothic horror in the attempts by McAdoo and Moralas to match the recovered skull with the photographs of missing women. They use a slide projector to superimpose photographs of the women onto that of the skull in an almost

FIGURE 6.1 Cinematographer John Alton's signature noir style: left, Vivian Heldon (Jan Sterling) confronts her lover and murderer, and right, Mrs. Smerrling (Elsa Lanchester) in "boarding-house gothic" surroundings in *Mystery Street* (John Sturges, 1950).

metaphysical series of what we might call "techno-gothic" representations (see Figure 6.2). All this is quite extraordinary for a film from 1950, especially with its bizarre and disquieting imagery.

The film is also interesting for its depiction of material that would have been quite impossible under former PCA strictures. For example, we see explicit crime-scene photographs in McAdoo's office, unsparing in their detail, and the narrative draws attention to the discovery of the remains of a fetus, showing that Vivian was pregnant at the time of her death. The narrative also deals with the miscarriage of Grace Shanway (Sally Forrest) when she is questioned by Moralas about her husband's involvement with Vivian on the night of her death. Moreover, there is an unequivocal depiction of Vivian as a "working" girl. Surrounded by the cheap erotica of the Grass Skirt Café and her practiced exploitation of many a drunken "john," her characterization is unequivocally that of a prostitute.

In a particularly macabre scene with necrophiliac accents, Vivian's murderer James Harkley (Edmon Ryan) is seen removing her body from the car when he is caught in the headlights of an approaching vehicle. Standing, he props up her body against the car, holding her as if in a lovers' embrace, her arm arranged around him before it drops down lifelessly. Hoisting the body over his shoulder, her head inadvertently bumps against the car door, the kind of cruel detail we occasionally see in film noir, providing casual emphasis on the desecrated body, the easy disposal of human life, and the sheer worthlessness of her corpse.

We can also see in *Mystery Street*, another example of the kind of "social film" subject identified by Borde and Chaumeton. Embedded within its noir stylistics is the melodrama of a murdered girl, but, as in *Outrage*, it is also a story about a victim of abuse with links to the social problem film. As we have seen, one of the recurrent themes in film noir is a critical treatment of those with wealth and power, often shown as vicious and corrupt. In *Mystery Street*

FIGURE 6.2 The "techno-gothic" forensic pathology in *Mystery Street* (John Sturges, 1950).

we know that at least two of the characters who have had sex with Vivian, including her murderer, are outwardly respectable and affluent men. We learn that Harkley is a family man, with three daughters, and we also see another of Vivian's clients, a mortician (Willard Waterman). Vivian's venal landlady, Mrs. Smerrling, is a curious parodic inversion of the femme fatale with her ridiculous fox stole and black gloves, feigning bereavement and poverty while trying to capitalize on her tenant's death by blackmailing Harkley. Like almost everyone else drawn into the investigation, she is motivated by greed and self-interest, willing to exploit even the grimmest situation for her own gain. Vivian's situation—where she lives, how she works, who she sees—exposes a social world that is rotten to the core.

Caper-movie noir

One significant development in the late noir period is the emergence of the caper film. This is a subcategory of the crime film often included in noir classifications which features an increased focus on the crime itself, usually a robbery or heist. It shows in detail the planning, execution, and aftermath of the crime with a narrative emphasis on the criminals rather than on the police or other agencies in pursuit of them. John Huston's *The Asphalt Jungle* (1950) is the first fully-fledged example of "caper-movie" noir that established several of its narrative conventions. Geoff Mayer's description of the film also delineates the category itself. It has a three-part narrative structure that shows "the recruitment of the criminals, each with specialist abilities; the rehearsal and execution of the robbery; and the bitter aftermath where . . . the criminals would either die or be captured by the police."[10] The term dates from around the late 1960s when it was retrospectively applied to films of the preceding decade such as *Armored Car Robbery* (1950), *5 Against the House*

(1955), *The Killing* (1956), *The Big Caper* (1957), and *Plunder Road* (1957).[11] By this time the caper film had become more comedic in tone and more readily associated with the comedy thriller or romantic comedy, often with tongue-in-cheek performances and fantastic plots involving the planning of absurdly unachievable robberies.[12] But if "caper" connotes the playfulness of the category as it developed during the 1960s, *The Asphalt Jungle* signaled the arrival of a new subgenre shaped to darker ends. The film is significant in several ways as a later film noir. It precipitated a new noir subgenre at the same time that it represented a swansong for Huston as a noir director, following such key films as *The Maltese Falcon* (1941) and *Key Largo* (1948). He went on to make adaptations of literary classics such as *The Red Badge of Courage* (1951) and *Moby Dick* (1956).

In *The Asphalt Jungle*, criminal mastermind Doc Riedenschneider (Sam Jaffe), newly released from prison, recruits a gang of local small-time criminals for an intricately planned jewel robbery and obtains financial backing from crooked lawyer Alonzo D. Emmerich (Louis Calhern). Due to "blind accidents" on the day and a treacherous double-cross by Emmerich, the meticulously executed robbery goes catastrophically wrong. Doc summarizes the fateful events:

> Put in hours and hours of planning. Figure everything down to the last detail. Then what? Burglar alarms start going off all over the place for no sensible reason. A gun fires of its own accord and a man is shot. And a broken-down old cop, no good for anything but chasing kids, has to trip over us. Blind accident. What can you do against blind accidents?

As we have seen in Chapter 4, film noir could demonstrate the work of criminals, enabling audiences to empathize with them, especially during the aftermath of the crime when everything is going wrong. Although criminal empathy isn't necessarily a prerequisite of the caper movie in the 1950s, it's certainly evident in *The Asphalt Jungle*.[13] Contemporary reviewers took note. Richard Griffith in the *LA Times*, for example, noted the "living, hopeful people" in the gang. "Their defeat and death is ours as well," he says.[14] Exploiting the familiar police procedural device of using an official spokesman to articulate the viewpoint of the police could make *The Asphalt Jungle* seem like another example of the "agency" film. Police Commissioner Hardy (John McIntire) makes a po-faced speech to the press in which he denounces the criminals as "predatory beasts" in a "jungle" while pointedly switching on, one by one, a bank of police radios behind him to dramatize the sheer volume of ongoing crime in the city. But his rhetoric is at odds with what he describes—a disparity that we can readily see in his description of Dix Handley (Sterling Hayden) as "a hardened killer, a hooligan, a man without human feeling or

FIGURE 6.3 Death in a Kentucky paddock: Dix Handley (Sterling Hayden) with Doll (Jean Hagen) in *The Asphalt Jungle* (John Huston, 1950).

human mercy." As Hardy is speaking, Dix is dying. We don't trust what Hardy says because we know it to be untrue, and we don't trust the forces of law and order because the case is being investigated by a corrupt police officer, Lieutenant Ditrich (Barry Kelley).

Dix's compulsive gambling can be seen as a link to his childhood and the family farm where he grew up. He clings to the dream of buying back the farm after it failed during the Depression. "The way I figure," he says, "my luck's just gotta turn. One of these days I'll make a real killing and then I'm gonna head for home." It's an impossible dream, of course. The end of the film sees Dix driving desperately toward his childhood home, even though he "hasn't got enough blood left in him to keep a chicken alive," accompanied by his devoted girlfriend Doll (Jean Hagen). He collapses and dies in a paddock, attended by Doll and the horses he has been dreaming about (see Figure 6.3). The lyrical fatalism of the scene evokes the Depression years as well as the French poetic-realist films of the same era.

There is none of the ethos of the aspirational gangster here. Dix embodies a rejection of the city as the site of gangster enterprise, where he cannot achieve even modest success. For Dix and the other members of the gang, the robbery holds out the promise of a way out of their hopeless lives. All the members of the gang are petty criminals with dismal prospects. Louis Ciavelli (Anthony Caruso), the cracksman, longs to escape the cramped apartment he shares with his family. He is accidentally shot during the robbery and, unable to go to hospital, is taken back home where he dies in front of his grieving wife Maria (Teresa Celli). The very idea of home seems broken or ailing in some way. Louis has a sick child; Emmerich has a bedridden wife, May (Dorothy Tree). He also has a young mistress Angela (Marilyn Monroe) who, in a kind of decadent parody of family life, is "some sweet kid" who calls him "uncle." Bankrupt and on the verge of arrest, he commits suicide. Doc imagines a future for himself in Mexico where he will be able to indulge his proclivity for young girls; but, lingering in a café to watch a teenage girl dancing, he is arrested before he can escape. When Doc invites Dix to accompany him after the botched robbery, Dix tells him that he's not interested. "I'm going home," he says. "Listen, Dix," says Doc. "You can always go home and when you do it's nothing. Believe me, I've done it. Nothing." For Dix, there is only the possibility of reaching "home" through death and, as Doc told him, it's "nothing."

"Un-American:" Cold War noir

"Before every free conscience in America is subpoenaed, please speak up! Say your piece. Write your Congressman a letter! Airmail special! Let the Congress know what you think of its Un-American Committee."

JUDY GARLAND (1948)[15]

"This is Humphrey Bogart. Is democracy so feeble it can be subverted merely by a look or a line, an inflection, a gesture?"

HUMPHREY BOGART (1947)[16]

The Asphalt Jungle inaugurated a new kind of subgenre, but it also represented one of the last noir films to contain an identifiable political critique of American institutions and their values. Postwar noir has often been read as a leftist critique of American capitalism through narratives critical of its corporate culture, national and local government, criminal justice system, and law enforcement agencies, all of which were represented as corrupt and deficient. As critics have often pointed out, it is in the narratives of film noir that the American Dream is most often held to account.[17] If the planned robbery in The Asphalt Jungle suggestively evokes a route to the American Dream, it provides an unremittingly bleak commentary on its unattainability. In the same way in which Dix's early prospects were tied to the failed economics of the Depression era, the social and economic milieu of the present sees the members of Doc's gang doomed to failure, criminals or not. Here, the caper film would provide an oblique noir critique of American institutions at a time when such criticism could be quickly branded as "un-American." As Mark Osteen points out, "heist pictures emerged when direct challenges to capitalism and law and order became taboo."[18]

All the films made in America after the end of the Second World War were produced in the climate of the Cold War. We should note here that historical periodization does not fall neatly into decades and that it is more useful for discussion of the period's Cold War noir to be situated in the "long" 1950s which, as we shall see, had its political origins in 1947, and even earlier than that. In that climate, questions of political affiliation became paramount in a discourse of national security. It was a period in which concerns with American national identity raised questions about patriotism, loyalty, freedom, and citizenship. The films subsequently defined as noir could scarcely be unaffected by Cold War concerns, especially when Hollywood itself would be seen as an agent in the cultural politics of the Cold War. We should also bear in mind, as Philip Kemp has pointed out, "that the key period of American film noir—roughly 1945 to 1954—coincides neatly with the years of the great anticommunist witch hunt of HUAC (House Committee on Un-American Activities), [Joseph] McCarthy and the blacklist."[19] What kind of impact did the Cold War have on American filmmaking and how did it affect film noir during the period?

In a speech at Fulton, Missouri, in March 1946, former British premier Winston Churchill warned that "from Stettin in the Baltic to Trieste in the Adriatic, an iron curtain has descended across the continent."[20] Churchill's phrase defined a line of demarcation between opposing ideological forces, between an expansionist, totalitarian Soviet Union and the West, a conflict that would become known as the Cold War. Amidst fears about communism abroad, President Truman instigated measures designed to curtail Soviet expansionism, a policy of "containment." The Cold War defense of American national interests against communism at home saw the adoption of what many saw as totalitarian measures of its own. "One lived in an occupied country," recalled Arthur Miller, "where anyone at all might be a spy for the enemy."[21] Within that "occupied country" people lived under what David Caute has called "The Great Fear."[22] Several agencies were active in its investigatory processes, although two predominated: the House Un-American Activities Committee (HUAC) and the Federal Bureau of Investigation (FBI). The HUAC hearings were conducted in an atmosphere calculated to browbeat, disorientate, and intimidate witnesses, whereby constitutional rights were routinely denied, where accusations contained the presumption of guilt, where individuals could be subpoenaed to appear before the committee at two hours notice, and where witnesses were encouraged to forego counsel. Routinely harassed and harangued at the hearings, witnesses were incessantly asked: "Are you now or have you ever been a member of the Communist Party of the United States?"

The committee exploited information provided by anonymous informers together with unsubstantiated allegations and other testimony, frequently perjured, from colleagues, neighbors, and acquaintances, some of it maliciously motivated. The committee made informing a duty in the national interest and, as Stephen Whitfield suggests, "insisted upon informing as the test of patriotism, as the price of full citizenship."[23] Information gathered in this way and through Senator McCarthy's "loyal American underground" network of informers was made available to employers and the threat of dismissal was used to elicit the cooperation of witnesses. In March 1947 president Truman issued Executive Order 9835, which launched a new loyalty program that would have a devastating impact on the country at large. "It contained," says Caute, "the most sinister and destructive departure in postwar domestic politics, one which was to ramify far beyond the federal service and poison wide areas of American working, educational and cultural life."[24] The rapid expansion of the FBI followed the Truman loyalty program in 1947 and the attorney general's subsequent list of subversive organizations provided the mandate for its extension beyond law enforcement and into the field of political surveillance in a role that Victor Navasky describes as "an ideological police force."[25] In this role, and with unprecedented powers of investigation, the bureau developed a vast bureaucratic apparatus that functioned outside any recognizable constitutional jurisdiction, using methods of investigation more readily associated with a totalitarian rather than a democratic state. Indeed, its director, J. Edgar Hoover, became "a state within the state" and the FBI "politically sacrosanct." As David Caute notes, "Hoover equated any criticism of the FBI's political role with un-Americanism."[26] By the use of its covert operations, the bureau amassed a phenomenal amount of information on individuals, while several other government agencies, as Caute puts it, "were all creeping up on people."[27]

In 1947, Hollywood found itself under investigation by HUAC, ostensibly to ascertain whether communist infiltration of the industry had led to the production of "subversive" films, an investigation that became likened to an inquisition.[28] Ten writers and directors—the "Hollywood Ten"—refused to testify before the committee and were subsequently cited for contempt of Congress and later imprisoned. Hundreds of people working in Hollywood and more widely in the entertainment industries were blacklisted in consequence of their suspected membership of or sympathies with the Communist Party, or for their refusal to cooperate with the committee. Many consequently lost their jobs. Some blacklisted screenwriters worked on the black market using a "front," usually for a fraction of their former pay, without screen credit, and with no say over the type of work they were given. In what sounds like an improbable scene from a film noir, one writer described how a frightened producer would bring him cash at a corner drugstore.[29] Some remained unemployed for years, while others left the United States for work abroad. Reputations were tarnished and careers destroyed, either by allegations of leftist political allegiance or, later, for informing on others.

In *The Front* (1976), Woody Allen's film about Hollywood blacklisting at this time, Howard Prince (Allen) has been acting as a "front" for blacklisted writers when he is himself summoned to appear before HUAC. There, he is confronted with a typical barrage of questions. "Fellahs," says Prince, rising from his chair, "I don't recognize the right of this committee to ask me these kind of questions, and furthermore, you can all go fuck yourselves." We might enjoy the chutzpah of such a principled stand, but the scene bears little resemblance to how most witnesses actually behaved at the time.

We should pause here for a moment to reflect, with no little incredulity, on the very notion of "Un-American," especially as a term designating a governmental body. What does it even mean? One of the problems with "un-American" is that it begs the question of what "American" is supposed to mean and what, therefore, is being negated or opposed by its "un" prefix. In his study of the relation between film noir and American citizenship, Jonathan Auerbach has drawn attention to the complex meaning of the term.[30] Unlike terms such as "anti-American" or "non-American," which have clear and precise meanings, "to be *un-American*," Auerbach says, "is not simply to be hostile toward or positioned against American values from some identifiable alternative perspective, but rather to somehow embody the very opposite of 'America'."[31] As Auerbach suggests, the term "made sense only when applied *to* Americans." Some later questioned whether the term itself constituted an expression that was un-American. In 1959 former president Truman pronounced HUAC itself "the most un-American thing in the country today." "In a telling circularity," as Auerbach nicely puts it, "Truman found it un-American for Americans to label other Americans un-American."[32]

Whatever the role of "un-American" in political discourse, it cannot be assumed that the causes of the "inquisition" were solely or even mainly ideological in their attacks on communism and the left. The purge of Hollywood leftists and fellow travelers, real or imagined, was part of a wider conservative campaign to eradicate the power of the industrial unions and "Roosevelt-style socialism."[33] The 1947 HUAC hearings were tactically evoked in opposition to the strikes organized by the Conference of Studio Unions (CSU).[34] Industrial action affecting Hollywood and an increasingly conservative Truman administration at this time enabled studio bosses to exploit fears of communism to defeat union activism.[35] All of this, of course, would have a bearing on the kinds of films that Hollywood would make, particularly on its noir productions.

With the consolidation of postwar conservatism, the period saw a strong right-wing sphere of influence take hold in Hollywood. For example, right-wing ideologue Ayn Rand published a *Screen Guide for Americans*,[36] produced on behalf of the tellingly named Motion Picture Alliance for the Preservation of American Ideals (MPAPAI), a militantly anticommunist organization.[37] Sections in the "Guide" carried titles such as "Don't Smear Wealth," "Don't Smear Success," and "Don't Smear American Political Institutions." These strictures might have been written in direct response to many films noir of the period, several of which do precisely what Rand's provisos sought to prohibit, while another, "Don't Glorify Failure," might serve an alternative description of film noir itself.

With the increasing use of social realism as a feature of postwar American film, the narrative treatment of social problems often blurred into films that would be categorized as film noir, indicating that Hollywood could articulate liberal or even leftist political viewpoints. As Thomas Schatz has suggested, the period saw the emergence of a new generation of writers and directors, "many of whom brought with them a progressive political agenda and a strong interest in film realism."[38] Schatz cites Elia Kazan, Robert Rossen, Jules Dassin, Abraham Polonsky, Nicholas Ray, Joseph Losey, Fred Zinnemann, and Anthony Mann. What is remarkable about his list is that *all* these directors made significant films noir: it constitutes a veritable *Who's Who* of some of the most notable directors of noir of the period.[39] But in what was becoming a fanatically conservative Hollywood, the leftist tenor of noir filmmaking would find a new kind of perspective for narrative expression. "After 1947," says Naremore, "many leftist filmmakers were treated as outlaws, and it is not surprising that they made some of their best pictures from the point of view of criminals."[40] Nevertheless, the kind of empathetic narrative treatment of criminals that we saw in a film like *The Asphalt Jungle* would become unsustainable in the new political climate of the 1950s. "Hollywood did not stop producing dark thrillers in 1947," says Naremore, "but about that time, a number of skilled craftspeople who had used such films for socially critical purposes were either silenced, destroyed, or driven underground."[41]

It is often assumed in studies of Cold War Hollywood that HUAC's allegations about "red" filmmakers having insinuated a radical political agenda into their films were untrue, even ludicrous. Hollywood, according to this view, is politically conservative, and so consequently are its films. But in an important contribution to noir debates, Thom Andersen has challenged this view, suggesting that a group of films produced between the HUAC hearings of 1947 and 1951, and usually designated as film noir, can be alternatively categorized as "film gris." This term is appropriate, Andersen argues, "because we have been taught to associate communism with drabness and grayness, and these films are often drab and depressing and almost always photographed in black-and-white."[42] This generic cycle comprises thirteen films, a sample which is small but significant.[43] Prior to this cadre of leftist filmmakers—"Browderite Communists and left-liberals"[44]—there had been little evidence of leftist political criticism in Hollywood film. "The only critique of capitalism in the American cinema," says Andersen, "came from the radical right, in the films of Frank Capra and King Vidor."[45] Andersen's useful term helps us to read these films with more historically informed understanding than is possible when they are classified under the blanket term "film noir."

A representative example from Andersen's list, *He Ran All the Way* (1951), demonstrates several "gris" characteristics. Nick Robey (John Garfield) goes on the lam after a botched robbery in which he shoots a policeman. Taking refuge in a public lido, he meets Peg Dobbs (Shelley Winters) who takes him back to the apartment where she lives with her working-class family. Nick holds the family hostage while planning his escape with Peg who has pledged to go with him. He entrusts her with buying a getaway car, but when it fails to materialize he believes she has deceived him. In a final showdown between Nick and her father, Peg shoots Nick.

The story is close to the "social" film discussed earlier. Nick's turn to crime is precipitated by poor social conditions as the opening scene makes emphatically clear: unemployed, feckless, and suggestible, he lives in a slum with his alcoholic mother, and although reluctant to participate in the robbery, he cannot resist the pressure to do so. Nick can be likened to the hapless criminals in *The Asphalt Jungle*, although with none of their ingenuity and expertise. His crime is ill-planned and vicious with a nasty aftermath as he terrorizes Peg's family. And yet Nick is a vulnerable and sympathetic figure too, especially as he tries to "belong" to Peg's family.[46] He compliments Peg's mother on her coffee and nurses her when she faints. He even cooks a turkey dinner for the family in his desperation to be part of it. But any prospect of a romantic future with Peg is as doomed as those of the French poetic-realist films of the 1930s. Fatally wounded, the last thing he sees as he falls into the gutter is the car that she has loyally got for him after all (see Figure 6.4).

The careers of the "gris" filmmakers behind *He Ran All the Way* all suffered from the anti-red purges in Hollywood. John Garfield, a working-class actor

FIGURE 6.4 Nick Robey (John Garfield) dies in the gutter in *He Ran All the Way* (John Berry, 1951).

and activist with a "proletarian" screen persona, was blacklisted by HUAC in 1951 and he died in the following year. Director John Berry was named as a communist by Edward Dmytryk and also blacklisted. Unable to work in Hollywood, he moved to Paris. Screenwriter Dalton Trumbo was jailed in 1947 for refusing to testify before HUAC and was subsequently blacklisted, as was co-screenwriter Hugo Butler. Both writers remained uncredited, their work appearing under the "front" of Guy Endore. *He Ran All the Way* represents the swansong of film gris: such narrative subjects were soon off limits and their filmmakers ostracized.

If Cold War politics was taking a rightward turn, so too was film noir, at least if we choose to accept that the spate of anticommunist films produced in the late 1940s and early 1950s can be categorized as such. It is a measure of the malleability of "film noir" as a critical term that the very qualities admired by the French critics could be effectively reversed. If film noir is identified with a leftist political stance and a critical or subversive viewpoint on American institutions, it would adopt in its Cold War incarnation an altogether different political stance. A subcategory of "Red Menace" noir emerged at this time which, drawing on many of the standard tropes of "agency" noir films, produced outright condemnations of communism and its threat to American democracy in films such as *Walk a Crooked Mile* (1948), *The Red Menace* (1949), *The Woman on Pier 13* [*I Married a Communist*] (1950), *I Was a Communist for the F.B.I.* (1951), *The Whip Hand* (1951), and *Pickup on South Street* (1953).[47]

Other films noir of the 1950s would bear the residue of Cold War conservatism, if rather less explicitly. Take for example Hitchcock's *Strangers on a Train* (1951), a film that might appear to have little to do with Cold War concerns. It has links to the Hitchcockian noir "wrong man" trope after Guy Haines (Farley Grainger) and Bruno Antony (Robert Walker) meet accidentally on a train and the innocent Guy becomes implicated in a murder plot. Bruno proposes a fanciful scheme whereby each would carry out a murder on behalf of the other, thereby making each perpetrator untraceable to "his" respective crime. Guy's promiscuous wife Miriam (Laura Elliott), pregnant by another man, refuses him a divorce, which would enable him to marry Anne Morton (Ruth Roman), the daughter of Senator Morton (Leo G. Carroll). Dismissing Bruno's scheme, Guy departs, discovering later that Miriam has been murdered at an amusement park. Afterward, Bruno keeps turning up to harass Guy about his failure to meet his end of the "agreement" by carrying out the murder of his father.

Adapted from Patricia Highsmith's 1950 novel of the same name, the film shifts the original setting from New York to Washington. There is no obvious explanation why the nation's capital should be used in preference, nor why it should have so many scenes that feature images of federal government

FIGURE 6.5 Guy Haines (Farley Grainger) arrives in Washington in *Strangers on a Train* (Alfred Hitchcock, 1951), the illuminated dome of the Capitol Building in the background.

buildings. Take for example the scene in which Guy returns home on the night of Miriam's murder. He is seen on the steps outside in a shot with an extremely canted angle as Bruno calls to him from the shadows. The illuminated dome of the Capitol Building is visible as an imposing presence in the upper-right section of the frame (see Figure 6.5). Later, when Bruno phones Guy at the senator's home, we see Bruno against a similarly composed shot with the Capitol Building in the background. Bruno later appears on the steps of the Jefferson Memorial, a tiny silhouetted figure against the monument's imposing white marble columns. Robert J. Corber has linked this image to a Cold War discourse in which fears of a "homosexual menace" as a risk to national security were gaining momentum following allegations about homosexual employees working in the State Department.[48] An ensuing investigation by the Senate Appropriations Committee in 1950 triggered a scare in which "homosexuals were said to pose as great a threat to the government as members of the Communist Party."[49]

The image of Bruno at the Jefferson Memorial, says Corber, "makes the government appear vulnerable and unprotected" with Bruno himself "a blight on the government."[50] (We should note too how the Memorial is symbolically such an *open* building, one that seems readily exposed to infiltration.) But it is Guy who ultimately poses the real security risk, and the narrative cannot be seen simply as an external threat by a malign homosexual psychopath. Guy is hardly the innocent "wrong man" in the equation: he is not only weak, careless, and suggestible but also vaguely complicit in Bruno's deranged scheme. Moreover, he is about to marry the senator's daughter, thereby putting him at the heart of Washington's political class, and with the stated intention of going into politics himself. Bruno repeatedly insinuates himself into this

FIGURE 6.6 The transmutation of the private eye: Mike Hammer (Ralph Meeker) in *Kiss Me, Deadly* (Robert Aldrich, 1955).

political world, but it is Guy who represents its weakness and vulnerability by being already part of it.

Another example of Cold War noir with a conservative, if not an extreme right-wing bias, is Robert Aldrich's *Kiss Me, Deadly* (1955). The film is based on the 1952 novel by Mickey Spillane and the second, after *I, the Jury* (1947), to feature private eye Mike Hammer. The character belongs to the hard-boiled private eye tradition derived from Dashiell Hammett and Raymond Chandler although one that represents a comprehensive transmutation of such predecessors as Sam Spade and Philip Marlowe, especially in their incarnations by Humphrey Bogart (see Figure 6.6). A clue to Hammer's characterization is already evident in the title *I, the Jury*, perhaps the most concisely phrased expression of a right-wing credo in fiction, as well as in his name. Mike Hammer (Ralph Meeker) is a brutal, sadistic, misogynistic thug with none of the qualities associated with his forebears, played by Meeker as a kind of muscular phallic automaton. Hammer's private eye is a despicable "bedroom dick" who uses his secretary Velda (Maxine Cooper) to seduce men in the interests of his matrimonial investigation work. At the same time, he represents a new kind of 1950s' *Playboy* masculinity as consumer and connoisseur, evident in his apartment, all mod cons and *objets d'art*, a far cry from the dark austerity of Sam Spade's in *The Maltese Falcon*.

Following a mysterious encounter with a woman called Christina (Cloris Leachman), Hammer begins to investigate her disappearance. Conducting his own investigation in antagonistic relation to that of the police, Lieutenant Pat Murphy (Wesley Addy) warns him guardedly about "Manhattan Project, Los Alamos, Trinity," terms pointing to the ultimate revelation that the "great whatsit" at the center of the intrigue is the atomic bomb, and the film ends with a spectacular apocalyptic detonation. Unlike the private eye of preceding decades, Hammer cannot sustain an autonomous, independent position for himself outside the law enforcement agencies. The narrative works to disabuse Hammer of the idea that there is any role for him in Cold

War America. Whether or not the film can be seen as a critique of Spillane or a parodic version of a hypermasculinized or fascistic private eye, it is a Cold War incarnation marking the culmination of this key noir figure.[51] This transmutation of the private eye was symptomatic of the "demise" of classic film noir itself.

Aftermath: Neo-noir

Attempts to historicize noir are complicated by the emergence and development of the related category of "neo-noir," surely the most prevalent subcategory of film noir today. Neo-noir is a term used to describe films derived from or influenced by "classic" noir, although produced after that period. Although largely beyond the scope of this book, it's worth noting some of the main features of neo-noir, especially as it's often seen as a continuation of the historical category. Neo-noir can also provide us with a useful perspective on the original films. What, then, is neo-noir? Once again, the term is resistant to definition. Given the problem of defining film noir itself, it's hardly surprising that further difficulties would arise in attempts to define neo-noir. Foster Hirsch sees it as the means by which film noir could "continue to reinvent itself, to bend and sway, to add and subtract in order to keep up with changing times."[52] What does this tell us? Certainly neo-noir is seen to draw on the stylistic and thematic tropes of classic noir, reworking them in revived forms.

Critical discourse based on the notion of a "post-noir" category arose in the 1970s. Richard Jameson's "Son of Noir" is one of the earliest attempts to link films of the 1970s to films noir of the 1940s. Jameson identifies a critical tendency for reviewers of contemporary films to "dive for prototypes" in such classic films noir as *The Big Sleep* (1946).[53] Significantly, Jameson discusses Roman Polanski's *Chinatown* (1974), a film now seen as a seminal neo-noir film, without ever using the term "neo-noir," describing it as one of "the new *films noirs*." Even ten years later with the release of *Body Heat* (1981), another film that would come to be seen as a key neo-noir, the term still wasn't in general use. The *New York Times*, for example, reviewed it under the rubric, "Film Noir Revisited."[54] Only later in the decade did "neo-noir" fully enter critical discourse to become a standard critical term.

We encounter in these critical accounts of neo-noir some of the same problems affecting classification of the original category. One problem is the extension of the term "film noir" to incorporate "neo-noir," often with no particular distinction between the two. This is a common characteristic of noir writing today, both populist and academic. Take for example Ballinger and Graydon's *Rough Guide to Film Noir* with its section on "The Canon: 50

Essential Film Noirs," nearly a third of which comprises neo-noir films. Another section, "The Top Ten" films noir, awards first place to *Chinatown* (1974). "It might be a Technicolor neo-noir and have arrived a few decades late," they say, but *Chinatown* is the "winner."[55] If *Chinatown* is cited as the best film noir of all, overriding all the canonical titles from the 1940s and 1950s, this raises questions about the latitude of the term's definition. Such studies typically deal in generalized timescales and often no timescales at all.[56]

Conversely, other definitions of neo-noir will claim a degree of exactitude that can seem as arbitrary as some of those used for classic noir. For example, Andrew Spicer pinpoints in remarkably precise terms a chronology for neo-noir. Neo-noirs, says Spicer, should be distinguished from what he calls "late noirs" (1960–67), a period, according to his given examples, dominated by Samuel Fuller with *Underworld U.S.A.* (1961), *Shock Corridor* (1963), and *The Naked Kiss* (1964). "The first true neo-noir was John Boorman's *Point Blank* (1967)," he says, a film that inaugurated a "modernist" phase of neo-noir (1967–80).[57] What are we to make of "true" here? Certainly such claims are characteristic of much noir criticism, especially in such sources as Spicer's *Dictionary* and Silver and Ward's *Encyclopedia* where they demonstrate a great deal of critical investment in the notion of a benchmark "true" noir as well as trading on the assumption that there are measurable degrees of "noirness." Such claims can appear authoritative, but they should be treated with skeptical caution.

A neo-noir film can appear in various forms. It may incorporate references to classic noir, perhaps quoting or imitating the original. *Body Heat*, for example, is a loose reworking of *Double Indemnity* (1944) without being an actual remake. Similarly, *Guncrazy* (1992) alludes to the title of Joseph H. Lewis's *Gun Crazy* (1950), but in its story of a naïve young couple on the lam it has more in common with another classic noir, Nicholas Ray's *They Live by Night* (1948). Other comparable neo-noir treatments of a murderous young couple include Terence Malick's *Badlands* (1973) and Oliver Stone's *Natural Born Killers* (1994) with each bearing traces of Lewis's original.

Neo-noir can also encompass period settings, such as in *Devil in a Blue Dress* (1995), *The Man Who Wasn't There* (2001), and *The Killer Inside Me* (2010). Neo-noir in the 1970s saw renewed interest in Raymond Chandler, author of the hard-boiled fiction that provided the source for several films noirs in the 1940s, when there was a "second wave" of adaptations of his novels. *Farewell, My Lovely* (1975) is one period adaptation of Chandler's 1940 novel with Robert Mitchum as Philip Marlowe, with Mitchum reprising the role in a remake of *The Big Sleep* (1978) updated to a 1970s' setting. *Farewell, My Lovely* was first adapted as *Murder, My Sweet* (1944) with Dick Powell as Marlowe. Robert Altman's *The Long Goodbye* (1973) updated the late 1940s' setting of the novel to 1970s' Hollywood, with Elliott Gould as Marlowe. These titles, whether modern or period settings, can all be seen to evoke a sense of nostalgia for Chandler's narrative world and for the original noir period of the 1940s.

Other neo-noirs "inhabit" the world of the original through parody or pastiche, sometimes comedically. In *Dead Men Don't Wear Plaid* (1982), for example, private eye Rigby Reardon (Steve Martin) is interpolated into actual scenes from several classic films noir to create a new noir "mash-up" structure where part of the viewing pleasure, especially for the cinephile spectator, is in recognition of the originals. Another kind of noir evocation can be seen in a later Martin film, *Novocaine* (2001). This reworks the familiar noir trope of an ordinary man, here as successful dentist Dr. Frank Sangster (Martin), whose well-ordered world is jeopardized by the arrival of "femme fatale" Susan Ivey (Helena Bonham Carter). Here, though, the noir plot template is transformed with a narrative treatment more akin to screwball comedy. Sangster's profession is subject to ridicule, although it also provides the macabre means by which he is able to extricate himself from his dull life, but only to achieve an almost farcical happy ending altogether at odds with those associated with film noir, the femme fatale transmogrified into a heavily pregnant "earth-mother" characterization, improbably relocated to an idyllic home in rural France.[58]

Several neo-noirs are remakes of classic noirs, and some of these recreate the period setting of the original, here categorized as "retro-noir." For example, *The Postman Always Rings Twice* (1981) retains the period setting of Tay Garnett's 1946 original. Other remakes create updated settings, such as Steven Soderbergh's *The Underneath* (1995), a remake of Robert Siodmak's *Criss Cross* (1949); or *No Way Out* (1987), a remake of *The Big Clock* (1948). Other remake titles are the same as the originals, such as *D.O.A.* (1988, 1950), *A Kiss Before Dying* (1991, 1956), and *Kiss of Death* (1995, 1955). Other "neo" titles may suggestively encapsulate those of classic noir, like *After Dark, My Sweet* (1990), an adaptation of Jim Thompson's 1955 novel, which sounds like a 1940s' noir, even if it wasn't one.

Other titles are directly derived from classic "hard-boiled" sources such as Martin Scorsese's *Mean Streets* (1973), a phrase taken from an essay by Raymond Chandler, while the Coen brothers' *Blood Simple* (1984) takes the phrase "blood-simple" from Dashiell Hammet's novel *Red Harvest*.[59] Such sources serve to authenticate the hard-boiled, noir credentials of these neo-noir films which are often replete with references to the originals. "Neo-noir" in this sense also functions as a marker of cultural pedigree, labeling the designated films in terms of a critically admired tradition as well as for their nostalgic appeal to a "golden age" of American cinema. It's no accident, then, that the term should be used so extensively in the films' publicity materials and by critics as a standard term of reference, conferring on the films a connection to the "classic" cultural status of the period's originals.

We can see something of how this works by looking at two films in more detail. My first example is Scorsese's *Cape Fear* (1990), a remake of J. Lee Thompson's *Cape Fear* (1962). A cinephile steeped in film history, Scorsese has done a great deal to validate and popularize film noir through books and documentaries, as a film historian, and through his work in film preservation. Scorsese is one of the most important figures in the film-school generation of filmmakers in the post-studio era. His early career coincided with the popularization of the term "film noir" in the 1970s, a period that saw the emergence of film studies as an academic discipline. During this period his own films were being studied alongside classic film noir together with European art-house cinema and the works of directors from around the world. Scorsese's early films at this time, *Mean Streets* (1973) and *Taxi Driver* (1976), were self-consciously drawing on noir influences, as would his later ones like *Goodfellas* (1990), *Casino* (1995), and *The Departed* (2006). Critics began to trace affinities between Scorsese's "neo-noir" films and their historical antecedents.

Such affinities were also apparent elsewhere. For example, Paul Schrader wrote the screenplay for *Taxi Driver* and a seminal essay on film noir around the same time, collapsing the divide between filmmaking and film criticism.[60] With the burgeoning study of film noir on the curriculum, classic noir films were being shown on college courses, campus screenings, at art-house movie theaters, and on television. Scorsese's neo-noir films of this period worked to endorse classical noir while simultaneously validating his own films by situating them in the historical context of a cinematic lineage which was being awarded cultural value for the first time. His films often reworked many of the thematic and stylistic characteristics of classic noir, such as the New York City night world of *Taxi Driver*, gangster culture in *Goodfellas*, and the plot device of the undercover cop infiltrating a criminal gang in *The Departed*, a trope drawn from such classic noirs as *The Street with No Name* (1948) and *House of Bamboo* (1955).

In another referential gesture, three of the actors appearing in the original *Cape Fear*—Gregory Peck, Robert Mitchum, and Martin Balsam—reappear in "ironic" cameos in the remake, with Mitchum now a police lieutenant after his role as the psychopath Max Cady in the original. Mitchum himself was a noir icon, having appeared in several major films noir of the 1940s and 1950s, including *The Night of the Hunter* (1955), in which he played the Reverend Harry Powell who, like Max Cady, is a predatory killer, stalking his prey downriver. Even De Niro's tattoos of biblical texts can be seen as amplified echoes of Powell's. The remake also has a reworking of Bernard Herrmann's score from the original. Scorsese's *Cape Fear* signals itself as a kind of knowing postmodern reconstruction of the original, a hyperbolic pastiche involving the noir tropes and stylistics of the original, reworked through myriad quotations.

My second neo-noir example is Brian De Palma's *The Black Dahlia* (2006). The film is based on a true story about the murder of Elizabeth Short whose mutilated body was found in a Los Angeles suburb in 1947. She was given the sobriquet "Black Dahlia" by the tabloid press. Like Scorsese's *Cape Fear*, *The Black Dahlia* self-consciously evokes a sense of its own noir lineage through several pointed references. Its title, for example, evokes *The Blue Dahlia* (1946), the wartime noir with two of the period's most iconic noir stars, Alan Ladd and Veronica Lake, a film explicitly mentioned by one of the detectives on the Black Dahlia case. *The Black Dahlia* features one of Hollywood's landmark locations, the Pantages Theatre, where a classic film noir, *Black Angel* (1946), is playing, itself a story about another murdered woman, Marvis Marlowe (Constance Dowling). That film was based on the 1943 novel by Cornell Woolrich, one of the major "pulp" writers, several of whose stories were made into films noir.[61] *The Black Dahlia* was itself an adaptation of the novel by James Ellroy, a writer often associated with latter-day hard-boiled crime fiction.

The Black Dahlia is a self-reflexive film with a Hollywood setting and a narrative partly about filmmaking, one that shows the failed Hollywood starlet Short reduced to making pornographic films. The film deploys two of the main narrative devices associated with noir: a flashback structure and voice-over narration, by Detective Bucky Bleichert (Josh Hartnett). One sequence deploys a bravura tracking shot, showing the discovery of Short's body, of the kind associated with Orson Welles and the celebrated opening sequence in *Touch of Evil* (1958). *The Black Dahlia* is replete with such noir themes as obsession, corruption, decadent wealth, and sadistic violence. It also revisits iconic LA locations like the City Hall building that appears in countless films noir of the 1940s and 1950s. The film even features a clip of *The Man Who Laughs* (1928) by German expressionist filmmaker Paul Leni which not only provides a narrative echo through Gwynplaine (Conrad Veidt), whose mouth has been deliberately disfigured into a hideous grin as Elizabeth Short's has been, but also establishes a more explicit connection between *The Black Dahlia* and the German expressionist roots of film noir.

Another self-reflexive Hollywood neo-noir is *L.A. Confidential* (1997), a narrative that sees a link between Hollywood and the pornography industry with a call-girl service in which girls undergo plastic surgery to make them resemble 1940s' movie stars like Veronica Lake. The narrative also explores a connection between a celebrity scandal sheet, *Hush-Hush*, based on *Confidential* magazine, and *Badge of Honor*, a television police procedural series based on *Dragnet* (1951–59) and a film version, *Dragnet* (1954), based on case files from the Los Angeles Police Department. *Dragnet* was designed to improve the public image of the police department following the "Zoot Suit" riots of 1943 and the 1951 "Bloody Christmas" scandal, each of which features, respectively, in *The Black Dahlia* and *L.A. Confidential*.

The films brought together under the rubric of neo-noir may be as difficult to define as their classical predecessors, but one of the characteristics they do have in common is that of a self-reflexive generic form. We have seen how neo-noir comprises a reworking of the stylistic and thematic tropes of the original noir films, but to what purpose? Leighton Grist has identified two distinct and opposing tendencies in neo-noir (although he doesn't use that term) in a critique that draws on Frederic Jameson's influential work on postmodernism. The first, dating from the late 1960s to the mid-1970s and characterized by such films as *Point Blank*, *Chinatown*, and *Taxi Driver*, represents a "modernist" phase associated with New Hollywood cinema, the deconstruction of noir's generic conventions, and demonstrates the kind of social and political critique of American ideology comparable to that often associated with film noir of the 1940s.[62] Grist's second phase occurs in the 1980s, with films like *Body Heat*, *Blade Runner* (1982), and *Fatal Attraction* (1987). The generic self-consciousness of *Body Heat*, Grist argues, is an example of postmodernist superficiality, nostalgia, and pastiche—all intrinsically conservative—a far cry from the modernist critiques of his 1970s' examples with their parodic power to analyze, satirize, and criticize.[63] Neo-noir, according to this argument, had become merely a series of exercises in genre stylization.

Notes

1 *Los Angeles Times* (February 17, 1952), 1.
2 Raymond Borde and Étienne Chaumeton, *A Panorama of American Film Noir, 1941–1953*, trans. Paul Hammond (San Francisco: City Lights, 2002), 97.
3 Ibid.
4 Ibid., 98.
5 Ibid., 99. Their examples include Billy Wilder's *The Big Carnival* (aka *Ace in the Hole*, 1951) and László Benedek's adaptation of Arthur Miller's *Death of a Salesman* (1951), following his *Port of New York* (1949), a film noir admired by Borde and Chaumeton. See Ibid., 88.
6 The earliest narrative treatment of rape in a mainstream film of the Production Code era is usually taken to be in Jean Negulesco's *Johnny Belinda* (1948) for Warner Bros.
7 For useful accounts of Lupino's career, see Wheeler Winston Dixon, "Ida Lupino" in *Senses of Cinema* (April 2009) at: http://sensesofcinema.com/2009/great-directors/ida-lupino/ (Accessed June 30, 2016); Annette Kuhn, ed., *Queen of the 'B's: Ida Lupino Behind the Camera* (Trowbridge: Flicks Books, 1995).
8 Lupino's directorial role on *Not Wanted* is uncredited.
9 Hitchhiking is a frequent trope in film noir, offering narrative scope for fateful encounters. See for example, *Detour* (1945), *The Postman Always Rings Twice* (1946), and *The Devil Thumbs a Ride* (1947).

10　Geoff Mayer, *Historical Dictionary of Crime Films* (Lanham, MD: Scarecrow Press, 2012), 62.

11　Perhaps the best-known example of the subgenre is the French film *Du rififi chez les hommes* (1955), widely known outside France as *Rififi*, directed by blacklisted filmmaker Jules Dassin, and heavily influenced by *The Asphalt Jungle*. The film is famed for its virtually silent twenty-five minute sequence depicting the intricately executed robbery of a Parisian jeweler.

12　See for example *Ocean's Eleven* (1960), which features synchronized raids on several Las Vegas casinos, with Frank Sinatra, Dean Martin, Sammy Davis Jr., and other members of the "Rat Pack" in a self-reflexive take on their own collective Las Vegas persona.

13　Released the same year, the caper film *Armored Car Robbery* differs from *The Asphalt Jungle*, first because there is little to empathize with in its depiction of criminal psychopath Dave Purvus (William Talman), and second because it has a more traditional narrative emphasis on the police investigation through the figure of Lieutenant Jim Cordell (Charles McGraw).

14　Richard Griffith, "'Asphalt Jungle' May Be Best Crime Movie," *Los Angeles Times* (June 27, 1950), A7.

15　Judy Garland, quoted in Gordan Kahn, *Hollywood on Trial: The Story of the Ten Who Were Indicted* (New York: Boni & Gaer, 1948), 215.

16　Humphrey Bogart, "Hollywood Fights Back," radio broadcast (October 26, 1947), quoted in Robert Sklar, *City Boys: Cagney, Bogart, Garfield* (Princeton: Princeton University Press, 1992), 195.

17　For an excellent account, see Mark Osteen, *Nightmare Alley: Film Noir and the American Dream* (Baltimore: Johns Hopkins Press, 2013).

18　Ibid., 240.

19　Philip Kemp, "From the Nightmare Factory: HUAC and the Politics of Noir," *Sight & Sound* 55, no. 4 (Autumn 1986): 266.

20　Quoted in Jeremy Isaacs and Taylor Dowling, *Cold War* (London: Bantam Press, 1998), 30.

21　Arthur Miller, *Timebends: A Life* (London: Minerva, 1990), 310–11. Miller's play *The Crucible* (1953) used the seventeenth-century Salem witch hunts as an allegory of HUAC's.

22　David Caute, *The Great Fear: The Anti-Communist Purge Under Truman and Eisenhower* (New York: Simon and Schuster, 1978).

23　Stephen J. Whitfield, *The Culture of the Cold War* (2nd edn, Baltimore: Johns Hopkins University Press, 1996), 104.

24　Caute, *Great Fear*, 269.

25　Victor S. Navasky, *Naming Names* (New York: Penguin, 1981), 22.

26　Caute, *Great Fear*, 113.

27　Ibid., 115.

28　See Larry Ceplair and Steven Englund, *The Inquisition in Hollywood: Politics in the Film Community, 1930–1960* (Berkeley: University of California Press, 1983).

29　Navasky, *Naming Names*, 345.

30 Jonathan Auerbach, *Dark Borders: Film Noir and American Citizenship* (Durham: Duke University Press, 2011), 3–5.

31 Ibid., 4.

32 Ibid.

33 James Naremore, *More than Night: Film Noir in its Contexts* (Berkeley: University of California Press, 1998), 123.

34 See Ceplair and Englund, *Inquisition in Hollywood*, 216–25.

35 Naremore, *More than Night*, 123.

36 *Screen Guide for Americans* (Beverly Hills, CA: The Motion Picture Alliance for the Preservation of American Ideals, 1947).

37 See Ceplair and Englund, *Inquisition in Hollywood*, 192–93, 209–15.

38 Thomas Schatz, *Boom and Bust: American Cinema in the 1940s* (Berkeley: University of California Press, 1999), 382.

39 Note the following examples of their work in film noir, virtually all of which were produced during the early stages of the HUAC investigations: Kazan, *Boomerang!* (1947), *Panic in the Streets* (1950); Rossen, *Body and Soul* (1947), *Johnny O'Clock* (1947), *All the King's Men* (1950); Dassin, *Brute Force* (1947), *The Naked City* (1948), *Thieves' Highway* (1949), *Night and the City* (1950); Polonsky, *Force of Evil* (1949); Ray, *They Live by Night* (1948), *In a Lonely Place* (1950); Losey, *The Lawless* (1950), *The Big Night* (1951); Zinnemann, *Act of Violence* (1949), and Anthony Mann, *The Great Flamarion* (1945), *Strange Impersonation* (1946), *Desperate* (1947), *Railroaded* (1947), *Raw Deal* (1948), *T-Men* (1948), *Border Incident* (1949), *Side Street* (1949).

40 Naremore, *More Than Night*, 128.

41 Ibid., 106.

42 Thom Andersen, *Red Hollywood* in Suzanne Ferguson and Barbara Groseclose, eds., *Literature and the Visual Arts in Contemporary Society* (Columbus: Ohio State University Press, 1985), 183.

43 Andersen's list comprises Robert Rossen's *Body and Soul* (1947), Abraham Polonsky's *Force of Evil* (1949), Jules Dassin's *Thieves' Highway* (1949) and *Night and the City* (1950), Nicholas Ray's *They Live by Night* (1948) and *Knock on Any Door* (1949), John Huston's *We Were Strangers* (1949) and *The Asphalt Jungle* (1950), Michael Curtiz's *The Breaking Point* (1950), Joseph Losey's *The Lawless* (1950) and *The Prowler* (1951), Cyril Endfield's *Try and Get Me* (aka *The Sound of Fury*, 1951), and John Berry's *He Ran All the Way* (1951). Ibid., 183–84.

44 Ibid., 187. The reference is to Earl Browder, general secretary of the American Communist Party USA (CPUSA) in the 1930s and 1940s.

45 Ibid., 186.

46 In his attempt to join in a family life denied him, Nick bears comparison with James Mason's Donnelly in *The Reckless Moment* (1949), discussed in the previous chapter.

47 These films noir form part of a broader category of anticommunist film. There were a spate of titles incorporating "Red," such as *The Red Danube* (1949) and *Red Snow* (1952).

48 Robert J. Corber, "Hitchcock's Washington: Spectatorship, Ideology, and the 'Homosexual Menace' in *Strangers on a Train*," in Jonathan Freedman and Richard Millington, eds., *Hitchcock's America* (New York: Oxford University Press, 1999), 103–06.

49 Ibid., 104.

50 Ibid., 112.

51 See Naremore, *More Than Night*, 151–55.

52 Foster Hirsch, *Detours and Lost Highways: A Map of Neo-Noir* (New York: Limelight, 1999), 6.

53 Richard T. Jameson, "Son of Noir," *Film Comment* 10, no. 6 (November to December 1974): 30–33.

54 Janet Maslin, "Screen: William Hurt as Fall Guy in 'Body Heat': Film Noir Revisited," *New York Times* (August 28, 1981), C14.

55 Ballinger and Graydon, *Rough Guide to Film Noir*, 56.

56 The first edition of Silver and Ward's *Film Noir* (1980) has a handful of neo-noir entries interspersed with the bulk of historical ones, incorporating titles such as *Dirty Harry* (1971), *Chinatown* (1974), *Night Moves* (1975), and *Taxi Driver* (1976). The latest edition (2010) sees neo-noir with separate categorization in a greatly expanded section with entries from *After Dark, My Sweet* (1990) to *The Zodiac* (2007).

57 Spicer, *Historical Dictionary*, 215.

58 Film noir and screwball comedy may not be as opposed as they seem and according to one film scholar there is a kinship between them. See Thomas C. Renzi, *Screwball Comedy and Film Noir: Unexpected Connections* (Jefferson, NC: McFarland, 2012). On the relation between screwball and noir in *In a Lonely Place*, see Dana Polan, *In a Lonely Place* (London: BFI, 1993), 16–18.

59 Raymond Chandler, "The Simple Art of Murder" (1944) in *The Simple Art of Murder* (New York: Vintage, 1988), 18; Dashiell Hammett, *Red Harvest* (1929; Vintage/Black Lizard, 1992), 154, 158.

60 Paul Schrader, "Notes on *Film Noir*," *Film Comment* (Spring 1972), repr. in Alain Silver and James Ursini, eds., *Film Noir Reader* (New York: Limelight, 1996), 53–63.

61 Woolrich's stories and novels provided the sources for more films noir than any other writer. See, for example, *Convicted* (1938), *Street of Chance* (1942), *The Leopard Man* (1943), *Phantom Lady* (1944), *Deadline at Dawn* (1946), *The Chase* (1946), *Fall Guy* (1947), *The Guilty* (1947), *Fear in the Night* (1947), *I Wouldn't Be in Your Shoes* (1948), *Night Has a Thousand Eyes* (1948), *The Window* (1949), *No Man of Her Own* (1950), *Rear Window* (1954), and *Nightmare* (1956). On Woolrich and film noir, see Thomas C. Renzi, *Cornell Woolrich: From Pulp Noir to Film Noir* (Jefferson, NC: McFarland, 2006).

62 Leighton Grist, "Moving Targets and Black Widows: Film Noir in Modern Hollywood," in Cameron, ed., *The Movie Book of Film Noir*, 267–72.

63 Ibid., 272–85.

PART THREE

Case study: The veteran problem and postwar film noir

7

The discourse of veteran readjustment

For the men of Barlow were coming home. Home over the seven seas from Australia and India; up from the swamps of Burma and the dragging of tired feet across the heavy sands of Africa; they had dropped down in a last swooping flight from the treacherous clouds over the Pacific and come out at last from the deep cold forests of the north. They were coming in over the clacking rails from the taking of Africa and their triumphant marches through war-torn Europe. Home with their wounds and their glory; their weariness and their pride; their bitter disillusion, longings, failures; their undefeated courage intact, the inexhaustible laughter still triumphant; home at last to hearthstone and a long rest on the deep bosom of love.

MARGARET RHODES PEATTIE, *The Return* (1944)[1]

Home. The way they said it to each other, it was more a word of anxiety and deep unexorcised fear, of despair even, than of relief, love or anticipation. What would it be like, now? What would they themselves be like?

JAMES JONES, *Whistle* (1978)[2]

There has been a longstanding tendency for critics to make generalized claims about the social factors presumed to have had a bearing on film noir. As we have seen in previous chapters, some critics have gestured toward such events as the Second World War and more vaguely toward "postwar disillusionment."[3] Much noir criticism has neglected more specific historical analysis, assuming that it is self-evident that the war and its aftermath would be likely to generate "dark" narratives. But what exactly was it about wartime and the postwar world that would find expression in postwar noir?

With the end of the war approaching, the figure of the returning veteran and the impact of his homecoming on postwar America became *the* issue of social concern. As Arthur Miller put it, "the danger lay in the return of the warriors, in the time when they were no longer webbed into the Army organization."[4] Fears and anxieties about the veteran would become a significant factor in shaping postwar noir, although few noir commentators have provided much analysis of this figure.[5] Why should the veteran's return precipitate such concern? The outpouring of textual commentaries on the veteran can be seen to constitute what Michel Foucault has termed "discourse," the means which enables, or produces, conditions of institutional power to define and delineate the terms of what is here given as "the veteran problem."[6] In this chapter, I examine the discourse of "the veteran problem" as the predominant social issue of the postwar years.

The aftermath of the Second World War witnessed military demobilization on a formidable scale and, in its wake, a vast influx of returning servicemen. The veterans' homecoming signaled a transition from military to civilian life which was often described as "readjustment." The term was predicated on the assumption that the servicemen's military experience had rendered them apart from mainstream society at home. The difference between military and civilian societies was often described as worlds apart— worlds not merely different but mutually incompatible to those at home. Even prior to their demobilization, veterans were beginning to appear as strange and incomprehensible. The purpose of readjustment would be to efface this difference. Ex-servicemen would undergo a process of social reconversion that would see them reabsorbed into the social system of home. Demobilization had brought the servicemen back, but readjustment would see them brought back *in*. The issue of returning veterans precipitated an unprecedented level of government intervention leading to an extensive series of measures, including the 1944 GI Bill (of Rights), legislation that would have far-reaching implications for the postwar reconstruction of American society.[7]

The figure of the veteran loomed large in postwar discourse and became the focus of intense scrutiny and speculation. When social scientists turned their attention to the postwar implications of returning servicemen, they identified two general areas of concern. First, there was broad consensus that "veteran" meant "the veteran problem" and that "readjustment," as defined by social scientists themselves, constituted the social mechanism necessary to solve it.[8] Few would have disagreed with Willard Waller's pronouncement on the magnitude of the problem. "The veteran who comes home is . . . certainly the major social problem of the next few years," says Waller. "*Unless and until he can be renaturalized into his native land, the veteran is a threat to society.*"[9]

Second, "the veteran problem" was seen as an aggregate of problems arising from the experience of military society. An extraordinary range of social, political, cultural, and economic issues were lumped together under the rubric of the veteran problem, often in absurd and contradictory ways. Benjamin Bowker has nicely summarized some of the contradictions implicit in the discourse of the veteran problem, where

> veterans had lost their moral sense in battle, but returned highly critical of the nation's peccadilloes; they had lost initiative in the routine of the services, yet they would organize so strongly that they would dominate the nation; they were physical and mental wrecks, yet they threatened to set up a reign of terror through brawny cunning; they vindictively hated the uniform, yet were planning to force universal military training upon their sons and brothers; they had gorged themselves on the "creature comforts" that had become short at home, yet they were returning to seize all remaining assets through communism; there were not atheists in foxholes, yet veterans were returning vicious and godless.[10]

A voluminous sociological literature about the veteran problem was accompanied by a plethora of self-help guides, advisory pamphlets, and articles in newspapers and popular magazines, all offering advice about every conceivable aspect of veteran readjustment.[11]

Demobilization

I'd been discharged from the Army at a good time, just before the rush began, all the brilliant young men with all the brilliant records, their discharge papers, their imitation gold buttons, all looking for a better job, a higher paying job, a job different from the one they'd had before the war. It took a few weeks, a few weary rounds of interviews, for the bright young veterans with bright war records to realize that they were available by the gross, the hundred, the thousand, the million. It took a little while to realize that the best thing to do about being a veteran was to forget it—quick. Throw away the imitation gold button. Place the discharge papers in the bottom of a trunk. Forget the possibility of five-figure salaries. Get to work, son. Get on the ball. Get busy. Catch up.

MERLE MILLER, *That Winter* (1948)[12]

The scale of demobilization was vast and its logistics formidable. A total of 16,353,000 men had been taken out of civilian life and put in uniform.[13] When the army began demobilization in May 1945, its ground and air forces numbered approximately 8,290,000 personnel. The navy began its demobilization in September with approximately 4,060,000. Veterans began returning home at the rate of 200,000–300,000 per month.[14] It was anticipated that the sheer scale of the operation would have a damaging, if not devastating, impact on the economy. Economic forecasts were pessimistic and polls confirmed a sense of foreboding about the prospects for economic reconversion. Estimates varied but none was encouraging. The Director of the Office of War Mobilization and Reconversion reported in September 1945 that the sudden termination of war contracts would precipitate an immediate and large-scale dislocation of the economy with a predicted rise in unemployment of "five million or more" within three months. Government economists foresaw that figure rising to ten million by the end of 1946.[15] The end of the war signaled a sudden halt to an economy geared to wartime production and the immediate cancellation of military contracts. With civilian employment in August 1945 at record levels of over 53,000,000, and with over 12,000,000 members of the armed forces scheduled for rapid demobilization, the economy appeared to many to be in imminent danger of collapse.

The social impact was immediate and extensive. Industries laid off thousands of workers, often in a single day.[16] Servicemen themselves shared these concerns and, according to a major official study by Samuel Stouffer, "all surveys" indicated that future employment prospects was the predominant concern of army personnel and the first of their "personal anxieties."[17] There was also a perception that military training and experience would be of little use in any civilian occupation. One study concluded that servicemen "may find the readjustment to civilian life difficult because the skill they learned in the army has no civilian counterpart."[18] Moreover, there was a prevailing view that the wartime economic boom had provided only a temporary respite from the Depression, echoes of which could be found among servicemen. "The saying, 'I hope I don't have to sell apples'," noted Wecter, "has become a wry joke in the ranks."[19]

Many social scientists stressed civilian employment as a crucial factor in the veteran's readjustment. Many of their concerns centered on the veteran's attitudes that, they anticipated, would cause various socially disruptive problems. Pratt described some of the "typical examples" already evident: "Job restlessness—a year or two of tramplike drifting from job to job . . . near neurotic choosiness in job selection . . . touchiness or even actual insubordination to industrial authority."[20] In some instances, the restlessness of the footloose veteran was seen as a direct result of his military experience. The inability to "settle down" and the drive to keep "moving on" were attributed to what Robert J. Havighurst called the "unusual mobility" of the military environment where servicemen were "almost continually" on the move. Here, servicemen acquired "a fast-moving introduction to diverse ways of life" and "the inclination to keep moving persisted long after the termination of their service careers."[21] According to one "Midwest" girl in Havighurst's study, "running around" was endemic: "It's 'Let's go here' and 'Let's go there'. That's all you hear—'Let's go here', 'Let's go there'."[22] The need to settle down with a steady job was seen as imperative.[23]

Many social scientists thought that the veteran could be incapable after military service of undertaking a civilian occupation at all. Surveys indicated high levels of reluctance by veterans to return to their prewar jobs. Havighurst reported that: "Usually, he did not want 'just a job'. Very often he did not even want his old job—if he had had one—back again. He wanted a better job. And . . . he was willing to wait stubbornly, for many months if need be, for this 'better job' to appear."[24] These forecasts contradicted the popular view that veterans had a nostalgic regard for their old jobs.[25] Many veterans didn't want to go straight back to work. Unemployed ex-servicemen were entitled to a "readjustment allowance" of $20 per week for fifty-two weeks and consequently found no immediate necessity to find work. Claimants of the allowance were known as members of the "52-20 Club" and as "rocking-chair vets." According to Havighurst, "most of the rocking-chair veterans *weren't* in a hurry."[26]

The readjustment allowance was one of several provisions in the GI Bill designed to assist returning servicemen and facilitate their readjustment. Although the bill was widely seen as necessary and pragmatic, the readjustment allowance was seen by some legislators as a license for malingerers and likely to encourage a dilatory attitude toward employment.[27] The testimony of veterans themselves was sometimes used to endorse criticism of the allowance. According to one, "this rocking-chair money is causing a lot of trouble. It's ruining a lot of these guys. They're sitting around on their dead asses forgetting what a day's work is like."[28] Social scientists would often acknowledge a veteran's right in principle to a well-earned rest, while simultaneously seeking to usher him toward a more socially integrated role—a role described by Walter Eaton, one of the contributors to Havighurst's study, as "a usefully participating member of his community."[29] Eaton cites one of the subjects in Havighurst's study, Bill, as an example of this problem with his "do-nothing" lifestyle of "just fooling around" or having "a few beers" and attending "all the veterans' meetings."[30] A socioeconomic role for the veteran, a *citizen* role, became for social scientists a significant criterion in the "measure of adjustment," which depended on the extent to which he was able to cast off his veteran identity. I discuss the issue of veteran citizenship in Chapter 9, but it is important to note here that his "continuing" veteran identity was a pressing concern. The key questions in this measure of adjustment, says Eaton were: "How long does the veteran continue to think of himself as a veteran? How long does he continue to rely upon veterans for moral . . . support? How long does it take him to re-enter into the associational and clique relationships which are available in the community?"[31]

Postwar sociology was beginning to assume considerable influence and the period saw the empowerment of social science as a significant new form of social power. As Terence Ball has pointed out, "there emerged for the first time a vast institutional infrastructure—government granting agencies, private foundations, and the modern multiversity, in which the increasing professionalization of the social sciences proceeded apace—for supporting research and training."[32] The emergence of social science as a political force was due to a large extent to the wartime role it was enabled to assume. "In some respects," Ball rightly suggests, "the war was a godsend for the social sciences."[33] It provided a unique opportunity for social scientists to undertake studies of the extraordinary social conditions imposed by war and, subsequently, of the social problems of postwar readjustment. With substantially increased funding, often through government agencies, the work of social science was increasingly linked to government interests and often undertaken on the government's behalf. Sociology, in particular, began to acquire an increasingly ideological function as a quasi-government agency with substantive influence on postwar social policy, often with an implication of "social engineering." Social science, in fact, would play a significant part in the construction of America's postwar social identity. Under the guise of disciplinary independence, scientific rationality and, with the rising authority of "the expert" in many walks of life, social science claimed the requisite expertise to define social problems and provide for their solutions. It was in these circumstances, then, that sociologists came to play a crucial role in defining the terms of "the veteran problem" and writing the agenda of readjustment with official status to do so through work that could assume a regulatory and supervisory function.[34]

Sociologists conducted a vast amount of wartime research into the nature of military society, and their perspectives on ex-servicemen were predicated on their earlier studies of servicemen in military service.[35] While the focus of sociological interest was on the social structures and practices of military life, it was also concerned with the transition from one type of society to the other and repeatedly emphasized the effects of this transition between the different worlds of military and civilian society. These accounts frequently contrasted descriptions of military social practices with those of civilian society, commonly finding the military as an aberration or deviation from the civilian "norm."

"Arriving as strangers": The veteran comes home

The veteran was often seen to be returning from a world that was remote and unaccountable to those at home, a figure in an emerging discourse of "the stranger." A product of military culture and society to which he no longer belonged, nor yet assimilated into civilian society at home, sociologists often saw the veteran as a dislocated, marginalized figure, as an outsider. Homecoming veterans "were arriving as strangers," says Bowker, "being met with the wary suspicion universally accorded strangers."[36] Even prior to his demobilization, a sense of growing apart had started to appear. According to Wecter, even the furlough, that crucial periodic connection with home, seemed to prefigure a sense of estrangement for the serviceman. He reports that, "on leave, outside his home town, the G.I. often has had the sense of being essentially a stranger."[37] Even the most eagerly anticipated visit was often found to cause disappointment and disillusionment, a condition known as "furlough syndrome."[38]

Sociologists found that the serviceman had become so comprehensively institutionalized that he often seemed to be unable to relate to home at all. Certainly, their accounts of military service were dominated by concerns with the effects of what Erving Goffman has called "total institutions."[39] The testimony of servicemen themselves was frequently enlisted to support this view. Waller cites a letter from a soldier to his wife in which he explains that even when home on furlough, the locus of "home" for him was the army base where he felt he belonged. "You don't feel you belong anywhere else—you can't when you're in uniform," he told her. "'The army seemed strange when I first got into it', he wrote, 'but now everything else but the army seems strange'."[40] "Once accustomed to the military environment," Havighurst noted, "servicemen often tended to think of civilian life as strange, distant, and unreal."[41]

The veteran's point of view often seemed to confirm his outsider status, especially through the "confessional" candor of many first-person accounts of the experience of homecoming. The veteran war correspondent Edgar L. Jones, for example, described himself as consigned to a kind of limbo in which he was "lost between two worlds" and suffering from a kind of emotional anesthesia that set him apart from everyday life. "I actually feel like a stranger in my own home," he says, "because everyday living in America requires emotional responses which I am incapable of giving."[42] For Pratt, the veteran had been rendered "different in hundreds of little ways from the man his family knew before he went away; different in his outlook on life; different in his manner of doing things; different in his sense of values; different in his likes and dislikes."[43] For Waller, the veteran had become an incomprehensible figure. "Civilians do not understand the veteran," he says. "He has become an alien."[44]

The veteran often appeared unable or unwilling to talk about his war experience. As Christopher La Farge has suggested, "he cannot tell a man or woman who has not been in combat what it is like: it is an incommunicable experience."[45] It was widely assumed that this gulf between the two worlds would set civilian and serviceman apart and pose major problems for the veteran's readjustment. Pratt, for example, supposed that the serviceman would have a "conviction that no one who had not been 'over there' possibly could understand how he feels about things," and he anticipated "loneliness, insecurity, and a sense of isolation" as the likely consequences.[46]

Many servicemen, especially those with combat experience, resented the anodyne or gung ho representations of combat in circulation at home, leading to false civilian perceptions of the war front. Wecter, for example, noted how much soldiers objected to press reports that treated the war "as if it were a kind of Rose Bowl game."[47] Moreover, as Wecter and other commentators often suggested, there were already many other aspects of the civilian world that the soldier disliked, especially when they seemed to him contrary to the war effort. He disliked "to hear of 'the gravy train' in civil life . . . black market, gas-stranded tourists in Florida, lavish spending in night clubs. . . . Rumors of chiseling, profiteering, indifference to the war." He was, suggests Waller, "contemptuous of civilians and 4Fs and all who are not doing their bit in uniform" as well as "slackers" and "swivel-chair heroes" at home.[48] "The soldier is bitter," says Waller, "because civilians see the glamor of war and gloss over its ugliness."[49] Jones saw GIs developing an increasingly rancorous view of home life as they showed their "bitter contempt for the home front's abysmal lack of understanding, its pleasures and comforts, and its nauseating capacity to talk in patriotic platitudes."[50] Although "home" was assiduously promoted in the discourse of national unity, there were concerns that for many servicemen it had become the target of resentment and contempt.

Sociologists were also concerned about civilian perceptions of the serviceman's experience of combat which, they believed, raised further obstacles to his readjustment. The post-combat veteran was seen as a particularly dangerous and unpredictable figure, especially in the media. In what was tantamount to a moral panic, the media exploited wartime terms of reference to define demobilization as a cataclysmic social phenomenon and the veteran as a dangerous figure. Demobilization, according to a media survey conducted by Bowker, was widely reported as an "invasion" by a new kind of "enemy" who, having fought abroad, would now turn against what they liked to call "PFCs" (Poor Fucking Civilians) at home.[51] In a discourse that linked the already newsworthy veteran with violent crime, a proliferation of sensationalist stories invariably defined the crime according to a veteran perpetrator. So many press reports made an implicit connection between the veteran and violent crime that the veteran-criminal became a ubiquitous postwar stereotype. Headlines such as "Former Soldier Charged in Wife's Bolo Knife Death" became a newspaper staple. These stories employed a standard technique by which the assault weapon was precisely specified, often the service-issue weapon that the veteran had brought home with him or, as here, an "exotic" acquisition brought back from the Pacific war. This typically produced other instances of the headline formula such as "VETERAN BEHEADS WIFE WITH JUNGLE MACHETE."[52] Other accounts made a more explicit connection between combat experience and fears of a postwar crime wave. There was a perception that veterans had been trained by the army to be reflexive, cold-blooded killers and that is what they would remain when they came home. Bowker cites a report in the *Boston Post* from February 1945 which warned of the dangers of those soldiers "educated to kill" who "cannot . . . readjust themselves to the ways of normal life" and who consequently "will lean to a life of crime." Both the police and the FBI were reported to be concerned about the criminological implications of the combat-trained veteran.[53]

Some commentators at home had already alluded to horrific wartime practices, especially in the Pacific war where atrocities were rife. There was a grim culture that saw the desecration of corpses and the use of body parts as souvenirs, ornaments, and trophies, some of which were mailed home. Jones gives an uncompromising synopsis of this culture.

> We shot prisoners in cold blood, wiped out hospitals, strafed lifeboats, killed or mistreated enemy civilians, finished off the enemy wounded, tossed the dying into a hole with the dead, and in the Pacific boiled the flesh off enemy skulls to make table ornaments for sweethearts, or carved their bones into letter openers.[54]

Awareness of this "souvenir" culture wasn't confined to the Pacific but was widely reported in the popular press at home through images such as Ralph Crane's well-known photograph of a sailor's sweetheart with a Japanese skull, which appeared in *Life* magazine in 1944.[55]

Amidst concerns about the psychological effects of combat, the veteran's readjustment became subject to a discourse of medicalization and defined in terms of psychopathology. Psychological science, especially psychiatry, was consolidating an increasingly influential position both in the military and society at large. As wartime had facilitated the development of social science, it similarly provided psychological science with the means to acquire influential military standing. Wartime also provided the opportunity to raise the professional profile of psychiatry with the publication of several major studies by military psychiatrists.[56] Military psychiatrists also wrote several "primers" on the psychology of readjustment.[57] Many sociological studies of the veteran were similarly concerned with the psychological effects of combat.[58]

The "intemperate environment" of military life

"Set 'em up." The sailor was high.—A sailor's money is loosely exchanged for pleasures for which he has a secret contempt. He does not calculate to have so many drinks for so many dollars, but he drinks until the money runs out, leaving a dollar to get back to the ship.

PAUL GOODMAN, "Sailor's Money" (1949)[59]

There were also concerns that the military had produced what Havighurst calls an "intemperate environment" in which servicemen were schooled in various forms of illicit behavior. Havighurst summarizes the intemperate curriculum as "to smoke, to gamble, to loot, to deal in stolen goods, and to pay for the attentions of prostitutes."[60] For Waller, this culture contributed toward the soldier's "moral irresponsibility" and his preoccupation with instant gratification and profligacy.[61] This was evident in his attitude to his pay. As one study pointed out, "complete exhaustion of the monthly paycheck within a few days was comparatively common" and the "soldier could squander his cash with equanimity, knowing that next month would see him 'flush' again; while, in the meantime, there was always the assurance of food and shelter." Money in these circumstances had only "immediate" value and "was used or loaned or gambled with considerable abandon."[62] For the soldier, unconstrained by the responsibilities of his civilian counterpart, there was no reason why he shouldn't do as he liked. For other commentators it was a culture that produced "delinquency" on such a vast scale as to be commonplace.[63] Looting, for example, was rife, even in Allied countries, and black marketeering was common practice. McCallum reports often hearing the sentiment that, "a man was a fool if he didn't leave the port of Le Havre with at least $1,000 in his pocket."[64] There were concerns that servicemen would return home with these attitudes and, perhaps, criminal tendencies as well.

The language of everyday life played a role in this culture, notably "bad" language.[65] Informal discourse was loaded with profanity and obscenity, especially in the multifarious use of "fuck." In virtually universal use, "fuck" was seen to convey a rebellious and contemptuous attitude to everything, including the army. It crops up everywhere, including in the ubiquitous army acronym SNAFU (Situation Normal, All Fucked Up).[66] The rampant use of such language was seen as an oppositional stance against the niceties of civilian life, as a kind of celebration of its own unsanctioned, uncouth culture. Such expressions could provide for the soldier "stronger ways of saying things and so manifest the image of a stronger self."[67] That "fuck" should have suffused everyday language to the extent that it did was seen as an expression of virility, constructed against the feminine world associated with home, and of what were often described as "baser instincts." To some commentators, the coarseness and crudity of the soldier appeared to be nothing short of a frontal assault on the feminized culture he had left behind. One commentator noted that, "by pronouncing those 'dirty words' which he never dared to utter in the presence of 'Mom' or his old-maid school-teachers, the G.I. symbolically throws off the shackles of the matriarchy in which he grew up."[68]

Commentators were particularly concerned about the soldier's detachment from the feminine sphere and his tendency to degrade the feminine. There was a blunt view of women in the servicemen's culture. After all, the common GI term for women was "cunt."[69] Moreover, for servicemen stationed overseas, the nature of sexual experience had changed. Prostitution was often widely available, and social scientists were concerned about the social implications of the serviceman's sexual relations abroad. As Elkin saw it, "the G.I. did not like or desire women other than as means of gratifying his self-respect and his primitive sexual desire." But he also "regarded the prostitute with special affection, because, unlike other women who were often formal and reserved, she had the friendly smile and democratic ways he had been accustomed to expect in social life. . . . Her approach to sex was as direct and casual as his own."[70] Commentators could barely conceal their distaste for the GI's sexual conduct. Bowker, for example, worried by the absence of a civilizing feminized milieu, describes how for the serviceman, "female company was . . . acquired under conditions so sordid as to be repellent," while Waller decried his "furtive amourettes with quick and easy women."[71]

Conversely, social scientists were also concerned about the readjustment implications of a masculine military culture. They found an environment that produced unusually close physical and emotional proximity with new patterns of intimacy within an exclusive conglomeration of men. This was a culture in which "all members of the group lived in the same section of the barracks, ate together, used the same latrine, took physical training and drill together, worked together, went to the movies together, and shared almost every other aspect of army life."[72] This new social experience wasn't necessarily as bad as it might have seemed. "Many," suggested Waller, "find something mysterious and rewarding in this comradeship of men at arms."[73] However, this comradeship was also seen as questionable. In a culture that saw the development of strongly forged "buddy" relationships, such associations could become, according to the vaguely coded expression of the period, "maudlin," and likely to meet with suspicion and disapproval at home. "Soldiers," warned Brotz and Wilson, "acquire some very queer friendships, which would have a dubious future in a civilian background."[74]

Sociologists also foresaw problems with other aspects of the veteran's readjustment. For example, if the serviceman felt that there would be a degree of recognition for his wartime endeavors, he may well have discovered on his return that his achievements would soon be disregarded. He might have been temporarily special at his homecoming, but soon after the end of the war he could be seen as an anachronism. Goulden draws attention to "the rapidly diminished novelty of the 'ex-serviceman', who by the end of 1945, in general public opinion, had been home long enough not to be considered anyone special."[75] His wartime experience didn't necessarily have much meaning in the context of a postwar society and wasn't necessarily worth much as it was now the wrong kind of experience. A civilian society, newly released from wartime anxieties, could regard the nature of military experience not only with indifference but also with antagonism. Hollingshead saw "heroic" wartime representations as already obsolete: "industry is not going to pay," he says, "for the rich personal pride a veteran carries because he helped storm the beaches on D-Day or for the skill a turret gunner on a multiengined bomber gained in combat with the Luftwaffe four miles up in the sky over Europe." These experiences, he contends, will be "of little value in making a living in our society."[76] There was a perception of a backward-looking veteran's undue preoccupation with a past, which would make it difficult for him to adjust to a forward-looking postwar nation. The veteran was emblematic of a past that many now preferred to forget. "Veterans," Bowker tellingly suggested, "were reminders of the universal tedium of the war," a war that was already receding from view. "And 'the war' was quickly rejected by the American public in its magazines, books and motion pictures."[77] Several commentators noted the veteran's preoccupation with the past, often demonstrated in his proclivity to "retreat" into the company of fellow veterans and his allegiance to veterans' organizations, both of which were seen as impediments to his readjustment.[78]

It was widely assumed that servicemen had been changed, perhaps irrevocably, by their military experience. Hollingshead, for example, described them as having "grown older . . . traveled widely, seen new lands and peoples, and gained a new viewpoint on life and the world. They have learned new ways of doing things and frequently . . . forgotten much that was once familiar and routine."[79] This experience was seen as ambivalent. On the one hand, military life seems to have had a positive value where travel provided new opportunities for a different kind of education, perhaps generating a more cosmopolitan outlook. Certainly, servicemen constituted the most widely traveled category of Americans.[80] On the other hand, it was possible that something new had displaced the "familiar and routine" and, perhaps, called into question an affirming view of home. Moreover, this sense of the new in his military experience could create in the serviceman not only a sense of remoteness from the more conventional aspects of civilian life but also, from this geographically and culturally distanced vantage point, a sharpened critical perspective from which to view society at home. Homecoming from such a perspective didn't necessarily mean a nostalgic conception of "home-sweet-home." In fact, home could begin to look jaded and take on a prospect of disenchantment. The experience of war, according to Robert E. Nisbet, had a tendency to cause in the soldier "a restlessness of spirit and a pervading dissatisfaction with the things he left behind him— old values and old aspirations."[81] Home, then, could become the object of resentment and disillusionment. "Not a few men," says Nisbet, "will return to civilian life with antagonisms pre-established, cynicism already crystallized."[82]

Dreaming of home

Ina Mae Harris had been part of the dream of his life: to marry her, to have kids with her, to be a man and leave his mother's home. Her picture was framed, a great big picture a foot tall, and placed on top his junk box at the foot of his bed. Morning and night he stared for several minutes at her simple oval face with large eyes and masses of curly hair. It was one of the few rituals of his army life he enjoyed—that and receiving letters from her on the scented pink paper decorated with her tiny unreadable backhand. Very short letters that had grown even shorter as he'd gone through his second and begun his third year overseas. But still talking of love, still promising faithfulness and marriage. Still from Her, the only Her in his life.

ROBERT LOWRY, *Casualty* (1946)[83]

In the wartime discourse of national unity, an affirmative discourse of "home" was constructed as a focal point of collective national purpose. It was axiomatic that for servicemen abroad, home was what they were fighting for and where they wanted to be. For many social commentators, homecoming held out the promise of marriage and family as the means to his readjustment. Historians too have often represented the period in ways that confirm the realization of a wartime dream of domestic longing, as a period in which, as William O'Neill puts it, "what men and women alike wanted was home, marriage, family. In the postwar world," he says, "their dreams would come true."[84] But to many social commentators, the postwar dream of home appeared less promising. They were concerned about the social effects of wartime separation which had fractured the traditional patterns of family life. Their studies often emphasized the effects of wartime separation and disruption which, as they saw it, had destabilized social relations and jeopardized the prospects for the domestically centered ideology of the family home as the structuring mechanism that was expected to play a crucial role in the readjustment of the returning serviceman.

They reported on several anxieties arising through wartime separation. Mail, for example, took on extraordinary significance in wartime, especially as the conduit that linked servicemen to their wives and sweethearts.[85] But although mail was seen as indispensable to morale, it didn't always fulfill its "good news" function. Letters from home could spell out bad news or imply it. For many husbands and wives, the long separation could cause a sense of growing apart and letters could confirm the demise of a relationship. A soldier might hear via the mail of his wife's sexual infidelity which, real or imagined, was a constant source of worry. Wecter describes how the soldier "searches her letters for clues that someone might be taking his place."[86] Whether true or not, he would be aware of the opportunities for her at home, particularly those arising from women's employment in the war industries.[87] Many servicemen were notified by letter that their wives intended to divorce them, and the "Dear John" letter was common. Jilted soldiers formed clubs such as the "Brush-Off Club" and the "Jilted G.I. Club" with admission by "Dear John" letter. But if this "club" response sounds lighthearted, a "Dear John" could have devastating consequences for the man who received it as well as on company morale. Such letters often provoked collective loathing for the women who sent them.[88]

The returning serviceman, particularly one who married before going overseas, could also find considerable disparity between the home life he imagined and how it actually turned out to be. His military life had been conducted exclusively in the absence of the family and many aspects of this life were, in fact, contrary to any sense of family values. Whenever off duty, for example, he could do whatever he liked: he could act without responsibility because he had none. But his return to family life could necessitate family responsibilities for which he was unprepared. Edward McDonagh cites the case of a private who "found himself adjusting to his wife in the new and unfamiliar role of mother to a child he had never seen, and a mother-in-law he had not expected to see in his home."[89] If he did return to find that his home was less than ideal, he might be inclined to idealize his former military life. "Once released from the Army and faced with the necessity of planning his own life, he looks with nostalgia on the regular paydays, the lack of responsibility, the freedom and anonymity that was his. Saddled with the responsibility of a wife and family, he thinks with longing of his carefree days."[90] In other words, wherever the soldier was, he would rather be somewhere else. For some, military service provided welcome opportunities for husbands to "escape" married life.[91] There was a view that many such wartime marriages had been undertaken prematurely and without benefit of maturing courtship. Certainly, wartime precipitated a sharp increase in the marriage rate.[92] Wartime marriages were often seen as impulsive and irresponsible, undertaken with only immediate or short-term interests in mind.[93] Marriages contracted on this basis were not expected to last and many didn't. As Reuben Hill put it: "Marriage in America has never been more popular, nor decisions to divorce more numerous."[94]

Homecoming could cause other anxieties. A wife may invest emotionally in the reconstruction of a too perfect past. Edward and Louise McDonagh see this reaction as a kind of "preservationist" syndrome, which they describe as "a pathetic eagerness on the part of many war wives to 'keep things exactly as they were' so that their husbands will not be disappointed and feel strange when they return."[95] Husband and wife may present to each other a figure altogether different from the one remembered. If absence, time, and distance had created a romanticized picture of the loved one, the actual reunion could be something of a disappointment, or worse. Social scientists frequently voiced concern with what Havighurst calls the "nostalgia effect," that is, "a sentimental overvaluing of everything the serviceman . . . has left behind," and this was a cause of major concern.[96]

It is difficult for us today to comprehend the sheer scale of these concerns about "the veteran problem" and the role that readjustment would play in postwar American life. These concerns with the veteran's return to civilian life had important social implications for postwar America and it's unsurprising that they should surface in the period's film noir, especially through its recurrent tropes of uncertainty, estrangement, and the destabilized spaces of home in the "readjustment" narratives of film noir, as we shall see in Chapter 8.

Notes

1 Margaret Rhodes Peattie, *The Return* (New York: William Morrow, 1944), 8–9.

2 James Jones, *Whistle* (1978; New York: Open Road Integrated Media, 2011), 41.

3 See for example Paul Schrader, "Notes on *Film Noir*," *Film Comment* (Spring 1972) in Silver and Ursini, *Film Noir Reader*, 54–55.

4 Arthur Miller, "Belief in America" from *Situation Normal* (1944), repr. in Steven R. Centola, ed., *Arthur Miller: Echoes Down the Corridor: Collected Essays 1944–2000* (New York: Penguin, 2001) 31.

5 For two notable exceptions, see Robert Francis Saxe, *Settling Down: World War II Veterans' Challenge to the Postwar* Consensus (Houndmills: Palgrave Macmillan, 2007), 83–115; Mark Osteen, *Nightmare Alley: Film Noir and the American Dream* (Baltimore: Johns Hopkins Press, 2013), 77–105.

6 On the Foucauldian concept of discourse, see for instance, Michel Foucault, *Discipline and Punish: The Birth of the Prison*, trans. Alan Sheridan (1975, London: Penguin, 1991).

7 Tellingly, the inclusion of "readjustment" in the formal title of the bill ("The Serviceman's Readjustment Act of 1944") had little popular appeal. On the GI Bill, see Michael J. Bennett, *When Dreams Came True: The GI Bill and the Making of Modern America* (Washington, DC: Brassey's, 1996); Edward Humes, *Over Here: How the G.I. Bill Transformed the American Dream* (New York: Houghton Mifflin Harcourt, 2006); Suzanne Mettler, *Soldiers to Civilians: The G.I. Bill and the Making of the Greatest Generation* (New York: Oxford University Press, 2007); Glenn C. Altschuler and Stuart M. Blumin, *The G.I. Bill: A New Deal for Veterans* (New York: Oxford University Press, 2009).

8 See George K. Pratt, *Soldier to Civilian: Problems of Readjustment* (New York: McGraw-Hill, 1944); Willard Waller, *The Veteran Comes Back* (New York: Dryden Press, 1944); Dixon Wecter, *When Johnny Comes Marching Home* (Cambridge, MA: Houghton Mifflin, 1944); Charles G. Bolte, *The New Veteran* (New York: Reynal and Hitchcock, 1945); Benjamin C. Bowker, *Out of Uniform* (New York: Norton, 1946); Samuel A. Stouffer et al., *The American Soldier*, Vol. 1, *Adjustment During Army Life* and Vol 2, *Combat and its Aftermath* (Princeton, NJ: Princeton University Press, 1949); Robert J. Havighurst et al., *The American Veteran Back Home: A Study of Veteran Readjustment* (New York: Longmans, Green, 1951); John C. Sparrow, *History of Personnel Demobilization in the United States Army* (Washington, DC: Department of the Army [No. 20-210] July 1952). Histories of the Second World War veteran include Davis R. B. Ross, *Preparing for Ulysses: Politics and Veterans During World War II* (New York: Columbia University Press, 1969); Thomas Childers, *Soldier From the War Returning: The Greatest Generation's Troubled Homecoming from World War II* (Boston: Houghton Mifflin Harcourt, 2009); Saxe, *Settling Down*. See also Studs Terkel, *"The Good War": An Oral History of World War II* (New York: New Press, 1984).

On the returning veteran in American history, see Richard Severo and Lewis Milford, *The Wages of War: When America's Soldiers Came Home—From Valley Forge to Vietnam* (New York: Simon and Schuster, 1989).

9 Waller, *Veteran Comes Back*, 13. (Italics in original.)

10 Bowker, *Out of Uniform*, 27.

11 See for instance Maxwell Droke, *Goodbye To G.I: How To Be a Successful Civilian* (New York: Abingdon-Cokesbury, 1945); Morton Thompson, *How To Be a Civilian* (Garden City, NY: Doubleday, 1946).

12 Merle Miller, *That Winter* (New York: William Sloane Associates, 1948), 65.

13 Cabell Phillips, *The 1940s: Decade of Triumph and Trouble* (New York: Macmillan, 1975), 275, 279.

14 Sparrow, *History of Personnel Demobilization in the United States Army*, 21–22.

15 Phillips, *1940s*, 276, 279. On economic reconversion, see Joseph C. Goulden, *The Best Years, 1945–1950* (New York: Atheneum, 1976), 91–107.

16 See for example Goulden, *Best Years*, 91–92.

17 Stouffer, *American Soldier*, Vol. 2, 598.

18 August B. Hollingshead, "Adjustment to Military Life," *American Journal of Sociology* 51 (1946), 446.

19 Wecter, *When Johnny Comes Marching Home*, 510.

20 Pratt, *Soldier to Civilian*, 149.

21 Havighurst et al., *American Veteran Back Home*, 26–27.

22 Ibid., 77.

23 See, for example, James H. Bedford, *The Veteran and His Future Job: A Guide-Book for the Veteran* (LA: Society for Occupational Research, 1946).

24 Ibid., 94. See also Wecter, *When Johnny Comes Marching Home*, 534–35.

25 See for example Edith Efron, "Old Jobs, or New Ones, for the Veterans?" *New York Times Magazine* (18 March 1945), 11, 41–42.

26 Havighurst, *American Veteran Back Home*, 117.

27 See for example Congressman John E. Rankin, chairman of the House
Veterans Committee, in Ross, *Preparing for Ulysses*, 108–10. See also
Bennett, *When Dreams Came True*, 154–80.

28 Havighurst, *American Veteran Back Home*, 117.

29 Walter H. Eaton, "Research on Veterans' Adjustment," *American Journal of
Sociology* 51 (1946), 486.

30 Havighurst, *American Veteran Back Home*, 116.

31 Eaton, "Research on Veterans' Adjustment," 486.

32 Terence Ball, "The Politics of Social Science in Postwar America," in Lary
May, ed., *Recasting America: Culture and Politics in the Age of the Cold War*
(Chicago: University of Chicago Press, 1989), 77.

33 Ball, "Politics of Social Science," 81.

34 Sociologists were frequently appointed to positions on bodies responsible
for the administration of veterans' issues, including legislation like the GI
Bill, and often served to chronicle the official accounts of demobilization and
readjustment as, for example, in Stouffer's account of *The American Soldier*,
undertaken through the Information and Education Division of the War
Department.

35 See, for example, the symposium issue, "Human Behavior in Military
Society," *American Journal of Sociology* 51 (1946).

36 Bowker, *Out of Uniform*, 24.

37 Wecter, *When Johnny Comes Marching Home*, 503.

38 See Lee Kennett, *G.I. The American Soldier in World War II* (New York:
Scribner's, 1987), 74–75.

39 That is, "a place of residence and work where a large number of like-situated
individuals, cut off from the wider society for an appreciable period of time,
together lead an enclosed, formally administered round of life." Erving
Goffman, *Asylums: Essays on the Social Situation of Mental Patients and
Other Inmates* (1961; Harmondsworth: Penguin, 1980), 11.

40 Waller, *Veteran Comes Back*, 31.

41 Havighurst, *American Veteran Back Home*, 23.

42 Edgar L. Jones, "The Soldier Returns," *Atlantic Monthly* (January 1944), 42.

43 Pratt, *Soldier to Civilian*, 7.

44 Waller, *Veteran Comes Back*, 193.

45 Christopher La Farge, "Soldier Into Civilian," *Harper's* (March 1945), 344. See
also Hollingshead, "Adjustment to Military Life," 446; Waller, *Veteran Comes
Back*, 32, 35.

46 Pratt, *Soldier to Civilian*, 13.

47 Wecter, *When Johnny Comes Marching Home*, 505.

48 Waller, *Veteran Comes Back*, 20, 98, 100. "4-F" is a designation of those
unfit for military service, a category of persons widely distrusted and disliked
by servicemen.

49 Ibid., 100.

50 Edgar L. Jones, "One War Is Enough," *Atlantic Monthly* (February 1946), 49.

51 Bowker, *Out of Uniform*, 25.

52 Ibid.

53 Ibid., 25–30.

54 Jones, "Soldier Returns," 49. On this "souvenir" culture, see John W. Dower, *War Without Mercy: Race and Power in the Pacific War* (New York: Pantheon, 1993), 61–66, 70–71; Gerald F. Linderman, *The World Within War: America's Combat Experience in World War II* (Cambridge, MA: Harvard University Press, 1999), 77–78, 180–83.

55 Ralph Crane, "Arizona war worker writes her Navy boyfriend a thank-you note for the Jap skull he sent her," *Life* (May 22, 1944), 35.

56 See for example, Edward A. Strecker and Kenneth E. Appel, *Psychiatry in Modern Warfare* (New York: Macmillan, 1945); Roy R. Grinker and John P. Spiegel, *Men Under Stress* (Philadelphia: Blakiston, 1945); William C. Menninger, *Psychiatry in a Troubled World: Yesterday's War and Today's Challenge* (New York: Macmillan, 1948).

57 See for example, Herbert I. Kupper, *Back To Life: The Emotional Readjustment of Our Veterans* (New York: Fischer, 1945); Howard Kitching, *Sex Problems of the Returned Veteran* (New York: Emerson, 1946).

58 See Bowker, *Out of Uniform*, 32–36, 80–85; Waller, *Veteran Comes Back*, 165–69; Wecter, *When Johnny Comes Marching Home*, 545–48; Pratt, *Soldier to Civilian*, 81–112.

59 Paul Goodman, "Sailor's Money," in Taylor Stoehr, ed., *The Facts of Life: Stories, 1940-1949* (Santa Barbara, CA: Black Sparrow Press, 1979), 315.

60 Havighurst, *American Veteran Back Home*, 31.

61 On profligacy, see Waller, *Veteran Comes Back*, 56–59.

62 Howard Brotz and Everett Wilson, "Characteristics of Military Society," *American Journal of Sociology* 51 (1946), 375.

63 On gambling, promiscuity, looting, and black marketeering, see Malcolm R. McCallum, "The Study of the Delinquent in the Army," *American Journal of Sociology* 51 (1946), 479–82.

64 Ibid., 481–82.

65 See Bowker, *Out of Uniform*, 117–35; Paul Fussell, *Wartime: Understanding and Behavior in the Second World War* (New York: Oxford University Press, 1989), 251–67.

66 See Frederick Elkin, "The Soldier's Language," *American Journal of Sociology* 51 (1946), 419.

67 Ibid.

68 Henry Elkin, "Aggressive and Erotic Tendencies in Army Life," *American Journal of Sociology* 51 (1946), 411.

69 Ibid.

70 Ibid., 413.

71 Bowker, *Out of Uniform*, 145; Waller, *Veteran Comes Back*, 128.

72 Anonymous, "Informal Organization in the Army," *American Journal of Sociology* 51 (1946), 367.

73 Waller, *Veteran Comes Back*, 38.

74 Brotz and Wilson, "Characteristics of Military Society," 374–75.

75 Goulden, *Best Years*, 50.

76 Hollingshead, "Adjustment to Military Life," 446.

77 Bowker, *Out of Uniform*, 21.

78 See Havighurst, *American Veteran Back Home*, 72; Wecter, *When Johnny Comes Marching Home*, 504; Waller, *Veteran Comes Back*, 42–43, 176–80.

79 Hollingshead, "Adjustment to Military Life," 445.

80 See Bowker, *Out of Uniform*, 62–67.

81 Robert E. Nisbet, "The Coming Problem of Assimilation," *American Journal of Sociology* 50 (1945), 262.

82 Ibid., 267.

83 Robert Lowry, *Casualty* (New York: New Directions, 1946), 56.

84 William O'Neill, *A Democracy at War: America's Fight at Home and Abroad in World War II* (Cambridge, MA: Harvard University Press, 1995), 266.

85 See Kennett, *G.I.*, 73–76; Linderman, *World Within War*, 302–04.

86 Wecter, *When Johnny Comes Marching Home*, 499.

87 See J.O. Reinemann, "Extra-Marital Relations With Fellow Employee in War Industry as a Factor in Disruption of Family Life," *American Sociological Review* 10 (1945), 399–404.

88 See Wecter, *When Johnny Comes Marching Home*, 499; Kennett, *G.I.*, 75–76; Linderman, *World Within War*, 310–11. For a fictional account of the effect of a "Dear John," see Lowry, *Casualty*, 56–68.

89 Edward C. McDonagh, "The Discharged Serviceman and His Family," *American Journal of Sociology* 51 (1946), 451.

90 W. Edgar Gregory, "The Idealization of the Absent," *American Journal of Sociology* 50 (1944), 54.

91 See Rose M. Rabinoff, "While Their Men Are Away," *Survery Midmonthly* 81(1945), 110–13.

92 See for example Susan M. Hartmann, *The Home Front and Beyond: American Women in the 1940s* (Boston: Twayne, 1982), 163–65.

93 See for example, Constantine Panunzio, "War and Marriage," *Social Forces* 21 (1943), 442–45.

94 Reuben Hill, "The American Family: Problem or Solution?" *American Journal of Sociology* 53 (1947), 125.

95 Edward C. McDonagh and Louise McDonagh, "War Anxieties of Soldiers and Their Wives," *Social Forces* 24 (1945), 198.

96 Havighurst, *American Veteran Back Home*, 26. See also McDonagh, "Discharged Serviceman and His Family," 453–54; Waller, *Veteran Come Back*, 31; Bowker, *Out of Uniform*, 143–44; Pratt, *Soldier to Civilian*, 113–16, 123–26; Donald Becker, "The Veteran: Problem and Challenge," *Social Forces* 25 (1946), 97–98.

8

The veteran and the readjustment narrative

The thing that scares me most is that everybody's going to try to rehabilitate me.

AL STEPHENSON (Fredric March), *The Best Years of Our Lives* (1946)

Such were the fears and anxieties about the returning veteran, it's unsurprising that he should figure as a presence in postwar films. Veterans feature explicitly as central characters in several postwar films noir, especially during the period 1946–49 where they can be seen as a noir subcategory. Concerns about veteran readjustment became increasingly pressing by the end of the war, concerns that often appeared in what we might call the "readjustment narrative," a generic category identifiable in postwar noir explicitly concerned with the figure of the returning veteran. These narratives constitute what can be seen as a production cycle during the period 1946–49 with an occasional earlier title such as *Cornered* (1945). The readjustment narrative deals with ex-servicemen characters and their problematic return to civilian life.[1]

Other readjustment narratives deal implicitly with veteran figures, often coded through characters who have been away and have recently returned, such as Johnny Farrell (Glenn Ford) in *Gilda* (1946) and Frank Chambers (John Garfield) in *The Postman Always Rings Twice* (1946). We can also see this figure in some of the period's other genres such as the "psychological" western which share some of the thematic and stylistic characteristics of film noir such as Jim Garry (Robert Mitchum) in *Blood on the Moon* (1948). As in many postwar film narratives, absence and return is a frequent trope. A character like Frankie Madison (Burt Lancaster) in *I Walk Alone* (1948), recently released after a prison sentence, can also imply the figure of a serviceman whose return necessitates coming to terms with a society that has changed in his absence and to which he no longer belongs. Such postwar gangster narratives, as Jonathan Munby has pointed out, were often "built around the metaphor of return," which can be seen as "allegorical structures for the GI returning home to find it irrevocably altered."[2]

Some veteran narratives have also been classified under the rubric of the "social problem" film. The social problem in such narratives often emanates from a physical injury where readjustment involves physical rehabilitation. Examples include *Pride of the Marines* (1945), a biopic based on the real-life story of Al Smidt (John Garfield), a marine blinded by a grenade at Guadalcanal, and the paraplegic lieutenant Ken (Marlon Brando) in *The Men* (1950).[3] Most veteran narratives of the period, however, are classified as film noir. Before investigating these, though, we can usefully consider what might be seen as a quasi-official version of the readjustment narrative: *The Best Years of Our Lives* (1946).

"Am I really home?" veteran readjustment in *The Best Years of Our Lives*

The Best Years of Our Lives was the period's most explicit dramatization of "the veteran problem" and a flagship production for the new postwar social problem film. It achieved phenomenal popular and critical success, winning nine Academy Awards, including Best Picture and Best Director for William Wyler.[4] The film was marketed as a uniquely American epic, with national advertising appeared under the rubric of "America" and assiduously promoted its "visionary" sense of postwar American society.[5] Its budget of $3,000,000 was far above the industry average of $665,000 for that year.[6] The religiose tenor of the advertisement describes the film's genesis quite literally in biblical terms ("In the beginning was the word"), casting producer Sam Goldwyn as a kind of Old Testament prophet. The advertising copy implies that Goldwyn underwent a kind of epiphany when, "providentially," he came upon a photograph of returning servicemen in *Time* magazine.[7] The film's critical reception was linked to the discourse of readjustment via reports by veteran commentators in which reviews often functioned as news about the veteran problem and the narrative's realism was equated with its social significance.[8] *Best Years of Our Lives* is the most self-consciously affirmative readjustment narrative that sets out the stories of three returning veterans.

The first to arrive home is Homer Parrish (Harold Russell). Russell, who lost both hands in a training accident, was the subject of a navy training film, *Diary of a Sergeant* (1945) and Wyler cast Russell as Homer after having seen this film. Several army orientation films showed disabilities in explicit terms, but such representation in a mainstream film was unprecedented.[9] The overwhelming concern for Homer is how his sweetheart Wilma (Cathy O'Donnell)—literally, the girl next door—will react to his disability, and there is a narrative implication that if he can reestablish his relationship with her, then he can reestablish himself in other walks of life too. Accompanied home by two other discharged servicemen, Fred Derry (Dana Andrews) and Al Stephenson (Fredric March), Fred commends the navy for its rehabilitation program ("they sure trained that kid how to use those hooks"); but when we see him arrive home standing almost paralyzed in Wilma's embrace, Al points out that "they couldn't train him to put his arms around his girl." We see him taunted by local children or otherwise treated as a tragic figure. Ultimately, he marries Wilma and it will be through her that his readjustment is assured. But the prospects for Homer and his friends are less assured than the narrative suggests. In the novel on which the film is based, Homer's inability to cope with his readjustment causes his attempted suicide, one of several instances in which the film ameliorates the novel's darker narrative.[10]

Fred's homeward journey is even more fraught. Indeed, he cannot even find out where home is and even the whereabouts of his wife are uncertain. Married to Marie (Virginia Mayo), their married life has amounted to less than three weeks together. Fred is returning to a war marriage in which husband and wife scarcely know each other. He learns that Marie has taken a downtown apartment and got a job in a nightclub. Even when he finally locates her address, he can't get into her apartment building and, portentously, it is only after another man has done so that he can. Marie may have been the airman's glamorous pinup bride, but she is now a "good-time" girl with a profligate, promiscuous lifestyle. He is ousted from Marie's apartment after challenging another ex-serviceman he finds making himself at home there ("Have *you* had any trouble getting adjusted?" Fred angrily demands of him.)

Fred also realizes that his employment prospects are poor following a demoralizing interview at the drugstore where he used to work with a store manager who, while noting Fred's "splendid" service record, points out that it is now irrelevant. Fred returns reluctantly to his old job as a soda-jerk, discovering how unprepossessing nonentities have prospered at home during the war years.[11] His drugstore uniform is now a caricature of his military one. The ex-flyer resolves to "bail out" and by the end of the film he has returned to the airport where he first arrived. Adrift and demoralized, he doesn't care about his future destination, nor even the direction he should take. He leaves the decision to chance, depending on which plane leaves first.[12] But like Homer's Wilma, the agent of Fred's readjustment will be Al's daughter Peggy (Teresa Wright), whose civic-mindedness is repeatedly contrasted with

Marie's "slacker" attitude. Marie, in this sense, represents Fred's prewar self and Peggy his postwar future.

Al's future appears to be more secure as he returns to his former job as a bank manager, now promoted to vice president with responsibility for GI loans. But his appointment may be more cynical than it might appear, with the bank's commercial interests likely to result in the rejection of a substantial number of loan applications from veterans lacking the requisite collateral. Siding with "the men," Al exceeds his authority and countermands official policy, jeopardizing his career. In a speech at a formal dinner, he bitterly attacks the bank's "collateral imperative" while getting determinedly drunk. He begins to look increasingly reckless and unstable. His wife Milly (Myrna Loy) marks off the number of drinks he consumes and she, like Wilma and Peggy, will establish the means by which he will be redeemed through the familiar patterns of domestic stability. Nevertheless, his disillusionment and alcoholic instability are so acute that they may not be so easily overcome as the narrative suggests. The former "hit-the-beach" sergeant finds himself being peremptorily forced back into an old familiar pattern that now looks very different or, perhaps, too much the same.

Wandering in the aircraft "graveyard" sequence at the end of the film, Fred assumes that the aircraft there are, like himself, destined to be scrapped until the foreman informs him otherwise. "This is no junk," he says. "We're using this material for building prefabricated houses." Fred asks the foreman for a job. The foreman, eyeing him with steady appraisal, recognizes in Fred the same doughty quality that the banker Al had earlier identified in the veterans with "GI collateral." Fred gets the job and is seen, symbolically, pulling off his old flying jacket in anticipation of his new prospects, helping to build the new houses in postwar suburbia. He has already confided in Peggy his dream of "a nice little house for my wife and me, out in the country, in the suburbs, anyway," and the narrative suggests that he will eventually achieve his dream. But despite the film's optimistic narrative agenda, it takes little account of how comprehensively Fred has been disavowed by civilian society since his return. (In the novel, Fred almost commits an armed bank robbery.)[13] The deus ex machina of a junkyard job and the narrative implication that from here he will eventually be able to "work his way up" remains an uncertain trajectory.

Film noir and the readjustment narrative

The quasi-official readjustment narrative of *Best Years of Our Lives* strives unconvincingly for an affirmative closure, but the period's "unofficial" noir narratives are invariably pessimistic about postwar prospects. Take, for example, *The Blue Dahlia* (1946), which can be seen as a kind of counter-version

FIGURE 8.1 "I didn't know these things were ever blue." Returning veteran Johnny Morrison (Alan Ladd) in *The Blue Dahlia* (George Marshall, 1946).

of *Best Years of Our Lives*, also featuring the return of three ex-servicemen. Johnny Morrison (Alan Ladd) returns home to find his wife Helen (Doris Dowling) at a raucous party, blatantly having an affair with Eddie Harwood (Howard Da Silva), owner of the Blue Dahlia nightclub. Like Fred's Marie, Johnny's wife Helen has spent the war years as a "good-time girl." A drunken Helen tells Johnny that their son Dicky didn't die of diphtheria as he had been led to believe but was killed in a car crash caused by Helen's drunk driving. The world to which Johnny has returned seems utterly corrupt and decadent. "I didn't know these things were ever blue," says Johnny, looking at a vase of dahlias sent as "calling cards" by Helen's lover, Harwood (see Figure 8.1). Like the nightclub's neon sign and Harwood's dandyish buttonholes, they are emblematic of falsity, corruption, and licentiousness.

Helen is found murdered and Johnny becomes the prime suspect. With the aid of his two navy buddies Buzz (William Bendix) and George (Hugh Beaumont) together with Harwood's wife Joyce (Veronica Lake), Johnny tries to clear his name. Evidence points to Buzz who has a neuropsychiatric condition. It is significant that Raymond Chandler's screenplay originally did have Buzz as the murderer, committed while suffering from a blackout, but Chandler was instructed by Paramount to alter the script following objections from the Navy Department who wouldn't countenance the portrayal of a serviceman with combat injuries (what we would call today posttraumatic stress disorder) as a murderer.[14] The unintended consequence of this screenplay change was not only to exonerate both ex-servicemen but also to enable them to carry out their own investigation, which would reveal some of the faults and failings of the civilian society to which they had returned.

This notion of a veteran assuming an investigatory role became a feature of several postwar films otherwise categorized as film noir, and it is through a cycle of private eye crime thrillers that we can find a useful point of entry into some of the key discourses surrounding the returning veteran. Nick Heffernan has identified a cycle of around a dozen films in the period 1945–49 which feature as their protagonist a veteran obligated to undertake an investigatory function.[15] The ideological work of these narratives can be seen in the veteran's investigations, which "compel him to re-evaluate domestic civilian life in the light of his overseas wartime ordeal. This experience," says Heffernan, "grants him the alienated, detached and in some cases oppositional consciousness of the social critic, forming a lens through which he interrogates the new social order constructed in his absence."[16] As we have seen in the previous chapter, the returning veteran was seen as an ambivalent figure, often as an outsider, and by using the investigative structure of the private eye narrative, the filmmakers in Heffernan's survey were able to create their own critique of the postwar social order via their screen protagonists. As Heffernan also points out, some of those filmmakers were "committed leftists" who would fall foul of the anticommunist blacklist. Conversely, these narratives were shaped by Hollywood's storytelling conventions and the "rising tide of postwar conservatism" which prescribed a comforting and affirmative view of the social order. "Vacillating between social critique and mythic reassurance, the war-veteran private-eye series points to a set of broader tensions within postwar America connected to the displacement of a New Deal ethos of progressive reform by the corporate authoritarianism of the emergent Cold War epoch."[17]

Heffernan's approach raises some useful questions, not only for the readjustment narrative but also for noir studies. First, we should note that *all* the films in his survey are invariably classed as film noir.[18] Second, Heffernan's methodology offers a welcome antidote to the paucity of those generalized claims often made about the presumed relation between film noir and the sociopolitical factors of the postwar period. This methodology has a sharp historical focus, drawing on a specific five-year period, precisely located within a specific generic subcategory providing generic coherence through the common protagonist of the veteran investigator. This is also a study that, remarkably, eschews any use of the term "film noir."

Too Late for Tears (1949) can be seen as a variation of the kind of veteran investigator discussed by Heffernan. In one of those spectacularly random noir occurrences, Jane Palmer (Lizabeth Scott) and her husband Alan (Arthur Kennedy) are driving to a party in the Hollywood Hills one night when their convertible is mistakenly taken for the drop of a bag containing $60,000 thrown onto the back seat. Clearly the proceeds of a crime, Alan wants to turn in the money to the police. Jane, however, desperately wants to keep it. "The money was literally thrown in our laps," she says. The conflict is between Jane's frustrated desire for wealth and social status and Alan's failure to provide it.

"We were white-collar poor, middle-class poor," she says, "the kind of people who can't quite keep up with the Joneses and die a little every day because they can't." Danny Fuller (Dan Duryea) arrives at the Palmers' apartment purporting to be a detective. Later, Jane kills her husband, aided and abetted by Fuller who, falling under her sway, becomes her accomplice. A stranger calling himself Don Blake (Don DeFore) arrives at the apartment, claiming to be a friend of Alan's, having served with him during the war. Blake later reveals to Alan's sister Kathy (Kristine Miller) that he is really called Blanchard and the brother of Jane's first husband assumed to have committed suicide but whom Blake believes was murdered by Jane while he was overseas. Through Blake's investigation as unofficial detective, Jane is revealed to have killed Alan, Fuller, and probably her first husband too. When the police move in on her in her luxury hotel in Mexico, she falls from the balcony, her corpse elegantly splayed out on the ground with banknotes fluttering down around her, a morbid noir image of futility (see Figure 8.2).

As with many films noir of the period, there is a deep dislike and distrust of conspicuous wealth and high living. We see Jane in an opulent suite, flirting with a tuxedoed playboy at the hotel, her insatiable desire for the high life represented as a form of pathology. In some ways she can be seen as a postwar incarnation of Phyllis Dietrichson in *Double Indemnity*, although she more closely resembles Margot Shelby (Jean Gillie) in *Decoy* (1946) in a kind of maniacal desire for riches. Certainly, the luxurious hotels and nightclubs such as those in films like *Too Late for Tears* and *The Blue Dahlia* are repeatedly criticized in films noir of the time. There are also several instances where servicemen like Johnny Morrison and Fred Derry return to find a corrupt and affluent society in which their cheating wives have found congenial places for themselves. Attracted to the glamorous high life provided by the crooked entrepreneurs who have profited opportunistically by their wartime business ventures, these women are similarly the object of narrative critique. See for example Toni Blackburn (Faye Emerson) in *Nobody Lives Forever* (1946);

FIGURE 8.2 Jane Palmer (Lizabeth Scott) falls to her death in *Too Late for Tears* (Byron Haskin, 1949).

Helen Kenet (Dorothy Patrick) in *The High Wall* (1948); Sally Lee (Dorothy Hart) in *Undertow* (1949); and Polly Faber (Barbara Lawrence) in *Thieves' Highway* (1949). The returning veteran husband/fiancé in these films—Nick Blake (John Garfield), Steven Kenet (Robert Taylor), Tony Reagan (Scott Brady), and Nick Garcos (Richard Conte)—cannot afford to provide his wife with the lavish lifestyle she wants. Paradoxically, it is often the figure of the returning veteran—the outsider—who is possessed of an integrity that enables him to challenge the values of an extravagant and decadent society at home.

Another key readjustment narrative is Elia Kazan's *Boomerang!* (1947), one of the "docu-noirs" produced after the war. Based on a true story, the narrative focuses on a veteran, John Waldron (Arthur Kennedy), who is accused of the murder of a priest, Father George Lambert (Wyrley Birch). The evidence against Waldron appears overwhelming. Seven witnesses pick him out in a police lineup and testify to having seen him commit the crime and Waldron later signs a statement admitting his guilt. Waldron's readjustment underwrites the narrative that is primarily concerned with the processes of a criminal justice system tied to the political and commercial ramifications of a Connecticut town. He has "a good war record" but has been unable to get the kind of job he wants, to "start a small business, make something of myself," he says. Mac McCreery (Robert Keith), a reform politician, and banker Paul Harris (Ed Begley) have vested political interests in the state's attorney Henry Harvey (Dana Andrews) securing Waldron's conviction and they offer him the inducement of the office of state governor if he wins the case. Meanwhile, T. M. Wade (Taylor Holmes), proprietor of the local newspaper and an opposition figure, exploits the situation for his own electoral advantage, attacking the police and the city government. "I don't care whether he's guilty or not," says Wade. "I've got to win an election."

The film opens with a 360° pan of a quiet Connecticut town with a voice-over extolling its ordinariness, part of the "backbone" of small-town America. This is followed by a scene at night where we see Father Lambert pausing on Main Street to light his pipe when a gun enters the frame, pointing at the back of his head before shooting him dead (see Figure 8.3). From here, we might expect the story to follow the kind of narrative pattern characteristic of the de Rochement semidocumentary style with an agency point of view demonstrating the police search for the killer and his eventual apprehension. However, the film sets up that expectation only to deny it. Far from being an agency narrative, *Boomerang!* represents a trenchant critique of several institutional aspects of the small-town ethos it seemingly extols. To begin with, there is a critique of the police. With increasing political pressure on the police to find the killer, a series of scenes show suspects—that is, any man wearing a dark coat and light hat—being picked up, and sometimes roughed up, as hundreds are brought in for questioning.

FIGURE 8.3 Murder on Main Street: Father Lambert (Wyrley Birch) in *Boomerang!* (Elia Kazan, 1947).

Waldron is subjected to a protracted interrogation conducted by police chief Robby Robinson (Lee J. Cobb) with psychiatrist Dr. Rainsford (Dudley Sadler). The psychiatrist already has a pat explanation for Waldron's demeanor. "Just out of the Army," he says. "That might account for his bitterness a little" and his "difficulty of readjustment." The psychiatrist plays a remarkable role in the interrogation, hectoring Waldron with his rapid-fire "explanation" of the veteran's guilt:

> But you told us before you were sick of the black market, you were tired of being pushed around, you were tired of handouts and advice. You resented the people that had good jobs and money when you came out of the Army with nothing. You brooded on that, you brooded over it till you took that gun. You took the gun with the idea of getting even and when you saw Lambert on the street you made him the personification of every handout, every word of advice, and in a rage you shot him.

Waldron is worn down by the tough, unrelenting interrogation. He is made to sign a statement that he is incapable of reading as the police chief and the psychiatrist, tightly framed around him, extract his confession, Rainsford actually guiding his hand as he is incapable of signing it himself. The veteran here conveniently provides a ready-made scapegoat, presenting from the outset a predictable veteran "case." For Robinson, though, it "doesn't feel right" and he struggles with his part in the proceedings. In a curious coda to this scene, Robinson lifts up Waldron who has by now passed out after signing his confession and places him gently on a bed. "What a way to make a living," he says, a disaffected cop caught up in the corrupt world of small-town politics. Acknowledging inconsistencies in his own case, Harvey later casts doubt on the testimony of his own eyewitnesses and scuppers his own prosecution case so that Waldron is ultimately acquitted. Nevertheless, the portrayal of criminal justice in small-town America is shown to be cynical and self-serving.

Other readjustment noirs deal with the shadow of the wartime events. In *Act of Violence*, for example, the opening sequence contains several characteristic noir tropes. An establishing shot shows the New York skyline at night. On a deserted street, we see the unidentified figure of a man limping toward a darkened doorway. Seen from behind, he goes up the stairs of a dimly lit boarding house and enters a room. We can see now that he is wearing a rain-soaked trench coat and snap-brim fedora as he takes a pistol from a drawer and loads a magazine clip into it. The camera pans up to reveal the man's face for the first time. He looks grim and determined, his movements driven by a sense of urgency. He boards a Greyhound bus. The action changes to another scene in contrast to the first, beginning with a close-up of another man's face, Frank Enley (Van Heflin), a building contractor and guest of honor at the opening of a new housing development at a small Californian town. With his wife Edith (Janet Leigh) and young child, Enley is shown as an honored veteran and respected citizen in the community. The sunlit scene, in which Enley is publicly congratulated for his civic contribution, is in marked contrast to those depicting the shadowy, solitary figure we have seen at the beginning, Joe Parkson (Robert Ryan).

The notion of an unspecified "dark past" has often been cited by noir critics as a thematic feature of film noir. But in the postwar cycle of veteran readjustment films, that dark past is specified as the war, and in *Act of Violence* the connection between Enley and Parkson is related to a wartime incident when they were both prisoners of war in a German prison camp. Here, Parkson was one of a group of prisoners planning a tunnel escape. Enley, as senior officer, tried to persuade Parkson and the others to abandon the attempt as too dangerous. Unable to convince them, Enley informed the camp commandant of the escape plan, hoping to secure leniency for the men, but they were killed in the attempt, leaving Parkson as sole survivor. Enley's action may have been well-intentioned, but he was rewarded for informing on his fellow prisoners with privileges of extra rations that he readily accepted.

Here, an unspoken "dark past" haunts the daylight present. The first incidence of this can be seen when Parkson, newly arrived in LA, is shown crossing a street while a veterans' parade is in progress, cutting across their official march-past in a symbolic interruption of the public commemoration. Parkson's presence there evokes an unofficial past. Parkson makes his way to Enley's house and later to the lake where he has gone fishing, apparently with the intention of killing him, although for reasons we, and Edith, don't yet know. "A lot of things happened in the war that you wouldn't understand," says Enley to Edith. "Why should you, I don't even understand them myself."

The film exploits noir and gothic stylistics to render Parkson as a malevolent psychotic, hell-bent on destroying Enley's life, his deranged condition signified by the sinister scraping sound of his dragging foot, a menacing threat to an upright citizen and a vicious assault on his family home. Enley, in contrast, is to all outward appearances a happy family man who has prospered in the postwar years with a successful business building houses. Indeed, the scene showing Enley's new housing project is reminiscent of the houses in Bailey Park in *It's a Wonderful Life* (1946) and similarly suggestive of postwar optimism with its promise of affordable housing for returning veterans and their families. That promise has eluded Parkson, however, who looks as if he's spent the postwar years in dingy rooming houses like the one we have seen him in at the beginning. As he says to Edith when he forces his way into to their house: "He's got it nice here, hasn't he? Real nice." And so he has, at least until Parkson confronts him with his hidden past.

Other readjustment narratives focus on the failure of economic prosperity. *Side Street* (1949), for example, is the last title in the series of films noir directed by Anthony Mann in the 1940s. Like other examples of Mann's noir films, this is shot in semidocumentary style with considerable footage shot on location in New York City. It is also similar to the kind of postwar agency films providing a police perspective on city crime, here provided in an avuncular voice-over narration by Captain Anderson (Paul Kelly). At the same time, the film represents a departure from some of the noir conventions in veteran narratives.

Veteran Joe Norson (Farley Granger) is working as a part-time mailman following the failure of his gas station business. With his young wife Ellen (Cathy O'Donnell) pregnant, the couple are struggling to get by and Ellen expects to have her baby in a hospital charity ward. Joe's low-status job and poor prospects make him feel inadequate as a provider when he wants a private hospital room for Ellen. Seeing the chance to steal $200 from one of the offices on his round, he can't resist the temptation. Finding the office empty, he tries to open the filing cabinet containing the cash, but it is locked. Thwarted, he leaves the office and hurries down the hall where he sees directly before him the silhouetted shape of a fire ax in a rack, the viewer's perspective seeing him from below and through the rack as he stares at it. He returns to the office with the ax, forces the drawer open and takes the file containing the cash, discovering there considerably more than he anticipated, $30,000, money belonging to gangsters. From this moment he becomes increasingly enmeshed in a criminal underworld from which he can't escape.

In some ways this appears to be a paradigmatic noir plot in which an ordinary man finds himself caught up in a web of criminality not of his making. "This is the story of Joe Norson," the narrator intones. "No hero, no criminal, just human, like all of us." Actually, this is not strictly true. When Joe first tried to open the filing cabinet, he is succumbing to temptation and opportunity. But when he returns for a second attempt, with an ax, it has become a different kind of act, willed and deliberate. The placement of the ax before him is seemingly random—that familiar noir trope of chance taking a hand in the outcome—and the image of it appears extraordinary and surreal. Certainly there is a difference between the hope of finding an unlocked drawer and the act of axing it open. In both attempts he is visibly anguished, torn between what he wants and what he knows to be wrong.

Joe's dilemma is rooted in what the narrative posits as a failed postwar economy. He has modest aspirations, merely to run his own small business and provide for his wife and child. He has "done the right thing" in serving his country during the war. And yet now he can only find work as "a part-time letter-carrier, dreaming of the unattainable—a fur coat for his wife." Many believed that the postwar economy had done little to provide realistic employment opportunities for returning servicemen. Indeed, when Joe is obliged to explain to Ellen where he got the money, he fabricates a story about being given a job in "selling," a description bordering on a fantasist's idea of a salesman's job.[19]

At the end of the film, following a police chase, Joe is almost killed in a car crash and he is taken away in an ambulance, even managing a smile as he is reunited with Ellen. The "happy ending" is provided courtesy of the police department as Captain Anderson's reassuring voice-over attests. "Now that we know some of the facts," he says, "we can help him. He's gonna be all right." In some ways *Side Street* shows a more benign and paternalistic view of police work than in some of Mann's other agency noirs like *T-Men* (1948), although there is a powerful sense of police surveillance at work here too. The figure of the police captain narrates the story as a figure of almost omniscient awareness as we see him at the end, standing and watching, judging events. In common with many films noir of the period, the aerial viewpoints of the city at the beginning of the film work to show the vastness of the metropolis; but, with the captain's narration, they also point up the extent of surveillance in operation. The veteran Joe comes perilously close to ruination but learns his lesson just in time. His readjustment will be facilitated by family life, tempered by more modest ambitions and more realistic aspirations, no longer needing to prove himself with a fur coat for his wife.

A comparable case can be seen in *Quicksand* (1950) in the figure of Daniel Brady (Mickey Rooney). Brady is a navy veteran who has just finished a relationship with his girlfriend Helen (Barbara Bates) as he doesn't want to be tied down. "I spent four years in the Navy fighting for freedom," he says, "why get anchored down now?" Now working as a mechanic in a Santa Monica garage, he meets Vera Novak (Jeanne Cagney), a seductive blonde waitress whom he invites on a date. Short of cash and anxious to impress Vera, he "borrows" some money from the cash register. Vera is besotted with the idea of a high life beyond her means, symbolized by the fur coat she sees in a shop window. On their date, they stand before a shop window with Vera admiring the mink coat she covets. The two diminutive figures are reflected in the shop window appearing superimposed on the coat, looking almost like children gazing up at a toyshop.[20] Like Joe in *Side Street*, Brady is drawn inexorably into the world of crime by incremental degrees. As he desperately tries to cover up the original theft of the cash, he buys an expensive watch on credit and immediately pawns it in order to replace the stolen money, thereby committing another crime for which he is threatened with prosecution. He is irrevocably trapped by his first, seemingly incidental, act. "I feel like I'm being shoved into a corner and if I don't get out soon it'll be too late," he says. "Maybe it's too late already."

One of the recurrent features of such readjustment noirs is the narrative emphasis on the youth of the veteran. Farley Granger in *Side Street* provides a particularly expressive example in his role as Joe. In early scenes he seems like a dreamer, callow and inexperienced despite his war service. This is similarly true of Cathy O'Donnell as his wife Ellen, one of several early roles that saw her playing the part of the young, innocent, and "good" in such roles as Wilma, Homer's loyal girlfriend in *Best Years of Our Lives*. In contrast to Ellen's optimistic outlook, Granger's Joe has a perpetually haunted look, only intermittently alleviated by Ellen's sunnier disposition. Granger had previously starred with O'Donnell as the doomed lovers Keechie and Bowie in Nicholas Ray's noir *They Live by Night* (1948), where the newlyweds seem like a dark, hopeless travesty of young love. We can see similar emphasis in the preternaturally youthful Rooney in *Quicksand*. His role here as Brady plays against Rooney's familiar "wholesome" juvenile screen persona, derived from the series of MGM films in which he played Andy Hardy, beginning with *A Family Affair* (1937), and through several pairings with Judy Garland at the studio.[21]

Another readjustment narrative that deals with a veteran's inadvertent criminality is *Ride the Pink Horse* (1947), an adaptation of the novel of the same name by Dorothy B. Hughes.[22] Here, an ex-soldier called Gagin (Robert Montgomery) arrives at a small Mexican border town by Greyhound bus. Smartly dressed in suit and hat, he descends from the bus and in a single continuous take we see him enter the bus depot where he takes a gun out of his small case (too small, surely, for him to be staying there) and puts it in his pocket. He then takes a slip of paper, possibly a check, from the case and places it in a deposit box. Then, oddly, he buys a pack of chewing gum from a vending machine, chews some, and uses it to fix the deposit box key to the back of a wall map, the camera lingering pointedly on these unexplained actions. Unlike most films noir featuring veterans, there is no recognizable

American city location to which he is returning. He appears unfamiliar with the Mexican town and certainly looks out of place there among the local population we see and hear in an ambience that occasionally anticipates that of *Touch of Evil* (1958). An inscrutable figure, we cannot as yet understand his actions nor have much idea of who he is or what he is doing there. By the end of this long opening take, we have been shown a great deal, but we know practically nothing about the character or his motives. In a constrained performance style, Montgomery's Gagin has an expressionless look and walks starchly, adding to the enigmatic impression.

His sense of alienation is intensified when he is unable to find anywhere to stay, all the hotels being full for the local fiesta. He enters a taverna whereupon the music immediately stops and the customers fall silent, all staring at him. He orders whiskey but is served tequila and told there is "no change." Later, one of the customers, Pancho (Thomas Gomez) offers Gagin a place to stay. This turns out to be a makeshift canopy at Pancho's fairground carousel ride. Pancho's "house" looks surreal, a parody of domestic normality, and when we see Gagin shaving and dressing the following morning, it is reminiscent of a GI's field camp to which he has readily adapted. To Pancho, Gagin is "the man with no place." Gagin has come to San Pablo with the intention of blackmailing a gangster and war profiteer named Frank Hugo (Fred Clark) who murdered his friend Shorty Thompson. Gagin is approached by FBI agent Bill Retz (Art Smith) who is also in pursuit of Hugo and suspects that Gagin is in possession of incriminating evidence that could be used against him. "Why you're not a bad feller," Retz tells Gagin, "like the rest of the boys, all cussed up because you fought a war for three years and got nothing out of it but dangled ribbons."

It is unsurprising that French critics Borde and Chaumeton should single the film out for praise for its "enigmatic situations" and "barbarous poetry."[23] The whole ambience of the film seems almost otherworldly, a strange and alien landscape through which Gagin moves awkwardly and uncertainly, a foreign country that he can scarcely understand. In one sense, it is as if he is still in the Pacific war. A local native girl, Pila (Wanda Hendrix), latches onto him and he takes her to lunch in a smart restaurant. "You know it's kinda funny," he tells Pila, "for a minute I thought I was back in New Guinea again, only in New Guinea they're darker." "Who is?" she asks. "Girls," he tells her.

As with several veteran noirs, there is an undercurrent of sadistic violence. Gagin is savagely beaten while Carla (Rita Conde) looks on with sadistic gratification. Another scene shows Pancho being assaulted by two of Hugo's henchmen next to the carousel on which the badly injured Gagin lies hidden by Pila. The camera follows the revolving carousel around, repeatedly glimpsing the attack every time it comes full circle, the faces of the children becoming increasingly distraught with the amplified sounds of the beating and Pancho's cries, intercut with the fairground music, creating an expressionist soundtrack to the violence. At one point, feverish and delirious, he imagines himself back in the jungle war with his helpmeet Pila now cast in the role of his army buddy: "Attaboy, Shorty," he says to her, addressing her by the name of his dead comrade. Although the Mexicans in the film initially appear as Hollywood's stereotypical caricatures of the period, Gagin's tough demeanor and his barely concealed contempt toward the townspeople change while he is there. Both Pila and Pancho are viciously beaten but neither will betray him, and it is in this Mexican community that the "Americano" is helped, protected, and nursed by strangers.

In his analysis of the film, Mark Osteen sees a reborn Gagin achieve "restitution" whereby "he is able to forget the war, remodel himself, and start anew with the support of a woman and a friend."[24] In this sense, Osteen argues, he is able to achieve restitution like the three servicemen in *The Best Years of Our Lives* and Johnny Morrison in *The Blue Dahlia*. But like them, the effort to establish a successful "readjustment" through an affirmative narrative closure is unconvincing. It is true that he finally returns the check to Retz and abandons his attempt to blackmail Hugo, and that the conclusion of the film sees him walking toward the bus with the Federal Agent having switched his allegiance to "Uncle Sam" in helping to secure Hugo's indictment. It is also true that he has softened in demeanor and outlook, forming close ties of friendship with his Mexican companions. But, poised to return home, his injured arm in a sling, what is he returning to? He has already bitterly confided to Pancho about his faithless wife back home ("She's busy, with another guy. He's okay. He's got what it takes. Dough.") He is not quite one of the "haywire veterans" as Hugo earlier described him, but it is the sheer fantasy of the space of this Mexican interlude with its central image of the merry-go-round that distances him from the homecoming that we don't see. ("I dream all my horses is alive," Pancho tells Gagin.) There is no place for him to stay in the town nor any prospect for him to remain there with Pila. Indeed, their parting, monitored by Retz, sees him uttering a string of platitudes to her, while she is later seen regaling her young friends with the story of a relationship already becoming myth.

Readjustment narratives tend toward empathetic depictions of their veteran figures, but there is at least one notable exception. *Cape Fear* (1962), a late entry in the noir catalogs, is based on John D. MacDonald's novel *The Executioners*, originally published in 1957. Although the film makes no mention of the war, the novel is rooted in a wartime incident. Attorney Sam Bowden (Gregory Peck), then an army lieutenant, was a key witness in the court-martial of a sergeant, Max Cady (Robert Mitchum), for the rape of a fourteen-year-old girl. Released after serving thirteen years of a life sentence, Cady traces Bowden and begins terrorizing him and his family. In the film, Cady pointedly addresses Bowden as "counselor," but in the novel he repeatedly evokes his wartime rank. "He called me Lieutenant. He used it in every sentence. He made it sound like a dirty word."[25] Cady's malevolence toward Bowden was forged at his court-martial but deepened during his years in prison. His hatred of Bowden is only partly explained by the Lieutenant's testimony that convicted him. He despises Bowden because he is privileged. Cady intrudes upon his domestic space as an expression of his resentment for what is essentially the class difference between them, Bowden having had the advantages of "a fancy education and a commission."[26] As in *The Desperate Hours* (1955), another narrative that sees the invasion of domestic space by criminals, there is a strong element of class antagonism and resentment. As Cady puts it: "A man has a nice family and a boat like that and a job where he can take off when he feels like it, it must be nice. Go out into the lake and mess around. When you're locked up you think of things like that. You know. Like dreaming."[27]

For Cady, it's a question of redress: his drive to harm the Bowden family represents a kind of compensation for everything he has been denied. Cady describes to Bowden in some detail how on his release from prison he abducted his former wife and subjected her over several days to grotesque sexual humiliation. He does this partly to intimidate Bowden and partly to ensure that he is "getting the picture," not only of his viciousness and depravity, but also of his ability to penetrate into his family life. Much is made of the Bowden home and family life in both the novel and the film, a representative example of middle-class domestic affluence and comfort which has established itself after the war, at least for some.

There remains a residual sense of the war in the film. The scene at the marina in which a lascivious Cady is seen looking down at Bowden's young daughter Nancy (Lori Martin) is held in shot for a disconcertingly long time, and his leering remark—"Say, she's getting to be almost as juicy as your wife, ain't she?"—is calculated to rile Sam Bowden (Gregory Peck) and remind him of Cady's original crime. Even the way he wears his hat looks like a calculated gesture of intimidation. Repeatedly described in the narrative as an animal, the pursuit of Sam Bowden's wife and daughter at Cape Fear show Mitchum's Cady exuding bodily threat, his bare, barrel-chested torso is rendered as a terrifying form of primal power. In one sense Cady is rendered as the monster figure of the horror genre, and the film exploits horror tropes such as in the scene in which he shows up at Nancy's school. Cady is a violent psychopath, but he is also a controlled killer. He is resourceful, cunning, and adept at listening and watching. At the houseboat, he stakes out the terrain like a military operation, and in his attack he resembles nothing less than a highly trained professional soldier, slipping into the water with practiced skill, silently killing the detective guarding the houseboat without the use of weapons and without leaving a mark on him (see Figure 8.4). Max Cady may be one of the most horrific characterizations of veteran madness on film, but it's a

FIGURE 8.4 Commando killer: Robert Mitchum as Max Cady in *Cape Fear* (J. Lee Thompson, 1962).

madness that also speaks to social injustice in the postwar world in which some veterans have prospered while others have not.

Bogartian noir: Humphrey Bogart and the readjustment narrative

"I'll make you look as if you've lived."

DR. COLEY (Houseley Stevenson)
to Vincent Parry (Humphrey Bogart) in *Dark Passage* (1947)

Humphrey Bogart is uniquely emblematic of film noir and plays a major role in its iconography. There are several reasons for this. He starred in what critics routinely see as the first film noir, *The Maltese Falcon* (1941), subsequently appearing in many others across the "classic" period: *Conflict* (1945), *The Big Sleep* (1946), *Dark Passage* (1947), *Dead Reckoning* (1947), *The Two Mrs. Carrolls* (1947), *Key Largo* (1948), *Knock on Any Door* (1949), *Tokyo Joe* (1949), *In a Lonely Place* (1950), *The Enforcer* (1951), *The Desperate Hours* (1955), and, his last film, *The Harder They Fall* (1956). He also played military roles during the war years in such films as *Sahara* (1943), *Action in the North Atlantic* (1943), and *Passage to Marseilles* (1944), as well as in films with war settings such as *Casablanca* (1942) and *To Have and Have Not* (1944). These roles cumulatively configured the Bogart persona as a serviceman and, later, a returned veteran. Also, with his scarred lip, he carried bodily the implication of combat experience.

This persona was complex and ambivalent. Following his Broadway role as escaped convict Duke Mantee in Robert Sherwood's play *The Petrified Forest* in 1935, Bogart reprised the role in Warner Brothers' highly successful film version the following year, making him a star. A series of gangster roles followed in the 1930s, which saw Bogart typecast as a gangster at Warner

Brothers.[28] He was then subject to reinvention as private eye Sam Spade in *The Maltese Falcon* and, early in the war, the cynical expatriate Rick in *Casablanca*. Here, Bogart's self-serving loner ("I stick my neck out for nobody") can be seen as an expression of America's isolationist stance before Pearl Harbor and his subsequent "conversion" to the Allied cause is linked to the imperative of America's entry into the war. A similar conversion can be seen in Bogart's Harry Morgan in *To Have and Have Not*.[29]

Bogart might seem an unlikely romantic hero and his appearance at odds with most conceptions of a Hollywood star. Despite, or perhaps because of, his unorthodox star persona, Bogart was widely admired by French critics, some of whom were instrumental in the invention of film noir. Borde and Chaumeton, for example, see him as "a key film noir figure."[30] Drawn to the idea of the noir hero as a contradictory figure, they cite the example of "a man who's already middle-aged, old almost, and not particularly handsome" with Bogart as the "model" for such a type.[31] He "appears to be over the hill," they say, but note that he will "carve out a new career in the [noir] series."[32] Bogart embodies what can seem like a contradiction of Hollywood conventions. "A happy end has always been somewhat ridiculous in the case of Bogart," they say, "whose sad, desperate look it is essential to vindicate."[33]

Bogart's noir persona was further consolidated in what might be described as a noir obituary in *Cahiers du Cinéma* in 1957 by André Bazin who lamented the star's death. Like Borde and Chaumeton, Bazin, saw Bogart's persona emerge with "the *noir* crime film whose ambiguous hero he was to epitomize."[34] But epitomize how? Bazin contrasted Bogart with the kind of prewar Hollywood heroes of which Gary Cooper was the prototype: "handsome, strong, noble, expressing much more the optimism and efficiency of a civilization than its anxiety."[35] Bazin sees Cooper as symbolic of an upbeat postwar Americanism, while Bogart is the very opposite, one who "epitomized the immanence of death." Bazin cites Robert Lachenay [François Truffaut] on Bogart's deathly presence. "Each time he began a sentence he revealed a wayward set of teeth. The set of his jaw irresistibly evoked the rictus of a spirited cadaver, the final expression of a melancholy man who would fade away with a smile."[36] The Bogart persona admired by Bazin and other French critics took shape through a series of noir's readjustment narratives.

Take, for example, *Dark Passage*. Like *Lady in the Lake* (1947), the film draws on the use of a subjective camera to convey the point of view of its protagonist, here Vincent Parry (Bogart), a convict who escapes from San Quentin prison. For the first half of the film we don't see Parry at all but only what he sees. *Dark Passage* is an example of one of the postwar gangster narratives suggestive of veteran return and we can see Parry's return to his home town of San Francisco in similar terms. Wrongly convicted for the murder of his wife, Parry was convicted on the basis of the perjured testimony of Madge Rapo (Agnes Moorehead). To escape and clear his name, Parry needs to change his identity and in *Dark Passage*, this familiar noir trope takes a literal form as he is taken to a backstreet plastic surgeon who will give him a new face. From this point *Dark Passage* borrows many of the "transformation" tropes of the horror film. The doctor about to perform the operation appears in grotesque close-up, smoking a cigarette, and his insalubrious "surgery" is a forbidding location for the illicit operation, necessarily performed at night. After the operation, we see Parry making his way through the streets of San Francisco in the early morning light, his face swathed in bandages, in scenes reminiscent of Universal horror films of the 1930s. These location scenes look surreal, but they also evoke the iconography of servicemen with combat injuries in hospital with many of the subsequent scenes dealing with Parry's recuperation, nursed by Irene Jansen (Lauren Bacall).

Parry's "readjustment" compels him to clear his name and redress the injustice that has put him in prison, but in fact he fails to accomplish this. The narrative sidesteps the issue of what should be his exoneration and acquittal, allowing him to escape to Peru in a romantic rendezvous with Irene, his facial features now restored to those of a recognizable Bogart, evocative of his romantic lead five years earlier as Rick in *Casablanca* and echoing his romantic union with Lauren Bacall at the close of *To Have and Have Not* and *The Big Sleep*.[37] Here, however, the narrative closure cannot credibly promise much of a postwar future for Parry, now a fugitive in a Peruvian refuge and still on the run as he was at the beginning. The prospect of a redemptive relationship with Irene seems like a strange, artificial epilogue to the film. Nor is this an exile from home only for Parry and Irene: the narrative has pointedly shown virtually all its other characters as hopelessly isolated and lonely.

In another film noir the same year, *Dead Reckoning*, Bogart plays Captain Rip Murdoch, a veteran paratrooper recuperating with his friend Sergeant Johnny Drake (William Prince) from war injuries. Rip is seen at the beginning of the film as a fugitive in a church, recounting his story to a priest almost in the form of a confession. In a flashback, Rip and Johnny are returning to Washington where Johnny is to be awarded the Congressional Medal of Honor. Johnny mysteriously flees from the train and Rip investigates his friend's disappearance, trailing him to Gulf City, Florida. Rip discovers that his friend is really called Johnny Preston and that Drake was an assumed name he used to enlist. Rip learns that Preston, wanted for murder, created a new military identity for himself to avoid prosecution. Before Rip can locate him, Johnny is killed in a car crash. Rip's investigation leads him to Johnny's seductive but duplicitous girlfriend Coral Chandler (Lizabeth Scott) to whom he is attracted before she too is killed.

An unusual feature of *Dead Reckoning* is its narrative treatment of the relationship between the two servicemen. An early flashback shows the two army buddies on the train to Washington bantering about women in general and Johnny's girlfriend—"that blond"—in particular. Their locker-room talk is typical of men talking suggestively about women and yet there is a sense in which their exchanges seem contrived and unconvincing. In fact, there is greater narrative emphasis on the closeness of their relationship than on any each has had with a woman, a homosocial relationship that may be homosexual. Their close-knit relationship was forged in the shared experience of combat. "After what we'd been through," Rip tells the priest, "we could read each other's minds." When Coral asks Rip if he loves her, he replies evoking the memory of his dead comrade: "I loved him more," he tells her. The earlier prospect of a relationship with Coral is rendered impossible, although unlike the brutal dispatch of Brigid O'Shaugnessy (Mary Astor) by Bogart's Sam Spade in *The Maltese Falcon*, Coral is given a tender deathbed scene with Rip forgivingly guiding her toward acceptance of her imminent death. She appears in lucent white, the surreal image of a parachute unfurling and falling through black space, becoming a kind of honorary paratrooper as she dies.

The narrative dramatizes Rip's emotional uncertainty about his transition from his army life to a civilian one through what Frank Krutnik describes as "a chaotic circuit of conflicting allegiances, with Coral as: (i) Johnny's girl; (ii) Rip's rival in love for Johnny, and (iii) Rip's replacement for Johnny."[38] With social commentators wary of the "queer friendships" among soldiers, as we have seen in the previous chapter, the narrative offers no prospect of a "heteronormative" happy ending, and the residue of Rip's "conflicting allegiances" is likely to remain. There is a powerful implication, though, that Rip's real loss was Johnny, expressed a little guardedly, as if to a lover, in private valediction (see Figure 8.5). "I was thinking, now I won't have to say goodbye to Johnny," says Rip. "I remembered him in Berlin—crazy song he always sang. I used to say, you drive me nuts with it. Yeah, I used to

FIGURE 8.5 Remembering Johnny: Humphrey Bogart as Rip Murdoch in *Dead Reckoning* (John Cromwell, 1947).

say to him—well, let's just say I remembered Johnny, laughing, tough and lonesome. Let's just say that."

It's significant that in both *Dark Passage* and *Dead Reckoning* the redemptive power of a romantic union between the Bogart character and the female looks unconvincing or impossible. Indeed, one of the characteristics of postwar noir in its narratives of returning servicemen is precisely in its repudiation of the notion of readjustment provided through the structure of marriage, especially given Hollywood's enduring myth of the happy ending and the power of narrative to imply marital continuity after the end of the film. Film noir would often see the promise of love and marriage, often given as the servicemen's dream of home, as a kind of wretched impossibility. This can be seen in another readjustment narrative, *Key Largo* (1948), in which Bogart plays disillusioned veteran Frank McCloud, a former army major who arrives at Key Largo in Florida to visit the family of George Temple, killed in combat under his command. Staying at the Temples' rundown hotel, he finds it has been taken over by gangster Johnny Rocco (Edward G Robinson) and his henchmen. McCloud is powerless to act. Socially dislocated and something of a drifter since getting out of the army, he has abandoned his civilian career as a newspaper circulation manager and seems feckless and rootless. Eventually, he does take action, which results in the death of Rocco, and is romantically united with George Temple's widow Nora (Lauren Bacall). However, the remote and inhospitable Key seems to hold little promise for the union between the embittered war widow and the disaffected veteran. As in *Dark Passage* and *Dead Reckoning*, the prospects for readjustment look as unpromising in Key Largo as they had in Peru.

The last readjustment narrative to exploit Bogart's noir persona is Nicholas Ray's *In a Lonely Place* (1950), based on the novel by Dorothy B. Hughes. The film is ostensibly about the question of whether Dix Steele (Bogart) murdered Mildred Atkinson (Martha Stewart). The film can be seen as yet another readjustment narrative to deviate from the affirmative narrative agenda of *Best Years of Our Lives*. Today, *In a Lonely Place* is routinely classified as a film noir, but its generic makeup is a complex amalgam of domestic melodrama, police procedural, "docu-noir," and, as Dana Polan has suggested, female gothic.[39] Early scenes in the film show Steele with a volatile temper, and described by Captain Lochner (Carl Benton Reid) as "an erratic violent man." Steele becomes the main suspect in Mildred's murder, partly on the basis of circumstantial evidence and partly because of his record of assaults. Detectives are seen examining a sheaf of reports documenting a series of Steele's violent incidents that began, significantly, in 1946, just after the end of the war. One scene shows him frenziedly attacking a driver, almost killing him.

The narrative makes much of Steele's status as an ex-serviceman. He resumes an acquaintance with an old army buddy, Brub Nicolai (Frank Lovejoy), who is now a detective working on the Mildred Atkinson case. Recently married

FIGURE 8.6 "As an ex-GI . . . you know how to kill a person without using your hands": Humphrey Bogart as Dix Steele in *In a Lonely Place* (Nicholas Ray, 1950).

to Sylvia (Jeff Donnell), he has "settled down" after the war to contented married life and a steady job. Brub has a home life with Sylvia which promises the kind of recuperative domesticity which has so far eluded Steele, at least until he meets Laurel Gray (Gloria Graham). As we see them falling in love, it is clear that they are good for each other. Unable to work, Steele has become a washed-up screenwriter, but his relationship with Laurel brings an emotional warmth and domestic stability that enables him to work again. "She's a good guy," he says, in a way that seems reminiscent of army life. "I'm glad she's on my side. She's not coy or cute or corny."

But the question of Steele's guilt persists. To Captain Lochner, Steele's unemotional response to the news of Mildred's death and his cool reaction to the sight of gruesome photographs of her body seem suspicious. In a scene at the Nicolais' home, Steele directs Brub and Sylvia in a reenactment of Mildred's murder, reminding Brub that as "an ex-GI . . . you know how to kill a person without using your hands" (see Figure 8.6). The simulation gets out of hand and Sylvia is hurt and frightened. Dix seems to relish the experiment and looks as though he knows enough about the murder to suggest that he may have been Mildred's killer after all. Increasingly, the relationship between Dix and Laurel is riven and ultimately destroyed by corrosive mistrust. Like women in the female gothic, Laurel has seen enough violence in Steele's behavior to fear for her own life, and she plans to escape from him. At the same time, he comes to distrust her every move.

In Hughes's novel, Steele really is a serial killer and in the film's screenplay, as well as in a scene actually shot by Ray, he does kill Laurel.[40] And yet the ending devised by Ray seems even more desolate and hopeless than the novel's. Following their final confrontation, a phone call from the police exonerates Dix, but it comes too late. "Yesterday this would have meant so much to us," Laurel says. "Now it doesn't matter, it doesn't matter at all." As she speaks, we see Dix go down the stairs and exit through the archway of the apartment building, one of the bleakest departures in film noir. This is a far cry from the upbeat ending of *The Best Years of Our Lives*. The phrase written by Dix for his screenplay—"I was born when she kissed me; I lived a few short weeks while she loved me; I died when she left me"—becomes a kind of epitaph for his destroyed relationship with Laurel, resonating with a sense of the deathly Bogart for whom there can be no hope of a happy ending.

* * *

That denial of a happy ending is a pervasive feature of the readjustment narrative, especially in its insistence on the failed prospects for postwar marriage. I will close with an example of one of the strangest characterizations in postwar noir: the nameless man (Paul Kelly) in *Crossfire* (1947) who enigmatically shows up in the apartment of "dancehall girl" Ginny (Gloria Grahame), purporting to be her husband while making a series of bizarre and contradictory claims about his relationship with her (see Figure 8.7). He says all this to the young corporal, Mitch Mitchell (George Cooper), whom Ginny has invited to the apartment to wait for her. The man tells Mitchell he is married to Ginny and then that he isn't, that he loves her and then that he doesn't. He says he joined the army to get away from her when he discovered that she was a "tramp," but now wants her back again. Is he her husband, perhaps estranged? We cannot tell. He is familiar with the apartment and may even "belong" there, but only in the strangest way. All the same, in a curious domestic detail, we see him making coffee in the kitchen as if he's often done so before, offering some to the bemused corporal. "You're wondering about this set-up, aren't you?" he asks Mitchell, and indeed we do wonder. With his disconcerting utterances, he speaks in a kind of Pinteresque dialogue with a mise-en-scène that resembles Theatre of the Absurd. A sinister intruder for whose presence there is no plausible narrative

FIGURE 8.7 "You're wondering about this set-up, aren't you?" The man (Paul Kelly) with Corporal Mitchell (George Cooper) in *Crossfire* (Edward Dmytryk, 1947).

logic, the man's characterization functions like a weird chorus, articulating a fantastic and chaotic commentary on the prospects for postwar married life. "We made a lot of plans," he says, "but they all fell through."

Notes

1 Examples include *Cornered* (1945), *Below the Deadline* (1946), *The Blue Dahlia* (1946), *The Chase* (1946), *The Dark Horse* (1946), *Johnny Comes Flying Home* (1946), *Somewhere in the Night* (1946), *Crossfire* (1947), *Dead Reckoning* (1947), *Desire Me* (1947), *The Guilty* (1947), *Ride the Pink Horse* (1947), *The High Wall* (1948), *Key Largo* (1948), *Kiss the Blood Off My Hands* (1948), *Perilous Waters* (1948), *Act of Violence* (1949), *The Clay Pigeon* (1949), and *The Crooked Way* (1949).

2 Jonathan Munby, *Public Enemies, Public Heroes: Screening the Gangster from Little Caesar to Touch of Evil* (Chicago: Chicago University Press, 1999), 8.

3 See also *The Enchanted Cottage* (1945), *Till the End of Time* (1946), and *From This Day Forward* (1946).

4 Thomas Schatz, *Boom and Bust: American Cinema in the 1940s* (Berkeley: University of California Press, 1999), 289, 370, 476.

5 See "America" in, for example, *Time* (October 28, 1946), 2–3.

6 Schatz, *Boom and Bust*, 343.

7 "Out of the window of a travel-soiled Pullman car stuck eleven pairs of khaki-clad shoulders, eleven faces, some smiling, some seemingly bewildered, some almost grimly expectant. Below the window were chalked two words. 'Home Again!!'" "America," 2. The original article seen by Goldwyn was "The Way Home," *Time* (August 7, 1944), 15–16. See also Goulden, *The Best Years: 1945-1950* (New York: Atheneum, 1976), 3–6.

8 See for example, Howard A. Rusk, "REHABILITATION," *New York Times* (November 24, 1946), 60.

9 See Thomas Doherty, *Projections of War: Hollywood, American Culture, and World War II* (New York: Columbia University Press, 1993), 269.

10 MacKinlay Kantor, *Glory for Me* (New York: Coward-McCann, 1945), 242–45.

11 Fred finds himself overseen by his own former assistant "Sticky" Merkle (Norman Phillips, Jr.). The unsympathetic characterization of such figures, often with an emphasis on their surveillance role, is a trope in several postwar films. For example, in *Holiday Affair* (1949), the department store sales assistant and veteran Steve Mason (Robert Mitchum) is closely monitored by a sinister floorwalker.

12 Many postwar films feature a Fred Derry type, either explicitly or implicitly a veteran, often characterized by a sense of dislocation, a breakdown in purpose and direction, perpetually in transit from one temporary location to another. For example, we see Frank Chambers at the beginning of *The Postman Always Rings Twice* compelled by "road fever" to keep on traveling with no particular destination in mind.

13 Kantor, *Glory For Me*, 224–31.

14 Frank MacShane, *Raymond Chandler: A Biography* (London: Vintage, 1998), 154.

15 Nick Heffernan "Acts of Violence: The World War II Veteran Private-Eye Movie as an Ideological Crime Series," in Jean Anderson, Carolina Miranda, and Barbara Pezzotti, eds., *Serial Crime Fiction: Dying for More* (London: Palgrave, 2015), 63–73.

16 Ibid, 63.

17 Ibid, 64.

18 *Act of Violence, The Blue Dahlia, The Chase, The Clay Pigeon, Cornered, The Crooked Way, Dead Reckoning, The Guilty, Ride the Pink Horse, Somewhere in the Night,* and *The Stranger* (1946). All these titles have entries in Silver and Ward's *Encyclopedia*.

19 It's worth noting that Arthur Miller's play *Death of a Salesman* opened on Broadway a few months before the release of *Side Street* and had a hugely successful run throughout the year.

20 Several films noir of the period see the fur coat as an emblem of conspicuous wealth and status. The object of desire by an avaricious female, she will often use a man to achieve it, such as Mona Stevens (Lizabeth Scott) in *Pitfall* (1948), Diane Peters (Joan Dixon) in *Roadblock* (1951), or Leonora Eames (Barbara Bel Geddes) in *Caught* (1949).

21 Topically, the last entry in the series, *Love Laughs at Andy Hardy* (1947), sees Andy as a returning veteran.

22 Dorothy B. Hughes, *Ride the Pink Horse* (1946; London: Canongate, 2002). Hughes wrote two other novels about returning veterans, both adapted as films noir: *The Fallen Sparrow* (1943) and *In a Lonely Place* (1947). A specialist in tough veteran fiction, she also wrote *"The Homecoming"* (1946), another veteran murder story. See, *"The Homecoming,"* in Mystery Writers of America, Inc., *Murder Cavalcade: An Anthology* (New York: Duell, Sloan and Pearce, 1946), 163–75. Hughes is one of several "hard-boiled" female writers, challenging the assumption that it was an exclusively masculine literary form.

23 Raymond Borde and Étienne Chaumeton, *A Panorama of American Film Noir, 1941-1953,* trans. Paul Hammond (San Francisco: City Lights, 2002), 66.

24 Mark Osteen, *Nightmare Alley: Film Noir and the American Dream* (Baltimore: Johns Hopkins Press, 2013), 92.

25 John D. MacDonald, *Cape Fear* (1957; London: Orion, 2014), 8.

26 Ibid., 59.

27 Ibid.

28 See for instance *Angels with Dirty Faces* (1938), *The Roaring Twenties* (1939), and as the doomed protagonist Roy Earle in *High Sierra* (1941).

29 On Bogart's wartime star persona, see Ian Brookes, "'A Rebus of Democratic Slants and Angles': *To Have and Have Not*, Racial Representation, and Musical Performance in a Democracy at War," in Graham Lock and David Murray, eds., *Thriving On a Riff: Jazz and Blues Influences in African American Literature and Film* (New York: Oxford University Press, 2009), 206–09.

30 Borde and Chaumeton, *Panorama of American Film Noir*, 34.

31 Ibid., 9.

32 Ibid., 16.

33 Ibid., 35.

34 André Bazin, "The Death of Humphrey Bogart," *Cahiers du Cinéma* 68 (February 1957), trans. Phillip Drummond, repr. in Jim Hillier, ed., *Cahiers du Cinéma: The 1950s: Neo-Realism, Hollywood, New Wave* (Cambridge, MA: Harvard University Press, 1985), 100.

35 Ibid.

36 Quoted, Ibid., 98.

37 Warner Brothers exploited the real-life romance between Bogart and Bacall, which began on the set of *To Have and Have Not*, including the animated short *Bacall to Arms* (1946) satirizing their roles in that film.

38 Frank Krutnik, *In a Lonely Street: Film Noir, Genre, Masculinity* (London: Routledge, 1991), 176.

39 Dana Polan, *In a Lonely Place* (London: BFI, 1993), 20–23.

40 Dorothy B. Hughes, *In a Lonely Place* (1947; New York: Feminist Press at the City University of New York, 2003); Patrick McGilligan, *Nicholas Ray: The Glorious Failure of an American Director* (New York: HarperCollins, 2011), 187–88.

9

Conformity, community, and citizenship

This is my last civilian day. . . . I am no longer to be held accountable for myself; I am grateful for that. I am in other hands, relieved of self-determination, freedom cancelled. Hurray for regular hours! And for the supervision of the spirit! Long live regimentation!

SAUL BELLOW, *Dangling Man* (1944)[1]

There's an osmosis in war, call it what you will, but the victors always tend to assume the . . . the, eh, trappings of the loser. We might easily go Fascist after we win.

NORMAN MAILER, *The Naked and the Dead* (1948)[2]

My idea is to let the generals run the country. Then everything would be shipshape. No trouble with unions. No trouble with traitors. No trouble of any kind.

RICHARD BROOKS, *The Brick Foxhole* (1945)[3]

We saw in Chapter 7 the various concerns that had accumulated under "the veteran problem" and to that catalog can be added a concern with military conformity. Social scientists identified in the "total organization" of the military a number of factors seemingly designed to produce a culture of conformity. Military society, they found, was a regime of discipline and control governed by orders, rules, and regulations, all strictly administered through a hierarchical model determined by rank. It was also, literally, a uniform society in which everything and everyone was subject to processes and procedures of standardization. Social scientists, through a remarkably consensual literature, discursively dramatized and pathologized military conformity.

Commentators noted that military society disavowed the very notion of personal initiative, self-reliance, and individual autonomy, effectively immobilizing the serviceman's capacity to think and act independently. They assumed that the serviceman had internalized the conformist tendencies of military culture and become conditioned to a life of institutionalized dependency. It followed that the serviceman had been so thoroughly inculcated with the conformist tendencies of military life that he couldn't help but return home with them. It was widely believed that this culture had impaired the serviceman's capacity for independence to the extent that the ex-serviceman could no longer assume personal responsibility for his own actions and decisions and, consequently, he had been rendered unfit for a place in civilian society. The serviceman's "readjustment," as we have seen, was designed to facilitate his return to civilian life. Readjustment has often been seen as a process of homogenization, bringing the veterans back into line with civilian society. Here, however, readjustment wasn't intended to reproduce conformity but to counteract it, to provide the means for the reconversion of the "conformist" ex-serviceman into the independent, autonomous citizen necessary for the functioning of a democratic society. The role of the nonconformist individual would become indispensable in the formation of postwar Americanism, especially in the construction of a national identity, which was being defensively positioned against foreign totalitarianism.

In their studies of wartime military society, social scientists found that the military environment fostered a culture of institutional dependency which immobilized the individual's capacity to think for oneself, engendering "a chronic incapacity for acting in any other way than under explicit orders."[4] Many commentators stressed the ways in which the military intentionally set out to erase the civilian's sense of himself—a process beginning with induction and basic training that "does much to generate conformity, because that was its intent."[5] Willard Waller describes how the soldier enters "a world in which his private personality and his private will no longer count," where "the self-will of the soldier must be systematically eradicated."[6] Because the military demanded reflexive obedience, it relieved the serviceman of all personal responsibility. Consequently, "all matters of food, clothing, and shelter are settled for the soldier in a way that leaves him unaware of them as processes, as responsibilities. Unconsciously he comes to take them for granted and indeed is encouraged to do so."[7] With his reliance on the military for the provision of all necessities, it was widely assumed that the serviceman couldn't help but develop a condition of institutional dependency on what was often seen as a kind of "welfare-state" society.

Social scientists were also concerned about the "welfare" implications of the Depression era. George Pratt, for example, noted how many servicemen had grown up during the Depression, becoming dependent on its "program of vast public relief." According to this view, the New Deal had fostered a culture of dependency in which the state, having assumed responsibility for providing "the bare necessities of existence," had also assumed the role of a surrogate parent. Many adolescents, Pratt says, "began imperceptibly to endow the Relief Bureau—and more remotely the 'Government'—with parental qualities of support and assumption of responsibility." Because they were habituated to being "taken care of," they had become "dependency-conditioned" and, consequently, would find it difficult—especially after military service—to assume for themselves the "responsibilities of independent living" on their return.[8] This perception of a New Deal "dependency culture" would be projected onto the military.

Sociologists were also concerned about the implications of a military system that seemed to negate the very values that supposedly constituted what America was fighting for. Bowker, for example, saw the "American-in-uniform" almost as a contradiction in terms because the "very qualities of individuality, independence and personal freedom of will and speech that he had been nurtured to consider his birthright became suddenly inoperative."[9] The military status of the GI was impersonal and anonymous in a culture where "his serial number is more important to the War Department than his name."[10] Absorbed into the military's numbers culture, commentators reported that the soldier found it comforting when "his own self was submerged in the anonymity of the mass."[11] It's significant, then, that the American soldier should be known as a GI, that is, Government Issue, a designation that defined him in the same terms as his equipment. "The individual soldier thus saw himself as an item of mass-production along with G.I. clothing, rations, and other materiel."[12]

Organization men: Postwar conformity

I'm just a man in a grey flannel suit. I must keep my suit neatly pressed like anyone else, for I am a very respectable young man. . . . I will keep my grey flannel suit spotless.

SLOAN WILSON, *The Man in the Grey Flannel Suit* (1956)[13]

To many social commentators, the conformist ex-serviceman was returning to a conformist postwar America. Many of its institutions seemed to confirm a national tendency toward conformity and uniformity. The postwar home, for example, would often be represented by the new suburban housing developments as serried ranks of seemingly identical, barrack-like units. For Lewis Mumford, every facet of suburbanization represented standardized mediocrity:

> a multitude of uniform, unidentifiable houses, lined up inflexibly, at uniform distances, on uniform roads, in a treeless communal waste, inhabited by people of the same class, the same income, the same age group, witnessing the same television performances, eating the same tasteless pre-fabricated foods, from the same freezers, conforming in every outward and inward respect to a common mold.[14]

The new suburban habitat was widely criticized as symptomatic of postwar conformity.[15]

Work was seen as another element in this conformist tendency, especially through the expansion of corporation employment. As corporate structures grew bigger, the employee began to look smaller, becoming one of the "new little people" described by C. Wright Mills and later personified in Whyte's telling phrase as an "organization man," an anonymous little cog in an enormous faceless machine.[16] In another contributing text to the discourse of conformity, *The Lonely Crowd*, David Riesman scrutinized the figure of the "other-directed man," a figure defined by his dependence on the approval of the group, adapting himself accordingly to fit in with it.[17] Even his clothing looked like a uniform, and terms that signified uniformity, like "white-collar" and "gray flannel suit," would become emblematic of the postwar years, especially the 1950s.[18] For many social commentators, large-scale forms of corporate organization were becoming a defining feature of postwar America and, in the discourse of readjustment, it often seemed as if the veteran had left one type of "total institution" to find himself in another.[19] Beyond that, Mills identified the emergence of a new form of state power, enlarged and centralized through an "interlocking directorate" of political, economic, and military institutions, which he designated the "power elite."[20]

Concerns about the conformist veteran were being articulated in the wider context of anxieties about postwar America becoming a mass society with a mass culture. To many, "mass" became one of the key terms to define a period which seemed geared to the mass production and consumption of conformity. Intellectuals were disconcerted by what they saw as a machine-age culture exemplified by the Hollywood studio system. They identified in the standardization of cultural production not only an aesthetically debased cultural form but also one with totalitarian traits. Many shared Bernard Rosenberg's view of mass culture as a double peril, threatening "not merely to cretinize our taste, but to brutalize our senses while paving the way to totalitarianism."[21] Similarly, Dwight Macdonald argued that "Kulturbolschewismus" (cultural bolshevism) was already "here" and he detected indications of "that *official* approach to culture" in America as "an ominous sign of the drift towards totalitarianism."[22]

Social commentators expressed concerns with what they saw as the totalitarian implications of an American mass culture. As Andrew Ross put it: "Mass culture, mass society, the masses. They have all come to sound 'un-American,' as if they suggested alarming foreign activities that surely 'can't happen here'." For Ross,

> these terms often function either as external limits or boundaries against which the official idea of a national democratic culture is defined, or, when applied internally, to denote a critical, dystopian view of profoundly undemocratic features within that culture. . . . In short, 'mass' is one of the key terms that governs the official distinction between American/Un-American, or inside/outside.[23]

In this sense, "mass" signaled a double danger because it suggested the antidemocratic forces of the totalitarian other on two fronts, foreign and domestic. Many intellectuals subscribed to the idea of a "center" alignment of consensual liberal pluralism, which would provide the basis for a national postwar culture strategically deployed in opposition to the threat of totalitarianism.[24]

But for Cold War intellectuals and social commentators alike, there were several impediments to the realization of a functioning democratic resistance to totalitarianism. The city, for example, was often blamed for its corrosive effects on community life, and social commentators became concerned about the loss of community and neighborhood, especially as structures of local democracy. "Without them," says Elmer Peterson, "democracy operates haltingly and often by remote control, which really means no democracy at all."[25] In a discourse linking the degraded quality of urban life to the demise of neighborhood and community, there were concerns that the very social structures through which grassroots democracy should be enacted were in themselves in decline. In order to counteract the "anti-democratic" tendencies of urbanism, a new concept of home would be realized through home ownership that would be distanced from the city and planned through suburbanization.[26] The city itself was often criticized as a failing habitat with its high rents, slum housing, traffic gridlocks, and rising crime. John Brooks has described how the new suburbs were "draining downtown of its nighttime population, except for night watchmen and derelicts." The city may have been bustling with commuters during the day but was "abandoned again at nightfall."[27] It became demonized in the popular imagination as a dark, dangerous, and crime-ridden space, precisely the kind of space that would feature as a recurrent trope in film noir.

There were few realistic opportunities to improve the urban environment when, "having scarcely any real citizens at all, it could hardly expect to have devoted and responsible ones able and willing to give it good government."[28] The city was also increasingly seen as the site of the racial other. Migration to the suburbs was tellingly described as a "white flight" from the city with black Americans taking their places.[29] In a society that remained racially segregated, the suburbs were largely white and the cities becoming black. Critics found other reasons to fear the cities too. Their densely populated areas would be especially vulnerable targets in the event of an atomic bomb attack. Dispersal of the urban population through suburbanization served the strategic purpose of reducing the risk to civilians.[30]

It was in these circumstances, then, that the suburban home became invested with symbolic national purpose and strategically deployed as an emblem of America's democratic freedom, individualism, and independence, defensively constructed against Cold War Soviet totalitarianism. As Kenneth Jackson has pointed out, both government and industry "played up" the prospect of the suburban house to the families of absent servicemen and, subsequently, the GI Bill "gave official endorsement and support to the view that the 16 million GI's of World War II should return to civilian life with a home of their own."[31] The earliest of the new housing developments was built by property developer William Levitt, progenitor of "Levittown" suburbanization, providing the means for home ownership on a hitherto unimaginable scale. Home ownership itself was conscripted to play a Cold War role. "No man who owns his own house and lot can be a communist," Levitt famously proclaimed. "He has too much to do."[32]

The "democratic counter-offensive" of *The Vital Center*

For intellectuals concerned with encroaching conformity, the local community would be mobilized to constitute the heartland of the diversified society envisaged by the Cold War intellectual Arthur Schlesinger in *The Vital Centre* (1949), one of the key postwar texts to advocate liberal democracy.[33] But in the discourse of readjustment, it was feared that the conformist veteran was returning not to a diversified society at all but to one in which the very notion of community appeared to be defunct. American society would consequently be incapable of mounting the kind of defense that Schlesinger and others saw as imperative to withstand the threat of incipient totalitarianism.

Many intellectuals in a demoralized Depression-era America had been attracted by the Russian "experiment" that seemed then to offer an inspirational alternative to their own collapsed economy. In fact, the two countries may not have been as ideologically far apart as they may have seemed. Soviet propaganda, as Richard Pells has pointed out, could sound "typically American" in emphasis.

> Both countries valued the material rewards of mass production, both respected the machine and its power to transform life, both celebrated industrialism and technology, both worshipped bigness as a sign of quality and progress, both preached the virtues of efficiency and physical growth.[34]

Later in the decade, however, disclosures about the Stalinist purges and Moscow show trials began to expose, if only partially, a horrifying picture of the Soviet police state, a picture that disabused many of their admiration for the Soviet experiment. With the war against a fascist enemy only recently over, and with news of the extent of Nazi atrocities appearing on American newsreels, American intellectuals began to undertake a reappraisal of American national identity vis-à-vis its totalitarian enemies.

For Cold War intellectuals, the development of a new kind of national identity became imperative for the reformation of postwar Americanism. This, they proposed, should be built on a new centrist alignment of reconstituted liberalism that Schlesinger called the "vital center." This center would represent a position from which, in one of Schlesinger's frequent military metaphors, "a democratic counter-offensive" would be strategically deployed against the threat of approaching totalitarianism. This was a tactical response to what was seen as a period of political uncertainty, a period often called "the age of anxiety."[35] If, "anxiety," as Schlesinger claims, "is the official emotion of our time," it was an existential prerequisite for democratic freedom.[36] It represented proof of individualism in a free society as opposed to totalitarianism's "*non-individual*" who was rendered incapable of feeling any "anxiety" at all.

This center would be "vital" because it connoted life in contradistinction to the condition of "unlife" often attributed to those living in the machine-like totalitarian state. We have seen in Chapter 5 something of the existential characteristics attributed to noir narratives. Here, the crucial dilemma in this culture of anxiety was that existential freedom imposed on the individual a responsibility to make choices and decisions which had become too much of an ordeal to make. The existential self was constituted by the act of choice, but to exercise that choice demanded the acceptance of personal responsibility that was preferable to avoid. Moreover, under the increasing dominance of capitalism's enlarged organizational authority, the individual was at risk of being overwhelmed by an overarching system of thought. "Man longs to escape the pressures beating down on his frail individuality," says Schlesinger, "and, more and more, the surest means of escape seems to be to surrender that individuality to some massive, external authority."[37] The individual, Schlesinger is saying, wants only "to flee" from the responsibility that freedom entails. The totalitarian state was dangerously alluring because it held out the promise of "meaning and purpose" and "security and comradeship," relieving the individual of personal responsibility.[38] Both communism and fascism similarly envisaged the individual as a component in the state apparatus. If the self is subordinated to the state, individual expression becomes conceptually meaningless, jeopardizing free discussion, criticism, and dissent. This, says Schlesinger, "is threatening to turn us all into frightened conformists; and conformity can only lead to stagnation."[39] Hence, the "vital center" would provide the means for the reconstituted "integrity of the individual" to withstand the pressures of conformity, to help us recapture a sense of the indispensability of dissent.[40]

For Cold War intellectuals like Schlesinger, the "center" represented a pluralist front in opposition to the ideological extremities of totalitarianism. Many liberal intellectuals believed that ideologically based proposals for postwar Americanism had become redundant and that ideology itself had come to a dead end. Ideology, it was argued, encouraged the abnegation of personal responsibility for asking questions by automatically providing the answers. Daniel Bell, one of the preeminent "end-of-ideology" apologists, described the conformist tendency implicit in ideological consumption. "One simply turns to the ideological vending machine," he says, "and out comes the prepared formulae."[41]

There were also concerns about the political susceptibility of the returning veteran and many sociologists saw him as a politically dangerous figure. They often saw the military as a "social machine" and frequently drew on the imagery of industrial machinery to suggest its own totalitarian implications. The soldier, according to Nisbet, even came to see himself as little more than an insignificant component in a vast military apparatus, "as the dependent cog of a gigantic mechanism."[42] For Waller, such a mechanism is "a machine . . . which enables a million men to act with a single will,"[43] an image more reminiscent of the *Wehrmacht* than America's wartime democracy, and one that clearly implies a fascist potential in the American army.

The returning veteran was often seen as politically dangerous and particularly susceptible to right-wing extremism.[44] Donald Becker, for example, saw veterans as a social force capable of being "agitated and directed toward self-aggrandizement by possible neo-totalitarian interests."[45] For Waller, the "highly organizable" veteran was suggestible to fascist demagoguery and vulnerable to exploitation by such groups as the Ku Klux Klan (then operating covertly as the "United Sons of America") that recruited ex-servicemen under the guise of veteran employment services.[46] Bolte similarly highlights the dangers of "Klannish" groups with "hidden alliances" and cites the "St. Sebastian's

Brigade"—a group associated with Father (Charles) Coughlin—which had enrolled "hundreds of thousands of servicemen."[47] Although Waller takes a patronizing view of the veteran's political acumen, seeing him as "the ready tool of the demagogue," his fear of the disaffected ex-soldier, steeped in martial ideology and primed for a "cause," was widely shared.[48] As commentators often emphasized the historical connection between the German veterans of the First World War and the rise of fascism, the prospect of a parallel development in postwar America seemed dangerously credible to them, a "warning," says Bolte, "of what *could* happen."[49] Wecter quotes a sergeant's warning: "'If this generation of soldiers returns home to a collapsed and chaotic economic system due to inflation . . . we shall not stand docilely on street corners selling apples; we shall not ashamedly wait in line to receive bread.'"[50] Wecter's sergeant represents a particularly ominous threat with its hint of the organized veteran as a politicized force.

Postwar film noir would often show that it was precisely in ordinary small-town life that American democratic liberalism was especially vulnerable to incursive totalitarian influence, where small-town life was repeatedly portrayed with a dubious sense of community.[51] At the core of many of these concerns was a preoccupation with the function of citizenship, especially as a democratic function, increasingly seen as under threat.[52] One of the more overtly political strands in postwar noir is with the dangers inherent in a moribund citizenship and ineffectual community life.

"In Harper, there's nothing to be afraid of": "renascent fascism" and Wellesian noir

In Orson Welles's *The Stranger* (1946), active citizenship is represented as the indispensable bulwark against a resurgent postwar fascism in America. Franz Kindler (Orson Welles) is a Nazi fugitive who has eluded capture in Germany and fled to America where he has assumed the identity of Charles Rankin, establishing himself as a schoolteacher in the Connecticut town of Harper. He is about to be married to Mary (Loretta Young), daughter of Judge Longstreet (Philip Merivale), a justice of the Supreme Court and a prominent liberal. Kindler is being pursued by the Allied War Crimes Commissioner, Wilson (Edward G. Robinson).

Kindler's American identity is authenticated through the guise of his professional role in Harper's community, where to all outward appearances he is exactly what he seems to be, an ordinary small-town American. But Wilson reveals that it was Kindler who "conceived the theory of genocide," linking him explicitly to Adolf Eichmann and other leading Nazis.[53] Here, as Wilson explains, Kindler's Nazism is unidentifiable. "Unlike Goebbels, Himmler and the rest of them," he says, "Kindler had a passion for anonymity. The newspapers carried no picture of him." This new Nazism has divested itself of all its characteristic paraphernalia to become unrecognizable as a covert force. The narrative shows nothing of Kindler's arrival in Harper, nor his metamorphosis into Rankin, nor his assimilation into the small-town community where he is already integrated, chameleon-like, into the familiar patterns of everyday life. In this sense, he is not a "stranger" at all but already there. His assimilation into town life is made plausible partly through Welles's performance that has none of the conventional inflections used to characterize stereotypical screen Nazis. Rankin remains a credible American because, through Welles, that's precisely what he is. It's worth bearing in mind how much this differs from earlier Nazi characterizations such as that of Dr. Kassel (Paul Lukas) in *Confessions of a Nazi Spy* (1939). Kassel is a Fuhrer-like demagogue whose histrionic speeches demonstrate a studied approximation to Hitler's own declamatory style. National Socialism is filtered through the German American Bund, a front for Kassel's rabble-rousing speeches, the dissemination of Nazi propaganda and the coordination of covert operations. Kassel's is a highly visible form of Nazism in comparison with Kindler's.

As a familiar figure in the local community, Rankin establishes a number of connections to the fundamental institutions of American society, providing him with the cover of ordinariness and respectability. At the same time, he exposes the vulnerability of these institutions to which he readily gains admittance. His forthcoming wedding will enable him to insinuate himself yet further into the social fabric of Harper, making Judge Longstreet his father-in-law and further consolidating his connections to the Judge's world of law and liberal politics. The elite school where he teaches provides the cover of respectability ("Who would think to look for the notorious Franz Kindler in the sacred precincts of the Harper School, surrounded by the sons of America's first families?") Also, his role in undertaking the restoration of the church clock puts him quite literally at the center of the town's civic and religious institutions.

This sense of vulnerability to incursive fascism is manifest throughout the narrative. Konrad Meinike (Konstantin Shayne) is a war criminal held prisoner by the Allies whose escape is planned by Wilson as a means of tracing Kindler. Meinike obtains a postcard establishing Kindler's whereabouts, and our initial view of Harper is this postcard image, a view of small-town America. Meinike stares at the postcard's depiction of a town center dominated by a church. The scene seems flat and lifeless before it dissolves into an establishing shot of the town itself where Meinike, trailed by Wilson, arrives by bus. The still image becomes animated as the orchestral score, by Bronislav Kaper, attributes a sense of alacrity to the town. But although the townscape is punctuated by an occasional automobile and passerby, it seems curiously vacant and lacking in any social dynamics. The following scene, at Potter's drugstore, also suggests a kind of social remoteness, where social interaction seems desultory, and customers look detached and uncommunicative. Potter (Billy House), a central figure in Harper, not only runs the drugstore but also officiates as town clerk. He is also one of the town's most unprepossessing citizens. Gossipy, lazy, mean-spirited, and devious, there is little about Potter that offers a positive view of Harper's community. In fact, there is little sense of any community at all. The townspeople will only be seen in any collective sense at the very end of the narrative when they are shown en masse, converging in a mob at the church tower to witness Rankin's death.

The family, as exemplified by the Longstreets, is found as wanting as the community. Mary is little more than a stalwart adherent to the social conventions of small-town life and a dutifully loyal wife. She is first glimpsed through the window of Rankin's house, putting up curtains. The scene not only illustrates her domestic preoccupations but also points to a proclivity for domestic insularity and shutting out external realities, later to become an obsessive, almost hysterical, repudiation of the world outside. Her own conformist disposition sees her as susceptible to, and complicit in, her husband's fascist world. We can see in Mary a particular kind of vulnerability with a naïve willingness to accept appearances. Even when confronted with evidence of her husband's guilt, she clings to her belief in his innocence. When Mary is forced by Wilson to watch newsreels of concentration camp atrocities, we see her caught in the flickering light of the projector and juxtaposed with the screen's horrific images, becoming herself a culpable figure in these crimes against humanity[54] (see Figure 9.1). Although she refutes the evidence of Kindler's war crimes, the scene sees her accused because in "failing to speak" she is implicated in them too. Moreover, with the Nuremberg Trials in session while Welles was shooting The Stranger, the scene has a didactic function which can be linked to the Allies' policy of making German civilians look at the bodies of Holocaust victims in the death camps. American audiences would have been aware of this practice through newsreels such as Nazi Murder Mills (1945).[55]

Mary's domestic situation is mapped onto tropes both of gothic melodrama and film noir which show a wife rendered vulnerable to the machinations of a malign foreigner—often her husband—and where the domestic space of home is itself the site of terror and threat.[56] Here, though, the gothic peril has a political dimension. Having deluded herself that her town is a haven of comfort and security—"In Harper, there's nothing to be afraid of," she says—she discovers that the community is as defenseless as she is. As in many female gothic narratives, female sexuality comes under assault by a malevolent masculine force within the domestic space of home. In The Stranger, this power penetrates the symbolic structure of home represented

FIGURE 9.1 Wellesian Noir: Mary Rankin (Loretta Young) watches newsreels of Nazi atrocities in *The Stranger* (Orson Welles, 1946).

by both the marital bed and the dinner table. Like many gothic/noir narratives, *The Stranger* incorporates a hallucinatory quality in which masculine terror is visited on the feminine, as in Mary's dream. When Rankin darkly enters their bedroom, casting a sinister shadow over her, she wakes from a dream in which she has seen Meinike, "walking all by himself, across a deserted square. Wherever he moved, he threw a shadow, but when he moved away, the shadow stayed there behind him." Mary's ominous nightmare reveals her subconscious anxieties about her unknown husband, where the import of the past haunts the present through its vestigial shadow. The sequence illustrates Mary's isolation and vulnerability as she is located, significantly, in the deserted town square.[57] There is no one in Harper to help her.

Nobody in Harper has noticed anything untoward about Rankin, including Mary's father. Longstreet may appear urbane and sophisticated, but he is really quite avuncular and parochial. Seen at home rather than at work, he occupies wood-paneled rooms filled with antiques where, with his collection of pewter, he retreats into an antique past. Although he is characterized uniquely among the citizens of Harper as politically informed, he is also, like them, politically out of touch. His connection to the Foreign Policy Association may have provided him with reports from Berlin of "men drilling by night" and other indications of a Nazi resurgence, but his "elder-statesman" liberalism seems ineffectual in the face of it. Certainly, he is unable to detect the presence of a Nazi at his own table. Nazism as a covert force was also becoming difficult to identify abroad. Reporting from occupied Germany in 1945, the *Collier's* war correspondent Martha Gellhorn discovered unanimous public disavowal of the country's Nazi past. "No one is a Nazi," she found. "No one ever was."[58]

Ultimately, only the forces of external agency, through Wilson, can set in motion the process by which the family and town are obligated to recognize the encroaching threat in their midst. Nevertheless, it is significant that Wilson should want to see Mary play such an active role in her husband's downfall. Although Wilson may appear callous in putting Mary in jeopardy, he does so because her own involvement is crucial to a wider narrative agenda that works toward a shift in the burden of responsibility. Wilson's agency provides the professional expertise necessary for identifying and locating Kindler, but it is ultimately through Mary's eventual acknowledgment of her own responsibility that she will be able to assume a more civically minded role in safeguarding the town and, by implication, the nation at large.[59]

Harper already bears several traces of a proto-fascist state. For example, the school is shown largely through its gymnasium, and the narrative emphasis on sports parallels the kind of paramilitary athleticism exemplified through *Hitlerjugend* programs. In a telling moment, a group of students is about to set off on a woodland paper-chase when their banter with Kindler is momentarily interrupted by a passing girl, enthusiastically hailed by the boys as "blondie." Another example can be seen in the clock tower. This might suggest a traditional New England townscape but it is merely a façade, another front for Kindler. He assiduously devotes himself to the restoration of the clock and often prefers to be in the tower rather than at home because the elaborately gothic clock (by "Hobrecht of Strasbourg"), with its grotesque figures and synchronized movements, provides for him a more symbolic sense of his real home (see Figure 9.2). As Harper's imposing centerpiece, it stands physically and symbolically at the very heart of the town. Prior to Kindler's arrival, the clock had fallen into disrepair and there was no official indicator of time. The townspeople feel ambivalent about its repair. While they are enthusiastic about its restoration as a matter of civic pride and effusive in their congratulations when it begins to work again, they also fear its disruptive effects on the rhythms of town life. This, in a sense, is Kindler's intention, to impose on the town a centrally determined form of temporal order. Moreover, his fascination for the clockwork mechanism implies a technological correlative to the regimented patterns of order of the Nazi state apparatus. This further suggests a relation between time, technology, and "will" as a combined expression of Nazi ideology. If "will" is the national power of determination and control, it works toward the logic of a planned future ("Till we strike again"). The clock tower is the highest point in Harper from which Kindler can survey the town below and, hence, in both spatial and temporal terms, he seeks to take control of the town. He is ultimately faced down in the same place and by the same means, killed at the top of the tower by the very mechanism that he has restored to use, the emblematic apparatus of a fascist-gothic technology.

These narrative concerns show up in other postwar films noir. In *The Big Clock* (1948), for example, it is the American corporation that is structured as a model of fascist organization. The Januth Corporation represents the

FIGURE 9.2 Franz Kindler as Charles Rankin (Orson Welles) at the top of the clock tower in *The Stranger* (Orson Welles, 1946).

corporatist state as a form of fascist modernity symbolized by the inexorable apparatus of the big clock itself, showcased in the lobby of the corporation building with a Langian "caged world" production design. The enormous clock functions as a "total" system of synchronization which centrally determines global time. Earl Januth (Charles Laughton) runs his "empire" from the top of the building, an explicitly Hitlerian space described as "the Berchtesgaden of the publishing world" and "the tycoon's lair," a reference to the "Wolf's Lair" (*Wolfsschanze*), Hitler's headquarters in Eastern Prussia.

The figure of "The Stranger" as a force of invasive fascism can also be seen is other 1940s' noir such as Hitchcock's *Shadow of a Doubt* (1943), in some ways a precursor of *The Stranger*. Here, Uncle Charlie (Joseph Cotten) is a kind of native counterpart to Kindler in a narrative that also draws attention to the predisposing factors in small-town America to fascism. Like Kindler, Uncle Charlie uses an assumed identity to infiltrate a small town and, like him, shuns any photographic record of himself. He is first seen in a desolate urban landscape (Philadelphia) that, like Harper, appears vacant and remote. We then see him arrive at Santa Rosa, the small-town community where his arrival is warmly anticipated at the family home. But as the train draws in, the ominous nature of his arrival is signaled by its voluminous clouds of black smoke darkly shadowing the station, a contrivance signifying his demonic entry.[60] Uncle Charlie is a glamorously attractive figure, especially to his niece Young Charlie (Teresa Wright) and he personifies for her a world of cosmopolitan sophistication lacking in her own home town. Like Harper, Santa Rosa is characterized as a typical American town, and there is narrative emphasis on the archetypal ordinariness of the family. When the detectives in pursuit of Uncle Charlie want to gain access to the family home, they pose as National Public Survey researchers purporting to document the "typical American family." But if Santa Rosa is ordinary, it is also banal and small minded. Uncle Charlie inveigles his way into this small-town world where he becomes a figure of irresistible allure, a star attraction feted by the unsuspecting community. Uncle Charlie, though, isn't simply a dandified charmer who exploits his appeal for murderous ends. His popularity derives from a kind of fascist appeal. Hence, we can see his punctilious dress as military uniform, his guest speaker as orator, his serial murderer as genocidal killer, and his misogyny as a displaced form of racial ideology.

Although Uncle Charlie, like Kindler, is ultimately eradicated from the community he threatened, his demise differs from Kindler's. In *The Stranger*, the narrative works to expose Kindler's criminal identity, and his death, as public spectacle, becomes public knowledge. In *Shadow of a Doubt*, there is no such exposure, and Uncle Charlie's reputation remains intact and his memory eulogized as the record of his crimes is effaced. Santa Rosa remains as it was before, ignorantly susceptible to a recurrence of the same incursive threat.

The Nazi theme of *The Stranger* is related to a discourse in which wider concerns with American fascism were being played out through the persona of Orson Welles. Welles is strongly identified with film noir with several of his films seen as canonical examples, including those often seen to bookend the noir period, *Citizen Kane* (1941) and *Touch of Evil* (1958) and including *The Lady from Shanghai* (1947) and *Mr. Arkadin* (aka *Confidential Report*, 1955). Welles also appeared as Colonel Haki in the Nazi espionage thriller *Journey into Fear* (1943) and, more famously, as Harry Lime in Carol Reed's *The Third Man* (1949). Fascism was a recurrent theme in his 1940s' films as well as in his Mercury Theater productions of the late 1930s.[61] Welles was himself a significant political figure in the 1940s, writing a column in the *New York Post* which provided him with a platform as a popular political commentator. He also gave lectures, made speeches, especially about the dangers of postwar fascism which, he believed, was the predominant concern in postwar America. Writing in his *Post* column in June 1945, Welles insisted that it wasn't communism but fascism that threatened the postwar world. "The phony fear of Communism," he wrote, "is smoke-screening the real menace of renascent Fascism."[62] Welles's unique synthesis of an antifascist strain with a noir aesthetic can be traced throughout his body of work, making him almost a subgenre of noir in his own right.[63]

A quasi-fascist American characterization is already evident in Welles's first film, *Citizen Kane*, a film often seen by critics as having an inaugural role in the formation of film noir.[64] The film's self-styled "March of Time" newsreel sequence ("News on the March") shows Charles Foster Kane (Welles) as a despotic press baron and self-serving propagandist who rules over a vast, ever-expanding empire. Kane is explicitly associated with Nazism through his meeting with Hitler that features in the mocked-up newsreel sequence, and implicitly in two narrative set-pieces. The first is political, as Kane, running

FIGURE 9.3 Charles Foster Kane's quasi-fascist political rally in *Citizen Kane* (Orson Welles, 1941).

for state governor, is shown at a political rally (see Figure 9.3). The scene's iconographic impact, styled after Leni Riefenstahl's *Triumph des Willens* [*Triumph of the Will*] (1935), derives from the colossal scale of a set depicting a mass audience in a vast auditorium where Kane addresses the rally standing before a towering image of himself. Here, his "K" logo acquires the force of a fascist emblem or insignia.

The second example is cultural, when Kane builds an opera house in Chicago as a showcase venue for his second wife, Susan Alexander (Dorothy Comingore). The opera is staged like his political rally, as a grandiose spectacle for his own self-aggrandizement in a production scored and visually stylized as Wagnerian pastiche.[65] But despite his attempts to control the event, he fails to manipulate the audience's reaction, manically attempting to galvanize their response through the insistent rhythm of his own solitary applause. But for them, the event has been boring and risible, and we can discern in their desultory response something of Welles's critique of the fascist Kane.[66]

Another noir version of Kane's fascist American reemerged at the end of the decade through the characterization of Harry Lime in *The Third Man* (see Figure 9.4). Lime, presumed dead, has been operating as a black marketeer in postwar Vienna and has become unrecognizable to his old friend Holly Martens (Joseph Cotten) who is seeking to solve the mystery of his friend's mysterious disappearance. Lime is eventually exposed as a racketeer trafficking in adulterated penicillin, the cause of countless children being maimed and killed. When Lime and Martens eventually meet, Lime justifies his operations by describing himself and his "business" in entrepreneurial terms. From his vantage point on the Ferris wheel high above the city, the people below are reducible to insignificant "dots" whose fate to Lime is inconsequential. In the same way that Kindler in *The Stranger* had surveyed from his tower the "little ants" below, Lime looks down godlike on his Viennese empire. He has

FIGURE 9.4 Harry Lime (Orson Welles) in *The Third Man* (Carol Reed, 1949).

assimilated in Vienna the vestiges of Nazi ideology and his "business" there has become analogous to genocide.

At the end of *The Stranger*, Wilson declares, "It's V-Day in Harper." This is a revealing expression in a postwar context: first, because it evokes a term officially designating the end of a war which, here, has not yet ended; and second, because it suggests that the war has carried home to the heartland of small-town America. If Harry Lime's Vienna is the site of a "renascent fascism" in Europe, it has also become, through him, a specifically Americanized form of it. But Charles Rankin's Harper, like Uncle Charlie's Santa Rosa, is the site of a "renascent fascism" at home. Its perpetrators were no longer the conspicuous foreign Nazis as they were in *Confessions of a Nazi Spy*, but Americans themselves. Fascism no longer looked "foreign" as it once did and these later noir narratives attest to the resurgence of a postwar fascism which was becoming institutionally and socially assimilated in American everyday life.

Other instances of "renascent fascism" would figure in postwar noir, some drawn from the American military itself. One of the key films to deal with a fascist dimension of the returning veteran is Edward Dmytryk's *Crossfire* (1947), a film in which noir themes and stylistics are harnessed to the "social problem" film. Its story parallels both *The Blue Dahlia* and *The Best Years of Our Lives* in its focus on a small group of returning servicemen.[67] The film draws on the standard noir plot of a murder investigation with a flashback narrative structure, although its subject—the racially motivated murder of a Jew by an American soldier—was unprecedented. The opening has none of noir's traditional establishing shots to set the scene but starts suddenly in a darkened room where a brutal assault is taking place, the action shown purely through the shadows of assailant and victim thrown up against the wall. Questioned shortly afterward by detective Captain Finlay (Robert Young) about the murder of Joseph Samuels (Sam Levine), Sergeant Montgomery

FIGURE 9.5 Robert Ryan as Sergeant Montgomery in *Crossfire* (Edward Dmytryk, 1947).

(Robert Ryan) denies any knowledge of Samuels in an exchange that betrays the "rationale" for his anti-Semitism.

> Montgomery: Course, seen a lot of guys like him.
> Finlay: Like what?
> Montgomery: Oh, you know, guys that played it safe during the war, scrounged around, keeping themselves in civvies—got swell apartments, swell dames, you know the kind.
> Finlay: I'm not sure that I do. Just what kind?
> Montgomery: Oh, you know. Some of them are named Samuels. Some of them got funnier names.

Montgomery is characterized as psychotically anti-Semitic, although his hatred is directed not only at Jews but also at blacks, foreigners, and 4-F civilians.[68] (Unbeknown to him, Samuels was himself a veteran, discharged from the service on medical grounds after being wounded at Okinawa.) In contrast to the postwar trend toward documentary realism, the film is one of the most self-consciously *un*realistic films noir of the postwar period, shot exclusively on studio sets and pushing to the extreme some of the more expressionistic and surrealistic features associated with noir. After the shadow play of the opening scene, a lamp is knocked over and the room is plunged into pitch blackness where it remains for several moments. Lighting throughout the film is set at low levels with large proportions of the frame obscured in shadow. Characters are often shot in close-up and lit to distort their facial features, especially Montgomery's, grotesque effects intensified by Ryan's disturbing performance (see Figure 9.5).[69]

It's also significant that this monstrous crime was committed by an American soldier in uniform, and in the nation's capital. We saw in Chapter 6 how in *Strangers on a Train* Washington was shown as politically vulnerable: here it is shown with a ubiquitous military presence that looks unpredictable and volatile. "We don't know what we're supposed to do," says Samuels in a kind of commentary on an unstable transition for military personnel: "we don't know what's supposed to happen. We're too used to fighting, but we just don't know what to fight. You can feel the tension in the air. A whole lotta fight and hate that doesn't know where to go." The film depicts the city as having a febrile, restless, hard-drinking culture, its soldiers full of pent-up discontent and, in Montgomery's case, racial hatred and xenophobia. Here, the issuing source of a renascent fascism comes not as an external threat but from within America's own demobilizing military.

Notes

1 Saul Bellow, *Dangling Man* (1944; Harmondsworth: Penguin, 1966), 159.

2 Norman Mailer, *The Naked and the Dead* (1948; London: Flamingo, 1999), 325.

3 Richard Brooks, *The Brick Foxhole* (New York: Harper & Brothers, 1945), 35.

4 Robert E. Nisbet, "The Coming Problem of Assimilation," *American Journal of Sociology* 50 (1945): 265.

5 Howard Brotz and Everett Wilson, "Characteristics of Military Society," *American Journal of Sociology* 51 (1946): 372. On induction and training, see Lee Kennett, *G.I.: The American Soldier in World War II* (New York: Scribner's, 1987), 24–65.

6 Willard Waller, *The Veteran Comes Back* (New York: Dryden Press, 1944), 20.

7 Nisbet, "Coming Problem of Assimilation," 264.

8 George K. Pratt, *Soldier to Civilian: Problems of Readjustment* (New York: McGraw-Hill, 1944), 31–32.

9 Benjamin C. Bowker, *Out of Uniform* (New York: Norton, 1946), 60.

10 August B. Hollingshead, "Adjustment to Military Life," *American Journal of Sociology* 51 (1946): 440–41.

11 Henry Elkin, "Aggressive and Erotic Tendencies in Army Life," *American Journal of Sociology* 51 (1946): 411.

12 Ibid., 408.

13 Sloan Wilson, *The Man in the Grey Flannel Suit* (1956; London: Pan, 1958), 104.

14 Lewis Mumford, *The City in History: Its Origins, Its Transformations, and Its Prospects* (London: Secker and Warburg, 1961), 486.

15 See for example William H. Whyte, "The New Suburbia: Organization Man At Home" in *The Organization Man* (1956; Harmondsworth: Penguin, 1963), 245–372; David Riesman, "The Suburban Sadness," in William M. Dobriner, ed., *The Suburban Community* (New York: Putnam, 1958), 375–408.

16 C. Wright Mills, *White Collar: The American Middle Classes* (1951; New York: Oxford University Press, 1956), xviii; Whyte, *Organization Man*.

17 David Riesman, with Nathan Glazer and Reuel Denney, *The Lonely Crowd: A Study of the Changing American Character* (New Haven, CT: Yale University Press, 1950).

18 See Sloan Wilson's best-selling novel *The Man in the Grey Flannel Suit* and its film adaptation (1956) with Gregory Peck as Tom Rath.

19 *The Man in the Grey Flannel Suit* is as much about the residual presence of its protagonist's military past as it is about his "organization man" present. Recollections of Tom Rath's previous role as a paratrooper repeatedly intrude upon his new one as an executive and the two are connected by his militarized sense of the postwar "standard issue" gray flannel suit he compulsorily wears. "'The uniform of the day,' Tom thought. 'Somebody must have put out an order.'" Ibid., 104.

20 C. Wright Mills, *The Power Elite* (New York: Oxford University Press, 1955).

21 Bernard Rosenberg, "Mass Culture in America," in Bernard Rosenberg and David Manning White, eds., *Mass Culture: The Popular Arts in America* (New York: Free Press, 1957), 9.

22 Dwight Macdonald, "Kulturbolschewismus Is Here," *Partisan Review* 8 (1941): 442–51.

23 Andrew Ross, *No Respect: Intellectuals and Popular Culture* (New York: Routledge, 1989), 42.

24 For a superb account of the role of intellectuals in the discourse of conformity, see Richard H. Pells, *The Liberal Mind in a Conservative Age: American Intellectuals in the 1940s and 1950s* (Hanover, NH: Wesleyan University Press, 1989), 183–261; and on intellectuals in the Cold War, see 262–345.

25 Elmer T. Peterson, "Cities Are Abnormal," in Peterson, ed., *Cities Are Abnormal* (Norman: University of Oklahoma Press, 1946), 11.

26 On suburbanization, see Kenneth T. Jackson, *Crabgrass Frontier: The Suburbanization of the United States* (New York: Oxford University Press, 1985).

27 John Brooks, *The Great Leap: The Past Twenty-Five Years in America* (London: Victor Gollancz, 1967), 114.

28 Ibid., 115.

29 See for example Richard Polenberg, *One Nation Divisible: Class, Race, and Ethnicity in the United States Since 1938* (New York: Penguin, 1980), 127–63.

30 See for example Warren S. Thompson, "The Atomic Threat," in Peterson, ed., *Cities Are Abnormal*, 226–38. Several press stories gave simulated accounts of atomic attacks on American cities. See for example "The 36-Hour War," *Life* (November 19, 1945), 27–35, which envisages the atomic destruction of Manhattan.

31 Jackson, *Crabgrass Frontier*, 232–3.

32 Quoted in Eric Larrabee, "The Six Thousand Houses That Levitt Built," *Harper's Magazine* (September 1948), 84.

33 Arthur M. Schlesinger Jr., *The Vital Center: The Politics of Freedom* (Cambridge, MA: Riverside Press, 1949).

34 Richard H. Pells, *Radical Visions and American Dreams: Culture and Social Thought in the Depression Years* (Middletown, CT: Wesleyan University Press, 1984), 64.

35 The phrase was popularized after publication of W.H. Auden's poem *The Age of Anxiety: A Baroque Eclogue* (New York: Random House, 1947).

36 Schlesinger, *Vital Center*, 52.

37 Ibid., 53.

38 Ibid., 54.

39 Ibid., 208.

40 Ibid.

41 Daniel Bell, "The End of Ideology in the West: *An Epilogue*," in *The End of Ideology: On the Exhaustion of Political Ideas in the Fifties* (rev. edn, New York: Collier, 1961), 400.

42 Nisbet, "Coming Problem of Assimilation," 263.

43 Waller, *Veteran Comes Back*, 19.

44 See for example, Charles G. Bolte, *The New Veteran* (New York: Reynal and Hitchcock, 1945), 147–52; Waller, *Veteran Comes Back*, 183–91; Bowker, *Out of Uniform*, 253.

45 Donald Becker, "The Veteran: Problem and Challenge," *Social Forces* 25 (1946): 99.

46 Waller, *Veteran Comes Back*, 188–89.

47 Bolte, *New Veteran*, 151. Father Coughlin was seen as a dangerous precedent for American fascism. His weekly radio broadcasts in the 1930s espousing pro-fascist views attracted mass audiences.

48 Waller, *Veteran Comes Back*, 188–91.

49 Bolte, *New Veteran*, 151.

50 Wecter, *When Johnny Comes Marching Home*, 510.

51 Similar concerns appear in other genres too. In the comedy *Colonel Effingham's Raid* (1946), for example, small-town life is characterized by easygoing complacency. The exercise of grassroots democracy has atrophied, enabling corrupt local government officials and businessmen to override the townspeople's interests with impunity. Colonel Effingham (Charles Coburn) challenges the authority of a corrupt and unrepresentative local government by mobilizing the dormant community against it, and his "raid" is as much against political apathy as it is with the intention of making the town fit for returning servicemen.

52 Critics have largely neglected the relation between film noir and citizenship but for a notable exception, see Jonathan Auerbach's *Dark Borders: Film Noir and American Citizenship* (Durham: Duke University Press, 2011).

53 When Welles was making *The Stranger*, Eichmann was one of the senior Nazis who remained at large. He fled to Argentina after the war where he lived under an assumed identity until 1960 when he was captured and later executed for war crimes.

54 According to Peter Bogdanovich, *The Stranger* was the first commercial film to show newsreel footage of concentration camp atrocities. See Orson Welles and Peter Bogdanovich, *This Is Orson Welles* (New York: HarperCollins, 1992), 189.

55 Universal's *Nazi Murder Mills* (1945) was among the first newsreel accounts to show Nazi atrocities in the death camps and included footage of local civilians being forced to witness them.

56 Many examples can be found at the intersection between the female gothic and film noir. See for instance Maxim de Winter (Lawrence Olivier) in *Rebecca* (1940), Johnnie Aysgarth (Cary Grant) in *Suspicion* (1941), Nick Bederaux (Paul Lukas) in *Experiment Perilous* (1944), Gregory Anton (Charles Boyer) in *Gaslight* (1944), Nicholas Van Ryn (Vincent Price) in *Dragonwyck* (1946), Richard Courtland (Don Ameche) in *Sleep, My Love* (1948), and Henry Stevenson (Burt Lancaster) with Morano (William Conrad) in *Sorry, Wrong Number* (1948).

57 According to the shooting script and production log, the original version of the film incorporated significantly more development of these noir features with a flashback structure and much greater narrative realization of the oneiric elements described here. For an account of these missing sequences, see James Naremore, *The Magic World of Orson Welles* (rev. edn, Dallas: Southern Methodist University Press, 1989), 269–71.

58 Martha Gellhorn, "Das Deutsches Volk," *Collier's* (April 1945), repr. in *The Face of War* (London: Virago, 1986), 155.

59 Welles originally wanted the Wilson character to be played by Agnes Moorehead. "I thought it would be much more interesting to have a spinster lady on the heels of this Nazi," he said. See Welles and Bogdanovich, *This Is Orson Welles*, 187. Welles may also have thought it interesting to have female agency actively deployed in the apprehension of the war criminal instead of passively facilitating him as Mary does.

60 "The black smoke," as François Truffaut has noted, "implies that the devil was coming to town." Quoted in Truffaut, with Helen G. Scott, *Hitchcock* (London: Secker & Warburg, 1967), 128.

61 Welles's 1937 Mercury Theater production of *Julius Caesar*, for example, featured a production design that drew on Nazi iconography such as newsreels of Nuremberg rallies. See Barbara Leaming, *Orson Welles: A Biography* (New York: Viking, 1985), 139–42.

62 Quoted in Naremore, *Magic World of Orson Welles*, 117.

63 For a superb account of Welles as an antifascist filmmaker, see Michael Denning, "The Politics of Magic: Orson Welles's Allegories of Anti-Fascism" in *The Cultural Front: The Laboring of American Culture in the Twentieth Century* (London: Verso, 1997), 362–402.

64 The first draft of *Citizen Kane* was titled "American." See Robert L. Carringer, *The Making of Citizen Kane* (London: John Murray, 1985), 18.

65 Wagner played a major ideological role in Nazi culture. See for example William L Shirer, *The Rise and Fall of the Third Reich: A History of Nazi Germany* (New York: Simon and Schuster, 1960), 101–02.

66 A number of postwar noirs featured stories about "fascist" American characters like Kane. *All the King's Men* (1949), for example, Robert Rossen's adaptation of Robert Penn Warren's novel of the same name, sees protagonist Willie Stark (Broderick Crawford) patterned after the political career of Huey P. Long, governor of Louisiana and later senator. Like Kane,

Stark begins as a populist figure—think of Kane's claim to be a champion of citizens' rights in his newspaper's "Declarations of Principles"—representing workers against big business until he becomes increasingly dictatorial and his speeches become more demagogic. Rossen's Stark resembles the kind of populist heroes of Frank Capra's films who can sometimes look close to fascist characterizations. The film also draws on the visual style of *Citizen Kane*, especially the scenes of his fascistic political rally, and deploys noir techniques such as a flashback narrative structure and voice-over narration by Stark's disillusioned aide Jack Burdon (John Ireland).

67 *Crossfire* is usually classified as a film noir but it also has affinities with the social problem film, an increasingly prominent postwar category. Its release preempted Elia Kazan's much-heralded Twentieth Century-Fox production, *Gentleman's Agreement* (1948), a social problem film also dealing with anti-Semitism.

68 *Crossfire* is based on the novel *The Brick Foxhole* by Richard Brooks, in which Monty Crawford is characterized as *the* absolute soldier, a characterization that links his violent racism and homophobia to his identity as a professional soldier. His victim in the novel is a homosexual. Richard Brooks, *The Brick Foxhole* (New York: Harper & Brothers, 1945).

69 Ryan's screen persona was powerfully inflected by the many noir roles in which he appeared following *Crossfire*. See for example, *Trail Street* (1947), *Berlin Express* (1948), *Caught* (1949), *The Set-Up* (1949), *The Woman on Pier 13* (1950), *The Secret Fury* (1950), *The Racket* (1951), *On Dangerous Ground* (1952), *Clash by Night* (1952), and *Odds Against Tomorrow* (1959). In addition to his psychopathic sergeant in *Crossfire*, Ryan's noir roles included other traumatized veterans such as Scott Burnett in *The Woman on the Beach* (1947), Joe Parkson in *Act of Violence* (1949), and (obliquely) Howard Wilton in *Beware, My Lovely* (1952). In a later addition to noir catalogs, in Samuel Fuller's *House of Bamboo* (1955), Ryan plays Sandy Dawson, the ex-soldier boss of a criminal gang operating in occupied Japan. The film draws on several of the traditional tropes of the gangster film, although Dawson's gang is recruited from the ranks of ex-servicemen, all with criminal records. "That's the way I built up my outfit," Dawson says. "All ex-cons before they were drafted. All stockade hounds in the army, dishonorably discharged." Dawson's veterans plan their criminal activities like military operations, exploiting their Army training with ruthless efficiency in what must be the first instance of militarized gangsterdom in film noir.

Coda: The end of film noir

Did film noir come to an end? Did it fizzle out in the late 1950s? Did it really end, as critics have commonly claimed, with *Touch of Evil* (1958), or did it linger on into the early 1960s? Did it, as others say, have an ongoing existence through "neo-noir," resurfacing as a facet of "New Hollywood" in the mid-1960s? One of the main problems we have encountered in this book has been that of determining the historical and generic parameters of film noir. Having discussed noir in its various contexts—industrial, social, cultural, political, economic, and intellectual—I have traced its evolution as an ex post facto critical entity and the application of the term to categories of American film in the 1940s and 1950s. But as film noir drew to the close of its historical cycle, there remains the question of what happened next. Where, if anywhere, does noir *go*? We can identify two transmutations of film noir in the 1960s which demonstrate its reemergence in other forms. The first example can be seen through American television series, and the second through French national cinema.

Film noir was produced within Hollywood's studio system which, by the 1950s, was effectively being dismantled. Reducing its output, the industry produced fewer films but with higher budgets, and big-budget filmmaking was scarcely conducive to noir production. At the same time, demographic trends such as postwar suburbanization saw a decline in box-office receipts as audiences for first-run movie theaters moved out of town. Moreover, with the concomitant rise of television and the comprehensive restructuring of the film industry, the major studios invested heavily in the new medium, soon to provide much of the television programming themselves.[1] Did film noir, in these circumstances, migrate to television? Did the thematic and stylistic characteristics of film noir translate to the television series? Some critics see "TV Noir" as a category in its own right although we should bear in mind their use of the term, often in a similarly elasticated way to their filmic counterparts, with "TV noir" standing more or less as a synonym for any television crime series up to the present day.[2]

Nevertheless, we can identify in some of the earlier series some noir influences that have been reworked for the serial form. Take, for example, *Richard Diamond, Private Detective* (CBS, 1957–59; NBC, 1959–60), starring

David Janssen. The opening credit sequence immediately evokes the familiar black-and-white visual style of 1940s' noir, its dark street lit by a single streetlamp with the shadowed figure of man pausing to light a cigarette, his face momentarily illuminated by the light of the match. But the significance of such scenes isn't merely an instance of stylistic quotation. We can see in a later series, *The Fugitive* (CBS, 1963–67), also starring Janssen, the most striking example of a noir theme transmuted to television. Dr. Richard Kimble (Janssen), falsely convicted of his wife's murder, is en route to prison to face execution when his train crashes, enabling him to escape. Kimble believes that the real killer is the one-armed man he encountered near his home on the night of the murder. The story is a reworking of the "wrong man" narrative (discussed in Chapter 2) and also reminiscent of *Dark Passage* (1947) in which Humphrey Bogart's Vincent Parry, also wrongly convicted of his wife's murder, escapes from prison and embarks on a search for her killer as Kimble does (see Chapter 8).[3]

How can a television series like *The Fugitive* be considered in terms of film noir? In some ways, the form itself might seem to deny meaningful comparison. After all, the technological limitations of television in the 1960s made for a poor-quality medium: its small screen and low-definition picture were incapable of reproducing anything like the rich black tones and low-key lighting effects associated with such noir filmmakers as, say, John Alton and Anthony Mann. Indeed, as with other television series of the 1950s and 1960s, the lighting is typically flat and gray. And yet there could be a "fit" between film noir and the TV series form. For example, program-making was relatively quick and cheap, sharing with the low-budget end of film noir production something of the budgetary aesthetic we examined in Chapter 5. However, the key noir element of *The Fugitive* is one which, paradoxically, sets it apart from its filmic predecessors. If films noir end darkly, at least there is the solace of closure, however bleak it may be. But with all of its 120 episodes spread over four seasons, the episodic structure of *The Fugitive* precludes narrative closure, or at least repeatedly defers it over a period of four years. Kimble is locked into a replicated cycle of angst-ridden survival in one episode after the other, continuously trying to evade detection and the inevitable return to death row, dogged by the grim figure of his nemesis, Lieutenant Gerard (Barry Morse), in inexorable pursuit. All the episodes are the same in that they see Kimble's arrival at a new location, living under an assumed name and working at whatever menial job he can find, his demeanor guarded and taciturn. Like the doomed protagonist Al Roberts in *Detour* (1945), Kimble can never return home nor settle elsewhere but must remain an outsider wherever he finds himself, continuously on the verge of capture. The noir tenor of *The Fugitive* also owes much to Janssen's performance, bringing to the role an intensely haunted look. Locked into a perpetual cycle of existential crisis in which he must always be someone else in order to survive, his fugitive existence is without parallel in film noir.

The second example of transmuted noir can be seen in French cinema during the same period. We have seen how film noir as a generic concept was shaped by French critics ("the Americans made it and then the French invented it"). Recalling how those critics in postwar Paris were predisposed to the reception of the new American crime films they saw there, we might say that the French then invented noir *again*, playing American noir tropes through their own films of the *nouvelle vague*. As we have seen in Chapter 1, the writers on *Cahiers du Cinéma* in the 1950s had drawn up a critical framework for the validation of the American filmmakers they admired—Howard Hawks, Alfred Hitchcock, Fritz Lang, Anthony Mann, Otto Preminger, Nicholas Ray— all of whom were strongly identified with film noir.[4] By the early 1960s, some of the key critics on *Cahiers* such as François Truffaut and Jean-Luc Godard had become filmmakers themselves when they effectively reinvented film noir, this time through their own films, during a period that roughly coincided with the decline of noir in America. Films of the early *nouvelle vague* often shared with American noir a predilection for low-budget filmmaking, location shooting, and semidocumentary style, often with existential themes and a leftist political bias.

Directors like Truffaut and Godard made films that were steeped in American cultural references, often specifically to film noir. Take, for example, Truffaut's *Tirez sur le pianiste* [*Shoot the Pianist*] (1960), based on the novel by David Goodis,[5] and Godard's *À bout de souffle* [*Breathless*] (1960). Godard's film is pointedly dedicated to Monogram Pictures, the Poverty-Row studio associated with "B" productions, and suffused with references to American cars, cigarettes, and jazz music, as well as to Humphrey Bogart, its most iconic noir star. Made two years after Bogart' death, the film sees petty criminal Michel Poiccard (Jean-Paul Belmondo) gazing at a poster of Bogart in his last film, *The Harder They Fall* (1956), while imitating Bogart's characteristic gesture of drawing his thumb over his lips, a gesture repeated by Patricia (Jean Seberg) at the end of the film. The late Bogart and his posthumous noir world were being revivified and reworked by Godard through Belmondo in a French idiom.

Other reworkings of American noir tropes can be found in French cinema of the 1960s and nowhere is this more evident than in the work of Jean-Pierre Melville, notably in his *policier* trilogy with Alain Delon: *Le Samouraï* (1967), *Le Cercle Rouge* [*The Red Circle*] (1970), and Un Flic [*A Cop*] (1972). In *Le Samouraï*, for example, as with the other films in the Delon trilogy, we see a muted color scheme that approximates to the monochrome of film noir through its cool, blue-gray palette. Melville famously talked about making "a black and white film in colour."[6] *Le Samouraï* is a loose remake of *This Gun for Hire* (1942), a key film for Borde and Chaumeton in their *Panorama* of

American noir, as we have seen in Chapter 5. Like Alan Ladd's Philip Raven in the original film, Delon's Jef Costello is a contract killer. The two are also facially similar, especially in their inexpressive demeanor, and similarly attired in trench coats and fedoras. We see Jef put on his coat and hat and study the effect in the mirror, running his fingers along the brim of his hat as if in a self-conscious effort to inhabit the iconography of 1940s' American noir. The self-reflexive gesture, narcissistically aware of its own effect, seems to be repackaging the noir style of what is now a bygone age. Melville draws particular attention to Jef's image during the police lineup sequence when he is brought in for questioning about the murder of a nightclub boss. Influenced by a corresponding scene in *The Asphalt Jungle* (1950), the sequence seems like an extended meditation on the design of gangster style. A witness who has briefly glimpsed Jef is brought in to identify him. In contrast to a regular lineup, Jef is positioned among rows of policemen, all conspicuously wearing different types of coat and hat. Jef is instructed to switch his hat with one policeman and his coat with another. "I have a composite image of the man I passed," says the witness before gesturing toward the policemen. "A trench-coat like that one. A hat like this one . . . or that one. And," he says, indicating the "misattired" Jef, "a face like his." The protracted sequence works to deconstruct Jef's noir characterization, dismantling and reassembling the different dress components that stylize his appearance.[7]

There are many instances in which the iconography of American noir is reconfigured in a Parisian milieu. In Truffaut's *Tirez sur le pianist*, for example, note the incongruous appearance of Charlie (Charles Aznavour) and Léna (Marie Dubois) in their matching trench coats, walking along the city streets where they look strangely out of place. Note too the opening sequence of Melville's *Bob le flambeur* (1956), where we see another trench-coated figure. Departing at dawn from an all-night gambling session, Bob (Roger Duchesne) pauses before a shop window and looks wryly at his reflection while adjusting his tie. "A real hood's face," says the aging gangster in a self-reflexive commentary on his "legendary" local status. The Pigalle and Montmartre districts are depicted in a "neo-realist" shooting style reminiscent of the New York of *The Naked City*. Here, as Ginette Vincendeau suggests, Bob represents Melville's "self-conscious citation of a Hollywood archetype," a figure "evocative of the 1940s iconic gangsters" such as Robert Mitchum in *Out of the Past* (1947) or Alan Ladd in *This Gun for Hire*, each emblematic of the period's noir stylization.[8]

As the cycle of film noir was drawing to a close in America, it was revisited by filmmakers of the *nouvelle vague* where a new modernist national cinema was being fashioned from the stylistic and thematic tropes of Hollywood noir. It seems like an apt coda to American noir that after its critical invention in postwar Paris it should reappear at the moment of its own demise as the subject of a valedictory address by French filmmakers.

Notes

1 See for instance, Janet Wasko, "Hollywood and Television in the 1950s: The Roots of Diversification" in Peter Lev, ed., *The Fifties: Transforming the Screen, 1950–1959* (Berkeley: University of California Press, 2003), 127–46.

2 See for instance, Steven Sanders, "Television Noir," in Andrew Spicer and Helen Hanson, eds, *A Companion to Film Noir* (Oxford: Wiley Blackwell, 2013), 440–57. Sanders's list of contemporary titles includes *Miami Vice* (NBC, 1984–89), *The X-Files* (Fox, 1993–2002), *The Sopranos* (HBO, 1999–2007), and *Dexter* (Showtime, 2006–13). For a useful survey, especially of earlier titles, see Allen Glover and David Bushman, "Lights Out in the Wasteland: The TV Noir," *Television Quarterly* (37:1) 2006 (67–75).

3 David Goodis, author of *Dark Passage* (1947), claimed that *The Fugitive* was based on his novel and in 1965 sued the network for copyright infringement.

4 For a representative selection of their writings, see "American Cinema" in Jim Hillier, ed., *Cahiers du Cinéma: The 1950s: Neo-Realism, Hollywood, New Wave* (Cambridge, MA: Harvard University Press, 1985), 71–172.

5 Originally published as *Down There* (New York: Gold Medal, 1956). Goodis was a "pulp" writer whose work had previously been adapted as film noir, including *Dark Passage* (1947), *Nightfall* (1957), and *The Burglar* (1957).

6 Quoted in Ginette Vincendeau, *Jean-Pierre Melville: An American in Paris* (2003; London: Palgrave/BFI, 2014), 186.

7 For a useful discussion of *Le Samouraï*, including this scene, see Jennifer Fay and Justus Nieland, *Film Noir: Hard-Boiled Modernity and the Cultures of Globalization* (Abingdon: Routledge, 2010), 204–10.

8 Vincendeau, *Jean-Pierre Melville*, 111.

Bibliography

Abel, Richard, *The Ciné Goes to Town: French Cinema 1896-1914* (Berkeley: University of California Press, 1998).

Altman, Rick, *Film/Genre* (London: BFI, 1999).

Altschuler, Glenn C., and Stuart M. Blumin, *The G.I. Bill: A New Deal for Veterans* (New York: Oxford University Press, 2009).

"America," *Time* (October 28, 1946), 2–3.

Andersen, Thom, "Red Hollywood," in Suzanne Ferguson and Barbara Groseclose, eds., *Literature and the Visual Arts in Contemporary Society* (Columbus: Ohio State University Press, 1985), 141–96.

Anonymous, "Informal Organization in the Army," *American Journal of Sociology* 51 (1946), 365–70.

Aragon, Louis, "On Décor," *Le Film* (September 1918), repr. in Hammond, ed., *Shadow and Its Shadow*, 55–59.

Asbury, Herbert, "Fiction," *The Bookman* (March 1929), 92.

Ashbery, John, "Introduction to *Fantômas*," in Marcel Allain and Pierre Souvestre, *Fantômas* (1911; London: Picador, 1986), 1–9.

Auden, W. H., *The Age of Anxiety: A Baroque Eclogue* (New York: Random House, 1947).

Auerbach, Jonathan, *Dark Borders: Film Noir and American Citizenship* (Durham: Duke University Press, 2011).

Auger, Emily E., *Tech-Noir Film: A Theory of the Development of Popular Genres* (Bristol: Intellect, 2011).

Ball, Terence, "The Politics of Social Science in Postwar America," in Lary May, ed., *Recasting America: Culture and Politics in the Age of the Cold War* (Chicago: University of Chicago Press, 1989), 76–92.

Ballinger, Alexander, and Danny Graydon, *The Rough Guide to Film Noir* (London: Rough Guides, 2007).

Basinger, Jeanine, *The World War II Combat Film: Anatomy of a Genre* (New York: Columbia University Press, 1986).

Basinger, Jeanine, *A Woman's View: How Hollywood Spoke to Women, 1930-1960* (London: Chatto & Windus, 1994).

Bazin, André, "The Death of Humphrey Bogart," *Cahiers du Cinéma* 68 (February 1957), trans. Phillip Drummond, repr. in Jim Hillier, ed., *Cahiers du Cinéma: The 1950s: Neo-Realism, Hollywood, New Wave* (Cambridge, MA: Harvard University Press, 1985), 98–101.

Becker, Donald, "The Veteran: Problem and Challenge," *Social Forces* 25 (1946), 95–99.

Bedford, James H., *The Veteran and His Future Job: A Guide-Book for the Veteran* (LA: Society for Occupational Research, 1946).

Bell, Daniel, *The End of Ideology: On the Exhaustion of Political Ideas in the Fifties* (rev. edn, New York: Collier, 1961).

Bellow, Saul, *Dangling Man* (1944; Harmondsworth: Penguin, 1966).

Belton, John, "Film Noir's Knights of the Road," *Bright Lights Film Journal* 12 (Spring 1994), 5–15.

Bennett, Michael J., *When Dreams Came True: The GI Bill and the Making of Modern America* (Washington, DC: Brassey's, 1996).

Bergala, Alain, "Weegee and Film Noir," in Miles Barth, ed., *Weegee's World* (Boston: Bullfinch, 2000), 69–117.

Biesen, Sheri Chinen, *Blackout: World War II and the Origins of Film Noir* (Baltimore: Johns Hopkins University Press, 2005).

Biesen, Sheri Chinen, *Music in the Shadows: Noir Musical Films* (Baltimore: Johns Hopkins University Press, 2014).

Bogdanovich, Peter, "Edgar G. Ulmer," in McCarthy and Flynn, eds., *Kings of the Bs* (New York: Dutton, 1975), 377–409.

Bolte, Charles G., *The New Veteran* (New York: Reynal and Hitchcock, 1945).

Borde, Raymond, and Étienne Chaumeton, *A Panorama of American Film Noir, 1941-1953*, trans. Paul Hammond (1955; San Francisco: City Lights, 2002).

Bowker, Benjamin C., *Out of Uniform* (New York: Norton, 1946).

Brean, Herbert, "A Case of Identity," *Life* (June 29, 1953), 97–107.

Brion, Patrick, *Le Film noir: L'âge d'or du film criminel américain d'Alfred Hitchcock à Nicholas Ray* (Paris: Éditions Nathan, 1991).

Britton, Andrew, "Detour," in Cameron, ed., *Movie Book of Film Noir*, 174–83.

Broe, Dennis, *Class, Crime and International Film Noir: Globalizing America's Dark Art* (New York: Palgrave Macmillan, 2014).

Brookes, Ian, "The Eye of Power: Postwar Fordism and the Panoptic Corporation in *The Apartment*," *Journal of Popular Film & Television* 37, no. 4 (Winter 2009), 150–60.

Brookes, Ian, "'A Rebus of Democratic Slants and Angles': *To Have and Have Not*, Racial Representation, and Musical Performance in a Democracy at War," in Graham Lock and David Murray, eds., *Thriving On a Riff: Jazz and Blues Influences in African American Literature and Film* (New York: Oxford University Press, 2009), 203–20.

Brookes, Ian, "Who the Hell Is Howard Hawks?" in Ian Brookes, ed., *Howard Hawks: New Perspectives* (London: Palgrave/BFI, 2016), 1–32.

Brooks, John, *The Great Leap: The Past Twenty-Five Years in America* (London: Victor Gollancz, 1967).

Brooks, Richard, *The Brick Foxhole* (New York: Harper & Brothers, 1945).

Brotz, Howard, and Everett Wilson, "Characteristics of Military Society," *American Journal of Sociology* 51 (1946), 371–75.

Buss, Robin, *French Film Noir* (London: Marion Boyars, 1994).

Cameron, Ian, ed., *The Movie Book of Film Noir* (London: Studio Vista, 1992).

Carringer, Robert L., *The Making of Citizen Kane* (London: John Murray, 1985).

Caute, David, *The Great Fear: The Anti-Communist Purge Under Truman and Eisenhower* (New York: Simon and Schuster, 1978).

Ceplair, Larry, and Steven Englund, *The Inquisition in Hollywood: Politics in the Film Community, 1930-1960* (Berkeley: University of California Press, 1983).

Chandler, Raymond, *The Big Sleep* (1939; Harmondsworth: Penguin, 1976).

Chandler, Raymond, *Farewell, My Lovely* (1940; Harmondsworth: Penguin, 1976).

Chandler, Raymond, "The Simple Art of Murder: An Essay," in *The Simple Art of Murder* (1950; New York: Vintage, 1988), 1–18.

Chartier, Jean-Pierre, "Les Américaines aussi font des films 'noirs' ('Americans Also Make *Noir* Films')" trans. Alain Silver, *La Revue du Cinéma* (November 1946), repr. in Silver and Ursini, eds., *Film Noir Reader 2*, 21–23.

Childers, Thomas, *Soldier from the War Returning: The Greatest Generation's Troubled Homecoming from World War II* (Boston: Houghton Mifflin Harcourt, 2009).

Christopher, Nicholas, *Somewhere In the Night: Film Noir and the American City* (New York: Owl, 1997).

Clarens, Carlos, *Crime Movies: An Illustrated History of the Gangster Genre From D.W. Griffith to Pulp Fiction* (1980 rev. edn, New York: Da Capo, 1997).

Clute, Shannon, and Richard L. Edwards, *The Maltese Touch of Evil: Film Noir and Potential Criticism* (Dartmouth: Dartmouth College Press, 2011).

Copjec, Joan, ed., *Shades of Noir: A Reader* (London: Verso, 1993).

Corber, Robert J., "Hitchcock's Washington: Spectatorship, Ideology, and the 'Homosexual Menace' *in Strangers on a Train*," in Jonathan Freedman and Richard Millington, eds., *Hitchcock's America* (New York: Oxford University Press, 1999), 99–121.

Cowie, Elizabeth, "*Film Noir* and Women," in Copjec, ed., *Shades of Noir*, 121–65.

Crane, Ralph, "Arizona War Worker Writes Her Navy Boyfriend A Thank-You Note For The Jap Skull He Sent Her," *Life* (May 22, 1944), 35.

Crowe, Cameron, *Conversations with Wilder* (New York: Alfred A. Knopf, 1999).

Crowther, Bosley, "It's an Ill Wind—But the Recent War Restrictions on Film Production Bode Some Good," *New York Times* (September 27, 1942), X3.

Crowther, Bosley, "The Screen: 'Christmas Holiday', Presenting Deanna Durbin in Serious and Emotional Role, Supported by Gene Kelly, Opens at Criterion," *New York Times* (June 29, 1944), 16.

Crowther, Bosley, "The Screen: 'Double Indemnity', a Tough Melodrama, With Stanwyck and MacMurray as Killers, Opens at the Paramount," *New York Times* (September 7, 1944), 21.

Crowther, Bruce, *Film Noir: Reflections in a Dark Mirror* (London: Columbus, 1988).

"DEAD!" *New York Daily News* (January 13, 1928), 1.

Denning, Michael, *The Cultural Front: The Laboring of American Culture in the Twentieth Century* (London: Verso, 1997).

Desser, David, "Global Noir: Genre Film in the Age of Transnationalism," in Barry Keith Grant, ed., *Film Genre IV* (Austin: University of Texas Press, 2012), 628–48.

Dixon, Wheeler Winston, "Ida Lupino," in *Senses of Cinema* (April 2009). http://sensesofcinema.com/2009/great-directors/ida-lupino/

Doane, Mary Ann, *Femme Fatales: Feminism, Film Theory, Psychoanalysis* (New York: Routledge, 1991).

Doherty, Thomas, *Projections of War: Hollywood, American Culture, and World War II* (New York: Columbia University Press, 1993).

Dower, John W., *War Without Mercy: Race and Power in the Pacific War* (New York: Pantheon, 1993).

Droke, Maxwell, *Goodbye To G.I: How To Be a Successful Civilian* (New York: Abingdon-Cokesbury, 1945).

Duhamel, Marcel, "Preface," in Borde and Chaumeton, *Panorama of American Film Noir*, trans. Paul Hammond, xxiii–xxv.

Duncan, Paul, ed., *Film Noir* (Köln: Taschen, 2004).

Duncan, Paul, and Jürgen Müller, eds., *Film Noir: 100 All-Time Favorites* (Köln: Taschen, 2014).

Durgnat, Raymond, "Paint It Black: The Family Tree of the *Film Noir*," *Cinema* (1970), repr. in Silver and Ursini, eds., *Film Noir Reader*, 37–51.

Dyer, Richard, "Resistance Through Charisma: Rita Hayworth and *Gilda*," in Kaplan, ed., *Women in Film Noir*, 91–99.

Eaton, Walter H., "Research on Veterans' Adjustment," *American Journal of Sociology* 51 (1946), 483–87.

Editors of *Look*, *Movie Lot to Beachhead: The Motion Picture Goes to War and Prepares for the Future* (New York: Doubleday, Doran, 1945).

Efron, Edith, "Old Jobs, or New Ones, for the Veterans?" *New York Times Magazine* (March 18, 1945), 11, 41–42.

Eisner, Lotte H., *The Haunted Screen: Expressionism in the German Cinema and the Influence of Max Reinhardt*, trans. Roger Greaves (London: Thames & Hudson, 1969).

Elkin, Frederick, "The Soldier's Language," *American Journal of Sociology* 51 (1946), 414–22.

Elkin, Henry, "Aggressive and Erotic Tendencies in Army Life," *American Journal of Sociology* 51 (1946), 408–13.

Erickson, Todd, "James Ellroy: Crime Fiction Beyond Noir," *L.A. Weekly* (July 21, 1989), 18–23.

Faison, Stephen, *Existentialism, Film Noir, and Hard-Boiled Fiction* (Amherst, NY: Cambria Press, 2008).

Fay, Jennifer, and Justus Nieland, *Film Noir: Hard-Boiled Modernity and the Cultures of Globalization* (Abingdon: Routledge, 2010).

Foucault, Michel, *Discipline and Punish: The Birth of the Prison*, trans. Alan Sheridan. (1975, London: Penguin, 1991).

Foucault, Michel, *The Order of Things: An Archeology of the Human Sciences* (New York: Vintage, 1994).

Frank, Nino, "Et la troisième dimension?" *L'Écran Français* (July 24, 1946), 5.

Frank, Nino, "An Exciting ... Put-You-To-Sleep Story," *L'Écran Français* (August 7, 1946), trans. Connor Hartnett, repr. in William Luhr, ed., *The Maltese Falcon: John Huston, Director* (New Brunswick, NJ: Rutgers University Press, 1995), 130–31.

Frank, Nino, "Un nouveau genre 'policier': L'aventure criminelle" ("A New Kind of Police Drama: The Criminal Adventure") trans. Alain Silver, *L'Écran Français* (August 1946), repr. in Silver and Ursini, eds., *Film Noir Reader 2*, 15–19.

Friedrich, Otto, *City of Nets: A Portrait of Hollywood in the 1940s* (London: Headline, 1987).

Frost, Adam, "Infographic: What makes a Film Noir?" (BFI, July 22, 2015). http://www.bfi.org.uk/news-opinion/news-bfi/features/infographic-what-makes-film-noir

Fussell, Paul, *Wartime: Understanding and Behavior in the Second World War* (New York: Oxford University Press, 1989).

Gates, Philippa, "Independence Unpunished: The Female Detective in Classic Film Noir," in Robert Miklitsch, ed., *Kiss the Blood Off My Hands: On Classic Film Noir* (Urbana: University of Illinois Press, 2014), 17–36.

Gellhorn, Martha, "Das Deutsches Volk," *Collier's* (April 1945), repr. in *The Face of War* (London: Virago, 1986), 155–63.

Gemünden, Gerd, *A Foreign Affair: Billy Wilder's American Films* (New York: Berghahn, 2008).

Gledhill, Christine, "*Klute* 1: A Contemporary Film Noir and Feminist Criticism," in Kaplan, ed., *Women in Film Noir*, 6–21.

Glover, Allen, and David Bushman, "Lights Out in the Wasteland: The TV Noir," *Television Quarterly* 37: 1 (2006), 67–75.

Goffman, Erving, *Asylums: Essays on the Social Situation of Mental Patients and Other Inmates* (1961; Harmondsworth: Penguin, 1980).

Goodis, David, *Down There* (New York: Gold Medal, 1956).

Goodman, Paul, "Sailor's Money", in Taylor Stoehr, ed., *The Facts of Life: Stories, 1940-1949* (1949; Santa Barbara, CA: Black Sparrow Press, 1979), 315–18.

Goulden, Joseph C., *The Best Years, 1945-1950* (New York: Atheneum, 1976).

Grant, John, *A Comprehensive Encyclopedia of Film Noir: The Essential Reference Guide* (Milwaukee: Limelight, 2013).

Gregory, W. Edgar, "The Idealization of the Absent," *American Journal of Sociology* 50 (1944), 53–54.

Griffith, Richard, " 'Asphalt Jungle' May Be Best Crime Movie," *Los Angeles Times* (June 27, 1950), A7.

Grinker, Roy R., and John P. Spiegel, *Men Under Stress* (Philadelphia: Blakiston, 1945).

Gunning, Tom, *The Films of Fritz Lang: Allegories of Vision and Modernity* (London: BFI, 2000).

Hamilton, Patrick, *Gas Light* (London: Constable, 1939).

Hammett, Dashiell, *The Maltese Falcon* (1930; New York: Vintage Crime/Black Lizard, 1992).

Hammett, Dashiell, *Red Harvest* (1929; New York: Vintage/Black Lizard, 1992).

Hammond, Paul, "Available Light, " in Hammond, ed., *Shadow and Its Shadow*, 1–48.

Hammond, Paul, ed., *The Shadow and Its Shadow: Surrealist Writings on the Cinema* (3rd edn, San Francisco: City Lights, 2000).

Hannsberry, Karen Burroughs, *Femme Noir: Bad Girls of Film* (Jefferson, NC: McFarland, 1998).

Hare, William, *Pulp Fiction to Film Noir: The Great Depression and the Development of a Genre* (Jefferson, NC: McFarland, 2012).

Hartmann, Susan M., *The Home Front and Beyond: American Women in the 1940s* (Boston: Twayne, 1982).

Harvey, Sylvia, "Woman's Place: The Absent Family of Film Noir," in Kaplan, ed., *Women in Film Noir*, 22–34.

Havighurst, Robert J., Walter H. Eaton, John W. Baughman, and Ernest W. Burgess, *The American Veteran Back Home: A Study of Veteran Readjustment* (New York: Longmans, Green, 1951).

Heffernan, Nick, "Acts of Violence: The World War II Veteran Private-Eye Movie as an Ideological Crime Series," in Jean Anderson, Carolina Miranda, and Barbara Pezzotti, eds., *Serial Crime Fiction: Dying for More* (London: Palgrave, 2015), 63–73.

Hemingway, Ernest, "The Killers" (1927), in *Men without Women* (Harmondsworth: Penguin, 1963), 57–69.

Higham, Charles, and Joel Greenberg, *Hollywood in the Forties* (New York: A.S. Barnes, 1968).

Hill, Reuben, "The American Family: Problem or Solution?" *American Journal of Sociology* 53 (1947), 125–30.

Hillier, Jim, ed., *Cahiers du Cinéma: The 1950s: Neo-Realism, Hollywood, New Wave* (Cambridge, MA: Harvard University Press, 1985), 71–172.

Hillier, Jim, and Alastair Phillips, *100 Film Noirs* (London: BFI, 2009).

Hirsch, Foster, *Film Noir: The Dark Side of the Screen* (New York: Da Capo, 1981).

Hirsch, Foster, *Detours and Lost Highways: A Map of Neo-Noir* (New York: Limelight, 1999).

Hollingshead, August B., "Adjustment to Military Life," *American Journal of Sociology* 51 (1946), 439–47.

Holmes, M. E., *Nino Frank: From Dada to Film Noir*, Chapter 8, "Nino Frank and the Fascination of Noir." http://rememberninofrank.org/chapters/6-nino-frank-and-the-fascination-of-noir Accessed January 5, 2016).

Horsley, Lee, *The Noir Thriller* (London: Palgrave Macmillan, 2009).

Hughes, Dorothy B., "*The Homecoming*," in Mystery Writers of America, Inc., *Murder Cavalcade: An Anthology* (New York: Duell, Sloan and Pearce, 1946), 163–75.

Hughes, Dorothy B., *Ride the Pink Horse* (1946; London: Canongate, 2002).

Hughes, Dorothy B., *In a Lonely Place* (1947; New York: Feminist Press at the City University of New York, 2003).

"Human Behavior in Military Society," [symposium issue] *American Journal of Sociology* 51 (1946).

Humes, Edward, *Over Here: How the G.I. Bill Transformed the American Dream* (New York: Houghton Mifflin Harcourt, 2006).

Hutchings, Peter, "Film Noir and Horror," in Spicer and Hanson, eds., *Companion to Film Noir*, 111–24.

Isaacs, Jeremy, and Taylor Dowling, *Cold War* (London: Bantam Press, 1998).

Jackson, Julian, *France: The Dark Years, 1940-1944* (New York: Oxford University Press, 2001).

Jackson, Kenneth T., *Crabgrass Frontier: The Suburbanization of the United States* (New York: Oxford University Press, 1985).

Jacobowitz, Florence, "The Man's Melodrama: *The Woman in the Window* and *Scarlet Street*," in Cameron, ed., *Movie Book of Film Noir*, 152–64.

Jameson, Fredric, *Postmodernism, Or, the Cultural Logic of Late Capitalism* (New York: Verso, 1991).

Jameson, Richard T., "Son of Noir," *Film Comment* 10, no. 6 (November–December 1974), 30–33.

Jones, Edgar L., "The Soldier Returns," *Atlantic Monthly* (January 1944), 42–46.

Jones, Edgar L., "One War Is Enough," *Atlantic Monthly* (February 1946), 48–53.

Jones, James, *Whistle* (1978; New York: Open Road Integrated Media, 2011).

Kahn, Gordon, *Hollywood on Trial: The Story of the Ten Who Were Indicted* (New York: Boni & Gaer, 1948).

Kantor, MacKinlay, *Glory for Me* (New York: Coward-McCann, 1945).

Kaplan, E. Ann, "Introduction," in Kaplan, ed., *Women in Film Noir*, 1–5.

Kaplan, E. Ann, ed., *Women in Film Noir* (London: BFI, 1978).

Kemp, Philip, "From the Nightmare Factory: HUAC and the Politics of Noir," *Sight & Sound* 55, no. 4 (Autumn 1986), 266–70.

Kennett, Lee, *G.I: The American Soldier in World War II* (New York: Scribner's, 1987).

Kerr, Paul, "Out of What Past? Notes on the B *Film Noir,*" *Screen Education* (Autumn/Winter 1979/1980), repr. in Silver and Ursini, eds., *Film Noir Reader,* 107–27.

Kitching, Howard, *Sex Problems of the Returned Veteran* (New York: Emerson, 1946).

Knight, Stephen, *Crime Fiction, 1800-2000: Death, Detection, Diversity* (Basingstoke: Palgrave Macmillan, 2004).

Koppes, Clayton R., and Gregory D. Black, *Hollywood Goes to War: How Politics, Profits, and Propaganda Shaped World War II Movies* (New York: Free Press, 1987).

Krutnik, Frank, *In a Lonely Street: Film Noir, Genre, Masculinity* (London: Routledge, 1991).

Kuhn, Annette, ed., *Queen of the 'B's: Ida Lupino Behind the Camera* (Trowbridge: Flicks Books, 1995).

Kupper, Herbert I., *Back To Life: The Emotional Readjustment of Our Veterans* (New York: Fischer, 1945).

La Farge, Christopher, "Soldier Into Civilian," *Harper's* (March 1945), 339–46.

Lally, Kevin, *Wilder Times: The Life of Billy Wilder* (New York: Henry Holt, 1996).

Larrabee, Eric, "The Six Thousand Houses That Levitt Built," *Harper's Magazine* (September 1948), 79–88.

Leaming, Barbara, *Orson Welles: A Biography* (New York: Viking, 1985).

Leff, Leonard J., and Jerold L. Simmons, *The Dame in the Kimono: Hollywood, Censorship, and the Production Code from the 1920s to the 1960s* (London: Weidenfeld and Nicolson, 1990).

Leibman, Nina C., "The Family Spree of Film Noir," *Journal of Popular Film and Television* 16, no. 4 (Winter 1989), 168–84.

Linderman, Gerald F., *The World Within War: America's Combat Experience in World War II* (Cambridge, MA: Harvard University Press, 1999).

Lowry, Robert, *Casualty* (New York: New Directions, 1946).

Lyons, Arthur, *Death on the Cheap: The Lost B Movies of Film Noir!* (New York: Da Capo, 2000).

Macdonald, Dwight, "Kulturbolschewismus Is Here," *Partisan Review* 8 (1941), 442–51.

MacDonald, John D., *Cape Fear* (1957; London: Orion, 2014).

MacShane, Frank, *Raymond Chandler: A Biography* (London: Vintage, 1998).

Madden, David, *Cain's Craft* (Metuchen, NJ: Scarecrow, 1985).

Mailer, Norman, *The Naked and the Dead* (1948; London: Flamingo, 1999).

Mainon, Dominique, and James Ursini, *Femme Fatale: Cinema's Most Unforgettable Lethal Ladies* (Milwaukee: Limelight, 2009).

Maltby, Richard, "The Politics of the Maladjusted Text," *Journal of American Studies* 18 (1984), repr. in Cameron, ed., *Movie Book of Film Noir,* 39–48.

Maltby, Richard, *Hollywood Cinema* (Oxford: Wiley Blackwell, 1995).

Maltby, Richard, "The Spectacle of Criminality," in J. David Slocum, ed., *Violence and the American Cinema* (New York: Routledge, 2001), 117–52.

Marling, William, *The American Roman Noir: Hammett, Cain, and Chandler* (Athens, GA: University of Georgia Press, 1995).

Maslin, Janet, "Screen: William Hurt as Fall Guy in 'Body Heat': Film Noir Revisited," *New York Times* (August 28, 1981), C14.

May, Lary, "Making the American Consensus: The Narrative of Conversion and Subversion in World War II Films," in Lewis A. Erenberg and Susan E. Hirsch, eds., *The War in American Culture: Society and Consciousness During World War II* (Chicago: University of Chicago Press, 1996), 71–102.

Mayer, Geoff, *Historical Dictionary of Crime Films* (Lanham, MD: Scarecrow Press, 2012).

Mayer, Geoff, and Brian McDonnell, *Encyclopedia of Film Noir* (Westport, CT: Greenwood Press, 2000).

McArthur, Colin, *Underworld U.S.A.* (London: Secker & Warburg, 1972).

McCallum, Malcolm R., "The Study of the Delinquent in the Army," *American Journal of Sociology* 51 (1946), 479–82.

McCarthy, Todd, and Charles Flynn, "The Economic Imperative: Why Was the B Movie Necessary?" in McCarthy and Flynn, eds., *Kings of the Bs*, 13–43.

McCarthy, Todd, and Charles Flynn, eds., *Kings of the Bs: Working Within the Hollywood System: An Anthology of Film History and Criticism* (New York: Dutton, 1975).

McDonagh, Edward C., and Louise McDonagh, "War Anxieties of Soldiers and Their Wives," *Social Forces* 24 (1945), 195–200.

McDonagh, Edward C., "The Discharged Serviceman and His Family," *American Journal of Sociology* 51 (1946), 451–54.

McGilligan, Patrick, *Alfred Hitchcock: A Life in Darkness and Light* (Chichester: Wiley, 2003).

McGilligan, Patrick, *Nicholas Ray: The Glorious Failure of an American Director* (New York: HarperCollins, 2011).

Meisel, Myron, "Edgar G. Ulmer: The Primacy of the Visual," in McCarthy and Flynn, eds., *Kings of the Bs*, 147–52.

Menninger, William C., *Psychiatry in a Troubled World: Yesterday's War and Today's Challenge* (New York: Macmillan, 1948).

Mettler, Suzanne, *Soldiers to Civilians: The G.I. Bill and the Making of the Greatest Generation* (New York: Oxford University Press, 2007).

Miller, Arthur, *Death of a Salesman* (1949; Harmondsworth: Penguin, 1972).

Miller, Arthur, *The Crucible* (1953; Harmondsworth: Penguin, 1974).

Miller, Arthur, *Timebends: A Life* (London: Minerva, 1990).

Miller, Arthur, "Belief in America," (1944), repr. in Steven R. Centola, ed., *Arthur Miller: Echoes Down the Corridor: Collected Essays 1944-2000* (New York: Penguin, 2001), 31–37.

Miller, Merle, *That Winter* (New York: William Sloane Associates, 1948).

Mills, C. Wright, *The Power Elite* (New York: Oxford University Press, 1955).

Mills, C. Wright, *White Collar: The American Middle Classes* (1951; New York: Oxford University Press, 1956).

Modleski, Tania, *Loving With a Vengeance: Mass Produced Fantasies For Women* (Hamden, CT: Archon, 1982).

Muller, Eddie, *Dark City: The Lost World of Film Noir* (London: Titan, 1998).

Mumford, Lewis, *The City in History: Its Origins, Its Transformations, and Its Prospects* (London: Secker and Warburg, 1961).

Munby, Jonathan, *Public Enemies, Public Heroes: Screening the Gangster from Little Caesar to Touch of Evil* (Chicago: Chicago University Press, 1999).

Naremore, James, *The Magic World of Orson Welles* (rev. edn, Dallas: Southern Methodist University Press, 1989).

Naremore, James, *More than Night: Film Noir in its Contexts* (Berkeley: University of California Press, 1998).

Naremore, James, "A Season in Hell or the Snows of Yesteryear?" in Borde and Chaumeton, *Panorama of American Film Noir*, vii–xxi.

Naremore, James, "Hitchcock at the Margins of Noir," in Naremore, ed., *An Invention Without a Future: Essays on Cinema* (Berkeley: University of California Press, 2014), 139–55.

Navasky, Victor S., *Naming Names* (New York: Penguin, 1981).

Neale, Steve, *Genre and Hollywood* (London: Routledge, 2000).

Neve, Brian, *Film and Politics in America: A Social Tradition* (London: Routledge, 1992).

Nicol, Bran, *The Private Eye: Detectives in the Movies* (London: Reaktion, 2013).

Nisbet, Robert E., "The Coming Problem of Assimilation," *American Journal of Sociology* 50 (1945), 261–70.

O'Brien, Charles, "Film Noir in France: Before the Liberation," *Iris* 21 (Spring 1996), 7–20.

O'Brien, Geoffrey, "The Return of Film Noir!" *New York Review of Books* (August 15, 1991), 43–46.

O'Brien, Geoffrey, *Hardboiled America: Lurid Paperbacks and the Masters of Noir* (1981; New York: Da Capo,1997).

Osteen, Mark, *Nightmare Alley: Film Noir and the American Dream* (Baltimore: Johns Hopkins Press, 2013).

Ottoson, Robert, *A Reference Guide to the American Film Noir, 1940-1958* (Metuchen, NJ: Scarecrow Press, 1981).

Ousby, Ian, *Occupation: The Ordeal of France, 1940-1944* (London: John Murray, 1977).

Palmer, R. Barton, *Hollywood's Dark Cinema: The American Film Noir* (New York: Twayne, 1994).

Palmer R. Barton, ed., *Perspectives on Film Noir* (New York: G.K. Hall, 1996).

Panunzio, Constantine, "War and Marriage," *Social Forces* 21 (1943), 442–45.

Peattie, Margaret Rhodes, *The Return* (New York: William Morrow, 1944).

Pells, Richard H., *Radical Visions and American Dreams: Culture and Social Thought in the Depression Years* (Middletown, CT: Wesleyan University Press, 1984).

Pells, Richard H., *The Liberal Mind in a Conservative Age: American Intellectuals in the 1940s and 1950s* (Hanover, NH: Wesleyan University Press, 1989).

Peterson, Elmer T., "Cities Are Abnormal," in Peterson, ed., *Cities Are Abnormal* (Norman: University of Oklahoma Press, 1946), 3–26.

Phillips, Cabell, *The 1940s: Decade of Triumph and Trouble* (New York: Macmillan, 1975).

Place, Janey, "Women in Film Noir," in Kaplan, ed., *Women in Film Noir*, 35–67.

Place, Janey, and Lowell Peterson, "Some Visual Motifs of *Film Noir*," *Film Comment* (January/February 1974), repr. in Silver and Ursini, eds., *Film Noir Reader*, 65–76.

Polan, Dana, *Power and Paranoia: History, Narrative, and the American Cinema, 1940-1950* (New York: Columbia University Press, 1986).

Polan, Dana, *In a Lonely Place* (London: BFI, 1993).

Polenberg, Richard, *One Nation Divisible: Class, Race, and Ethnicity in the United States Since 1938* (New York: Penguin, 1980).

Porfirio, Robert, "Interview with Otto Preminger," in Porfirio, Silver, and Ursini, eds., *Film Noir Reader 3*, 87–99.

Porfirio, Robert, "No Way Out: Existential Motifs in the *Film Noir*," *Sight and Sound* (Autumn 1976), repr. in Silver and Ursini, eds., *Film Noir Reader,* 77–93.

Porfirio, Robert, "The Strange Case of Film Noir," in Spicer and Hanson, eds., *Companion to Film Noir*, 17–32.

Prakash, Gyan, ed., *Noir Urbanisms: Dystopic Images of the Global Modern City* (Princeton, NJ: Princeton University Press, 2010).

Pratt, George K., *Soldier to Civilian: Problems of Readjustment* (New York: McGraw-Hill, 1944).

Rabinoff, Rose M., "While Their Men Are Away," *SurveryMidmonthly* 81(1945), 110–13.

Reinemann, J.O., "Extra-Marital Relations With Fellow Employee in War Industry as a Factor in Disruption of Family Life," *American Sociological Review* 10 (1945), 399–404.

Renzi, Thomas C., *Cornell Woolrich: From Pulp Noir to Film Noir* (Jefferson, NC: McFarland, 2006).

Renzi, Thomas C., *Screwball Comedy and Film Noir: Unexpected Connections* (Jefferson, NC: McFarland, 2012).

Rey, Henri-François, "Hollywood Makes Myths Like Ford Makes Cars (Last Installment): Demonstration by the Absurd: Films Noirs," *L'Écran Français* (June 1948), in R. Barton Palmer, ed., *Perspectives on Film Noir* (New York: G.K. Hall, 1996), 28–29.

Riesman, David, "The Suburban Sadness," in William M. Dobriner, ed., *The Suburban Community* (New York: Putnam, 1958), 375–408.

Riesman, David, with Nathan Glazer and Reuel Denney, *The Lonely Crowd: A Study of the Changing American Character* (New Haven, CT: Yale University Press, 1950).

Rosenberg, Bernard, "Mass Culture in America," in Bernard Rosenberg and David Manning White, eds., *Mass Culture: The Popular Arts in America* (New York: Free Press, 1957), 3–12.

Ross, Andrew, *No Respect: Intellectuals and Popular Culture* (New York: Routledge, 1989).

Ross, Davis R.B., *Preparing for Ulysses: Politics and Veterans During World War II* (New York: Columbia University Press, 1969).

Rusk, Howard A., "REHABILITATION," *New York Times* (November 24, 1946), 60.

Sammon, Paul M., *Future Noir: The Making of Blade Runner* (New York: Harper, 1996).

Sanders, Steven, "Television Noir," in Spicer and Hanson, eds., *Companion to Film Noir*, 440–57.

Santos, Marlisa, *The Dark Mirror: Psychiatry and Film Noir* (Lanham, MD: Lexington, 2011).

Sartre, Jean-Paul, "Paris Under the Occupation," *La France libre* (November 15, 1944), in J. G. Weightman, ed., *French Writing On English Soil: A Choice of French Writing Published in London Between November 1940 and June 1944* (London: Sylvan Press, 1945), 122–34.

Saxe, Robert Francis, *Settling Down: World War II Veterans' Challenge to the Postwar Consensus* (New York: Palgrave Macmillan, 2007).

Schatz, Thomas, *Boom and Bust: American Cinema in the 1940s* (Berkeley: University of California Press, 1999).

Scheuer, Philip K., "Film History Made by 'Double Indemnity'," *Los Angeles Times* (August 6, 1944), C1, 3.

Schlesinger, Arthur M. Jr., *The Vital Center: The Politics of Freedom* (Cambridge, MA: Riverside Press, 1949).

Schrader, Paul, "Notes on *Film Noir,*" *Film Comment* (Spring 1972), repr. in Silver and Ursini, eds., *Film Noir Reader,* 53–63.

Scorsese, Martin, and Michael Henry Wilson, *A Personal Journey with Martin Scorsese Through American Movies* (London: Faber and Faber, 1997).

"Screen Guide for Americans" (Beverly Hills, CA: The Motion Picture Alliance for the Preservation of American Ideals, 1947).

Selby, Spencer, *Dark City: The Film Noir* (Jefferson, NC: McFarland, 1884).

Server, Lee, Ed Gorman, and Martin H. Greenberg, *The Big Book of Noir* (New York: Carroll & Graff, 1998).

Severo, Richard, and Lewis Milford, *The Wages of War: When America's Soldiers Came Home—From Valley Forge to Vietnam* (New York: Simon and Schuster, 1989).

Shearer, Lloyd, "Crime Certainly Pays on the Screen: The Growing Crop of Homicidal Films Poses Questions for Psychologists and Producers," *New York Times* (August 5, 1945), 17, 37.

Shirer, William L., *The Rise and Fall of the Third Reich: A History of Nazi Germany* (New York: Simon and Schuster, 1960).

Silver, Alain, and James Ursini, "Docu-Noir," in Duncan, ed., *Film Noir,* 80–95.

Silver, Alain, and James Ursini, eds., *Film Noir Reader* (New York: Limelight, 1996).

Silver, Alain, and James Ursini, eds., *Film Noir Reader 2* (New York: Limelight, 1999).

Silver, Alain, and James Ursini, eds., *Film Noir Reader 3: Interviews with Filmmakers of the Classic Noir Period* (New York: Limelight, 2002).

Silver, Alain, and James Ursini, eds., *Film Noir Reader 4: The Crucial Films and Themes* (New York: Limelight, 2004).

Silver, Alain, Elizabeth Ward, James Ursini, and Robert Porfirio, eds., *Film Noir: The Encyclopedia* (New York: Overlook Duckworth, 2010).

Sklar, Robert, *City Boys: Cagney, Bogart, Garfield* (Princeton: Princeton University Press, 1992).

Sklar, Robert, *Movie-Made America: A Cultural History of American Movies* (1975; rev. edn, New York: Vintage, 1994).

Sobchack, Vivian, "Lounge Time: Postwar Crises and the Chronotype of Film Noir," in Nick Browne, ed., *Refiguring Film Genres: Theory and History* (Berkeley: University of California Press, 1998), 129–70.

Sparrow, John C., *History of Personnel Demobilization in the United States Army* (Washington, DC: Department of the Army [No. 20-210] July 1952).

Spicer, Andrew, ed., *European Film Noir* (Manchester: Manchester University Press, 2007).

Spicer, Andrew, *Historical Dictionary of Film Noir* (Lanham, MD: Scarecrow Press, 2010).

Spicer, Andrew, and Helen Hanson, eds., *A Companion to Film Noir* (Oxford: Wiley Blackwell, 2013).

Stephens, Michael L., *Film Noir: A Comprehensive, Illustrated Reference to Movies, Terms and Persons* (Jefferson, NC: McFarland, 2006).

Stouffer, Samuel A., Arthur A. Lumsdaine, Marion H. Lumsdaine, Robin M. Williams, Jr., M. Brewster Smith, Irving L. Janis, Shirley A. Star, and Leonard S. Cottrell, Jr., *The American Soldier*, Vol. 1, *Adjustment During Army Life* (Princeton, NJ: Princeton University Press, 1949).

Stouffer, Samuel A., Arthur A. Lumsdaine, Marion H. Lumsdaine, Robin M. Williams, Jr., M. Brewster Smith, Irving L. Janis, Shirley A. Star, and Leonard S. Cottrell, Jr., *The American Soldier*, Vol. 2, *Combat and its Aftermath* (Princeton, NJ: Princeton University Press, 1949).

Strecker, Edward A., and Kenneth E. Appel, *Psychiatry in Modern Warfare* (New York: Macmillan, 1945).

Telotte, J.P., *Voices in the Dark: The Narrative Patterns of Film Noir* (Urbana: University of Illinois Press, 1989).

Terkel, Studs, *"The Good War": An Oral History of World War II* (New York: New Press, 1984).

"The 36-Hour War," *Life* (November 19, 1945), 27–35.

Thomas, Deborah, "How Hollywood Deals With the Deviant Male," in Cameron, ed., *Movie Book of Film Noir*, 59–70.

Thompson, Kristin, and David Bordwell, *Film History: An Introduction* (New York: McGraw-Hill, 1994).

Thompson, Morton, *How To Be a Civilian* (Garden City, NY: Doubleday, 1946).

Thompson, Warren S., "The Atomic Threat," in Peterson, ed., *Cities Are Abnormal*, 226–38.

"Tillie Scrubbed On," *Reader's Digest* (December 1, 1946), 81–84.

Truffaut, François, with Helen G. Scott, *Hitchcock* (London: Secker & Warburg, 1967).

Tuska, Jon, *Dark Cinema: American Film Noir in Cultural Perspective* (Westport, CT: Greenwood Press, 1984).

"250 Quintessential Noir Films (1940–1964)" http://www.theyshootpictures.com/noir250noirs1.htm

Vernet, Marc, "*Film Noir* on the Edge of Doom," in J. Swenson, trans., Joan Copjec, ed., *Shades of Noir: A Reader* (London: Verso, 1993), 1–31.

Vincendeau, Ginette, "French Film Noir," in Spicer, ed., *European Film Noir*, 23–54.

Vincendeau, Ginette, *Jean-Pierre Melville: An American in Paris* (2003; London: Palgrave/BFI, 2014).

Vincendeau, Ginette, "Noir Is Also a French Word: The French Antecedents of Film Noir," in Cameron, ed., *Movie Book of Film Noir*, 49–58.

Vinen, Richard, *The Unfree French: Life under the Occupation* (London: Allen Lane, 2006).

Wagstaff, Sheena, ed., *Edward Hopper* (London: Tate Publishing, 2004).

Waller, Willard, The *Veteran Comes Back* (New York: Dryden Press, 1944).

Walker, Michael, "Film Noir: Introduction," in Cameron, ed., *Movie Book of Film Noir*, 8–38.

Walz, Robin, "Serial Killings: *Fant ô mas*, Feuillade, and the Mass-Culture Genealogy of Surrealism," *Velvet Light Trap* 37 (Spring 1996), 51–57.

Wasko, Janet, "Hollywood and Television in the 1950s: The Roots of Diversification," in Peter Lev, ed., *The Fifties: Transforming the Screen, 1950-1959* (Berkeley: University of California Press, 2003), 127–46.

"The Way Home," *Time* (August 7, 1944), 15–16.

Wanger, Walter, "Upheaval in Hollywood," *Los Angeles Times* (November 15, 1942), H4.

Wecter, Dixon, *When Johnny Comes Marching Home* (Cambridge, MA: Houghton Mifflin, 1944).

Weegee, *Naked City* (New York: Essential Books, 1945).

Welles, Orson, and Peter Bogdanovich, *This Is Orson Welles* (New York: HarperCollins, 1992).

Whitfield, Stephen J., *The Culture of the Cold War* (2nd edn, Baltimore: Johns Hopkins University Press, 1996).

Whyte, William H., *The Organization Man* (1956; Harmondsworth: Penguin, 1963).

Wilson, Sloan, *The Man in the Grey Flannel Suit* (1956; London: Pan, 1958).

Filmography

Abandoned. USA: Universal-International Pictures. Newman, Joseph M., dir. 1949.
Accused of Murder. USA: Republic Pictures. Kane, Joe, dir. 1956.
Act of Violence. USA: Metro-Goldwyn-Mayer. Zinnemann, Fred, dir. 1949.
Action in the North Atlantic. USA: Warner Bros. Bacon, Lloyd, dir. 1943.
Affairs of Jimmy Valentine. USA: Republic Pictures. Vorhaus, Bernard, dir. 1942.
After Dark, My Sweet. USA: Avenue Pictures. Foley, James, dir. 1990.
After the Thin Man. USA: Metro-Goldwyn-Mayer. Van Dyke, W. S., dir. 1936.
Air Force. USA: Warner Bros. Hawks, Howard, dir. 1943.
Algiers. USA: Walter Wanger Productions. Cromwell, John, dir. 1938.
Alien. USA: Twentieth Century-Fox. Scott, Ridley, dir. 1979.
All the King's Men. USA: Columbia Pictures. Rossen, Robert, dir. 1950.
Angels with Dirty Faces. USA: Warner Bros. Curtiz, Michael, 1938.
Another Thin Man. USA: Metro-Goldwyn-Mayer. Van Dyke, W. S., dir. 1939.
Apartment, The. USA: Mirisch Company. Wilder, Billy, dir. 1960.
Appointment with a Shadow. USA: Universal-International Pictures. Carlson,
    Richard, dir. 1958.
Armored Car Robbery. USA: RKO Radio Pictures. Fleischer, Richard, dir. 1950.
Asphalt Jungle, The. USA: Metro-Goldwyn-Mayer. Huston, John, dir. 1950.
L'Assassinat du Duc de Guise [*The Assassination of the Duke of Guise*]. France:
    Pathé Frères. Calmettes, André and Charles Le Bargy, dir. 1908.

Bacall to Arms. USA: Warner Bros (Merrie Melodies). Clampett, Bob, dir. 1946.
Bachelor and the Bobby-Soxer, The. USA: RKO Radio Pictures. Reis, Irving, dir. 1947.
Back to Bataan. USA: RKO Radio Pictures. Dmytryk, Edward, dir. 1945.
Backfire. USA: Warner Bros. Sherman, Vincent, dir. 1950.
Badlands. USA: Pressman-Williams/Badlands Ltd. Malick, Terence, dir. 1973.
Ball of Fire. USA: Samuel Goldwyn Productions. Hawks, Howard, dir. 1942.
Band Wagon, The. USA: Metro-Goldwyn-Mayer. Minnelli, Vincente, dir. 1953.
Bataan. USA: Metro-Goldwyn-Mayer. Garnett, Tay, dir. 1943.
Batman Begins. USA: Warner Bros. Nolan, Christopher, dir. 2005.
Battle of Midway, The. USA: US Navy. Ford, John, dir. 1942.
Battle of San Pietro, The. USA: US Army Pictorial Services. Huston, John, dir. 1945.
Beat the Devil. USA: Santana Pictures/Romulus Films/Rizzoli-Haggiag/Dear Film.
    Huston, John, dir. 1954.
Below the Deadline. USA: Monogram Productions. Beaudine, William, dir. 1946.
Berlin Express. USA: RKO Radio Pictures. Tourneur, Jacques, dir. 1948.
Best Years of Our Lives, The. USA: Samuel Goldwyn Productions. Wyler, William,
    dir. 1946.
Bête Humaine, La [*The Human Beast*]. France: Paris Film. Renoir, Jean, dir. 1938.
Between Midnight and Dawn. USA: Columbia Pictures. Douglas, Gordon, dir. 1950.

Beware, My Lovely. USA: The Filmakers/RKO Radio Pictures. Horner, Harry, dir. 1952.

Bewitched. USA: Metro-Goldwyn-Mayer. Oboler, Arch, dir. 1945.

Big Caper, The. USA: PTS Productions. Stevens, Robert, dir. 1957.

Big Carnival, The. USA: Paramount Pictures. Wilder, Billy, dir. 1951.

Big Clock, The. USA: Paramount Pictures. Farrow, John, dir. 1948.

Big Combo, The. USA: Theodora Productions/Security Pictures. Lewis, Joseph H., dir. 1955.

Big Gamble, The. USA: RKO Pathé Pictures. Niblo, Fred, dir. 1931.

Big Heat, The. USA: Columbia Pictures. Lang, Fritz, dir. 1953.

Big Knife, The. USA: Associates and Aldrich Co. Aldrich, Robert, dir. 1955.

Big Lebowski, The. USA: Working Title Films. Coen, Joel, dir. 1998.

Big Night, The. USA: Philip A. Waxman Productions. Losey, Joseph, dir. 1951.

Big Sleep, The. USA: Warner Bros. Hawks, Howard, dir. 1946.

Big Sleep, The. USA: Winkast. Winner, Michael, dir. 1978.

Bigamist, The. USA: The Filmakers Productions. Lupino, Ida, dir. 1953.

Birds, The. USA: Alfred J. Hitchcock Productions. Hitchcock, Alfred, dir. 1963.

Bishop's Wife, The. USA: Samuel Goldwyn Productions. Koster, Henry, dir. 1948.

Black Angel. USA: Universal Pictures. Neill, Roy William, dir. 1946.

Black Book, The. USA: Walter Wanger Pictures. Mann, Anthony, dir. 1949.

Black Dahlia, The. USA: Millenium Films. De Palma, Brian, dir. 2006.

Blade Runner. USA: The Ladd Company/Sir Run Run Shaw. Scott, Ridley, dir. 1982.

Blaue Angel, Der [*The Blue Angel*]. Germany: Universumfilm. Von Sternberg, Josef, dir. 1930.

Blind Alley. USA: Columbia Pictures. Vidor, Charles, dir. 1939.

Blonde Alibi. USA: Universal Pictures. Jason, Will, dir. 1946.

Blonde Ice. USA: Martin Mooney Productions. Bernhard, Jack, dir. 1948.

Blonde Venus. USA: Paramount Publix. Von Sternberg, Josef, dir. 1932.

Blood on the Moon. USA: RKO Radio Pictures. Wise, Robert, dir. 1948.

Blood Simple. USA: River Road Productions. Coen, Joel, dir. 1984.

Blue Dahlia, The. USA: Paramount Pictures. Marshall, George, dir. 1946.

Blue Velvet. USA: Blue Velvet Productions. Lynch, David, dir. 1986.

Blueprint for Murder, A. USA: Twentieth Century-Fox. Stone, Andrew, dir. 1953.

Bob le flambeur [*Bob the Gambler*]. France: Organisation Générale Cinématographique/Play Art/Productions Cyme. Melville, Jean-Pierre, dir. 1956.

Body and Soul. USA: Enterprise Productions/Roberts Productions. Rossen, Robert, dir. 1947.

Body Heat. USA: The Ladd Company. Kasdan, Lawrence, dir. 1981.

Boomerang! USA: Twentieth Century-Fox. Kazan, Elia, dir. 1947.

Border Incident. USA: Metro-Goldwyn-Mayer. Mann, Anthony, dir. 1949.

Bout de soufflé, À [*Breathless*]. France: Les Films Impéria/Les Productions Georges Beauregard/Société Nouvelle de Cinématographie. Godard, Jean-Luc, dir. 1960.

Brasher Doubloon, The. USA: Twentieth Century-Fox. Brahm, John, dir. 1947.

Brazil. UK: Embassy International Pictures. Gilliam, Terry, dir. 1985.

Breaking Point, The. USA: Warner Bros. Curtiz, Michael, dir. 1950.

Brick. USA: Bergman Lustig. Johnson, Ryan, dir. 2006.

Brute Force. USA: Mark Hellinger Productions. Dassin, Jules, dir. 1947.

Büchse der Pandora, Die [*Pandora's Box*]. Germany: Nero-Film AG. Pabst, G. W., dir. 1929.

Burglar, The. USA: Samson Productions. Wendkos, Paul, dir. 1957.
Bury Me Dead. USA: Eagle-Lion Films. Vorhaus, Bernard, dir. 1947.

Caged. USA: Warner Bros. Cromwell, John, dir. 1950.
Call Northside 777. USA: Twentieth Century-Fox. Hathaway, Henry, dir. 1948.
Cape Fear. USA: Melville-Talbot Productions. Thompson, J. Lee, dir. 1962.
Cape Fear. USA: Amblin Entertainment/Cappa Films/Tribeca Productions. Scorsese, Martin, dir. 1991.
Captive City, The. USA: Aspen Productions. Wise, Robert, dir. 1952.
Carmen Jones. USA: Twentieth Century-Fox. Preminger, Otto, dir. 1955.
Casablanca. USA: Warner Bros. Curtiz, Michael, dir. 1942.
Casbah. USA: Marston Pictures/Universal-International Pictures. Berry, John, dir. 1948.
Casino. USA: Universal Pictures. Scorsese, Martin, dir. 1995.
Cat People. USA: RKO Radio Pictures. Tourneur, Jacques, dir. 1942.
Caught. USA: Enterprise Productions. Ophuls, Max, dir. 1949.
Cercle Rouge, Le [*The Red Circle*]. France: Euro International Film/Les Films Corona/Selenia Cinematografica. Melville, Jean-Pierre, dir. 1970.
Chase, The. USA: Nero Films. Ripley, Arthur D., dir. 1946.
Chien jaune, Le [*The Yellow Dog*]. France: Les Établissements Braunberger-Richebé. Tarride, Jean, dir. 1932.
Chienne, La [*The Bitch*]. France: Les Établissements Braunberger-Richebé. Renoir, Jean, dir. 1931.
Chinatown. USA: Long Road Productions. Polanski, Roman, dir. 1974.
Chinatown Nights. USA: Paramount Famous Lasky. Wellman, William A., dir. 1929.
Christmas Holiday. USA: Universal Pictures. Siodmak, Robert, dir. 1944.
Citizen Kane. USA: Mercury Productions/RKO Radio Pictures. Welles, Orson, dir. 1941.
City for Conquest. USA: Warner Bros. Litvak, Anatole, dir. 1940.
City of Fear. USA: Orbit Productions. Lerner, Irving, dir. 1959.
City Streets. USA: Paramount Publix. Mamoulian, Rouben, dir. 1931.
City That Never Sleeps. USA: Republic Pictures. Auer, John H., dir. 1953.
Clash by Night. USA: Wald-Krasna Productions/RKO Radio Pictures. Lang, Fritz, dir. 1952.
Clay Pigeon, The. USA: RKO Radio Pictures. Fleischer, Richard, dir. 1949.
Clockwork Orange, A. USA/UK: Polaris Productions/Hawks Films. Kubrick, Stanley, dir. 1971.
Colonel Effingham's Raid. USA: Twentieth Century-Fox. Pichel, Irving, 1946.
Confessions of a Nazi Spy. USA: Warner Bros. Litvak, Anatole, dir. 1939.
Conflict. USA: Warner Bros. Bernhardt, Curtis, dir. 1945.
Convicted. USA: Columbia Pictures. Levin, Henry, dir. 1950.
Cop Hater. USA: Barbizon Productions. Berke, William, dir. 1958.
Corbeau, Le [*The Raven*]. France: Continental Films. Clouzot, Henri-Georges, dir. 1943.
Convicted. USA: Central Films. Barsha, Leon, dir. 1938.
Cornered. USA: RKO Radio Pictures. Dmytryk, Edward, dir. 1945.
Crimson Kimono, The. USA: Globe Enterprises. Fuller, Samuel, dir. 1959.
Crimson Pirate, The. USA: Warner Bros/Norma Productions. Siodmak, Robert, dir. 1952.

Criss Cross. USA: Universal-International Pictures. Siodmak, Robert, dir. 1949.

Crooked Way, The. USA: La Bria Productions. Florey, Robert, dir. 1949.

Crooked Web, The. USA: Clover Productions. Juran, Nathan Hertz, dir. 1955.

Crossfire. USA: RKO Radio Pictures. Dmytryk, Edward, dir. 1947.

Cry of the City. USA: Twentieth Century-Fox. Siodmak, Robert, dir. 1948.

Damaged Lives. USA: Beacon Productions/Columbia Pictures. Ulmer, Edgar G.,
    dir. 1933.

Dark City. USA: Paramount Pictures. Dieterle, William, dir. 1950.

Dark Corner, The. USA: Twentieth Century-Fox. Hathaway, Henry, dir. 1946.

Dark Horse, The. USA: Universal Pictures. Jason, Will, dir. 1946.

Dark Knight, The. USA: Legendary Pictures/Syncopy Productions. Nolan,
    Christopher, dir. 2008.

Dark Knight Rises, The. USA: Legendary Pictures/Syncopy Films. Nolan,
    Christopher, dir. 2012.

Dark Mirror, The. USA: Inter-John. Siodmak, Robert, dir. 1946.

Dark Passage. USA: Warner Bros. Daves, Delmer, dir. 1947.

Dark Past, The. USA: Columbia Pictures. Maté, Rudolph, dir. 1948.

Dark Waters. USA: Benedict Bogeaus Productions. De Toth, Andre, dir. 1944.

Day the Earth Stood Still, The. USA: Twentieth Century-Fox. Wise, Robert, dir. 1951.

Dead Men Don't Wear Plaid. USA: Aspen Film Society/Universal Pictures. Reiner,
    Carl, dir. 1982.

Dead Reckoning. USA: Columbia Pictures. Cromwell, John, dir. 1947.

Deadline at Dawn. USA: RKO Radio Pictures. Clurman, Harold, dir. 1946.

Death of a Salesman. USA: Columbia Pictures/Stanley Kramer Co. Benedek,
    Laslo, dir. 1951.

Deception. USA: Warner Bros. Rapper, Irving, dir. 1946.

Decoy. USA: Monogram Productions. Bernhard, Jack, dir. 1946.

Departed, The. USA: Warner Bros. Scorsese, Martin, dir. 2006.

Dernier tournant, Le [*The Last Turn*]. France: Gladiator Productions. Chenal,
    Pierre, dir. 1939.

Desire Me. USA: Metro-Goldwyn-Mayer. Cukor, George, dir. 1947.

Desperate. USA: RKO Radio Pictures. Mann, Anthony, dir. 1947.

Desperate Hours, The. USA: Paramount Pictures. Wyler, William, dir. 1955.

Destination Tokyo. USA: Warner Bros. Daves, Delmer, dir. 1944.

Detour. USA: Producers Releasing Corporation. Ulmer, Edgar G., dir. 1945.

Devil in a Blue Dress. USA: Tristar Pictures. Franklin, Carl, dir. 1995.

Devil Is a Woman, The. USA: Paramount Productions. Von Sternberg, Josef, dir.
    1935.

Devil Thumbs a Ride, The. USA: RKO Radio Pictures. Feist, Felix, dir. 1947.

Devil's Doorway. USA: Metro-Goldwyn-Mayer. Mann, Anthony, dir. 1950.

Dial M for Murder. USA: Warner Bros. Hitchcock, Alfred, dir. 1954.

Diary of a Sergeant. USA: US War Department. Newman, Joseph M., dir. 1945.

Dirty Harry. USA: Malpaso Company. Siegel, Don, dir. 1971.

Dishonored. USA: Paramount Publix. Von Sternberg, Josef, dir. 1931.

D.O.A. USA: Cardinal Pictures. Maté, Rudoph, dir. 1950.

D.O.A. USA: Bigelow Films. Morton, Rocky, dir. 1988.

Docks of New York, The. USA: Paramount Famous Lasky. Von Sternberg, Josef,
    dir. 1928.

Doorway to Hell, The. USA: Warner Bros. Mayo, Archie, dir. 1930.

Double Indemnity. USA: Paramount Pictures. Wilder, Billy, dir. 1944.
Dr Mabuse, der Spieler [*Dr. Mabuse, The Gambler*]. Germany: Uco-Film GmbH.
    Lang, Fritz, dir. 1922.
Dracula. USA: Universal. Browning, Todd, dir. 1931.
Dragnet. USA: Mark VII Ltd. Webb, Jack, dir. 1954.
Dragonwyck. USA: Twentieth Century-Fox. Mankiewicz, Joseph L., dir. 1946.
Drive a Crooked Road. USA: Columbia Pictures. Quine, Richard, dir. 1954.
Du Rififi chez les hommes. France: Pathé Consortium Cinéma/Indusfilms/Société
    Nouvelle Pathé Cinéma/Primafilm. Dassin, Jules, dir. 1955.
Duel in the Sun. USA: Vanguard Films. Vidor, King, dir. 1947.

Easter Parade. USA: Metro-Goldwyn-Mayer. Walters, Charles, dir. 1948.
Egg and I, The. USA: Universal-International Pictures. Erskine, Chester, dir. 1947.
Enchanted Cottage, The. USA: RKO Radio Pictures. Cromwell, John, dir. 1945.
Enforcer, The. USA: United States Pictures. Windust, Bretaigne, dir. 1951.
Experiment Perilous. USA: RKO Radio Pictures. Tourneur, Jacques, dir. 1944.

Fall Guy. USA: Monogram Productions. Le Borg, Reginald, dir. 1947.
Fallen Angel. USA: Twentieth Century-Fox. Preminger, Otto., dir. 1945.
Fallen Sparrow, The. USA: RKO Radio Pictures. Wallace, Richard, dir. 1943.
Family Affair, A. USA: Metro-Goldwyn-Mayer. Seitz, George B., dir. 1937.
Fantômas. France: Gaumont. Feuillade, Louis, dir. 1913.
Fantômas contra Fantômas [*Fantômas versus Fantômas*]. France: Gaumont.
    Feuillade, Louis, dir. 1914.
Farewell, My Lovely. USA: EK/ITC. Richards, Dick, dir. 1975.
Fargo. USA: Working Title Films. Coen, Joel, dir. 1996.
Fatal Attraction. USA: Jaffe/Lansing. Lyne, Adrian, dir. 1987.
Faux Magistrat, Le [*The False Judge*]. France: Gaumont. Feuillade, Louis, dir. 1914.
F.B.I. Story, The. USA: Warner Bros. LeRoy, Mervyn, dir. 1959.
Fear in the Night. USA: Pine-Thomas Productions. Shane, Maxwell, dir. 1947.
Fight Club. USA: Fox 2000 Pictures/New Regency Productions. Fincher, David,
    dir. 1999.
Fighting 69th, The. USA: Warner Bros. Keighley, William, dir. 1940.
5 Against the House. USA: Dayle Production. Karlson, Phil, dir. 1955.
Flic, Un [*A Cop*]. France. Euro International Film/Oceania Produzioni Internazionali
    Cinematografiche. Melville, Jean-Pierre, dir. 1972.
For Me and My Gal. USA: Metro-Goldwyn-Mayer. Berkeley, Busby, dir. 1942.
Force of Evil. USA: Enterprise Studios/Roberts Productions. Polonsky, Abraham,
    dir. 1949.
Framed. USA: Columbia Pictures. Wallace, Richard, dir. 1947.
Frau im Mond [*Woman in the Moon*]. Germany: Fritz Lang-Film/Universum Film.
    Lang, Fritz, dir. 1929.
From This Day Forward. USA: RKO Radio Pictures. Berry, John, dir. 1946.
Front, The. USA: Columbia Pictures. Ritt, Martin, dir. 1976.

Gaslight. UK: British National Films. Dickinson, Thorold, dir. 1940.
Gaslight. USA: Metro-Goldwyn-Mayer. Cukor, George, dir. 1944.
Gentleman's Agreement. USA: Twentieth Century-Fox. Kazan, Elia, dir. 1948.
Gilda. USA: Columbia Pictures. Vidor, Charles, dir. 1946.
Girl in Every Port, A. USA: Fox Film Corp. Hawks, Howard, dir. 1928.
Glass Key, The. USA: Paramount Pictures. Heisler, Stuart, dir. 1942.

Glass Webb, The. USA: Universal-International Pictures. Arnold, Jack, dir. 1953.
Golem: wie er in die Welt kam, Der [*The Golem: How He Came into the World*].
  Germany: Projektions-AG Union. Wegener, Paul, dir. 1920.
Gone with the Wind. USA: Selznick International Pictures/MGM. Fleming, Victor,
  dir. 1939.
Goodfellas. USA: Irwin Winkler Productions/Warner Bros. Scorsese, Martin, dir.
  1990.
Great Flamarion, The. USA: Filmdom Productions. Mann, Anthony, dir. 1945.
Guest in the House. USA: Guest in the House Inc/Hunt Stromberg Productions.
  Brahm, John, dir. 1944.
Guilty, The. USA: Monogram Productions. Reinhardt, John, dir. 1947.
Gun Crazy. USA: King Bros. Productions. Lewis, Joseph H., dir. 1950.
Guncrazy. USA: Zeta Entertainment/First Look Pictures. Davis, Tamra, dir. 1992.

Hail the Conquering Hero. USA: Paramount Pictures. Sturges, Preston, dir. 1944.
Hangover Square. USA: Twentieth Century-Fox. Brahm, John, dir. 1945.
Harder They Fall, The. USA: Columbia Pictures. Robson, Mark, dir. 1956.
He Ran All the Way. USA: Roberts Pictures. Berry, John, dir. 1951.
He Walked by Night. USA: Eagle-Lion Films. Werker, Alfred, dir. 1948.
High Sierra. USA: Warner Bros. Walsh, Raoul, dir. 1941.
High Wall, The. USA: Metro-Goldwyn-Mayer. Bernhardt, Curtis, dir. 1948.
Hitch-Hiker, The. USA: The Filmakers/RKO Radio Pictures. Lupino, Ida, dir. 1953.
Holiday Affair. USA: RKO Radio Pictures. Hartman, Don, dir. 1949.
Hollow Triumph. USA: Hollow Triumph. Sekely, Steve, dir. 1948.
Home of the Brave. USA: Screen Plays II. Robson, Mark, dir. 1949.
Hôtel du Nord. France: Societé d'Exploitation et de Distribution de Films. Carné,
  Marcel, dir. 1938.
House of Bamboo. USA: Twentieth Century-Fox. Fuller, Samuel, dir. 1955.
House on 92nd Street, The. USA: Twentieth Century-Fox. Hathaway, Henry, dir.
  1945.
How Green Was My Valley. USA: Twentieth Century-Fox. Ford, John, dir. 1941.
Human Desire. USA: Columbia Pictures. Lang, Fritz, dir. 1954.

I Died a Thousand Times. USA: Warner Bros. Heisler, Stuart, dir. 1955.
I Shot Jesse James. USA: Lippert Productions. Fuller, Samuel, dir. 1949.
I Walk Alone. USA: Hal Wallis Productions. Haskin, Byron, dir. 1948.
I Want You. USA: Samuel Goldwyn Productions. Robson, Mark, dir. 1951.
I Was a Communist for the FBI. USA: Warner Bros. Douglas, Gordon, dir. 1951.
I Wouldn't Be in Your Shoes. USA: Monogram Productions. Nigh, William, dir. 1948.
Impact. USA: Cardinal Pictures. Lubin, Arthur, dir. 1949.
In a Lonely Place. USA: Santana Pictures. Ray, Nicholas, dir. 1950.
Inner Sanctum. USA: MRS Pictures. Landers, Lew, dir. 1948.
Invaders from Mars. USA: National Pictures. Menzies, William Cameron, dir. 1953.
Invasion of the Body Snatchers. USA: Walter Wanger Pictures. Siegel, Don, dir. 1956.
It's a Wonderful Life. USA: Liberty Films. Capra, Frank, dir. 1946.
Ivy. USA: Inter-Wood Productions. Wood, Sam, dir. 1947.

Jackie Brown. USA: Mighty, Mighty Afrodite Productions. Tarantino, Quentin, dir.
  1997.
Jane Eyre. USA: Twentieth Century-Fox. Stevenson, Robert, dir. 1944.
Johnny Belinda. USA: Warner Bros. Negulesco, Jean, dir. 1948.

Johnny Comes Flying Home. USA: Twentieth Century-Fox. Stoloff, Benjamin, dir. 1946.

Johnny Guitar. USA: Republic Pictures. Ray, Nicholas, dir. 1954.

Johnny O' Clock. USA: JEM Productions. Rossen, Robert, dir. 1947.

Jour se lève, Le [*Daybreak*]. France: Productions Sigma. Carné, Marcel, dir. 1939.

Journey into Fear. USA: RKO Radio Pictures. Foster, Norman, dir. 1943.

Juve contra Fantômas. [*Juve versus Fantômas*]. France: Gaumont. Feuillade, Louis, dir. 1913.

Kabinet des Dr Caligari, Das [*The Cabinet of Dr Caligari*]. Germany: Decla-Bioscop AG. Wiene, Robert, dir. 1920.

Key Largo. USA: Warner Bros. Huston, John, dir. 1948.

Killer Inside Me, The. USA: MuseFilm Productions/Cyclone Productions/Revolution Films/Curiously Bright Entertainment. Winterbottom, Michael, dir. 2010.

Killer's Kiss. USA: Minotaur Productions. Kubrick, Stanley, dir. 1955.

The Killers. USA: Mark Hellinger Productions/Universal Pictures. Siodmak, Robert, dir. 1946.

Killing, The. USA: Harris-Kubrick Pictures. Kubrick, Stanley, dir. 1956.

Kind Hearts and Coronets. UK: Ealing Studios. Hamer, Robert, dir. 1949.

King Kong. USA: Radio Pictures. Cooper, Merian C. and Ernest B. Schoedsack, dir. 1933.

Kiss Before Dying, A. USA: Crown Productions. Oswald, Gerd, dir. 1956.

Kiss Before Dying, A. USA: Kellgate/Initial Film. Dearden, James, dir. 1991.

Kiss Me, Deadly. USA: Parklane Pictures. Aldrich, Robert, dir. 1955.

Kiss of Death. USA: Twentieth Century-Fox. Hathaway, Henry, dir. 1947.

Kiss of Death. USA: Twentieth Century-Fox. Schroeder, Barbet, dir. 1995.

Kiss the Blood Off My Hands. USA: Norma Productions. Foster, Norman, dir. 1948.

Klute. USA: Warner Bros/Gus Productions. Pakula, Alan J., dir. 1971.

Knock on Any Door. USA: Santana Pictures. Ray, Nicholas, dir. 1949.

L.A. Confidential. USA: Regency Enterprises. Hanson, Curtis, dir. 1997.

Lady from Shanghai, The. USA: Columbia Pictures. Welles, Orson, dir. 1948.

Lady in the Lake, The. USA: Metro-Goldwyn-Mayer. Montgomery, Robert, dir. 1947.

Lady on a Train. USA: Universal Pictures. David, Charles, dir. 1945.

Laura. USA: Twentieth Century-Fox. Preminger, Otto, dir. 1944.

Lawless, The. USA: Pine-Thomas Productions. Losey, Joseph, dir. 1950.

Leave Her to Heaven. USA: Twentieth Century-Fox. Stahl, John M., dir. 1946.

Leopard Man, The. USA: RKO Radio Pictures. Tourneur, Jacques, dir. 1943.

Letter, The. USA: Warner Bros. Wyler, William, dir. 1940.

Letter from an Unknown Woman. USA: Rampart Productions. Ophuls, Max, dir. 1948.

Little Caesar. USA: First National Pictures. LeRoy, Mervyn, dir. 1931.

Little Foxes, The. USA: Samuel Goldwyn Productions. Wyler, William, dir. 1941.

Locket, The. USA: RKO Radio Pictures. Brahm, John, dir. 1947.

Long Goodbye, The. USA: Lion's Gate Films. Altman, Robert, dir. 1973.

Long Night, The. USA: Select Productions. Litvak, Anatole, dir. 1947.

Lost Highway. USA: CIBY 2000/Asymmetrical Productions. Lynch, David, dir. 1997.

Lost Weekend, The. USA: Paramount Pictures. Wilder, Billy, dir. 1945.

Love Laughs at Andy Hardy. USA: Metro-Goldwyn-Mayer. Goldbeck, Willis, dir. 1947.

Lured. USA: Oakmont Pictures. Sirk, Douglas, dir. 1947.

M: Eine Stadt sucht einen Mörder [*M: A City Searches for a Murderer*] (1931). Germany: Nero-Film AG. Lang, Fritz, dir. 1931.

Macomber Affair, The. USA: Award Productions/Benedict Bogeaus Productions. Korda, Zoltan, dir. 1947.

Magic Town. USA: Robert Riskin Productions. Wellman, William A., dir. 1947.

Maltese Falcon, The. USA: Warner Bros. Del Ruth, Roy, dir. 1931.

Maltese Falcon, The. USA: Warner Bros. Huston, John, dir. 1941.

Man in the Dark. USA: Columbia Pictures. Landers, Lew, dir. 1953.

Man in the Gray Flannel Suit, The. USA: Twentieth Century-Fox. Johnson, Nunnally, dir. 1956.

Man Who Laughs, The. USA: Universal Pictures. Leni, Paul, dir. 1928.

Man Who Wasn't There, The. USA: Working Title Films. Coen, Joel, dir. 2001.

Manpower. USA: Warner Bros. Walsh, Raoul, dir. 1941.

Marlowe. USA: Beckerman Productions/Cherokee Productions/Katzka-Berne Productions. Bogart, Paul, dir. 1969.

Mean Streets. USA: Taplin-Perry-Scorsese Productions. Scorsese, Martin, dir. 1973.

Meet Me in St Louis. USA: Metro-Goldwyn-Mayer. Minnelli, Vincente, dir. 1944.

Memphis Belle: A Story of a Flying Fortress, The. USA: US Army Air Forces/First Motion Picture Unit. Wyler, William, dir. 1944.

Men, The. USA: United Artists. Zinnemann, Fred, dir. 1950.

Menschen am Sonntag [*People on Sunday*]. Germany: Filmstudio Berlin. Siodmak, Curt and Robert Siodmak, dir. 1930.

Metropolis. Germany: Universum Film. Lang, Fritz, dir. 1926.

Mildred Pierce. USA: Warner Bros. Curtiz, Michael, dir. 1945.

Ministry of Fear. USA: Paramount Pictures. Lang, Fritz, dir. 1944.

Miracle of Morgan's Creek, The. USA: Paramount Pictures. Sturges, Preston, dir. 1944.

Moby Dick. USA: Warner Bros/Moulin Productions. Huston, John, dir. 1956.

Morocco. USA: Paramount Publix. Von Sternberg, Josef, dir. 1930.

Mort qui tue, Le [*The Murderous Corpse*]. France: Gaumont. Feuillade, Louis, dir. 1913.

Mother Wore Tights. USA: Twentieth Century-Fox. Lang, Walter, dir. 1947.

Moulin Rouge. USA: Romulus Films/Moulin Productions. Huston, John, dir. 1953.

Mr Arkadin. USA: Cervantes Films/Filmorsa/Sevilla Studios. Welles, Orson, dir. 1955.

Mr Lucky. USA: RKO Radio Pictures. Potter, H. C., dir. 1943.

Mrs Miniver. USA: Metro-Goldwyn-Mayer. Wyler, William, dir. 1942.

Müde Tod, Der [*Destiny*]. Germany: Decla-Bioscop AG. Lang, Fritz, dir. 1921.

Mulholland Drive. USA: Asymmetrical Productions/Imagine Entertainment/Picture Factory/Touchstone Pictures. Lynch, David, dir. 2001.

Mummy, The. USA: Universal. Freund, Karl, dir. 1932.

Murder Is My Beat. USA: Masthead Productions. Ulmer, Edgar G., dir. 1955.

Murder, My Sweet. USA: RKO Radio Pictures. Dmytryk, Edward, dir. 1944.

Murders in the Rue Morgue. USA: Universal. Florey, Robert, dir. 1932.

Musketeers of Pig Alley, The. USA: Biograph. Griffith, D. W., dir. 1912.

Mutiny. USA: King Bros. Productions. Dmytryk, Edward, dir. 1952.

My Darling Clementine. USA: Twentieth Century-Fox. Ford, John, dir. 1946.

My Favorite Brunette. USA: Hope Enterprises. Nugent, Elliott, dir. 1947.

My Name Is Julia Ross. USA: Columbia Pictures. Lewis, Joseph H., dir. 1945.

Mystery Street. USA: Metro-Goldwyn-Mayer. Sturges, John, dir. 1950.

Naked Alibi. USA: Universal-International Pictures. Hopper, Jerry, dir. 1954.
Naked City, The. USA: Mark Hellinger Productions. Dassin, Jules, dir. 1948.
Naked Kiss, The. USA: Leon Fromkess/Sam Firks. Fuller, Samuel, dir. 1964.
Naked Spur, The. USA: Metro-Goldwyn-Mayer. Mann, Anthony, dir. 1953.
Narrow Margin, The. USA: RKO Radio Pictures. Fleischer, Richard, dir. 1952.
Natural Born Killers. USA: NBK. Stone, Oliver, dir. 1994.
Night and the City. USA: Twentieth Century-Fox. Dassin, Jules, dir. 1948.
Night Holds Terror, The. USA: Columbia Pictures. Stone, Andrew, dir. 1955.
Night Has a Thousand Eyes. USA: Paramount Pictures. Farrow, John, dir. 1948.
Night Moves. USA: Hillier Productions-Layton. Penn, Arthur, dir. 1975.
Night of the Hunter, The. USA: Paul Gregory Productions. Laughton, Charles, dir.
    1955.
Night Runner, The. USA: Universal-International Pictures. Biberman, Abner, dir. 1957.
Night Without Sleep. USA: Twentieth Century-Fox. Baker, Roy, dir. 1952.
Nightfall. USA: Copa Productions. Tourneur, Jacques, dir. 1957.
Nightmare. USA: PTS Productions. Shane, Maxwell, dir. 1956.
Nightmare Alley. USA: Twentieth Century-Fox. Goulding, Edmund, dir. 1947.
No Escape. USA: Matthugh Productions. Bennett, Charles, dir. 1953.
No Man of Her Own. USA: Paramount Pictures. Leisen, Mitchell, dir. 1950.
No Way Out. USA: Twentieth Century-Fox. Mankiewicz, Joseph L., dir. 1950.
Nobody Lives Forever. USA: Warner Bros. Negulesco, Jean, dir. 1946.
Nosferatu: eine Symphonie des Grauens [*Nosferatu: A Symphony of Horrors*].
    Germany: Jofa-Atelier/Berlin-Johannisthal/Prana-Film GmbH. Murnau, F. W.,
    dir. 1922.
Not Wanted. USA: Emerald Productions. Clifton, Elmer, dir. 1949.
Notorious. USA: RKO Radio Pictures. Hitchcock, Alfred, dir. 1946.
Novocaine. USA: Artisan Entertainment. Atkins, David, dir. 2001.
Now, Voyager. USA: Warner Bros. Rapper, Irving, dir. 1942.
Nuit du Carrefour, La [*Night at the Crossroads*]. France: Europa Films. Renoir,
    Jean, dir. 1932.

Ocean's Eleven. USA: Dorchester Productions. Milestone, Lewis, dir. 1960.
Odd Man Out. UK: Two Cities Films. Reed, Carol, dir. 1947.
Odds Against Tomorrow. USA: Harbel Productions. Wise, Robert, dir. 1959.
On Dangerous Ground. USA: RKO Radio Pictures. Ray, Nicholas, dir. 1952.
One Way Street. USA: Universal-International Pictures. Fregonese, Hugo, dir. 1950.
Orchestra Wives. USA: Twentieth Century-Fox. Mayo, Archie, dir. 1942.
Ossessione [*Obsession*]. Italy: Industrie Cinematografiche Italiane. Visconti,
    Luchino, dir. 1943.
Out of the Past. USA: RKO Radio Pictures. Tourneur, Jacques, dir. 1947.
Outrage. USA: The Filmakers. Lupino, Ida, dir. 1950.
Ox-Bow Incident, The. USA: Twentieth Century-Fox. Wellman, William A., dir. 1943.

Panic in the Streets. USA: Twentieth Century-Fox. Kazan, Elia, dir. 1950.
Passage to Marseilles. USA: Warner Bros. Curtiz, Michael, dir. 1944.
Pépé le Moko. France: Paris Film. Duvivier, Julien, dir. 1937.
Perilous Waters. USA: Norwalk Productions. Bernhard, Jack, dir. 1948.
Perils of Pauline, The. USA: Pathé. Gasnier, Louis J. and David MacKenzie, dir. 1914.

Petrified Forest, The. USA: Warner Bros. Mayo, Archie, dir. 1936.

Phantom Lady. USA: Universal Pictures. Siodmak, Robert, dir. 1944.

Pickup on South Street. USA: Twentieth Century-Fox. Fuller, Samuel, dir. 1953.

Pitfall. USA: Regal Films. De Toth, Andre, dir. 1948.

Plunder Road. USA: Regal Films. Cornfield, Hubert, dir. 1957.

Point Blank. USA: Metro-Goldwyn-Mayer. Boorman, John, dir. 1967.

Port of New York. USA: Contemporary Productions. Benedek, Laslo, dir. 1949.

Possessed. USA: Warner Bros. Bernhardt, Curtis, dir. 1947.

Postman Always Rings Twice, The. USA: Metro-Goldwyn-Mayer. Garnett, Tay, dir. 1946.

Postman Always Rings Twice, The. USA: Lorimar Productions/Metro-Goldwyn-Mayer/Northstar International. Rafelson, Bob, dir. 1981.

Pride of the Marines. USA: Warner Bros. Daves, Delmer, dir. 1945.

Private Hell 36. USA: The Filmakers. Siegel, Don, dir. 1954.

Prowler, The. USA: Eagle Productions/Horizon Pictures. Losey, Joseph, dir. 1951.

Psycho. USA: Shamley Productions. Hitchcock, Alfred, dir. 1960.

Public Enemy, The. USA: Warner Bros. Wellman, William A., dir. 1931.

Pulp Fiction. USA: A Band Apart/Jersey Films. Tarantino, Quentin, dir. 1994.

Pursued. USA: United States Pictures. Walsh, Raoul, dir. 1947.

Quai des brumes, Le [*Port of Shadows*]. France: Ciné-Alliance. Carné, Marcel, dir. 1938.

Quicksand. USA: Samuel H. Stiefel Productions. Pichel, Irving, dir. 1950.

Racket, The. USA: RKO Radio Pictures. Cromwell, John, dir. 1951.

Railroaded. USA: Eagle-Lion Films. Mann, Anthony, dir. 1947.

Ramrod. USA: Enterprise Productions. De Toth, Andre, dir. 1947.

Rancho Notorious. USA: Fidelity Pictures. Lang, Fritz, dir. 1952.

Raw Deal. USA: Reliance Pictures. Mann, Anthony, dir. 1948.

Razor's Edge, The. USA: Twentieth Century-Fox. Goulding, Edmund, dir. 1946.

Rear Window. USA: Paramount Pictures/Patron Inc. Hitchcock, Alfred, dir. 1954.

Rebecca. USA: Selznick International Pictures. Hitchcock, Alfred, dir. 1940.

Reckless Moment, The. USA: Columbia Pictures. Ophuls, Max, dir. 1949.

Red Badge of Courage, The. USA: Metro-Goldwyn-Mayer. Huston, John, dir. 1951.

Red Danube, The. USA: Metro-Goldwyn-Mayer. Sidney, George, dir. 1949.

Red Light. USA: Roy Del Ruth Productions. Del Ruth, Roy, dir. 1949.

Red Menace, The. USA: Republic Pictures. Springsteen, R. G. dir. 1949.

Red Shoes, The. UK: The Archers. Powell, Michael and Emeric Pressburger, dir. 1948.

Red Snow. USA: All American Film Corp. Petroff, Boris L., dir. 1952.

Règle du jeu, La [*The Rules of the Game*]. France: Nouvelles Éditions de Films. Renoir, Jean, dir. 1939.

Report from the Aleutians. USA: US Army Signal Corps. Huston, John, dir. 1943.

Reservoir Dogs. USA: A Band Apart Productions. Tarantino, Quentin, dir. 1992.

Ride the Pink Horse. USA: Universal-International Pictures. Montgomery, Robert, dir. 1947.

Road to Utopia. USA: Paramount Pictures. Walker, Hal, dir. 1946.

Road House. USA: Twentieth Century-Fox. Negulesco, Jean, dir. 1948.

Roadblock. USA: RKO Radio Pictures. Daniels, Harold, dir. 1951.

Roaring Twenties, The. USA: Warner Bros. Walsh, Raoul, dir. 1939.

RoboCop. USA: Orion Pictures. Verhoeven, Paul, dir. 1987.

Roman d'un tricheur, Le [*Confessions of a Cheat*]. France: Cinéas. Guitry, Sacha, dir. 1936.

Roman Holiday. USA: Paramount Pictures. Wyler, William, dir. 1953.

Rope. USA: Transatlantic Pictures. Hitchcock, Alfred, dir. 1948.

Rosie the Riveter. USA: Republic Pictures. Santley, Joseph, dir. 1944.

Sahara. USA: Columbia Pictures. Korda, Zoltan, dir. 1943.

Samouraï, Le [*The Samourai*]. France: Compagnie Industrielle et Commerciale Cinématographique/Fida Cinematografica/Filmel/TC Productions. Melville, Jean-Pierre, dir. 1976.

Satan Met a Lady. USA: Warner Bros. Dieterle, William, dir. 1936.

Scarface. USA: The Caddo Co. Hawks, Howard, dir. 1932.

Scarlet Empress, The. USA: Paramount Productions. Von Sternberg, Josef, dir. 1934.

Scarlet Street. USA: Universal Pictures. Lang, Fritz, dir. 1945.

Searchers, The. USA: C.V. Whitney Pictures. Ford, John, dir. 1956.

Secret Fury, The. USA: Loring Theater Corp/RKO Radio Pictures. Ferrer, Mel, dir. 1950.

Sergeant York. USA: Warner Bros. Hawks, Howard, dir. 1941.

Set-Up, The. USA: RKO Radio Pictures. Wise, Robert, dir. 1949.

Shadow of a Doubt. USA: Jack H. Skirball Productions/Universal Pictures. Hitchcock, Alfred, dir. 1943.

Shadow of a Woman. USA: Warner Bros. Santley, Joseph, dir. 1946.

Shadow of the Thin Man. USA: Metro-Goldwyn-Mayer. Van Dyke, W. S., dir. 1941.

Shadow on the Wall. USA: Metro-Goldwyn-Mayer. Jackson, Patrick, dir. 1950.

Shanghai Express. USA: Paramount Publix. Von Sternberg, Josef, dir. 1932.

Shanghai Gesture, The. USA: Arnold Productions. Von Sternberg, Josef, dir. 1942.

Shed No Tears. USA: Equity Pictures. Yarbrough, Jean, dir. 1948.

Shock. USA: Twentieth Century-Fox. Werker, Alfred, dir. 1946.

Shock Corridor. USA: F & F Productions. Fuller, Samuel, dir. 1963.

Shockproof. USA: Columbia Pictures. Sirk, Douglas, dir. 1949.

Side Street. USA: Metro-Goldwyn-Mayer. Mann, Anthony, dir. 1949.

Since You Went Away. USA: Selznick International Pictures. Cromwell, John, dir. 1944.

Sleep, My Love. USA: Triangle Productions. Sirk, Douglas, dir. 1948.

Sleeping City, The. USA: Universal-International Pictures. Sherman, George, dir. 1950.

Snake Pit, The. USA: Twentieth Century-Fox. Litvak, Anatole, dir. 1948.

So Dark the Night. USA: Darmour Inc. Lewis, Joseph H., dir. 1946.

Somewhere in the Night. USA: Twentieth Century-Fox. Mankiewicz, Joseph L., dir. 1946.

Son of Frankenstein. USA: Universal Pictures. Lee, Rowland V., dir. 1939.

Song of the Thin Man. USA: Metro-Goldwyn-Mayer. Buzzell, Edward, dir. 1947.

Sorry, Wrong Number. USA: Hal Wallis Productions. Litvak, Anatole, dir. 1948.

Spellbound. USA: Selznick International Pictures/Vanguard Films. Hitchcock, Alfred, dir. 1945.

Spione [*Spies*]. Germany: Fritz Lang-Film/Universum Film. Lang, Fritz, dir. 1928.

Spiral Staircase, The. USA: RKO Radio Pictures. Siodmak, Robert, dir. 1945.

Steel Helmet, The. USA: Deputy Corp. Fuller, Samuel, dir. 1951.

Steel Trap, The. USA: Thor Productions. Stone, Andrew, dir. 1952.

Story of GI Joe, The. USA: Lester Cowan Productions. Wellman, William A., dir. 1945.

Strange Illusion. USA: Producers Releasing Corporation. Ulmer, Edgar G., dir. 1945.

Strange Impersonation. USA: Republic Pictures/William Wilder Productions. Mann, Anthony, dir. 1946.

Strange Intruder. USA: Allied Artists Pictures/Lindsley Parsons Productions. Rapper, Irving, dir. 1956.

Strange Life of Martha Ivers, The. USA: Hal Wallis Productions. Milestone, Lewis, dir. 1946.

Strange Woman, The. USA: Mars Film Corp. Ulmer, Edgar G., dir. 1946.

Stranger, The. USA: International Pictures. Welles, Orson, dir. 1946.

Stranger on the Third Floor. USA: RKO Radio Pictures. Ingster, Boris, dir. 1940.

Strangers in the Night. USA: Republic Pictures. Mann, Anthony, dir. 1944.

Strangers on a Train. USA: Warner Bros. Hitchcock, Alfred, dir. 1951.

Strasse, Die [*The Street*]. Germany: Stern-Film. Grune, Karl, dir. 1923.

Street of Chance. USA: Paramount Pictures. Hively, Jack, dir. 1942.

Street with No Name, The. USA: Twentieth Century-Fox. Keighley, William, dir. 1948.

Sunrise: A Song of Two Humans. USA: Fox Film Corp. Murnau, F. W., dir. 1927.

Sunset Boulevard. USA: Paramount Pictures. Wilder, Billy, dir. 1950.

Suspicion. USA: RKO Radio Pictures. Hitchcock, Alfred, dir. 1941.

Swing Shift Maisie. USA: Metro-Goldwyn-Mayer. McLeod, Norman Z., dir. 1943.

T-Men. USA: Edward Small Productions. Mann, Anthony, dir. 1947.

Talk About a Stranger. USA: Metro-Goldwyn-Mayer. Bradley, David, dir. 1952.

Taxi Driver. USA: Columbia Pictures/Bill/Phillips Productions/Italo/Judeo Productions. Scorsese, Martin, dir. 1976.

Tender Comrade. USA: RKO Radio Pictures. Dmytryk, Edward, dir. 1944.

Terminator, The. USA: Hemdale Productions. Cameron, James, dir. 1984.

Tête d'un homme [*A Man's Head*]. France: Les Films Marcel Vandal et Charles Delac. Duvivier, Julien, dir. 1933.

Them! USA: Warner Bros. Douglas, Gordon, dir. 1954.

They Drive by Night. USA: Warner Bros. Walsh, Raoul, dir. 1940.

They Live by Night. USA: RKO Radio Pictures. Ray, Nicholas, dir. 1948.

They Won't Believe Me. USA: RKO Radio Pictures. Pichel, Irving, dir. 1947.

Thieves' Highway. USA: Twentieth Century-Fox. Dassin, Jules, dir. 1949.

Thin Man, The. USA: Metro-Goldwyn-Mayer. Van Dyke, W. S., dir. 1934.

Thin Man Goes Home, The. USA: Metro-Goldwyn-Mayer. Thorpe, Richard, dir. 1936.

Third Man, The. UK: London Film Productions. Reed, Carol, dir. 1949.

13 Rue Madelaine. USA: Twentieth Century-Fox. Hathaway, Henry, dir. 1947.

13th Letter, The. USA: USA: Twentieth Century-Fox. Preminger, Otto, dir. 1951.

This Above All. USA: Twentieth Century-Fox. Litvak, Anatole, dir. 1942.

This Gun for Hire. USA: Paramount Pictures. Tuttle, Frank, dir. 1942.

This Land Is Mine. USA: RKO Radio Pictures. Renoir, Jean, dir. 1943.

Tight Spot. USA: Columbia Pictures. Karlson, Phil, dir. 1955.

Till the End of Time. USA: RKO Radio Pictures. Dmytryk, Edward, dir. 1946.

Time To Kill. USA: Twentieth Century-Fox. Leeds, Herbert I., dir. 1943.

Tirez sur le pianist [*Shoot the Pianist*]. France: Les Films de la Pléiade. Truffaut, François, dir. 1960.

To Have and Have Not. USA: Warner Bros. Hawks, Howard, dir. 1944.

Tokyo Joe. USA: Santana Pictures. Heisler, Stuart, dir. 1949.

Tomorrow Is Another Day. USA: Warner Bros. Feist, Felix, dir. 1951.

Too Late For Tears. USA: Republic Pictures. Haskin, Byron, dir. 1949.

Total Recall. USA: Carolco. Verhoeven, Paul, dir. 1990.

Touch of Evil. USA: Universal-International Pictures. Welles, Orson, dir. 1958.

Trail Street. USA: RKO Radio Pictures. Enright, Ray, dir. 1947.

Trapped. USA: Contemporary Productions. Fleischer, Richard, dir. 1949.

Triumph des Willens [*Triumph of the Will*]. Germany: Leni Riefenstahl-Produktion/ Reichspropagandaleitung der NSDAP. Riefenstahl, Leni, dir. 1935.

Truman Show, The. USA: Paramount Pictures/Scott Rudin Productions. Weir, Peter, dir. 1998.

Try and Get Me. USA: Robert Stillman Productions. Endfield, Cyril, dir. 1951.

Two Mrs Carrolls, The. USA: Warner Bros. Godfrey, Peter, dir. 1947.

Two Smart People. USA: Metro-Goldwyn-Mayer. Dassin, Jules, dir. 1946.

Undercover Man, The. USA: Columbia Pictures. Lewis, Joseph H., dir. 1949.

Undercurrent. USA: Metro-Goldwyn-Mayer. Minnelli, Vincente, dir. 1946.

Underneath, The. USA: Populist Pictures. Soderbergh, Steven, dir. 1995.

Undertow. USA: Universal-International Pictures. Castle, William, dir. 1949.

Underworld. USA: Paramount Famous Lasky. Von Sternberg, Josef, dir. 1927.

Underworld USA. USA: Globe Enterprises. Fuller, Samuel, dir. 1961.

Unfaithfully Yours. USA: Twentieth Century-Fox. Sturges, Preston, dir. 1948.

Union Station. USA: Paramount Pictures. Maté, Rudolph, dir. 1950.

Unknown, The. USA: Metro-Goldwyn-Mayer. Browning, Todd, dir. 1927.

Unknown Man, The. USA: Metro-Goldwyn-Mayer. Thorpe, Richard, dir. 1951.

Vampires, Les [*The Vampires*]. France: Société des Etablissements L. Gaumont. Feuillade, Louis, dir. 1915–16.

Videodrome. Canada: Filmplan International. Cronenberg, David, dir. 1983.

Walk a Crooked Mile. USA: Edward Small Productions. Douglas, Gordon, dir. 1948.

We Were Strangers. USA: Horizon Pictures. Huston, John, dir. 1949.

Web, The. USA: Universal-International Pictures. Gordon, Michael, dir. 1947.

West Side Story. USA: Beta Productions/Mirisch/Seven Arts Productions/B & P Enterprises. Wise, Robert, dir. 1961.

Westworld. USA: Metro-Goldwyn-Mayer. Crichton, Michael, dir. 1973.

Where the Sidewalk Ends. USA: Twentieth Century-Fox. Preminger, Otto, dir. 1950.

While the City Sleeps. USA: Bert Friedlob Productions. Lang, Fritz, dir. 1956.

Whip Hand, The. USA: RKO Radio Pictures. Menzies, William Cameron, dir. 1951.

Whirlpool. USA: Twentieth Century-Fox. Preminger, Otto, dir. 1950.

White Heat. USA: Warner Bros. Walsh, Raoul, dir. 1949.

Who Killed Who? USA: Metro-Goldwyn-Mayer. Avery, Tex, dir. 1943.

Window, The. USA: RKO Radio Pictures. Tetzlaff, Ted, dir. 1949.

Witness to Murder. USA: Chester Erskine Pictures. Rowland, Roy, dir. 1954.

Woman in Hiding. USA: Universal-International Pictures. Gordon, Michael, dir. 1949.

Woman in the Window, The. USA: International Pictures. Lang, Fritz, dir. 1945.

Woman on Pier 13, The. USA: RKO Radio Pictures. Stevenson, Robert, dir. 1950.

Woman on the Beach, The. USA: RKO Radio Pictures. Renoir, Jean, dir. 1947.

Woman on the Run. USA: Fidelity Pictures. Foster, Norman, dir. 1950.

Wrong Man, The. USA: Warner Bros. Hitchcock, Alfred, dir. 1956.

Yellow Sky. USA: Twentieth Century-Fox. Wellman, William A., dir. 1948.

Young at Heart. USA: Warner Bros. Douglas, Gordon, dir. 1955.

Zodiac, The. USA: Phoenix Pictures. Fincher, David, dir. 2007.

Phantom Lady (Robert Siodmak, 1944).

Index

Lightning Source UK Ltd.
Milton Keynes UK
UKHW021103250122
397661UK00004B/84